New Directions in Public Opinion

Edited by Adam J. Berinsky

NEW YORK AND LONDON

First published 2012
by Routledge
711 Third Avenue, New York, NY 10017

Simultaneously published in the UK
by Routledge
2 Park Square, Milton Park, Abingdon, Oxon OX14 4RN

Routledge is an imprint of the Taylor & Francis Group, an informa business

Library of Congress Cataloging in Publication Data
New directions in public opinion / edited by Adam Berinsky.
p. cm. – (New directions in American politics)
Includes bibliographical references and index.
1. Public opinion–United States. 2. United States–Politics and government–Public opinion. I. Berinsky, Adam J., 1970–
HN90.P8N49 2011
303.3'80973–dc23

2011024007

ISBN: 978-0-415-88528-7 (hbk)
ISBN: 978-0-415-88529-4 (pbk)
ISBN: 978-0-203-83983-6 (ebk)

Typeset in Minion
by Wearset Ltd, Boldon, Tyne and Wear

Printed and bound in the United States of America on acid-free paper by Edwards Brothers, Inc.

To Don and Nancy

New Directions in Public Opinion

The field of public opinion is one of the most diverse in political science. Over the last 60 years, scholars have drawn upon the disciplines of psychology, economics, sociology, and even biology to learn how ordinary people come to understand the complicated business of politics. But much of the path breaking research in the field of public opinion is published in journals, taking up fairly narrow questions one at a time and often requiring advanced statistical knowledge to understand these findings. As a result, the study of public opinion can seem confusing and incoherent to undergraduates. To engage undergraduate students in this area, a new type of textbook is required.

New Directions in Public Opinion brings together leading scholars to provide an accessible and coherent overview of the current state of the field of public opinion. Each chapter provides a general overview of topics that are at the cutting edge of study as well as well-established cornerstones of the field. Suitable for use as a main textbook or in tandem with a lengthier survey, it comprehensively covers the topics of public opinion research and pushes students further to explore critical topics in contemporary politics.

Adam J. Berinsky is Associate Professor of Political Science at Massachusetts Institute of Technology.

New Directions in American Politics

The Routledge series *New Directions in American Politics* is composed of contributed volumes covering key areas of study in the field of American politics and government. Each title provides a state-of-the-art overview of current trends in its respective subfield, with an eye toward cutting edge research accessible to advanced undergraduate and beginning graduate students. While the volumes touch on the main topics of relevant study, they are not meant to cover the "nuts and bolts" of the subject. Rather, they engage readers in the most recent scholarship, real-world controversies, and theoretical debates with the aim of getting students excited about the same issues that animate scholars.

Titles in the Series:

New Directions in American Political Parties
Edited by Jeffrey M. Stonecash

New Directions in the American Presidency
Edited by Lori Cox Han

New Directions in Campaigns and Elections
Edited by Stephen K. Medvic

New Directions in Congressional Politics
Edited by Jamie Carson

New Directions in Public Opinion
Edited by Adam J. Berinsky

New Directions in Judicial Politics
Edited by Kevin McGuire

Contents

Contributors

Matthew Baum is Marvin Kalb Professor of Global Communications and Professor of Public Policy at Harvard University's John F. Kennedy School of Government and Department of Government. His research focuses on delineating the effects of domestic politics on international conflict and cooperation in general and American foreign policy in particular, as well as on the role of the mass media and public opinion in contemporary politics. His research has appeared in over a dozen leading scholarly journals, such as the *American Political Science Review*, *American Journal of Political Science*, and *Journal of Politics*. His books include *Soft News Goes to War: Public Opinion and American Foreign Policy in the New Media Age* (2003) and *War Stories: The Causes and Consequences of Public Views of War* (with Tim Groeling, 2010). He has also contributed op/ed articles to a variety of newspapers and magazines in the United States and abroad. Before coming to Harvard, Baum was Associate Professor of Political Science and Communication Studies at UCLA. Baum received his PhD in political science at UC San Diego in 2000.

Adam J. Berinsky is an Associate Professor of Political Science at MIT. Berinsky received his PhD from the University of Michigan in 2000. He is a specialist in the fields of political behavior and public opinion. He is the author of *In Time of War: Understanding American Public Opinion from World War II to Iraq* (2009) and *Silent Voices: Public Opinion and Political Participation in America* (2004) and has published articles in the *American Journal of Political Science*, *Journal of Politics*, *Political Behavior*, *Political Psychology*, *Public Opinion Quarterly*, *Quarterly Journal of Political Science*, *American Politics Research*, and *Communist and Post-Communist Studies*. He has won several scholarly awards, is the recipient of grants from the National Science Foundation, and was a fellow at the Center for Advanced Study in the Behavioral Sciences.

Ted Brader is Associate Professor of Political Science at the University of Michigan and Research Associate Professor in the Center for Political Studies at the Institute for Social Research. He is the author of *Campaigning for*

Hearts and Minds (2006) and currently serves as Associate Principal Investigator for the American National Election Studies and Associate Principal Investigator for Time-sharing Experiments for the Social Sciences. His research focuses on the role of emotions in politics, political partisanship, media effects on public opinion, and other topics in political psychology. He received his PhD from the Department of Government at Harvard University.

Nancy Burns is the Warren E. Miller Professor of Political Science and Director of the Center for Political Studies at the University of Michigan. Her work focuses on gender, race, public opinion, and political action. Burns served as Principal Investigator of the National Election Studies from 1999 to 2005. She is a Fellow of the American Academy of Arts and Sciences.

Andrea Louise Campbell is Associate Professor of Political Science at the Massachusetts Institute of Technology. Her research interests include American politics, political behavior, public opinion, and political inequality, particularly their intersection with social welfare policy, health policy, and tax policy. She is the author of *How Policies Make Citizens: Senior Citizen Activism and the American Welfare State* (2003) and, with Kimberly J. Morgan, *The Delegated Welfare State: Medicare, Markets, and the Governance of Social Policy* (forthcoming in 2011). She is also completing a book manuscript on public opinion and taxes in the United States. Her research has appeared in the *American Political Science Review, Political Behavior, Comparative Political Studies, Politics & Society, Studies in American Political Development*, and *Health Affairs*, among others.

David E. Campbell is the John Cardinal O'Hara, CSC Associate Professor of Political Science and Director of the Rooney Center for the Study of American Democracy at the University of Notre Dame. He is the author of *Why We Vote: How Schools and Communities Shape Our Civic Life* (2010) and, most recently, *American Grace: How Religion Divides and Unites Us* (with Robert Putnam, 2010). He has also edited *A Matter of Faith: Religion in the 2004 Presidential Election* (2007). In addition to publishing in scholarly journals such as the *American Journal of Political Science* and the *Journal of Politics*, his work has been featured in the *New York Times, Wall Street Journal, Economist, USA Today*, and many other general media outlets.

Erica Czaja is a PhD candidate in the Department of Politics at Princeton University, specializing in political psychology, inequality, and racial politics in the United States. Prior to studying at Princeton, she spent two years working in survey research at the RAND Corporation. She earned her MA in the social sciences from the University of Chicago, and her MA thesis about the impact of Hurricane Katrina on public views of racial inequality has been published in *SOULS: A Critical Journal of Black*

Politics, Culture and Society (2007) as well as in *Seeking Higher Ground: The Race, Public Policy and Hurricane Katrina Crisis Reader* (2008). She also holds a BA with high distinction in psychology from the University of Michigan, Ann Arbor.

Christopher M. Federico is Associate Professor of Psychology and Political Science at the University of Minnesota and the director of the University of Minnesota's Center for the Study of Political Psychology. He received his PhD in psychology from the University of California, Los Angeles, in 2001. His research and teaching interests include the psychological bases of ideology and belief systems, political sophistication, and racial attitudes. His work has appeared in the *Journal of Personality and Social Psychology*, the *Personality and Social Psychology Bulletin*, *Public Opinion Quarterly*, the *American Journal of Political Science*, the *Journal of Politics*, and *Political Psychology*.

Martin Gilens teaches in the Politics Department at Princeton University. His research examines public opinion and mass media, especially in relation to inequality, public policy, and democratic responsiveness to public preferences. Professor Gilens is the author of *Why Americans Hate Welfare: Race, Media and the Politics of Antipoverty Policy* (2000), and has published on political inequality, mass media, race, gender, and welfare politics in the *American Political Science Review*, *American Journal of Political Science*, *Journal of Politics*, *British Journal of Political Science*, *Public Opinion Quarterly*, and *Berkeley Journal of Sociology*. He holds a PhD in sociology from the University of California Berkeley, and taught at Yale University and UCLA before joining the faculty at Princeton. His research has been supported by grants from the Russell Sage Foundation, the National Science Foundation, and the Social Science Research Council.

John C. Green is Distinguished Professor of Political Science and director of the Ray C. Bliss Institute of Applied Politics at the University of Akron as well as a Senior Research Advisor for the Pew Forum on Religion and Public Life. He has written extensively on religion and American politics, including *The Faith Factor* (2007) and *The Assemblies of God: Godly Love and the Revitalization of American Pentecostalism* (2010).

Jake Haselswerdt is a PhD candidate in political science at George Washington University. He is currently working on a dissertation on Congress and the politics of tax expenditures. Before coming to GWU he worked for six years as a lobbyist at Lewis-Burke Associates LLC, a Washington-based government relations firm specializing in the representation of universities and other science and education organizations.

Susan Herbst is the President of the University of Connecticut, where she is also Professor of Political Science. She is author of several books on public opinion including *Numbered Voices: How Opinion Polls Have Shaped American Politics* (1993), *Politics at the Margin: Historical Expression Outside of the Mainstream* (1994), *Reading Public Opinion: Political Actors View the Democratic Process* (1998), and, most recently, *Rude Democracy: Civility and Incivility in American Politics*. She has held academic positions at Northwestern University, Temple University, and the University at Albany.

Marc Hetherington is Professor of Political Science at Vanderbilt University. He does research on public opinion and political behavior, with particular interests in public trust in government and party polarization. He is the author of *Why Trust Matters: Declining Political Trust and the Demise of American Liberalism* (2005) and *Authoritarianism and Polarization in American Politics* (with Jonathan Weiler, 2009). He has also published numerous articles in journals, such as the *American Political Science Review*, *American Journal of Political Science*, *Journal of Politics*, *Public Opinion Quarterly*, and *British Journal of Political Science*.

Matthew V. Hibbing is an Assistant Professor of Political Science at the University of California, Merced. His research focuses on American political behavior, with emphasis on public opinion, political psychology, and biology and politics. He has published research in *Science*, *American Political Science Review*, *Legislative Studies Quarterly*, *British Journal of Political Science*, and *Political Behavior*.

D. Sunshine Hillygus is an Associate Professor of Political Science and Director of the Initiative on Survey Methodology at Duke University. Her research areas focus on public opinion, voting behavior, campaigns and elections, and survey methodology. She is author of *The Persuadable Voter: Wedge Issues in Presidential Campaigns* (with Todd Shields, 2008) and *The Hard Count: The Political and Social Challenges of the Census Participation* (with Norman Nie, Ken Prewitt, and Heili Pals, 2006). She received her PhD in political science from Stanford University in 2003.

Jane Junn is Professor of Political Science at the University of Southern California. She specializes in U.S. political behavior and public opinion, with emphasis on race, ethnicity, and the politics of immigration. She has published three books on political participation in the United States. Her first book, *Education and Democratic Citizenship in America* (with Norman H. Nie and Kenneth Stehlik-Barry, 1996), won the Woodrow Wilson award from the American Political Science Association for the best book published that year.

Donald Kinder is the Philip E. Converse Collegiate Professor of Political Science at the University of Michigan. He has held fellowships from the Guggenheim Foundation and from the Center for Advanced Study in the

Behavioral Sciences and is a member of the American Academy of Arts and Sciences. His books include *News that Matters* (1987), *Divided by Color* (1996), *Us against Them* (2009), and *The End of Race?* (2011).

Geoffrey C. Layman is Associate Professor of Political Science at the University of Notre Dame and specializes in political parties, public opinion, electoral behavior, and religion and politics. He is the author of *The Great Divide: Religious and Cultural Conflict in American Party Politics* (2001). His articles have appeared in the *American Political Science Review*, *American Journal of Political Science*, *Journal of Politics*, *British Journal of Political Science*, *Annual Review of Political Science*, and several other journals and edited volumes. His current work focuses on the growth of partisan issue polarization, the rise of secularism and non-religion in the U.S. and its political causes and consequences, and American attitudes toward Muslims and their implications for electoral behavior.

Tali Mendelberg is the author of *The Race Card: Campaign Strategy, Implicit Messages, and the Norm of Equality* (2001), winner of the American Political Science Association's 2002 Woodrow Wilson Foundation Award for "the best book published in the United States during the prior year on government, politics or international affairs." She has also published articles in the *American Journal of Political Science*, *Journal of Politics*, *Public Opinion Quarterly*, *Perspectives on Politics*, *Political Behavior*, *Political Psychology*, and *Political Communication*. Her work has been supported by grants and fellowships from the National Science Foundation, the University of Pennsylvania, and Harvard University. In 2002 she received the Erik H. Erikson Early Career Award for Excellence and Creativity in the Field of Political Psychology. She holds a PhD from the University of Michigan.

Jeffery J. Mondak is James M. Benson Chair in Public Issues and Civic Leadership in the Department of Political Science at the University of Illinois at Urbana-Champaign. Mondak's research has examined numerous aspects of American and cross-national political behavior. His most recent work focuses on the political significance of personality traits. Mondak is the author of *Personality and the Foundations of Political Behavior* (2010) and *Nothing to Read: Newspapers and Elections in a Social Experiment* (1995), and coeditor of *Fault Lines: Why the Republicans Lost Congress* (2009). Mondak's articles appear in numerous journals, including the *American Political Science Review*, *American Journal of Political Science*, *British Journal of Political Science*, *Cognitive Brain Research*, *Political Behavior*, *Political Psychology*, and *Public Opinion Quarterly*.

David O. Sears received his AB in History (Stanford University, 1957), his PhD in Psychology (Yale University, 1962), and then was appointed as Assistant Professor in Psychology at UCLA (1961) and Professor of Psychology and Political Science (1971). He has served as Dean of Social

Sciences and Director of the Institute for Social Science Research at UCLA, and as President of the International Society of Political Psychology. He has co-authored *Public Opinion* (with Robert E. Lane, 1964), *The Politics of Violence: The New Urban Blacks and the Watts Riot* (with John B. McConahay, 1973), *Tax Revolt: Something for Nothing in California* (with Jack Citrin, 1982), 12 editions of *Social Psychology* (with Shelley E. Taylor and L. Anne Peplau, 1970–2005), *Obama's Race: The 2008 Election and the Dream of a Post-Racial America* (with Michael Tesler, 2010), and co-edited *Political Cognition* (with Richard Lau, 1986), *Racialized Politics: The Debate about Racism in America* (with Jim Sidanius and Lawrence Bobo, 2000), and the *Oxford Handbook of Political Psychology* (with Leonie Huddy and Robert Jervis, 2003).

John Sides is Associate Professor of Political Science at George Washington University. He studies political behavior in American and comparative politics. His current research focuses on political campaigns, the effects of factual information on public opinion, citizenship laws and national identity, and measurement equivalence. His work has appeared in the *American Political Science Review*, *American Journal of Political Science*, *American Politics Research*, *British Journal of Political Science*, *Journal of Politics*, *Political Communication*, *Political Studies*, *Presidential Studies Quarterly*, and *Legislative Studies Quarterly*. He helped found and contributes to *The Monkey Cage*, a political science blog.

Acknowledgments

An edited volume is only as good as the chapters it contains. Every one of the authors who contributed to this volume produced an excellent chapter. The final product is a testament to their hard and careful work. Above all, I am grateful to them.

I am also grateful to Michael Kerns who approached me to write this manuscript and guided it seamlessly through the editorial process. Seth Dickinson and Timothy McKinley both provided outstanding research assistance. Gabe Lenz, Michele Margolis, and Michael Sances provided helpful comments on drafts of the introduction.

This book is dedicated to my former advisors Don Kinder and Nancy Burns, who sparked my interest in public opinion while I was a graduate student at Michigan (and provided a timely chapter for this volume to boot).

Introduction

Adam J. Berinsky

Why do some citizens approve of same-sex couples having the right to marry, while others are vehemently opposed? Why can't Democrats and Republicans seem to agree on anything? Should we trust opinion polls? Are some polls better than others? How much does the average American really care about politics anyway? These are the types of important questions that are central to the study of public opinion.

The field of public opinion is one of the most diverse in political science. Over the last 60 years, scholars have drawn upon the disciplines of psychology, economics, sociology, and even biology to answer these questions and more. As a field we have learned a great deal about how ordinary people come to understand the complicated business of politics.

This diversity makes the study of public opinion an especially interesting area of political science, but diversity comes with a cost. Much path breaking research in the field of public opinion is published in professional journals, whose target audience is professors and advanced graduate students. These papers take up fairly narrow questions one at a time and often require advanced statistical knowledge to understand. As a result, the study of public opinion can seem confusing and incoherent to novices and specialists alike.

This book is intended to expand the audience for cutting edge public opinion research by providing an accessible and coherent overview of the current state of the field. In this volume, I have brought together leading scholars of public opinion to provide an understandable introduction to new and exciting research. Each of the authors of the chapters in this volume provide both an overview of their field of specialization as well as a lively review of their own research. In order to stimulate interest among readers and students, these examples focus on contemporary and ongoing political controversies. My hope is that this book will serve as a comprehensive introduction to the field, while at the same time piquing the interest of students to further explore the frontiers on their own. Each chapter is intended to be self-contained, but, together, this volume serves as a gateway to the study of public opinion.

The Measure and Meaning of Public Opinion

Before we can begin to study public opinion, we need to have some sense of what we mean by "public opinion." As you might expect, this is easier said than done. As the eminent political scientist V.O. Key aptly noted 50 years ago, "To speak with precision of public opinion is a task not unlike coming to grips with the Holy Ghost."[1] Indeed, the term has long been used to mean many different things. The ancient Greeks assessed opinion through public rhetoric and oratory, embracing a notion of public opinion that befit their restrictive notions of citizenship.[2] With the emergence of expanded male suffrage throughout the nineteenth century, a notion of public opinion as an aggregation of the preferences of individuals began to take hold. But this view did not go unchallenged. In the 1940s, sociologist Herbert Blumer argued that public opinion was a purely collective phenomenon. Public opinion emerged through the communication and clash of group interests and, as a result, could not be gauged through individual survey responses. It was, instead, "the product of a society in operation."[3] It is no surprise, then, that a review of the academic literature on public opinion in the 1960s uncovered scores of different definitions of this central concept.[4]

While it may be difficult to come to a consensus on a single definition of public opinion, Key ultimately arrived at a working view of public opinion—one that is a useful starting point for this book: "Those opinions held by private persons which governments find it prudent to heed."[5] Key's definition is an expansive one. Public opinion is a property of individuals, but acquires its power in the public sphere. Moreover, there is a place both for the strongly formed, crystallized opinions of citizens that we might think of as reasoned public opinion and the lightly held beliefs and transient preferences that are decried by politicians and journalists as fickle judgments, but which sometimes guide government.

Once we have defined public opinion, we must figure out how best to measure it. Almost certainly, the most familiar technique for the readers of this volume is opinion polls or surveys. Over the course of the twentieth century, polls emerged as an important tool to measure the public will. Today, polls pervade the political scene. Indeed, writing for the fiftieth anniversary of the leading journal for public opinion research, *Public Opinion Quarterly*, noted political scientist Philip Converse (whose crucial contributions to the field are discussed below) argued that opinion polls *were* public opinion. This view is at least implicitly shared by nearly all scholars of public opinion. Indeed, in this volume, when scholars speak of public opinion, they almost always mean the results of polls.

There are, however, dissenting views. Opinion polls have only existed for 80 years, but scholars and practitioners of politics have been talking about public opinion for centuries. Before the development of polls, as Susan Herbst argues in her excellent book *Numbered Voices*, there were many ways that interested parties could measure public opinion.[6] Citizens could listen in at coffeehouses or follow the partisan press. Politicians could attend to public speeches or follow mail from their constituents. In Chapter 1, Herbst expands this argument, both reviewing the history of opinion expression and looking forward to possible changes in the years to come. Over time, she reminds us, public opinion has meant many things to many different people. In the future, it may change again. An exclusive focus on polls provides us with a restricted and perhaps incomplete picture of the public will.

But given that polls are the dominant way to measure opinion, practitioners should be careful about how they conduct surveys—and citizens should be careful about how they interpret them. In Chapter 2, D. Sunshine Hillygus describes the key challenges that face those who wish to conduct and use surveys as a measure of public opinion. Above all, Hillygus reminds us that we need to pay close attention to the quality of the data gathered by particular surveys.

Data quality is especially important in the twenty-first century, because we are undergoing great changes in the way we measure opinion through surveys. In the early days of surveys, pollsters went door-to-door to interview survey respondents. Beginning in the 1970s, the industry started conducting polls by telephone, a cheaper and more convenient form of data collection that facilitated an explosion in the number of polls in the United States. In recent years, however, this model of data collection has been threatened on several fronts. For one, the rise in the use of cell phones puts the representativeness of phone polls at risk. Over a quarter of all Americans have dropped their land lines in favor of a cell phone and these numbers are growing, especially among younger Americans. As of December 2010, more than half of Americans aged 25 to 29 lived in households that had a cell phone but no traditional land line telephone.[7] Polling exclusively through land lines will therefore miss a large portion of the citizens that comprise the mass public. In addition, the Internet holds promise as a method of data collection but, as Hillygus notes, it is difficult to translate the time-tested mechanics of collecting opinions to this new medium. For instance, it is almost impossible to define the universe of Internet users, making it a challenge to draw representative samples.

With the future of opinion polling uncertain, scholars and practitioners must be even more careful about how they collect and report measures of public opinion. Consider, for example, the reporting of poll results by the media. Traditionally, media outlets such as the *New York Times* and the *Washington Post* (in conjunction with CBS and ABC, respectively) maintained polling units that would conduct polls across the course of a campaign. In the last few election cycles, websites that aggregate *all* available polling information—such as Real Clear Politics, Mark Blumenthal's Pollster.com (now under the umbrella of the *Huffington Post*) and Nate Silver's fivethirtyeight.com (now published under the banner of the *New York Times*)—have become extremely popular. These sites provide polling consumers with a vast array of information. But this information is not all of equal quality. Some surveys, Hillygus reminds us, are more worthy of trust than others. In the end, as Hillygus argues, no survey is perfect, but by making the decisions that go into collecting survey data more transparent, it is possible for policy makers, journalists, and ordinary citizens to decide how much faith to put into any single measure of the public will.

The Question of Democratic Competence

Even if we draw a high-quality sample and conduct our poll to minimize survey errors, sometimes it is not clear what it is that we can measure with opinion polls. If, as Walter Lippmann once wrote, politics is a "swarming confusion of problems," can ordinary people make sense of it?[8] Perhaps, when confronted with a complex world, ordinary citizens simply *don't* think about politics in a coherent manner—or even at all.

Lippmann did not have much faith in the common man. And he was not alone in his beliefs: for most of American history politicians and commentators have been skeptical that the mass public is—or ever could be—engaged enough with the political world to make reasonable and temperate political decisions. There was a reason, after all, that the founders established a *representative* democracy rather than let citizens directly govern themselves.

However, it was not until the early twentieth century that the capability of the citizenry became a pressing concern. In the early republic, the political sphere was restricted in numerous ways to keep "undesirables" away from the political process. But gradually more and more citizens were brought into the political sphere. With the expansion of the franchise to women in 1920, all Americans (at least nominally) had the right to vote. The capacity of the mass public, then, became a critical subject of interest to politicians and scholars alike. A. Lawrence Lowell, for example, argued that individual differences in political knowledge must be taken into account when determining the proper role of the public in the process of government—some people, according to Lowell, *should* count more than others.[9] To return to Key's conception of public opinion, Lowell's worry was that without some mechanism to filter opinion, public opinion would reflect *only* lightly held views and ill-thought-out transient demands.

The early days of opinion polling confirmed the worst suspicions of the skeptical. Survey researchers in the 1930s and 1940s painted a rather bleak picture of the capabilities of the mass public. Summing up the findings of one of the first large-scale academic studies of voter decision making in the 1948 election, Bernard Berelson, Paul Lazarsfeld, and William McPhee wrote that their surveys "reveal that certain requirements commonly assumed for the successful operation of democracy are not met by the behavior of 'average' citizen."[10] For instance, in 1947, one-quarter of the public could not even name the Vice President and 40 percent did not know who controlled the Senate, essentially failing a multiple choice question with two options. The passage of time has done little to alleviate these concerns. Even with a remarkable increase in the educational attainment of the average American and the rapid development of the mass media since in the 1940s, American citizens remain largely ignorant of the goings-on in the political world. Moreover, survey researchers have consistently found that even minor differences in the wording of questions can dramatically change the shape of opinions expressed in polls. Americans support "assistance to the poor" but reject spending on "welfare." It is a legitimate question, then, whether American citizens hold meaningful policy preferences worthy of serving as the basis of democratic governance.

Martin Gilens addresses this very question in Chapter 3. As he concedes, much evidence suggests that citizens lack the knowledge or motivation to form sensible policy preferences. Few Americans, for example, understand the content of complex legislation like the recent health care reforms under President Obama. But, as Gilens notes, individuals do not navigate the political world on their own. For instance, citizens can draw on cues from prominent politicians to help them form meaningful attitudes. And while any individual might fall short of the democratic ideal, groups of citizens can be drawn together into a meaningful aggregate. As James Stimson has argued, once we think of public opinion as property of whole electorates, rather than individuals, it appears orderly and functions as a sensitive barometer to events in the political world.[11]

Aggregation does not, however, solve all the problem of public opinion. The aggregation of disparate preferences may lead to a rational and reasonable opinion, but in practice not all individuals have an equal voice. For instance, Gilens finds that the policies enacted by government reflect aggregate public preferences, but this policy is strongly biased toward the preferences of the most economically advantaged Americans. Still, Gilens does not blame the public; the inequality in democratic responsiveness, he concludes, results not from a failure of the broader public to form meaningful preferences, but from the failure of the political decision makers to take those preferences into account.

The Foundations of Political Preferences

That said, the opinions of individual members of society remain a critical object of study. Shifting the focus to the aggregate level, as Gilens argues we should, might address some of the concerns raised by critics of direct democracy, such as Berelson and his colleagues. But it remains a fact that even if the American public, taken as a whole, can reason effectively, individual citizens are often distracted by more pressing concerns. Setting aside the noble impulse to accept the wisdom of the collective, to fully understand the relationship between the mass public and politicians, we must not lose our focus on individual citizens. After all, as Christopher Achen aptly noted, if individuals do not possess even meaningful attitudes, let alone well-defined policy preferences, then "democratic theory loses its starting point."[12] A great deal of public opinion research therefore tries to understand exactly how people *do* reason about politics. Answering this question is the task of the second part of this book.

Ideology and Political Reasoning

For the first few decades of the academic study of public opinion, the search for the principles that shaped public opinion did not stray far from ideology. From the 1950s through the 1970s, scholars were occupied by the search for a single overarching belief system that could guide political opinions. The seminal work in this tradition was Philip Converse's 1964 chapter, "The Nature of Belief Systems in Mass Publics." Converse defined a belief system as "a configuration of ideas and attitudes in which the elements are bound together by some form of constraint or functional interdependence."[13] Political ideology, as commonly conceived, is a belief system with a broad range of political objects serving as referents for the ideas and attitudes in the system. Ideology therefore provides a relatively abstract and far-reaching structure for a large variety of political attitudes and preferences.

Converse argued that very few citizens thought of politics in an ideological manner. Analyzing survey data from the 1950s, Converse found that the vast majority of citizens did not use ideological terms, such as "liberal" or "conservative," when talking about politics. Moreover, their opinions were largely unconnected across different issues and seemed to vary in random ways across time.

Converse's work is perhaps the most provocative piece of public opinion scholarship of the last 50 years. It is provocative not only because it focused researchers on questions central to the functioning of democracy, but also because it generated a tremendous amount of reaction—most of it trying to rehabilitate the picture of the general public. For instance, in the 1970s, Norman Nie, Sidney Verba, and John Petrocik published *The Changing American Voter*.[14] These authors found that "constraint"—the correspondence between attitudes on related issues examined by Converse—suddenly increased in 1964. Nie et al. attributed this change to a shift in the larger political context—from the placid Eisenhower era of the 1950s to the ideologically charged events of the 1960s. These findings, however, turned out to be largely illusory. Both Converse and Nie et al. examined data collected by the American National Election Study (ANES). While the ANES is careful to preserve the continuity of its survey questions, at times the ANES does change its wordings. One important such change in question wording was … in 1964! It turns out that the ANES shifted from asking questions in a form where respondents were given a statement that asked if they agree or disagree with it, to a format where they were asked to choose between a pair of competing alternatives. In a series of clever experiments, John Sullivan, James Pierson, George Marcus, and Stanley Feldman demonstrated that most of the change found by Nie et al. could be attributed to these changes in question wording.[15] By the end of the 1970s, the field was in many ways back where it started in the 1950s—with the dismal findings of the early days of survey research at the forefront.

Was there, then, nothing left to say about public opinion? Perhaps the answer was to ask different kinds of questions. In early 1980s, Donald Kinder made a call to reframe the study of public opinion from the search for a single overarching principle to a finer grained investigation of what, exactly, *does* structure the political thought of ordinary Americans.

This call to expand the study of public opinion beyond a debate over the power of ideology has been taken up to good effect: indeed the chapters in this book on the role of race, religion, emotion, personality, and other topics provide testament to the fruitfulness of this research agenda. However, what may have gotten somewhat lost in the renaissance of the last 30 years is that ideology is still an important topic, as demonstrated by Christopher M. Federico's contribution to this volume. In Chapter 4, Federico presents evidence that ideology has deep roots in citizens' social circumstances, their psychological characteristics, and perhaps even in biology. Federico also notes that there are conditions under which ideology is a powerful determinant of citizens' opinions on the matters of day. Admittedly, not all citizens are able to reason in an ideological manner—they must possess both political information and a strong desire to appraise things as "good" or "bad" in order to think ideologically and express ideologically consistent opinions. Among these citizens, though, ideology is a powerful force.

Moving Beyond Ideology

That said, Kinder's call to move beyond ideology has greatly expanded the scope of the field of public opinion. For those citizens who do not reason in an ideological manner, there are many other possible bases of political reasoning. Perhaps the most obvious determinant of public opinion is partisanship—the degree to which individual citizens identify with one of the major political parties in America. Republicans and Democrats, after all, differ greatly on the major issues of the day. For instance, a poll taken right after the 2010 midterm election by CBS News demonstrated that Americans were evenly split on the question of whether Congress should try to repeal the health care bill passed in March of 2010. Forty-five percent of respondents supported repeal, 45 percent opposed repeal, and another 10 percent were undecided. This seemingly balanced judgment, however, concealed a strong divide between the parties; 76 percent of Republicans favored repeal, compared with 19 percent of Democrats. These stark partisan differences extend to evaluations of major political figures. In that same poll, 78 percent of Democrats approved of the way Barack Obama was handling his job as president, but only 10 percent of Republicans expressed support.[16]

Given the magnitude of these differences it might surprise today's readers to learn that for much of the history of the field, the power of partisanship was not a given. In fact, if this book was written 20 or 25 years ago we would be bemoaning the death of parties. While the heyday of the literature on the decline of parties occurred in the 1970s and 1980s—with works such as David Broder's 1972 book, *The Party's Over* and William Crotty's 1984 book, *American Parties in Decline*—Martin Wattenberg's seminal work, *The Decline of American Political Parties* was updated several times into the late 1990s. Ironically, at the precise moment that political scientists were writing about the decline of parties and attachments to parties as a central determinant of public opinion, parties were beginning a steep ascent. Examining the votes that occur on the floor of the House and the Senate, Keith Poole and Howard Rosenthal have found that beginning in the mid-1970s Democrats and Republicans began voting in more unified and distinct ways. Over time, the emergence of these distinct ideological positions among politicians began to trickle down to the level of ordinary citizens.

In Chapter 5, Marc Hetherington chronicles the rise in the importance of party identification over the last 30 years. He first describes the different ways in which political scientists have conceived of party identification. Some scholars have argued that party identification is akin to a summary judgment about the current state of the political world. If times are good when a Democrat is in power, as they were in the early 1960s, individuals are more likely to think of themselves as Democrats. If times are bad—think, for instance, late 2008 to 2010—they are less likely to identify as Democrats. The more dominant view, however, is to think of party identification as an intense attachment to a political group. Over a lifetime, party identification is generally stable for most people. Identification with a particular party therefore provides even casually engaged citizens with a useful shortcut to arrive at an understanding of a complicated political world. This seemingly simple fact, though, has important political implications. Over the last 30 years, the beliefs, preferences, and even knowledge of politically relevant facts among Republicans, has increasingly diverged from those of Democrats. Hetherington details these changes and explores their significance for the study of public opinion.

The Importance of Groups

Attachments to political parties are not the only group connections that matter in American politics. As noted above, Converse's landmark work on belief systems is primarily remembered for its conclusions regarding the limits of ideological thinking among members of the mass public. But Converse did not merely document the shortcomings of the citizenry; he also considered the ways that individuals could come to reasoned political decisions, even in the absence of an overarching guiding ideology. Chief among these was social groups.

Converse claimed that visible groups in a society provide structure to individual political judgments, mentioning race, religion, and nationality as clear referents on the political scene in the 1950s. Converse placed a great deal of weight on the power of groups because they were relatively simple concepts, requiring a lower threshold of sophistication than needed to employ abstract concepts, such as ideology. As Converse argued, to make use of group-based reasoning, citizens need only "be endowed with some cognitions of the group and with some interstitial 'linking' information indicating why a given party or policy is relevant to the group."[17] Converse concluded that reference group cues could serve as the foundation of "ideology by proxy," creating meaningful patterns in the attitudes and behaviors of ordinary citizens.[18]

In America, for better or for worse, race has long served as such a guide. The political implications of the relationships between blacks and whites have a long history in this country, from pre-Civil War debates about the role of slavery, through today. But racial politics is not simply about these relationships. As America becomes a more diverse society, other racial groups have risen in prominence. For instance, over the last 30 years, the percentage of the population that is Hispanic has increased greatly. Moreover, the "multi-racial" population—individuals who identify with more than one racial group—is among the fastest growing group in America. Thus, as Jane Junn, Tali Mendelberg, and Erica Czaja remind us, racial politics in the United States is in flux. In Chapter 6, they argue that the contours of the relationships between racial group identity, racial group consciousness, and public opinion—especially for Latinos and Asian Americans—are particularly challenging for scholars. In their chapter, they try to make sense of these diverse measurements by focusing on individual-level measurements of psychological attachment to groups, namely group identity and consciousness which are critical intervening variables between racial group classification and the formation of political preferences.

Junn, Mendelberg, and Czaja are primarily concerned with the consequences of attachment to particular groups for public opinion. This in-group identification is indeed an important component of political attitudes. But also important is an individual's relationships with other groups in society. In Chapter 7, Nancy Burns and Donald Kinder explicitly take up both these concerns in the context of race and gender. Specifically, they consider how the groupings of "man" and "woman" and "black" and "white" matter for politics. As mental categories, gender and race are important and consequential features of how we think about ourselves and others. In some ways, these categories have similar political implications. Both gender and race,

Burns and Kinder note, are sites of persistent and serious inequality in America. However, in practice, race and gender have very different effects on opinion. Examining a wide range of policy attitudes, Burns and Kinder find that the differences between men and women in the domain of gender policy are present, but often quite small. Differences between blacks and whites on policy in the domain of racial policy, on the other hand, are enormous. They argue that the distinction in the power of gender and racial politics is a function of the differences in the social organization of these two powerful groups. Women spend much of their lives in close relationships with men: as daughters, sisters, and mothers. As a matter of course, Burns and Kinder argue, women acquire interests and values in common with the men whose lives they share. The story of race in America, on the other hand, is one of segregation—enforced during the Jim Crow era by law, but continuing today through patterns of de facto racial segregation. Burns and Kinder therefore remind us that the power of group identity is in many ways contextually dependent. Different aspects of group identity may come into play in different ways depending on the particular social and political circumstances that create, shape, and activate that identity.

Race and gender do not exhaust the scope of groups that matter in American politics. Another set of groups that Converse mentioned, almost in passing, were religious organizations. Despite a constitutional provision against state religion, throughout American history religion and politics have been intertwined. In Chapter 8, David E. Campbell, Geoffrey C. Layman, and John C. Green examine the religious bases of public opinion. Today, when commentators speak of religion and politics, they often mean the growing link between evangelical denominations and conservative politics. Indeed, as Layman has convincingly demonstrated elsewhere, through the 1980s and into the 1990s, members of evangelical denomination became increasingly Republican in partisanship and conservative in political orientation relative to mainline denominations.[19]

However, a devotion to a religious identity does not always shift opinion to the right; it can also move attitudes in a liberal direction. While, today, religiosity is strongly correlated with conservative attitudes on "sex and family" issues like abortion, there are many more issues where religion has no effect. And there are a few issues—like the death penalty—where higher religiosity leads to a more liberal position.

Finally, Campbell, Layman, and Green demonstrate that religion may also function as a guide for those individuals who reject religious affiliation. Even as religion has emerged as an increasingly important factor in politics, the number of Americans who do not identify with a particular religious sect has risen as well. Identification as a religious "none" therefore has important implications for public opinion.

The New Psychological Foundations of Opinion

In addition to political and group attachments, there are a host of other factors that help to shape public opinion. An important new direction in recent years is the incorporation of insights from psychology and biology about the roots of public opinion. One line of research concerns the role of emotion in shaping political preferences. At the forefront of this fast-growing subfield is Ted Brader, who provides an overview of the emotional foundations of democratic citizenship in Chapter 9. While emotions are a complex set of reactions to external circumstances, individuals experience emotions via their gut reactions to particular stimuli. Thus, as Brader notes, emotions are best understood as the processes that generate feelings, and serve as a motivation for action. For instance, a feeling of fear causes individuals to become more alert and focused on external threats. People therefore shift from the status quo to actively reconsider their options.

While emotions are not explicitly political, such feelings often have important political implications. Of the plethora of emotional reactions, scholars have found that three stand out: fear, anger, and enthusiasm. These emotions affect public opinion by altering whether and how citizens pay attention to political events, learn about political developments, think through their decisions, and act on their opinions. For example, in his work on campaign advertising reviewed in Chapter 9, Brader has found that campaign ads that elicit fear—through the use of ominous music and unsettling images—cause voters to reconsider their standing decisions and make decisions based on their assessment of a candidate's issue positions and leadership qualities.

A second area of research that has gained steam in recent years is of the relationship between personality and politics. Personality played an important role in some early studies of political behavior—for example, Herbert McClosky's work on personality and ideology.[20] But this line of research largely went dormant in the 1960s, perhaps because of the lack of standard measures and concepts led the field of personality and psychology to acquire, as Paul Sniderman aptly puts it, "a jerry-built appearance," one without a coherent theory or set of findings.[21] The last 15 years, however, has seen a resurgence of this line of work. Beginning in the mid-1990s, scholars such as Stanley Feldman and Karen Stenner began exploring the power of authoritarianism.[22] This research harkens back to work done in the wake of World War II that sought to tie the rise of fascism in Europe to a particular "authoritarian" personality type, one prone to intolerance and obedience to authority.[23] While the early work had a number of measurement flaws that were quickly discovered and debated, this more recent work demonstrated that with a more careful eye toward questions of validity, the intersection of personality and politics could prove a fruitful and important area of inquiry.

More recent work has built on developments in basic measurement from psychology. In Chapter 10, Jeffery J. Mondak and Matthew V. Hibbing focus on the "Big Five" approach developed in personality psychology. This approach represents personality trait structure via attention to five trait dimensions: openness to experience, conscientiousness, extroversion, agreeableness, and emotional stability. They then present original survey research that demonstrates the importance of these personality traits on a wide range of political attitudes ranging from basic political ideology to specific attitudes on moral policies, such as same-sex marriage. They also touch on an interesting new direction in public opinion research that draws on insights from biology, namely the genetic roots of political orientation. Mondak and Hibbing contend that biological differences matter both for personality and for political behavior. This work is still in its early stages, and studies of biology and politics have generated a great deal of controversy. However, this is certainly a promising and interesting area that remains to be explored in the years to come.

The Public and Society

Understanding the structure of public opinion is an important step in assessing its political significance. But it is also important to actually detail the role it plays in the political world. The last part of this book explicitly examines how public opinion is shaped by political events and the rhetoric of politicians and how, in turn, public opinion shapes and guides the conduct of politics.

In Chapter 11, John Sides and Jake Haselswerdt begin by observing that what was true in 1948 is true today. Months before an election, political scientists can predict election results. For instance, at a meeting of political scientists held over Labor Day weekend in 2008—even before the start of the Republican National convention, much less the economic meltdown that began in October—a panel of political scientists each presented a forecast of the final vote tally. Almost all of them predicted the exact outcome within a couple of percentage points. The average of their predictions was a 53 percent vote share for the Democrats, and that is exactly the national percentage of the vote Barack Obama received on Election Day.

At the same time, there are lots of reasons to think that campaigns should matter. Journalists focus incessantly on the ups and downs of campaigns and analyze each day's events in the search for critical turning points. Furthermore, polls are variable, changing from day to day and week to week. This leads to an important question: How is it possible that elections are so predictable even amidst the apparently volatility of the campaign?

The answers to this question can, in part, be found in the other chapters in this volume. Voters, Sides and Haselswerdt remind us, almost never arrive at a campaign as a blank slate, devoid of ideas about politics or the candidates. In most elections, voters can draw on their long-standing political identities to guide their choices, even without any detailed information about the candidates. These identities include race, ethnicity, socioeconomic status, religion, and—above all—partisanship. The predictability of elections stems from how these fundamental factors affect how citizens vote and, by association, who wins the election. Put another way, campaign outcomes are predictable because pre-existing ties to particular choices are so strong.

This, of course, is not to say that campaigns serve no function in a democratic society. True, most voters can draw on social and partisan identities to make decisions about candidates, but there will still be some citizens who are uncertain about or unfamiliar with the candidates. For these citizens, campaigns can serve a critical function. Moreover in primary or nonpartisan election, voters cannot draw on familiar heuristics and decisions rules, such as straight-party voting. Here, too, campaigns can matter greatly. In the second half of their chapter, Sides and Haselswerdt therefore detail *how* campaigns can reinforce some existing decisions and change others' minds.

In Chapter 12, Matthew Baum explores how changes in the media environment have revolutionized the ways in which politicians reach out to the mass public when building support for their policies and programs. With the rise of the Internet and the fragmentation of the television audience among a growing number of cable channels, politicians can no longer mobilize the public through a single source. Instead, the changing media landscape means they must work harder to communicate with citizens, and to be far more precise in tailoring their messages to particular sub-constituencies who might otherwise dismiss what they hear. As the media become more specialized—and as voters flock to different sources that share their pre-existing political views, in line with the rise of partisanship as a motivating force (as discussed by Hetherington in Chapter 5)—politicians face a difficult task. The opportunities to mobilize to action those citizens who already agree with a politician by "preaching to the choir" have increased as the media have become more specialized. However, opportunities to "convert the flock"—actually persuade citizens who are not inclined to share the preferences and political stances of politicians—are in increasingly short supply. Thus, while a common civic space for public affairs has not entirely disappeared, the potential for reaching across the partisan aisle through the media has certainly been shrinking in recent years.

Another important topic of research is the dynamics of democratic elections. Though the study of campaigns and elections is itself a thriving subfield in political science, it has been deeply informed by insights from the field of public opinion. In fact, many of the fundamental insights about the nature of public opinion discussed in this book came out of data collected on voter reactions to political campaigns in the 1940s and 1950s. Consider the Columbia studies led by Berelson, Lazarsfeld, and McPhee, discussed above. These scholars went into their study expecting that voters during a campaign would treat candidates as something akin to products in a supermarket—citizens would shop around, consider (and reconsider) their options, and finally arrive at a choice on Election Day. In fact, the Columbia researchers found something very different. Most people did not change their preferences. The campaign, it seemed, had little effect on voters' decisions.

Finally, in Chapter 13, Andrea Louise Campbell examines the relationship between public opinion and public policy, including processes of policy feedback. Political scientists have spent decades examining whether public opinion shapes the policies of government. But, as Campbell notes, an exclusive focus on the public opinion side of the equation paints an incomplete picture. On the one hand, the public's preferences influence policy outcomes, although this varies across time and across issues. Moreover, privileged and politically active groups are more likely to see their preferences fulfilled than others. But once policies are created, they acquire a life of their own. Thus, public policies themselves influence public opinion, so that existing policy shapes the political landscape and the possibilities for future policy. Opinion and policy move together, each influencing the other.

Campbell uses a case study of the Medicare reform of 2003, which added a prescription drug benefit to the public health insurance program for older Americans, to illustrate these effects. At the moment of passage, the reform bill was the largest social policy expansion in a generation. But its passage begs three questions. Why, Campbell asks, was a new benefit added for seniors, who already enjoyed national health insurance, when one-sixth of the population had no health insurance at all? Why was the main focus of the bill the addition of a new prescription drug benefit to Medicare rather than other provisions that might better serve Medicare recipients, such as long-term care? And why did the specific features of drug benefit conform more to interest groups' preferences than those of seniors? The answers illustrate both the effects of past policies on subsequent policy making and the limits of public opinion's influence. She argues that seniors were the focus of new health policy making rather than the uninsured because of the formidable political power older Americans accrued as a result of previous policies—the development of Social Security, which over time made seniors the most politically active age group. The focus became prescription drugs because they are a highly salient expense to seniors and, as a result, their coverage was an extremely popular provision. And interest groups shaped specific features of the law rather than seniors because public opinion's influence is often blunt—helping set broader agendas rather than giving instructions about specific policy alternatives. Interestingly, she finds that unlike the case of Social Security, the creation of a large-scale government prescription drug program did not change the attitudes of the recipients. Perhaps over the coming decades, this will change, but for now the impact of policy on public opinion has been limited.

Final Thoughts

Though I have tried to provide a comprehensive overview of the field of public opinion, this volume has only scratched the surface of the excellent research that is out there. Of necessity, there is a great deal of material that I could not cover. For instance, besides political and group attachments and personality and emotion, there are a host of other factors that help to shape public opinion. There is a large and rich literature on the power of core political values, such as subscription to principles of political equality or individualism.[24] Other scholars have explored the relationship between self-interest and opinion.[25] For instance, some political scientists have examined whether those individuals with the greatest stake in a policy—parents who might be directly affected by policies designed to ensure school integration, for instance—are more likely to take a clear stance on questions relating to that policy. Here, the evidence is very mixed; somewhat surprisingly, the relationship between self-interest and opinion is often quite weak. Recently, however, scholars have begun exploring other ways in which direct economic interests could matter for political choice.[26]

Beyond research on the structure of opinion, there is also a great deal of interesting work being done on the role of public opinion in society. For example, a number of researchers have explored the nature of social influence in opinion formation and dissemination, some of which harkens back to Blumer's work in the 1940s.[27] And even this work merely scratches the surface of the field.

But this book is intended to be just the starting point for most students. Hopefully, the chapters will pique your interest and give you the tools and motivation you need to go off and explore the field on your own.

Notes

1. Key, V.O. (1963) *Public Opinion and American Democracy*. New York: Alfred Knopf, p. 8.
2. Herbst, Susan (1993) *Numbered Voices: How Opinion Polling has Shaped American Politics*. Chicago, IL: University of Chicago Press.
3. Blumer, Herbert (1948) "Public Opinion and Public Opinion Polling." *American Sociological Review* 13: 542–549.
4. Childs, H. (1964) *Public Opinion*. Princeton, NJ: D. Van Nostrand.
5. Key (1963), p. 14.
6. Herbst (1993).
7. Blumberg, S., Julian Luke, Gestur Davidson, Michael Davern, Tzy-Chyi Yu, and Karen Soderberg. (2007) "Wireless Substitution: State-level Estimates From the National Health Interview Survey, January–December 2007." *National Health Statistics Report* 14.
8. Lippmann, Walter (1925) *The Phantom Public*. New York: MacMillan Company, pp. 24.
9. Lowell, Abbot Lawrence (1922) *Public Opinion in War and Peace*. Cambridge, MA: Harvard University Press.

10. Berelson, B., P. Lazarsfeld, and W. McPhee (1954) *Voting*. Chicago, IL: University of Chicago Press, p. 207.
11. Stimson, James A. (2004) *Tides of Consent: How Public Opinion Shapes American Politics*. Cambridge: Cambridge University Press.
12. Achen, Christopher H. (1975) "Mass Political Attitudes and the Survey Response." *American Political Science Review* 69: 1227.
13. Converse, Philip (1964) "The Nature of Belief Systems in Mass Publics." In *Ideology and Discontent*, ed. David Apter: 206–261. New York: The Free Press of Glencoe, p. 207.
14. Nie, N.H., S. Verba, and J.R. Petrocik (1979) *The Changing American Voter*. Cambridge, MA: Harvard University Press
15. Sullivan, John L., James Pierson, and George E. Marcus (1979) "An Alternative Conceptualization of Political Tolerance: Illusory Increases, 1950s–1970s." *American Political Science Review* 73: 233–249.
16. CBS News (2011, 11 10). "Looking Ahead to the 112th Congress." Retrieved from http://www.cbsnews.com/stories/2010/11/11/politics/main7045964.shtml.
17. Converse (1964), pp. 236–237.
18. Converse, Phillip (1975) "Public Opinion and Voting Behavior." In *Handbook of Political Science*, eds. F.W. Greenstein and N.W. Polsby, 4: 75–169. Reading, MA: Addison-Wesley.
19. Layman, Geoffrey C. (1997) "Religion and Political Behavior in the United States: The Impact of Beliefs, Affiliations, and Commitment from 1980 to 1994." *Public Opinion Quarterly* 61: 288–316.
20. McClosky, Herbert (1958) "Conservatism and Personality." *American Political Science Review* 52: 27–45.
21. Sniderman, Paul M., W. Russell Neuman, Jack Citrin, Herbert McClosky, and J. Merrill Shanks (1975) "The Stability of Support for the Political System: The Impact of Watergate." *American Politics Quarterly* 3: 437–457.
22. Feldman, Stanley and Karen Stenner (1998) "Perceived Threat and Authoritarianism." *Political Psychology* 18: 741–770. Also, Stenner, Karen (2005) *The Authoritarian Dynamic*. New York: Cambridge University Press. For more recent work in this vein, see Hetherington, Marc and Jonathan Weiler (2009) *Authoritarianism and Polarization in American Politics*. New York: Cambridge University Press.
23. Adorno, T.W., E. Frenkel-Brunswik, D.J. Levinson, and R.N. Sanford (1950) *The Authoritarian Personality*. New York: Harper and Row.
24. For an excellent review, see Feldman, Stanley (2003) "Values, Ideology, and the Structure of Political Attitudes." In *Oxford Handbook of Political Psychology*, eds. David O. Sears, Leonie Huddy, and Robert Jervis, 477–508. New York: Oxford University Press.
25. See, for example, Sears, David O., Richard Lau, Tom Tyler, and Harris Allen, Jr. (1980) "Self-interest vs. Symbolic Politics in Policy Attitudes and Presidential Voting." *American Political Science Review* 74: 670–684. Also, Citrin, Jack, Beth Reingold, and Donald Green (1990) "American Identity and the Politics of Ethnic Change." *Journal of Politics* 52: 1124–1154.
26. Gerber, Alan S. and Gregory A. Huber (2010) "Partisanship, Political Control and Economic Assessments." *American Journal of Political Science* 54: 153–173.
27. See, for example, Huckfeldt, R. and J. Sprague (1995) *Citizens, Politics, and Social Communication: Information and Influence in an Election Campaign*. New York: Cambridge University Press; Baybeck, Brady and Scott McClurg (2005) "What Do they Know and How Do they Know It? An Examination of Citizen Awareness of Context." *American Politics Research* 33: 492–250; Mutz, Diana (2006) *Hearing the Other Side: Deliberative versus Participatory Democracy*. New York: Cambridge University Press; Nickerson, David (2008) "Is Voting Contagious? Evidence from Two Field Experiments." *American Political Science Review* 102: 49–57.

Part I

The Meaning and Measurement of Public Opinion

Chapter 1

The History and Meaning of Public Opinion

Susan Herbst

While the phrase "public opinion" was not formally coined until the eighteenth century, the concept has been with us since biblical times and the ancient Greek democracies. It seems that understanding the sentiment of common people is a chronic desire of leaders and citizens alike, no matter the form of government, nation in question, or moment in history.

In our day, the definition of public opinion seems more complex than ever before due to the intensity of global communication: Changes in communication have upset all of our apple carts, making us question the value of opinion surveys, demonstrations, letters to the editor, punditry, and all of the other conventional vehicles for opinion expression and measurement we have become accustomed to. I will close this historical overview with a few reflections about the future of public opinion meaning and measures, based on the recent evolution of media like the Internet. But my central focus will be on the past, taking time to underscore pivotal eras and events, when the meaning of public opinion changed in significant ways.

The chapter is organized into four sections, reflecting my own periodization—designed for this volume—of public opinion history. First, however, a few notes of preface.

This is a Western history of public opinion with a focus on America, in part because of my own training, but primarily because we have little documentation of public opinion expression and assessment from Africa and Asia. This is not to say that popular sentiment was not important or interesting on those continents, but simply that we are challenged by the lack of a written historical record focused on public opinion before the twentieth century. Second, this chapter is most akin to intellectual history, due to the deficit of historical data that might better represent the perspectives of lower or middle class Europeans and Americans in a systematic way. Finally, my tour through hundreds of years is by nature a superficial one, and those wishing to explore different periods in more depth might begin with the bibliographic sources provided.

Public Opinion as Community: From Ancient Times to the Seventeenth Century

The phrase "public opinion" was not in common usage in ancient Greece or Rome (it was coined during the Enlightenment), but the *vox populi* was an intriguing phenomenon in both civilizations. We know far more about what the ancient Greeks believed, and it is clear that popular sentiment played a larger role than in Rome, where the public was called the "vulgus."[1]

In the Greek city-states, public opinion was a valued—if limited—dimension of the political sphere, given the narrow definition of citizenship (confined to only a category of men), and the many contradictions of early democracy (e.g., slavery). Yet despite these limits, the Greeks were extraordinary in their attention to public opinion and its many forms—theater, rhetoric, oratory, festivals, juries, and the like.[2] These mechanisms for the expression and assessment of public opinion were abundant, creative, and very much in keeping with the outward expression of the period. If we are to gather clues about the meaning of public opinion, from these many forms of expression, they would add up to a sense of public opinion as *community*: People came together for entertainment, for debate, and even the goal of consensus. This is not to say that all participated with equal footing or that the discourse was an inchoate model of strong democratic activity; we have far too little empirical evidence to draw such conclusions. But there is a sense that public opinion was very much tied to interpersonal networks, since ancient societies were small and built on kinship, friendship, and the face-to-face nature of tiny polities. This is a very different way of thinking about public opinion than we see in later centuries, where the scale of democracies makes an interpersonal model impossible to sustain. But suffice it to say that public opinion was formed through relationships, and expressed in much the same way, deeply embedded in social life—in the gathering of small groups, crowds, and even mobs.

The pre-eminent ancient philosophers debated public opinion, while the populace created it and went about their business.[3] Plato and Aristotle differed greatly in how they viewed public opinion, with Plato more skeptical of its role. The Aristotelian view likely matches better the hopes of at least the elite citizenry of early democracies, with their devotion to voting, juries, and political participation. Aristotle's view is worth quoting at length, the earliest and most profound views of public opinion as the aggregation of views within a community—a foreshadowing of polls and surveys to come much later:

> It is possible that the many, no one of whom taken singly is a good man, may yet taken all together be better than the few, not individually but collectively, in the same way that a feast to which all contribute is better than one given at one man's expense. For where there are many people, each has some share of goodness and intelligence, and when these are brought

> together, they become as it were one multiple man with many pairs of feet and hands and many minds. So too in regard to character and the powers of perception. That is why the general public is a better judge of works of music and poetry; some judge some parts, some others, but their joint pronouncement is a verdict upon the whole. And it is this assembling in one what was before separate that gives the good man his superiority over any individual man from the masses.[4]

This view of public opinion is both ancient and very contemporary at the same time. It appeals to our current view of public opinion as the aggregation of individual opinions, yet embeds public opinion in everyday life. One gets the sense that—at Aristotle sees it—citizens can and should move from politics to art and music seamlessly, with valuable opinions on all.

My point is that early views and practices of public opinion were based in community in ways that are difficult to fathom in mass democratic societies of today. Put another way, the norms and values of a community *were* in fact its public opinion. This meaning of public opinion is the dominant one until the eighteenth century, when societies grew larger and urban life dominated the political scene and the nature of intellectual life. Nonetheless, the notion of public opinion being deeply rooted in the values and day-to-day life of a community can still be found today when a polity or organization is tiny—a neighborhood, a PTA, or a place of business. And, as I mention in closing, threads of this definition of public opinion are also with us in Internet communication, as electronic communities form and social networking imitates at least some aspects of timeless community life.

The history of public opinion is nearly impossible to trace with much vigor between the ancient Greek and Roman states until the Renaissance, although of course the population grew and evolved during these centuries. Daily life was difficult, and citizens expressed their opinions in both older ways and newer ones, with petitions and bread riots characterizing the fifteenth and sixteenth centuries. I discuss these and other mechanisms elsewhere, but, without question, the most important advance between the early democracies and the Renaissance was the development of the printing press, which transformed the notion of a public: While communities were often cohesive in previous centuries, print tied people together across geography, made possible the diffusion of ideas, and profoundly changed conceptions of democracy and citizenship.[5] The printing and distribution of bibles, books, pamphlets, and newspapers enabled the formation of attitudes, as well as the linear development of public thought, argument, and national identity. Print legitimated views and social groups, but, most of all, led to the intensive and widespread cognitive engagement of people who previously had local conversation only, to shape their world.

One last intellectual note about the pre-seventeenth century period that deserves mention is the appearance of Machiavelli's *Prince*, one of the few compelling works on public opinion before the Enlightenment. As is well known, the essays are written as advice to the prince, by a shrewd observer of politics, alliances, and people.[6] Machiavelli was a civil servant and warrior, but also a philosopher and advisor to political leaders. In *The Prince*, Machiavelli views people as fickle, greedy, and generally weak, hence the successful leader must adopt a kind and paternalistic style. Yet, as he notes, the populace must also be kept in line through fear, and a successful prince uses fear as his most powerful weapon, given the fragile power of love, hardly a way for a leader to maintain social control. With regard to public opinion, of course Machiavelli's views are undemocratic: The people are not capable of self-rule. Nonetheless, Machiavelli's perspectives are much in keeping with the conception of public opinion as based in community, in interpersonal networks, and reflects the norms and values of society at large. Most interesting for us, in our age where polling is so dominant, is what is missing in his thought: There is no trace of public opinion as the aggregation of individuals, nor of the persuasion necessary to move them. Machiavelli's prince must persuade, but it is still his force and his power that moves public opinion, or, better stated, keeps it unperturbed and in a relative state of ignorance.

Independent, Conversational Publics: From the Enlightenment to Early America

During the late seventeenth and early eighteenth centuries, we see the emergence of public opinion in a form far closer to what we understand it to be today. In fact, the phrase "public opinion" is often attributed to Jacques Necker, finance minister to King Louis XIV of France in heady days before the revolution.[7] He coined the phrase to describe the talk of the salons and parlors of Enlightenment Paris, part of the "public sphere" identified by Jürgen Habermas in his narrative about the history of political communication.[8]

The decades before the French Revolution are without question the first truly important period in the intellectual and social history of public opinion, and so have received intensive scholarly treatment by historians and those with an interest in political development. While the ancient democracies and communities in the medieval period were defined by norms and interpersonal networks, the largely rural and agrarian economies meant that public opinion was largely underdeveloped as an idea and a reality. Print communication, often religious in nature, but eventually resulting in news-sheets and newspapers, led to increased sophistication about citizenship and public expression that come to fruition in the decades of the Enlightenment. A few key modes of public opinion expression are worth exploring, since they led Necker to coin the phrase, but also exemplify what I mean by "conversational" public opinion.

Among the most important means of public opinion expression during the decades before the great revolutions in Europe and America, were coffeehouses, salons, and taverns. Of course, people have always gathered to eat, drink, and make merry, but these venues took on a far different character in the seventeenth and eighteenth centuries. By this era, printed news, pamphlets, and political tracts were commonplace and read in public, given their cost (home delivery and individual subscription to newspapers is a late nineteenth century phenomenon). News was part of coffeehouse conversation—driving it, and being formed by it—since editors and journalists mingled with merchants and common folk in London coffeehouses. Information about politics, policy, commerce, and culture readily available through newspapers, and the urbanization of the population, led directly to a far more intense, dynamic, and coherent public opinion than had ever been imagined. As Habermas has noted, coffeehouses symbolize the emergence of a "public sphere"—an arena for free expression apart from the court and outside of the domestic realm. These profound changes in public life—indeed the emergence of a public life that had legitimacy and energy—would eventually lead to revolutions and the modern form of democracy.

Less democratic and open than the coffeehouse, but perhaps even more critical in the evolution of public opinion practice and philosophy, was the *salon* of pre-revolutionary Paris.[9] These were elite gatherings of statesmen, philosophers, writers, financiers, and other opinion leaders, typically held in the homes of wealthy and charismatic women. During these dinners, participants staged plays, argued about politics and the existence of God, tried out their theories of social life, and, most important, sustained criticism of the king and his court. In fact, there is evidence that the king sent emissaries to the salons to report on conversations there, presumably to keep a finger on the pulse of public opinion. It might seem odd to us today, particularly in Western democracies, to view the salon as a vehicle for public opinion formation and expression, given the tiny number of privileged Parisians who took part. But, the bulk of the population, even in a large and sophisticated city like Paris, was illiterate and too busy struggling to survive to have the time or opportunity for political theory.

This all changed with the onslaught of violent revolutionary fervor in France, the ideas of which were—somewhat ironically—developed in the salons of the elite. In an unusually direct mention of public opinion, the writer and literary critic Louis-Sébastien Mercier noted in 1782:

> Today, public opinion has a preponderant force in Europe that cannot be resisted. Thus in assessing the progress of enlightenment and the change it must bring about, we may hope that it will bring the greatest good to the world and that tyrants of all stripes will tremble before this universal cry that continuously rings out to fill and awaken Europe.[10]

In this period of public opinion development, expression of sentiment began energetically in salons and coffeehouses, was reflected in newspapers, and took on the occasional underclass formation of bread riots, strikes, and petitioning (during this period, petitions were presented both peacefully and violently).

These very same European-born techniques for the expression and assessment of public opinion take root, albeit in a different style, in the American revolution and early decades of the nation, described so well by Alexis de Tocqueville in his masterwork, *Democracy in America*. Tocqueville is quite interesting on this point, admiring public opinion and its democratic voice in a new nation, but seeing seeds of danger as well—the "tyranny of the majority," as he called it. As Leo Damrosch notes in his scholarly treatment of Tocqueville's travels of 1831:

> Only in hindsight could Americans appreciate the real force of Tocqueville's insight: public opinion was indeed the true danger, and prejudices might actually be strongest where expression was free. A self-governing people could internalize rigid attitudes and inhibitions, and in effect police its own behavior.[11]

To summarize this extraordinary period, from the inchoate public opinion of salons to the great revolutions and the birth of an American nation, we can detect some of the ancient threads—people still lived in communities that valued face-to-face relationships, conversation, kinship, and friendship. The social imagination of most people—from elites to the lower classes—was largely a local one and public opinion took on this flavor. But it was becoming far more national and far reaching, with the development of print. Public opinion was suddenly a more powerful force to be reckoned with, whether an elite-driven revolution like the American one or a more proletariat French revolution. The power of public opinion, even if often illiterate and uneven, was clear and compelling, and theorists of the nineteenth century—Tocqueville, Marx, Bryce, Tönnies—recognized it with equal fervor. It was still a period characterized by human relations and towns, but the independent voice of the public had emerged never to be entirely silenced again, no matter the authoritarian intentions of a leader.

Numbered Voices and the Diffusion of Media: Mid-Nineteenth Century through the 1950s

While public opinion as a phenomenon is largely European in character, the accelerated development of the United States in the mid-nineteenth century made America the most interesting and complex site for the practice and philosophy of public opinion. In fact, Tocqueville, then the British visitor Lord Bryce a few decades later, were among many European travelers drawn overseas. Many from the old world sought an understanding of democratic institutions, of political behavior, federalism, industry, and, most of all, the strange and compelling force that is public opinion.

As is well documented by historians, the American nineteenth century was a confluence of profound changes in manufacturing, demographics, communication, and transportation, all of which were reflected in the growth and complexity of public opinion. Political parties evolved quickly, reflecting and shaping the popular sentiment, through hand-to-hand combat in the urban precincts and the highly partisan newspapers of the time. Immigration and urbanization led to an extraordinarily stratified, even booming, population and public opinion reflected the mobility and volatility of the time. Perhaps it was inevitable that, in trying to understand the complex nature of public opinion, journalists, statesmen, party operatives, and citizens themselves took to more quantitative methods for opinion expression and measurement. In new larger-scale democracies, where elections determined the course of a community and a nation, the aggregation of individual opinions through counting and straw polling was vital.

While voting and pre-election straw polling can be traced as far back as biblical times, counting heads and opinions fit a growing democracy perfectly, hence the explosion of these polls in the nineteenth century. As I note elsewhere, citizens polled themselves and sent the counts into their local newspapers for publication, journalists counted votes and opinions as they traveled the rails of the Midwest, and of course party operatives polled in private, as they do today, to get a sense of the prevailing winds. The intensity of polling, partisanship, and campaigning was fierce by century's end and indeed many aspects of the 1896 U.S. presidential election reflect this change (the race was between William McKinley and William Jennings Bryan). This particular election foreshadowed the culture of politics we experience in the twenty-first century—highly emotional issues, new demographic coalitions of voters, wild campaign spending, hyperbolic oratory, mud-slinging, and the extensive use of train travel to move candidates and voters. For example, there was a fierce debate between the candidates about the gold standard, which Bryan believed hurt rural working people, deeply in trauma due to the 1893 economic downturn. He gave one of the most famous speeches in American political history (the "Cross of Gold" speech) at the 1896 Democratic Presidential Convention. It was one of the earliest "rock star" type performances in our history, inspiring many and waging class warfare in rhetorical terms. Bryan's populism was unique in its power and formulation, and unforgettable in its effects on American politics even today.

Most of all, the election highlighted the centrality of public opinion—its measurement and persuasion. After 1896, no campaign manager or candidate would ever conceive of running without strategizing an approach to the ever-evolving American public.

And everyone thought they owned the right to poll, from women in quilting bees and college students to factory workers and drinking clubs. During the 1896 election, a railroad worker wrote a typical, colorful partisan polling report to the *Chicago Tribune*:

> John J. Byrnes, General Passenger Agent and Auditor of the Southern California railroad, reached Chicago yesterday morning on a Santa Fe train on which, among other passengers, were seventy-five Californians. Some one polled the denizens of the Far West and Bryan got fifteen votes. Just before Mr. Byrnes came East a large manufacturing plant in Lost Angeles in which 1000 men are employed was polled, and McKinley was the choice of 997. Mr. Byrnes, who until this campaign has been a Democrat, is confident McKinley will carry California by a big majority.[12]

The nineteenth century was a period of tremendous quickening in the quantification of public opinion in the United States, in part because of the increasing intensity and partisanship, but also fed by the rise of the sciences, where measurement was central. If we could calculate the best ways to assess crop production or speed factory assembly lines, a booming industrial nation could also bring science to its democratic practices. Polling—unscientific though it was at the turn of the century—was as democratic as voting, and as satisfying, in a nation with so many people and opinions to count.

At the turn of century and into the pre-war period, public opinion gained in thoughtfulness and sophistication due to a proliferation of print media then, eventually, radio. Most interesting was the explosion of magazines during these decades, the era when many periodicals still with us—the *New Republic*, the *Atlantic*, and *Harper's*—began or gained subscribers at an impressive pace. The rising literacy of the population enabled the appearance of thoughtful publications, leading to an even more engaged, serious public. As a result, polling the public became an extraordinarily attractive political and financial endeavor in the 1920s and 1930s. This is the period when a magazine called the *Literary Digest* began extensive polling of the public, and many of the polling firms still with us today were born. For example, George Gallup—a marketing expert—got his start as a pollster in the 1930s. In 1936, he correctly predicted victory for Franklin Roosevelt in his presidential bid against Alf Landon. The *Digest*, by contrast, had predicted a win for Landon, and so this year marked the ascendency over Gallup's more scientific methods. The *Digest* soon halted publication, and Gallup led the development of a far more sophisticated polling industry in the United States.[13]

As radio diffused in the early century and through World War II, a nation bound by communication was taken for granted: no one was out of reach, from the great plains to the depths of Appalachia. But what is interesting for our purposes here is the solidity of the notion of an *American public*, whose opinions could and would be counted.

From an Atomized Public to a Connected One: Broadcast Media and the Internet

By the 1950s, with the diffusion of television, Americans saw themselves as a diverse but unified public, brought together by culture, habits, media, the struggles of a depression, and two world wars of enormous consequence. We were never a cohesive nation, a fairy tale that no scholar can support. But by mid-century, the notion that publics could exist, even if momentarily, and that they could "speak," was as concrete as the massive skyscrapers of Chicago or the new highways that crisscrossed every state in the nation.

As so many have pointed out, television brought Americans together through shared programming, media events both planned and unexpected (e.g., the Kennedy assassination), but it also separated or atomized them. Even more compelling than radio, television in the United States was a domestic technology, one that drew viewers home and away from streets, bars, parks, and public space. Americans had been a people who, weather permitting, lived life in the open, from the giant torchlight political parades of the 1800s to amusement parks, movie theaters, urban street life of the tenements, and state fairs. Television began to affect this public culture, and, some would argue, had a hand in abolishing it. While one could argue for multiple forces steering people toward the nuclear family, this turn inward was an undeniable reality in the latter half of the twentieth century to the present day.[14]

What did this type of cultural transformation mean for public opinion? With regard to measurement, it coincided with the rise of the sample survey, a systematic and scientific way to sample Americans' opinions either through visits to homes or phone calls to households.[15] So the "turning inward" of Americans, to their families, moving out of inner cities and toward the suburbs, fit squarely with a means of opinion measurement that relied on people sitting still: Americans were home and available to opine. The engagement of Americans with television, ever evolving and expanding in its offerings, focused them on the news and made the networks enormously powerful and influential. Politicians used the new medium, some better than others, but there was no question by the mid-1960s that visual electronic media would be the most dominant tool one could find to shape public opinion.

In terms of the four grand periods of this chapter, the televisual age drops much of the earlier sense—present in the three previous eras—that public opinion was based in interpersonal community and dialogue. With the advent of television, Americans were more closely tethered to the medium—to Walter Cronkite or Ed Sullivan—than they were to each other. The communities of ancient Greece, of the Enlightenment coffeehouses, of colonial taverns, and the local gatherings so attractive to a visiting Tocqueville, were no longer interchangeable with the notion of public opinion. Public opinion in the twentieth century was based less in community norms, values, and exchange and more suitably defined as the aggregation of atomized household and their inhabitants. The conversational and interpersonal meanings of public opinion—the phenomena that prompted Necker to coin the phrase—no longer meant much in a modern world that lived in single family suburban houses or longed to.

Television had a profound effect on the nature of publics themselves—how they are formed and how they interact. And it still does: Americans get their news from cable television in great numbers and newer organizations like *MSNBC* and *Fox News* are tremendously influential in shaping both opinion and public discourse. But try as they might to modernize, by reading Twitter messages on air or providing social networking opportunities, cable news programs are still very much in the "one to many" mode of early television. We don't interact with television hosts, they are not our friends, and we have no relationship with them.

Interestingly, the emergence of the Internet has brought us back around—although perhaps not full circle—to a more conversational mode of public opinion. I would argue that we live now in the most complex of times, with regard to the meaning of public opinion: All at once, it makes sense to define, express, and measure public opinion through traditional local means (local zoning board hearings), Facebook, opinion polls, demonstrations, Internet chat, and so many other means of communication. Perhaps Jacques Necker's meaning of public opinion—the wide-ranging, undisciplined, but engaging talk of the salons—fits America in the early twenty-first century?

The Return of the Repressed: Conversation and the Internet

It remains to be seen how American public opinion will be shaped by social networking, the abundance of political blogs, and upcoming forms of face-to-face chat that will make teleconferencing easy for the individual citizen. Much has changed already, as the Internet breaks down barriers and speeds the news cycle, forcing constant action and reaction by our candidates and leaders. Citizens try to keep up or not, but we all know that a world of debate about political and social issues awaits us at all hours on our screens, should we choose to lurk or actually participate. Internet literacy is booming, and young people know of no other way to learn of public opinion than the Internet, rich with data and full of serendipity. The immediacy of communication that we experience is perhaps the most gratifying aspect of all: There is no more trying to get one's modest letter to the editor published, or hoping in vain for a scene of the president on the basketball court. Images, ideas, debates, and screeds abound, and link us to a complex, but seemingly smaller world.

Public opinion—its dynamic and its meaning—evolve very slowly as my lengthy sweep of history demonstrates. Change seems to come at a faster pace now, but predicting the future of political discourse and popular sentiment would be a dangerous game. All that said, I close with three insights about public opinion in our current period, informed by history:

Citizens will have more control over the shape of public opinion and how it is measured. With the easy access afforded by the web, most people can express their opinions to large audiences, no matter their thoughtfulness, or accuracy of their facts. Whether this direct expression of public opinion—pursued without the gatekeepers and editors of previous periods—enhances the nature of free expression or the quality of public policy remains to be seen. But it is clear that we shall never return to a political realm where elites tightly regulate the nature and flow of popular beliefs. This is a profound change in the nature of public opinion, unique to the early twenty-first century and our technological environment. It is democratizing and it levels the communicative playing field, even if not the economic one.

Media organizations will need a fundamentally different business model. As has been pointed out repeatedly over the past few years, both advertising and subscriber-based models for sustaining a journalistic enterprise, are failing even our most esteemed elite newspapers and networks. The future is unclear, but as more regional newspapers collapse or turn to shared wire services for content, a loss of professional, sophisticated, reporting, and investigative journalism will fundamentally change the nature of public opinion. A narrowing of news sources, and a media sphere where the same content is spread far and wide, will not enable the marketplace of ideas we hope for in a lively democracy. It is a dire moment for media professionals, and their organizational infrastructure matters immensely for the formation of intelligent public opinion.

Political participation is in danger of disappearing. Despite the abundance of information and opinions we now have, through our many Internet and broadcast sources, participation in politics has not risen in parallel. Turnout in presidential elections, for example, has not increased dramatically, nor do we see a rise in demonstrations or political participation at the local levels. While candidate fundraising has become easier, and there are some odd, media-induced political movements springing up (e.g., the Tea Party of 2010), it would be difficult to locate an uptick in actual political behavior. Perhaps the sociologists Robert Merton and Paul Lazarsfeld were right, in 1948, when they predicted that mass media (radio, in their time) would lull us into an *informed yet inactive state*. They wrote, famously:

> Exposure to this flood of information may serve to narcotize rather than to energize the average reader or listener. As an increasing meed [*sic*] of time is devoted to reading and listening, a decreasing share is available for organized action. The individual reads accounts of issues and problems and may even discuss alternative lines of action. But this rather intellectualized, rather remote connection with organized social action is

> not activated. The interested and informed citizen can congratulate himself on his lofty state of interest and information and neglect to see that he has abstained from decision and action. In short, he takes his secondary contact with the world of political reality, his reading and listening and thinking, as a vicarious performance. He comes to mistake *knowing* about problems of the day *for doing* something about them. His social conscience remains spotlessly clean. He *is* concerned. He *is* informed. And he has all sorts of ideas as to what should be done. But, after he has gotten through his dinner and after he has listened to his favored radio programs and after he has read his second newspaper of the day, it is really time for bed. In this peculiar respect, mass communications may be included among the most respectable and efficient of social narcotics. They may be so fully effective as to keep the addict from recognizing his own malady.[16]

It seems a fine note on which to conclude this brief history of public opinion, as public opinion is not just a political phenomenon but a fundamental, endangered aspect of democracy. Without an unhindered yet intelligently engaged *vox populi* effective democratic institutions are elusive to us, hence the centrality of public opinion to the ambitions of both developed and developing nations around the world. Throughout human history, the popular sentiment has inevitably found vehicles and thousands of expressive forms. But it is fragile as well, crushed by many a dictator or authoritarian government. Public opinion as a practice and an ideal is very much in the hands of the people, should they choose to value it.

Notes

1. See Paul Palmer, "The Concept of Public Opinion in Political History," in Carl Wittke, ed., *Essays in History and Political Theory in Honor of Charles Howard McIlwain* (Cambridge, MA: Harvard University Press. 1937).
2. An excellent starting point for learning about the history of public opinion is Wilhelm Bauer's "Public Opinion," in E. Seligman, ed., *Encyclopaedia of the Social Sciences* (New York: Macmillan, 1930).
3. See David Minar's brilliant intellectual history of public opinion, "Public Opinion in the Perspective of Political Theory," *Political Research Quarterly* 13 (1960): 31–44.
4. Aristotle, *The Politics*, ed. and trans. T.A. Sinclair (Baltimore, MD: Penguin Books, 1962).
5. See my *Numbered Voices: How Opinion Polling Has Shaped American Politics* (Chicago, IL: University of Chicago Press, 1993). On the history of printing, see Elizabeth Eisenstein, *The Printing Press as an Agent of Change: Communications and Cultural Transformations in Early-Modern Europe* (Cambridge: Cambridge University Press, 1979).
6. Niccolò Machiavelli, *The Prince*, trans. N.H. Thompson (Buffalo, NY: Prometheus, 1986).
7. See Palmer, p. 238.

8. Jürgen Habermas, *The Structural Transformation of the Public Sphere: An Inquiry into a Category of Bourgeois Society* (Cambridge: MIT Press).
9. Much of the best work on Parisian salons is by Dena Goodman: see "Enlightenment Salons: The Convergence of Female and Philosophic Ambitions," *Eighteenth Century Studies* 22 (Spring 1989): 329–350.
10. Keith Baker, "Politics and Public Opinion Under the Old Regime," in J. Censer and J. Popkin, eds., *Press and Politics in Pre-Revolutionary France* (Berkeley, CA: University of California Press, 1987).
11. Leo Damrosch, *Tocqueville's Discovery of America* (New York: Farrar, Straus and Giroux, 2010), p. 101.
12. *Chicago Tribune*, August 11, 1896, p. 4. McKinley lost narrowly in California that year.
13. See my *Numbered Voices* for more commentary on the *Digest.*
14. Robert Putnam, *Bowling Alone: The Collapse and Revival of American Community* (New York: Simon and Schuster, 2001).
15. For a history of academic and industry survey research, see Jean Converse, *Survey Research in the United States: Roots and Emergence, 1890–1960* (Berkeley, CA: University of California Press, 1987). Also see Sarah Igo, *The Averaged American: Surveys, Citizens, and the Making of a Mass Public* (Cambridge, MA: Harvard University Press, 2007).
16. Paul Lazarsfeld and Robert Merton, "Mass Communication, Popular Taste, and Organized Social Action," in J.D. Peters and P. Simonson, eds., *Mass Communication and American Thought: Key Texts 1919–1968* (Boulder, CO: Rowman and Littlefield, 2004), p. 235.

Chapter 2

The Practice of Survey Research

Changes and Challenges

D. Sunshine Hillygus

After pre-election polls predicted the wrong winner of the 2008 Democratic primary in New Hampshire, a *Washington Post* headline asked "Can we ever trust the polls again?"[1] Concerns about the increasing methodological challenges facing survey research in recent years have undermined confidence in the entire survey enterprise. Surveys rely on the cooperation of people to check boxes and answer questions, yet people today are harder to reach, and when contacted they are less likely to answer questions. At the same time, there has been a proliferation in the amount of polling—from horserace numbers in the newspaper headlines to opt-in "polls" predicting sports outcomes on ESPN.com or judging celebrity outfits in *US Weekly* magazine. With so many polls, it is hard to figure out which ones are accurate and reliable.

It would be easy to blame the media for blurring the line between quality and junk polls. After all, many mainstream news organizations sponsor both open-access "straw polls" on their websites as well as traditional, scientific surveys—and fail to distinguish the methodological differences between the two. ABC polling director Gary Langer chides the news media for indulging in "the lazy luxury of being both data hungry and math phobic."[2] Journalists value the credibility and authority that survey numbers add to a story, but they often fail to scrutinize those numbers for methodological rigor. The media, however, are not the only ones to blame. In academia, we have also seen increasing variability in survey quality. Surveys that would fail to meet the minimum quality standards of the top news organizations are currently being published in social science journals.[3] Some scholars justify their use by arguing that because all surveys are flawed it is just as valid to use inexpensive, opt-in samples. Others are simply unaware of how to evaluate survey quality or naive about the way survey design decisions can affect the validity of their research conclusions.

In this chapter, I will outline some of the key methodological challenges in conducting, using, and evaluating surveys as a measure of public opinion. This chapter has three "take-home" messages. First, I will explain why all surveys are not created equal. Some surveys should be trusted more than others, and, unfortunately, it is not sufficient to make assumptions about survey quality based on polling topic (say, politics rather than entertainment), sample size, or sponsorship. The total survey error perspective provides a framework for evaluating how various aspects of the survey method can shape survey accuracy and reliability. Second, I hope this chapter makes clear that *no* survey is perfect. While there is significant variation in survey quality, not even our "gold standard" surveys like the American National Election Study (ANES) should be immune from scrutiny. Finally, I will appeal for journalists and scholars at all levels to provide enough information about their survey methods for readers to assess the knowledge claims being made. While no survey is perfect, increased transparency should make clear that not all survey methods are equal.

The Data Stork Myth

Despite increasing concerns about survey quality, surveys remain the cornerstone of research on economic, political, and social phenomena across academic, commercial, nonprofit, and government sectors. When properly designed, surveys are a powerful tool for collecting information about the attitudes, characteristics, and behaviors of individuals, households, and organizations. Too often, however, scholars and journalists tend to treat survey data as if it has been delivered by a data stork, failing to question where they came from, how they were produced, and by what methodology. Yet a survey involves a number of different steps and decisions, and, with each one, error can be introduced into the resulting survey statistics. A significant part of the difficulty in establishing survey quality standards is not that our scientific understanding of survey methodology is flawed or inadequate, but rather that scientific research in survey methodology has not permeated the broader community of survey consumers. In the survey methodology literature, scholars have adopted a total survey error perspective that recognizes the need to consider a variety of different types of error in evaluating survey quality.[4] A high-quality survey is one that tries to minimize all sources of error within the inevitable time and budgetary constraints of the project. I will discuss some of these sources—sampling error, coverage error, nonresponse error, and measurement error—highlighting specific challenges and controversies. I first provide an overview of the survey process and introduce some key terminology.

Overview of the Survey Process

When we think of surveys, we often have in mind the resulting survey statistics. A recent news story, citing a CNN poll, reported that 67 percent of Americans favor allowing gays and lesbians to openly serve in the military. Such a conclusion about public opinion is the product of a very specific survey process that involves a series of consequential methodological decisions and assumptions. In small print at the end of the article, we find some of that methodological information: "Interviews with 1,010 adult Americans were conducted by residential telephone on September 21–23, 2010. The margin of sampling error is ±3 percentage points." In this section, I will outline the basic process involved in reaching conclusions about public opinion on the basis of a smaller sample of respondents.

The first step in the survey process is deciding on the *target population*; that is, the group to whom the survey is intended to generalize. CNN obviously did not ask all Americans their opinion on this issue; rather, they surveyed 1,010 individuals that they believed were representative of the broader American public. Their target population was the entire adult U.S. population.[5] Pre-election polls, in contrast, typically want to generalize to the U.S. voting population—adult citizens who will cast a ballot in the election (the so-called "likely voters"). Other surveys are interested in even more specialized populations; for example, a recent survey on alcohol and drug use at Duke University was meant to represent only those undergraduates currently enrolled at the university.

After determining the target population, the next step in the survey process is specifying a *sample frame*—lists or procedures that identify all elements of the target population. The sample frame may be a list of telephone numbers, maps of areas in which households can be found, or a procedure (like random digit dialing) that could identify the target population. At their simplest, sampling frames just list the phone numbers, addresses, or emails of individuals in the target population, such as the list of student email addresses for the Duke University students survey. In the case of the CNN poll, random digit dialing (RDD) was likely used. In random digit dialing, a computer generates a random set of seven-digit numbers (in this case, excluding nonresidential and cellular exchanges). Compared to using a telephone book or other list of telephone numbers, an RDD sample frame has the advantage of including unlisted numbers.

Often, the list will not perfectly capture the entire target population. For example, the target population of the CNN poll is U.S. adults, but the sample frame excludes individuals living in households without landline telephones. This can result in *coverage error*—the error that arises when the sampling approach is not representative of the target population. That is, when there is a failure to give some persons in the target population a chance of selection into the sample. There is a growing concern that the recent rise in the number of cell only households threatens the generalizability of telephone surveys—a coverage error concern.

Once a sample frame has been identified, individual cases are randomly selected to be in the survey. Because the survey is administered to a sample, rather than all, of the target population, it is subject to random sampling error. This is the "margin of error" mentioned in the methodological disclosure of the CNN poll. Of course, these selected cases are just the people asked to be in the survey—many of them will be difficult to reach, will refuse to participate, or will drop out during the survey. *Nonresponse error* occurs when the individuals invited to take the survey do not actually take the survey. Finally, the *respondents* are the subsample of the selected cases who actually complete the survey and on which the analysis is conducted.[6]

Figure 2.1 illustrates the key steps in the survey sampling process using the CNN poll as an example. As shown in the figure, each step in the survey sampling process can introduce uncertainty and bias in the resulting survey statistics. These errors can threaten the ability to generalize from the sample to the target population.

Traditionally, survey users have focused on sampling error as the metric for evaluating survey quality. As mentioned, *sampling error* represents the uncertainty or imprecision in estimates based on random chance that occurs simply because we observe data on a sample of individuals in the population rather than on every individual in the population. Sampling error is often reported as margin of error. In the case of the CNN poll, we should interpret the results as showing that public approval for gays serving openly in the military is 67% ±3 percentage points. This tells us how precise we are in our estimate of public opinion on this issue—the larger the margin of error, the less confidence we have in our estimate. The literal interpretation of the margin of error is that, in repeated sampling, we would expect the true level of public support for gays in the military to fall between 64 percent and 70 percent in 95 out of 100 samples.

Critically, the size of sampling error depends only on the size of the sample collected—the larger the sample, the less uncertainty in the estimate. Sampling error does not tell us about whether our estimates are biased or inaccurate.

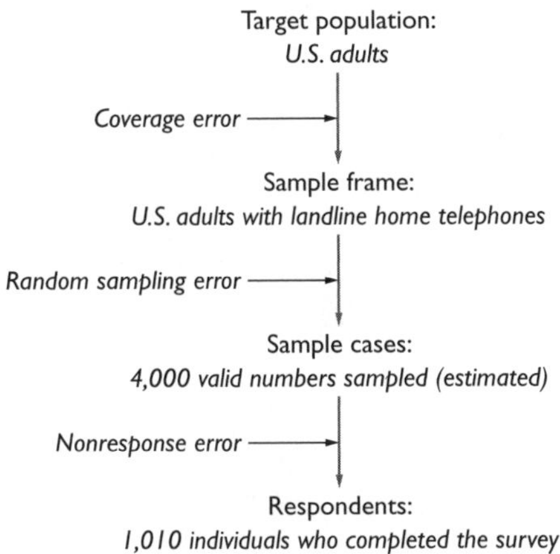

Figure 2.1 Steps and Potential Error in Survey Sampling Process, CNN poll example.

Thus, despite the traditional focus on sampling error, it may well be the *least* important aspect of survey error; for a survey of a given size sampling error simply "is what it is," whereas other sources of error—coverage error, nonresponse error, measurement error—can be minimized through various design decisions.[7]

The total survey error perspective highlights the need to take into account both sampling error and *nonsampling* error in evaluating survey quality. Figure 2.2, reproduced from Herb Weisberg's textbook *The Total Survey Error Approach*, summarizes the various sources of error in the survey process.[8] This perspective highlights the need to evaluate additional sources of error in the survey sampling process—coverage error and nonresponse error. At the same time, it recognizes that the substantive conclusions drawn from surveys also depend on the measurement process, in which scholars have to make decisions about how to operationalize and measure their theoretical constructs and then have to make decisions about how to code and adjust the resulting data. In the remainder of this chapter, I will use the total survey perspective to outline some of the key contemporary threats to survey quality.

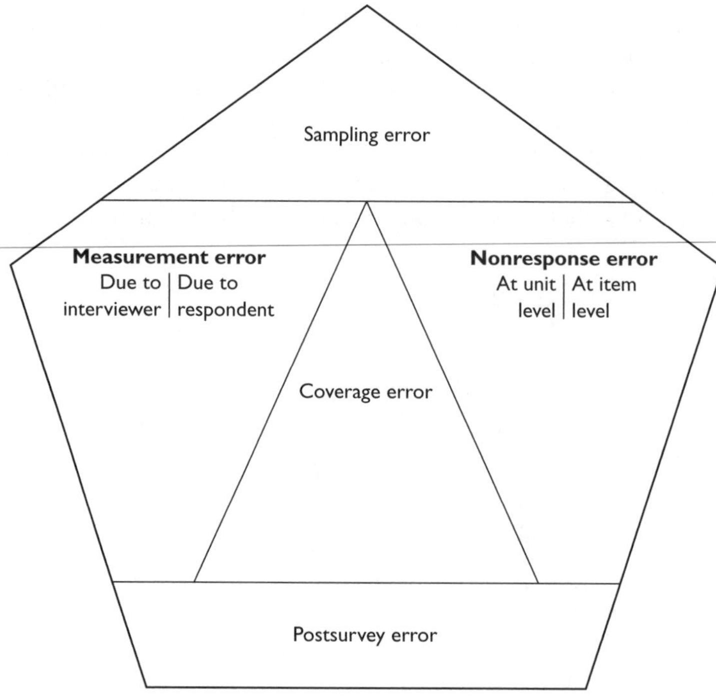

Figure 2.2 The Total Survey Error Perspective (source: Weisberg 2005).

Probability vs. Nonprobability Sampling

Surveys are typically conducted in order to make generalizations about a target population using data collected from a smaller subset—the sample. The ability to generalize from the sample to the population rests on the use of *probability sampling*. Probability samples are ones that use some form of random selection. As pollsters like to joke, "If you don't believe in random sampling, the next time you have a blood test tell the doctor to take it all." Random selection of respondents means that errors—both those observed and unobserved—cancel out over the long run. In order to have a random selection method, it's necessary for each member of the target population to have a chance of being selected into the sample. With a random probability sample, the results will be close (within the "margin of error") to what we would have found had we interviewed the entire population. George Gallup liked to compare sampling public opinion to sampling soup—"as long as it was well-stirred pot, you only need a single sip to determine the taste."

In contrast, *nonprobability samples* select respondents from the target population in some nonrandom manner, so that some members of the population have no chance of selection. For example, many media organizations invite visitors to their websites to answer "straw polls." This type of nonprobability sampling is often called *convenience sampling* because members of the population are chosen based on their relative ease of access. A variant, *quota sampling*, identifies a set of groups (e.g., men, women, 18–25 year olds, 26–40 year olds, etc.) and specifies a fixed number of people to be recruited for each group. Interviewing then proceeds until the quota is reached for each group. For example, convenience samples might be designed so that they match the population proportions on age, gender, and socio-economic status. Unfortunately, some people will be more likely to visit the website than others and some website visitors will be more likely to participate than others, so the results are not representative of any broader population—even if they look demographically similar.

The *Literary Digest* polling fiasco of 1936 is the classic example of how nonprobability samples can lead to biased conclusions. The popular magazine had correctly predicted the winner in the previous five presidential elections, but in 1936 incorrectly predicted that Alf Landon would beat FDR in that year's election by 57 to 43 percent (FDR won with 60.8 percent of the popular vote). The *Digest* had mailed over ten million survey questionnaires to their subscribers and to names drawn from lists of automobile and telephone owners. More than 2.3 million people responded, but it turns out that, in 1936, those who owned automobiles, telephones, or had the disposable income to subscribe to a magazine were not a random cross-section of the voting public.

More recently, a *Scientific American* online poll illustrated the perils of nonprobability surveys. The popular science magazine's online poll asked their readers about climate change, which attracted the attention of climate skeptic bloggers who directed their own readers to participate in the poll. The resulting poll results found that 80 percent of respondents denied climate change and 84 percent answered that "The Intergovernmental Panel on Climate Change is … A corrupt organization, prone to groupthink, with a political agenda." Although it's not unusual for online polls to be hijacked by activists, these skewed polling results have since been reported in a *Wall Street Journal* editorial and included in congressional testimony with no mention of the unscientific methodology.[9]

Probability sampling allows us to calculate sampling error so we can estimate how much our sample might differ from the target population (the margin of error). With nonprobability sampling, in contrast, the degree to which the sample differs from the population remains unknown and unknowable. Even if the sample looks demographically similar to the target population (as with quota sampling), we have no way to evaluate if the sample is representative on unobserved characteristics.

One of the key contemporary debates in public opinion research regards the quality of nonprobability based online panel surveys. New technologies have both made probability sampling more difficult and made nonprobability sampling—especially with online panels—easy and inexpensive. The main concern with Internet based surveys is not just that they will miss those without Internet access—Internet usage rates are quickly approaching the same coverage rate of landline telephones. The key hurdle is that, in most cases, it is difficult to define an appropriate sample frame from which to draw a random sample that is a reasonable approximation of the target population.[10] In other words, there is typically no list of Internet users from which a random sample can be drawn. While not a problem in cases where a population list exists and is reachable online (e.g., email addresses of students at a university), for general population surveys, the nature of the Internet means that "frames of Internet users in a form suitable for sampling do not—and likely will not—exist."[11]

This issue is a source of confusion for academics and journalists alike. For one, not all Internet surveys are the same. In cases where the population list is known and reachable online (e.g., email addresses of students at a university or business CEOs), web surveys are appropriate—even preferable.[12] It is also possible to draw a probability based sample using a traditional technique (such as RDD or address based sampling), and then provide Internet access to those without it. This is the approach of the survey firm, Knowledge Networks. But the majority of web based surveys, including those by well-known firms like YouGov/Polimetrix, Harris Interactive, and Zogby Internet, rely on nonprobability online panels. In such cases the respondents are (nonrandomly) recruited through a variety of techniques: website advertisements, targeted emails, and the like.[13] Individuals are then signed up in an online panel in which they are regularly invited to answer surveys in exchange for financial incentives or other awards. Even if a poll is randomly selected from this online panel, the pool of potential respondents are all people who initially "opted in" to the respondent pool.

A second source of confusion is that nonprobability samples are often claimed to be "representative" because the sample looks like the target population on a set of observed characteristics; often through adjustments (e.g., weighting and/or matching) of the opt-in sample to census benchmarks.[14] These surveys are then reported to be comparable to population estimates on race, age, gender, and the like.

Inherently, however, there are only a limited number of benchmarks on which the sample can be compared, so these samples still require the untestable assumption that unmatched characteristics are ignorable.[15] And research has shown, for instance, that those who volunteer to participate in surveys are often more informed, knowledgeable, and opinionated about the survey topic even if they look demographically similar to the general population.[16] A recent taskforce of the American Association for Public Opinion Research (AAPOR), the leading professional organization of public opinion and survey research professionals in the United States, tackled the issue of online panels and forcefully concludes that "There currently is no generally accepted theoretical basis from which to claim that survey results using samples from nonprobability online panels are projectable to the general population.... Claims of 'representativeness' should be avoided." Pollsters Gary Langer and Jon Cohen offer a similar, if more colorful, conclusion:

> anyone following the polls is probably finding it increasingly difficult to separate signal from noise.... In reality, there are good polls and bad, reliable methods and unreliable ones. To meet reasonable news standards, a poll should be based on a representative, random sample of respondents; "probability sampling" is a fundamental requirement of inferential statistics, the foundation on which survey research is built. Surrender to "convenience" or self-selected samples of the sort that so many people click on the Internet, and you're quickly afloat in a sea of voodoo data.... Probability sampling has its own challenges, of course. Many telephone surveys are conducted using techniques that range from the minimally acceptable to the dreadful. When it's all just numbers, these, too, get tossed into the mix, like turpentine in the salad dressing.[17]

To be sure, there are many research questions for which a probability sample will not be a priority. For example, scholars conducting survey experiments are often more concerned with internal validity (a clear causal effect) than external validity (generalizability). Likewise, focused exploratory research might use a nonprobability sample to generate hypotheses or pilot various measurements. There may also be times when the researcher simply wants to demonstrate that a particular trait occurs in a population. These are all cases in which the researcher does not intend to draw inferences to the broader population, so a nonprobability sample can be a cost effective method for the research goals.

In sum, the validity of inferences from a sample to a larger population rests on random probability sampling. In contrast, nonprobability samples—no matter their size—are not generalizable because there is no way to know how respondents and nonrespondents might differ across an infinite number of characteristics related to the outcome of interest. Procedures such as quota sampling, matching, or weighting that ensure a convenience sample looks like the target population on a set of observed characteristics inherently assume that unobserved characteristics do not influence the phenomenon being studied—an often unrealistic, untestable, and unstated assumption. This does not mean that nonprobability samples should never be conducted, but given the fundamental distinction between probability and nonprobability samples, it is critical that scholars are transparent about the methodology being used. AAPOR, for example, recommends the following wording when documenting surveys with non-probability samples:

> Respondents for this survey were selected from among those who have [volunteered to participate/registered to participate in (company name) online surveys and polls]. The data (have been/have not been) weighted to reflect the demographic composition of (target population). Because the sample is based on those who initially self-selected for participation [in the panel] rather than a probability sample, no estimates of sampling error can be calculated. All sample surveys and polls may be subject to multiple sources of error, including, but not limited to sampling error, coverage error, and measurement error.

Unfortunately, there is a deep and growing schism in academia, journalism, and politics over the value of nonprobability samples. On one side are those who insist that statistical theory renders all nonprobability samples useless; on the other side are those who believe that nonprobability samples likely get us "close enough" to the right answer. Wherever one falls in this debate, we have an obligation to fully disclose the research methodology being used. At minimum, we should explicitly discuss the assumptions underlying our substantive conclusions.

Nonresponse Error

Nonresponse errors refer to errors introduced by the practical reality that surveys almost never collect data from all sampled cases. People are often difficult to reach or refuse to participate. In fact, most of us have probably contributed to nonresponse in a survey if we have ever hung up the phone when we realized it was a pollster on the other end of the line interrupting our dinner. There has been considerable focus on nonresponse error in recent decades and rightfully so. In recent decades, response rates have declined precipitously across government, academic, and media surveys. Given the barrage of telemarketing calls, spam, and junk mail, people are increasingly hesitant to participate in surveys. And technologies like voicemail and caller i.d. make it easier than ever to avoid intrusions from strangers.

The most common marker for nonresponse error has traditionally been the survey response rate. In its most basic form, response rate is calculated as the number of people actually surveyed divided by the number of people you tried to survey. Figure 2.3 graphs the response rates in the General Social Survey and the ANES in recent years, and illustrates that declining response rates are affecting even the high-budget "gold standard" academic studies.[18] For example, the ANES response rate declined from 74 percent in 1992 to less than 60 percent in 2008. Although not shown in the graph, these declines are largely due to increasing rates of refusal. For example, the ANES refusal rate increased from less than 15 percent in 1972 to over 24 percent in 2004. Response rates for media polls have been especially hard hit by declining cooperation. Although the response rate was not reported for the CNN poll example, it is unlikely that survey with a three day field period exceeded a

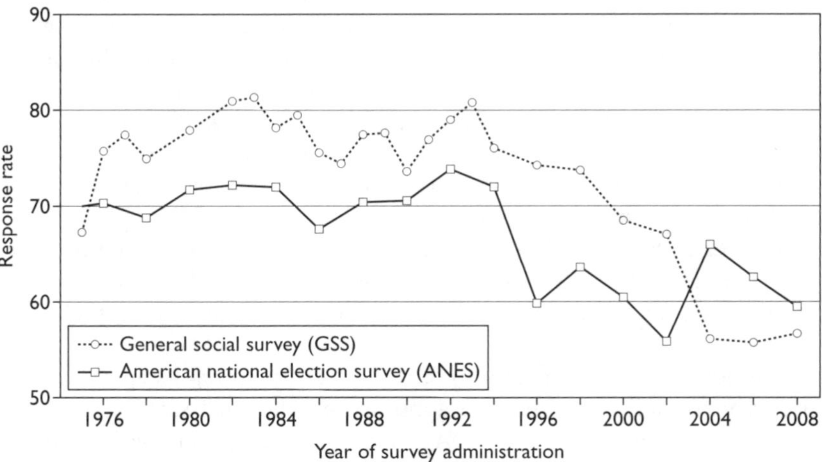

Figure 2.3 Response Rate Trends in Major Academic Surveys (source: for GSS, all rates reported in James Allan Davis, Tom W. Smith, and Peter V. Marsden, *General Social Surveys, 1972–2008: Cumulative Codebook* (Chicago, IL: National Opinion Research Center, 2009). For ANES, numbers through 2000 reported in American National Election Studies. "Data Quality." Retrieved from: http://www.electionstudies.org/overview/dataqual.htm. Subsequent numbers compiled from individual study year codebooks.).

25 percent response rate (1,010/4,000). In reality, many media polls—especially those conducted as overnight "snapshot" polls on a salient topic that may have a limited number of callbacks—now have response rates that hover around 10 percent.

The question is whether these lower response rates actually lessen data quality. Certainly, the low response rates of telephone polls are often used as justification for using nonprobability samples. Some argue that the bias introduced by those who "opt out" from survey requests (nonresponse) is no different from the bias introduced by people choosing to "opt in" to online nonprobability panels. An increasing body of research has evaluated the link between response rate and nonresponse bias, and, perhaps surprisingly, has concluded that a low response rate by itself does not indicate the results are inaccurate.[19] Multiple studies have found that lower response rates do not significantly reduce survey quality.[20] Nonresponse bias depends not just on the rate of nonresponse but the extent to which those who answer are different from those who did not. So, a low response rate indicates a risk of lower accuracy, but does not guarantee it. Thus, the nonprobability "opt-in" samples discussed above likely present a greater threat to inferences about the target population than the declining response rates in probability samples.

The reassuring news on response rates does not mean we can ignore nonresponse error. To the contrary, it remains a significant concern—we have just been using an incomplete metric for evaluating its impact. In thinking about nonresponse error, it's first worth clarifying that nonresponse can be classified in two different categories: unit and item nonresponse. Unit nonresponse is where an individual fails to take part in a survey. This is the basis of response rate calculations. Another type of nonresponse, item nonresponse, occurs when the individual answering the questionnaire skips a question, giving us incomplete data on an individual respondent. Questions on income, for instance, are often susceptible to item nonresponse. Once again, the key concern is with potential differences between nonrespondents and respondents. For instance, in his book *Silent Voices*, Adam Berinsky shows that item nonresponse in racially sensitive survey questions can reflect prejudicial sentiments.[21]

For both unit and item nonresponse, the most important step in reducing nonresponse bias is to create an appropriately designed survey in the first place. Many of the fundamental design decisions, including mode, interviewer characteristics, length of survey, question wording, and response options, can directly affect the extent of nonresponse bias. For example, research on the 2004 exit polls found that using college-aged interviewers resulted in higher rates of nonresponse among Republican voters compared to Democratic voters, thereby biasing estimates of vote choice.[22] Self-administered surveys (mail and Internet) have higher levels of item nonresponse than interviewer-administered surveys, but answers in self-administered surveys tend to be more accurate because of reduced pressures to give a socially desirable answer.

Respondents are more likely to skip questions that are long, burdensome, confusing, vague, or do not provide the preferred response, so it becomes especially important that the questionnaire itself follows best practice principles for the particular mode being used.

Again, while response rates are perhaps not the key marker of nonresponse bias, it is nonetheless important for those conducting surveys to try to minimize nonresponse error and those consuming surveys to consider the nature and extent of nonresponse bias in any reported data.

Coverage Error

One of the growing issues of concern about survey quality comes from coverage error. Coverage error is the failure to give some persons in a target population a chance of being selected into the sample, such as when those without Internet access have no chance of ending up in an Internet survey. The extent of bias resulting from coverage error depends both on the rate of noncoverage and difference between those covered by the survey and those not. So, if Internet users were no different from non-Internet users on most dimensions then we might have coverage error, but our resulting estimates could still accurately reflect the characteristics of the target population we are interested in.

Much of the focus on coverage bias has concerned the impact of cell phone only households on telephone surveys. It is widely recognized that there is a growing cellular only population, so that surveys that omit people who are exclusively or primarily reached through their cell phones may not be representative. Figure 2.4 shows the growth in cell phone only households in the

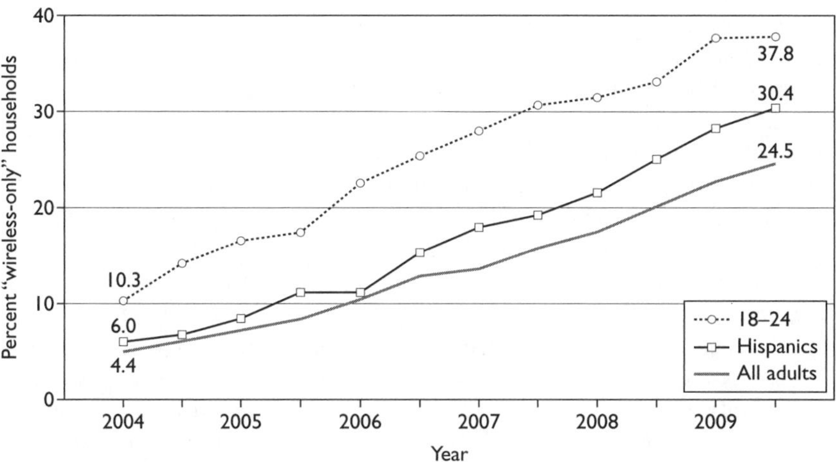

Figure 2.4 Trend in Cell Only Households (source: National Health Interview Surveys).

last few years. Cell phone usage is particularly prevalent among young people and minorities—24.5 percent of the U.S. population is cell phone only, while 30.4 percent of Hispanics, and 37.8 percent of those age 18–24 live in houses with wireless only telephones. It is also the case that cell phone only respondents often differ in their views than those with landline telephones. For instance, research from the 2008 presidential campaign found that cell phone only respondents were significantly more likely to support Obama—60.5 percent of those with only a cell phone reported voting for Obama, compared to his actual vote share of 52.9 percent.[23]

It is worth first pausing to explain why cell phone numbers are often excluded from telephone surveys. Although there are some quality issues (e.g., blurry geographic associations, shorter questionnaires possible, lower response rates), mainly it's an issue of cost. Specifically, the 1991 Telephone Consumer Protection Act prohibits the use of automated dialers for all unsolicited calls to cell phones, including surveys. Pollsters typically use automated dialers—a device that automatically calls telephone numbers until reaching a live respondent—because it is much faster (and thus less expensive) than having interviewers manually dial the numbers.

To determine the extent of coverage bias introduced by excluding cell phone only households, we must take into account not only the difference in opinions between cell phone only and landline response but also their expected proportion in the target population. For example, support for Obama was higher among cell phone only individuals than the electorate at large, but those who relied solely on cell phones were also significantly less likely to vote. Thus, there was not as much bias in the polls as might otherwise be expected. Still, the problem is worsening, and a 2010 Pew Research Center study found that landline samples "tend to slightly underestimate support for Democratic candidates when compared with estimates from dual frame landline and cell samples in polling."[24] There is a related concern about the "cell phone mostly crowd," although there is limited research on this group to date. It is known that this group is nearly impossible to reach on a landline, and they look quite different—highly educated, white, homeowners, and married—from both the cell phone only and the other landline crowds.

Returning to the example of the CNN poll, cell phone only households were excluded from the sample frame. Because younger age groups tend to have more liberal positions on gay rights, we might suspect that the poll actually underestimates public support for allowing gays and lesbians to serve openly in the military because younger age groups might not be adequately represented. Given the clear implications of cell only households on the generalizability of survey estimates, many top media organizations, including *ABC News*, *CBS News*, *New York Times*—have started routinely including cell phone respondents in their samples, despite the increased cost.

Measurement Error

Thus far, we have focused on sources of error that shape the ability to generalize from a sample of respondents to a population of interest. But the quality of a survey depends not only on the ability to generalize, but also on the ability to accurately measure the theoretical concepts of interest. Ideally, the survey questions result in measures that are both valid—they fully and accurately measure the concept that is supposed to be measured—and reliable—they measure the concept in a reproducible manner. Measurement error occurs when recorded responses to a survey fail to reflect the true characteristics of the respondents, and it can influence both the accuracy and reliability of our results.

There are many different sources of measurement error: the questionnaire, the data collection method, the interviewer, and the respondent. Questionnaire factors like question wording, question order, length of questions and questionnaire, number of response categories, presence of a "don't know" or middle response option can all influence measurement error. Even very small differences in question wording can generate very different findings. For example, asking about attitudes toward "assistance for the poor" generates much higher levels of support than a question asking about attitudes toward "welfare."[25] In another example, party identification questions that are otherwise identical besides the beginning phrase, either "In politics today" or "Generally speaking," result in entirely different conclusions regarding the stability of partisanship.[26]

Measurement error can also be affected by the mode of survey administration (e.g., telephone, in-person, mail). A survey that uses an interviewer in the administration, for example, can introduce measurement error from that interaction. Numerous studies have found that whites express more liberal racial attitudes to black interviewers than to white interviewers.[27]

Finally respondents themselves introduce error based on their comprehension or interpretation of the question in addition to any editing of the responses they might make because of fears of disclosure, concerns about privacy, or a desire to give a response that would be viewed favorably by others. People are especially reluctant to provide honest answers on sensitive topics, like sexual history, drug use, or racial attitudes. Voter turnout is another sensitive question—people tend to overreport voting because they want to appear to be good citizens. Thus, the ANES does not simply ask "Did you vote in the 2008 election? (yes or no?)." Rather, they attempt to reassure the respondent that it really is okay to admit to not voting:

> In talking to people about elections, we often find that a lot of people were not able to vote because they weren't registered, they were sick, or they just didn't have time. Which of the following statements best describes you:

1. I did not vote (in the election this November)
2. I thought about voting this time—but didn't
3. I usually vote, but didn't this time
4. I am sure I voted.

For those conducting their own surveys, it is worth remembering that substantive expertise on a topic is the only skill needed to conduct a survey. There is a rich body of research on the nature and extent of measurement error in surveys, and emerging best practices for reducing that error.[28] The single best way to improve measurement is to do extensive pretesting of the survey instrument.[29] For instance, *cognitive pretesting*, in which draft survey questions are administered for the purpose of collecting information about how people interpret and process the questions, can be used to identify any questions that are difficult to interpret or that can be interpreted in ways different from what the researcher intends. And for those introducing a new measure, it is especially important to explicitly evaluate the operationalization of that measure for validity and reliability. In this regard, political science as a field could take guidance from fields like psychology or education, where it is standard practice to take measurement seriously.

For those using secondary survey data, there is often a tendency to take for granted that the survey questions adequately measure the concepts of interest. However, many questions in major infrastructure surveys were written before the development of rigorous question-wording practices. Moreover, because over time inferences depend on having identical question wording, recurring surveys like the ANES face a tension between the need for continuity in question wording and the need for innovation to keep up with developing knowledge in the field of survey methodology. Ultimately, we often must "work with what we got," but any analysis that uses survey research should pay careful attention to the potential for measurement error.

Disclosure

As the previous discussion highlights, there are many different threats to survey quality. Ultimately, the ability to assess survey quality—across all sources of survey error—rests on having sufficient information about the survey methodology. Although most academic journals and media organizations do not have formal disclosure requirements in place, there are increasing pressures on survey users to improve methodological transparency. In the last few years, there have been at least two well-publicized incidents in which survey firms appear to have made up or manipulated survey results. The liberal blog, DailyKos, discovered that weekly polling results they had paid for and featured from the organization Research 2000 (R2K) were "largely bunk."[30] Likewise, blogger Nate Silver of fivethirtyeight.com concluded that pollster Strategic Vision LLC was "disreputable and fraudulent."[31] AAPOR publicly reprimanded Strategic Vision for failure to disclose basic methodological information about the studies. Not long after, AAPOR announced a transparency initiative aimed at encouraging and making it as easy as possible for survey users to be transparent about their research methods. Basic standards for minimal disclosure include reports of the following information about a survey:[32]

1. Who sponsored the survey, and who conducted it.
2. The exact wording of questions asked, including the text of any preceding instruction or explanation to the interviewer or respondents that might reasonably be expected to affect the response.
3. A definition of the population under study, and a description of the sampling frame used to identify this population.
4. A description of the sample design, giving a clear indication of the method by which the respondents were selected by the researcher, or whether the respondents were entirely self-selected.
5. Sample sizes and, where appropriate, eligibility criteria, screening procedures, and response rates computed according to AAPOR Standard Definitions. At a minimum, a summary of disposition of sample cases should be provided so that response rates could be computed.
6. A discussion of the precision of the findings, including estimates of sampling error, and a description of any weighting or estimating procedures used.
7. Which results are based on parts of the sample, rather than on the total sample, and the size of such parts.
8. Method, location, and dates of data collection.

With this basic information, readers can determine if the survey is a probability or nonprobability sample, and thus whether the sample is generalizable to the population of interest. It also offers some indication about the potential for nonsampling error, including coverage error, nonresponse error, and measurement error.

Full methodological disclosure should make clear that *every* survey is flawed in some way. There is no perfect survey design in part because there are inevitable trade-offs involved in balancing the various sources of survey error. In reducing one source of survey error a researcher could inadvertently increase another source of error. For example, new technologies such as Interactive Voice Response have the potential to reduce measurement bias introduced by the interactions of human interviewers, but they simultaneously increase nonresponse error or exacerbate coverage problems because people are less inclined to answer questions from a robocall. Likewise, best practices for measurement error would have multiple questions about each concept of interest, but doing so lengthens the survey and thus might increase the number of people who skip questions or drop out of the survey because of the time burden. Because no survey is perfect, every analysis of survey data should explicitly discuss how the results might or might not be affected by various survey errors.

Greater levels of transparency will give readers the ability to evaluate whether the knowledge claims being made are warranted given the methodology used. Increased transparency might also offer incentives for researchers to employ higher quality methods because it should make clear that not all survey methods are equal. Currently there seem to be two standards for surveys: gold and tin. The budgets of some of the most important federal and academic "gold standard" surveys are increasing dramatically in an effort to maintain the same levels of quality by traditional metrics; yet even these budgets are often not sufficient to maintain traditional metrics. At the same time, an extraordinary amount of research is currently conducted on modest budgets, yet falls dramatically short on many standards. A clearer understanding of the sources of survey errors and a full disclosure of survey methodology will help survey practitioners and consumers better understand and evaluate the potential trade-offs involved in using new or emerging technologies. Most importantly, it will make clear that there is no one answer to the question asked by the *Washington Post*, "Can we ever trust the polls again?"

Notes

1. George Bishop, "Why We Keep Getting Snowed by the Polls," *Washington Post*, February 3, 2008, B03.
2. "Tracking Polls" transcript, On the Media, March 26, 2010. Retrieved from http://www.onthemedia.org/transcripts/2010/03/26/04.
3. Indeed, top media organizations are more likely than academic journals to have written survey-quality standards. The Associated Press, *New York Times*, and *ABC News*, among others, have developed internal standards for judging whether or not they should report a survey. Media organizations often maintain a list of survey vendors—based on their methodology—that do not pass minimum quality standards.
4. Herb Weisberg, *The Total Survey Error Approach: A Guide to the New Science of Survey Research* (Chicago, IL: University of Chicago Press, 2005); Robert M. Groves, Floyd J. Fowler Jr., Mick P. Couper, James M. Lepkowski, Eleanor Singer, and Roger Tourangeau, *Survey Methodology* (New York: John Wiley and Sons, 2004).
5. We could even be more specific in defining our target population: in this case, as adults reachable at home September 21–23, 2010.
6. Not mentioned are a number of other important steps, including choosing the precision level necessary, choosing the response mode, drafting the questionnaire, pretesting the instrument, data processing, and analysis. These steps, too, can introduce error in the resulting statistics.
7. It is perhaps also worth noting that estimates of sampling error (margin of error; standard errors) almost always are calculated assuming the survey was collected using simple random sampling. Yet, most major data collections use a more complex probability sampling design such as clustered or stratified sampling. Although procedures exist in statistical packages like R and STATA for correcting

the standard errors to account for complex designs, it is rarely ever done in political science. As such, published political science research often underestimates standard errors.

8. Weisberg, *The Total Survey Error Approach.*
9. Retrieved from http://online.wsj.com/article_email/SB10001424052748703305404575610402116987146-lMyQjAxMTAwMDEwNjExNDYyWj.html; http://democrats.science.house.gov/Media/file/Commdocs/hearings/2010/Energy/17nov/Michaels_Testimony.pdf.
10. There are also heightened concerns about data quality, particularly for Internet panels. For instance, it can be difficult for researchers to verify that the person taking the survey is the desired respondent. Also, scholars have shown that web respondents are more likely to satisfice when inputting responses to survey items. See Dirk Heerwegh and Geert Loosveldt, "Face to Face Versus Web Surveying in a High-Internet Coverage Population: Differences in Response Quality," *Public Opinion Quarterly* 72 (2009). In this mode, the authors found respondents provided "don't know" responses at a higher rate, were less likely to provide differentiated responses across items, and were more likely to avoid responding to individual items altogether. On these points, see also Scott Fricker, Mirta Galesic, Roger Tourangeau, and Ting Yan, "An Experimental Comparison of Web and Telephone Surveys," *Public Opinion Quarterly* 69 (2005).
11. Mick Couper and Peter Miller, "Web Survey Methods," *Public Opinion Quarterly* 72 (2008).
12. Indeed, the web, as a mode, has a number of unique advantages. For instance, web based surveys are convenient for both interviewers and subjects—respondents can decide when to answer rather than having dinner interrupted by a phone survey. Researchers have shown that the web based mode is quite resistant to social desirability biases. See Frauke Kreuter, Stanley Presser, and Roger Tourangeau, "Social Desirability Bias in CATI, IVR, and Web Surveys," *Public Opinion Quarterly* 72 (2008); Don Dillman, "Why Choice of Survey Mode Makes a Difference," *Public Health Reports* 121 (2006).
13. Researchers have evaluated the success rates from various recruitment strategies. See R. Michael Alvarez, Robert Sherman, and Carla VanBeselaere, "Subject Acquisition for Web-Based Surveys," *Political Analysis* 11 (2003). They found, for instance, that their banner ad was displayed over 17 million times, resulting in 53,285 clicks directing respondents to the panel website, and ultimately 3,431 panel members.
14. The matching procedure might work as follows. First, the survey is administered to a sample of opt-in respondents. Next, a random sample of individuals from existing consumer and voter registration files is drawn but not administered the survey. Finally, a matching procedure is used to find the opt-in respondent (who answered the survey) who most closely matches the randomly selected individual (who did not answer the survey). Survey weighting is a post-survey procedure that adjusts the sample to look more representative on some observed characteristics. For example, if the sample of respondents is 60 percent female, 40 percent male, but the target population is evenly split between the two, then we might weight each man in the sample a bit more and each woman a bit less.
15. A large number of studies—at least 19—have examined survey results with the same questionnaire administered to probability samples and online to nonprobability samples. See, for instance David Yeager, Jon Krosnick, LinChiat Chang, Harold Javitz, Matthew Levindusky, Alberto Simpser, and Rui Wang, "Comparing the Accuracy of RDD Telephone Surveys and Internet Surveys Conducted with Probability and Non-Probability Samples," working paper (Knowledge Networks, 2009), retrieved from http://www.knowledgenetworks.com/insights/docs/Mode-04_2.pdf.

All but one found significant differences in the results that could not be substantially reduced by weighting. Unfortunately, most of these studies cannot adequately distinguish differences due to sampling design effects and differences due to mode effects.

16. Mick Couper, "Web Surveys: A Review of Issues and Approaches," *Public Opinion Quarterly* 64 (2000); Jill Dever, Ann Rafferty, and Richard Valliant, "Internet Surveys: Can Statistical Adjustments Eliminate Coverage Bias?" *Survey Research Methods* 2 (2008); Linchiat Chang and Jon Krosnick, "National Surveys via RDD Telephone Interviewing versus the Internet: Comparing Sample Representativeness and Response Quality," *Public Opinion Quarterly* 73 (2009); Neil Malhotra and Jon Krosnick, "The Effect of Survey Mode and Sampling on Inferences about Political Attitudes and Behavior: Comparing the 2000 and 2004 ANES to Internet Surveys with Nonprobability Samples," *Political Analysis* 15 (2007).
17. Gary Langer and Jon Cohen, "5 Tips for Decoding Those Election Polls," *Washington Post*, December 30, 2007, B03.
18. The response rates for the GSS were computed by dividing the number of completed cases by the "net" original sample, which excludes sampled households not deemed "eligible." The ANES response rates were computed by the American National Election Studies. Response rates for 2002 and 2004 were computed as described above, by dividing the number of completed cases by the number of "eligible" households included in the original sample. The response rate for the 2008 ANES was computed according to AAPOR's "minimum response rate" (RR1). It is referred to as the "minimum" because it assumes that in all households at which the eligibility of residents was not determined, at least one eligible adult lived there.
19. Emilia Peytcheva and Robert Groves, "Using Variation in Response Rates of Demographic Subgroups as Evidence of Nonresponse Bias in Survey Estimates," *Journal of Official Statistics* 25 (2009).
20. Scott Keeter, Courtney Kennedy, Michael Dimock, Jonathan Best, and Peyton Craighill, "Gauging the Impact of Growing Nonresponse on Estimates from a National RDD telephone Survey," *Public Opinion Quarterly* 70 (2006); Penny Visser, Jon Krosnick, Jesse Marquette, and Michael Curtin, "Mail Surveys for Election Forecasting? An Evaluation of the Columbus Dispatch Poll," *Public Opinion Quarterly* 60 (1996).
21. Adam Berinsky, *Silent Voices: Opinion Polls and Political Representation in America* (Princeton, NJ: Princeton University Press, 2004).
22. Warren Mitofsky, "Evaluation of Edison/Mitofsky Election System of 2004," Retrieved from http://www.exit-poll.net/electionnight/EvaluationJan192005.pdf.
23. Michael Mokrzycki, Scott Keeter, and Courtney Kennedy, "Cell Phone Only Voters in the 2008 Exit Poll and Implications for Future Noncoverage Bias," *Public Opinion Quarterly* 73 (2009).
24. Leah Christian, Scott Keeter, Kristen Purcell, and Aaron Smith, "Assessing the Cell Phone Challenge" Pew Research Center, May 20, 2010. Retrieved from http://pewresearch.org/pubs/1601/assessing-cell-phone-challenge-in-public-opinion-surveys.
25. Tom Smith, "That Which We Call Welfare by any Other Name would Smell Sweeter: An Analysis of the Impact of Question Wording on Response Patterns," *Public Opinion Quarterly* 51 (1987).
26. Paul Abramson, and Charles Ostrom, Jr., "Macropartisanship: An Empirical Reassessment," *American Political Science Review* 85 (1991). Paul Abramson, and Charles Ostrom, "Question Form and Context Effects in the Measurement of Partisanship: Experimental Tests of the Artifact Hypothesis," *American Political Science Review* 88 (1994).

27. See, for example, Darren Davis, "Nonrandom Measurement Error and Race of Interviewer Effects among African-Americans," *Public Opinion Quarterly* 61 (1997).
28. Paul Biemer, Robert Groves, Lars Lyberg, Nancy Mathiowetz, and Seymour Sudman, *Measurement Errors in Surveys* (New York: John Wiley and Sons, Inc., 1991). Colm O'Muircheartaigh (1997) "Measurement Error in Surveys: a Historical Perspective," overview chapter in L. Lyberg, P. Biemer, M. Collins, E. de Leeuw, C. Dippo, N. Schwartz, and D. Trewin (Eds.), *Survey Measurement and Process Quality*, pp. 1–25. New York: John Wiley and Sons.
29. Stanley Presser, Mick Couper, Judith Lessler, Elizabeth Martin, Jean Martin, Jennifer Rothgeb, and Eleanor Singer, *Methods for Testing and Evaluating Survey Questionnaires* (New York: Wiley, 2004).
30. For more complete discussion of the controversy and evidence, see http://www.dailykos.com/storyonly/2010/6/29/880185/-More-on-Research-2000.
31. Retrieved from http://www.fivethirtyeight.com/search/label/strategic%20vision.
32. Retrieved from http://www.aapor.org/AM/Template.cfm?Section=Standards_andamp_Ethics&Template=/CM/ContentDisplay.cfm&ContentID=2397.

Chapter 3

Two-Thirds Full?

Citizen Competence and Democratic Governance

Martin Gilens

The eminent political theorist Robert Dahl asserted that "a key characteristic of democracy is the continuing responsiveness of the government to the preferences of its citizens, considered as political equals."[1] This formulation implies first that citizens must have meaningful preferences for democratic government to be possible, and second that in order to gauge the democratic quality of any given government we must be able both to discern what its citizens' preferences are, and to assess how strongly and how equally government policy responds to those preferences.

The ideal democratic citizen "is expected to be well informed about political affairs. He is supposed to know what the issues are, what their history is, what the relevant facts are, what alternatives are proposed … [and] what the likely consequences are."[2] Observers of American democracy have long questioned not only citizens' ability to meet this lofty goal, but citizens' ability to play any truly meaningful role in shaping government policy. Political issues in contemporary societies are numerous, complex, and often remote from citizens' everyday lives. The American public, it is often claimed, simply lacks the interest, motivation, or ability to form meaningful preferences on most of these issues.

In this chapter I ask first whether American citizens hold meaningful policy preferences and whether such preferences, if they exist, are accurately reflected in surveys of political attitudes. I argue that despite the limited political knowledge and engagement typically displayed by the American public, public preferences—at least in the aggregate—are "enlightened enough" to serve as a reasonable basis for guiding government decision makers on a wide range of issues. Given this positive evaluation, I then ask how the preferences of the public are related to the policy decisions of the national government, and how equally influence over government policy extends to more and less well off Americans.

To evaluate the link between public preferences and government policy, I rely on a dataset consisting of over 2,000 survey questions in which random samples of Americans were asked whether they favored or opposed specific changes in government policy. Some of these proposed changes were extremely popular (like confiscating money from bank accounts linked to terrorism), others were quite unpopular (like reducing Social Security benefits), and some were favored by the poor but opposed by the affluent or vice versa. In each case, I determined whether the change in government policy posed in the survey question took place. Using these data, I assess how much the probability of a proposed policy change being adopted depends on the extent to which that change is favored or opposed, and how this association between preferences and policies differs for poor, middle class, and affluent Americans.

Conflicting Views of Citizen Competence

Scholars of public opinion can be roughly divided into two schools of thought. One concludes that Americans' low level of political knowledge and apparent lack of clear and consistent policy preferences shows that the public is incapable of providing meaningful guidance to government decision makers on policy matters. The other school of thought acknowledges the gap between the traditional expectations of democratic citizens and the public's performance, but believes that compensatory mechanisms allow citizens to form meaningful preferences, at least in the aggregate, even in the face of low information levels and considerable inconsistency in survey responses.

In his seminal paper "The Nature of Belief Systems in Mass Publics," Philip Converse[3] painted a bleak picture of the American public as largely lacking coherent political preferences. Converse observed that survey respondents were apt to express different preferences when presented with the identical question on different occasions, that preferences on one policy issue were at best weakly associated with questions on seemingly related issues, and that broad organizing principles like liberalism or conservatism were poorly understood by most Americans. Confronted with this evidence, Converse concluded that the preferences respondents report on surveys consist largely of "non-attitudes" and that "large portions of [the] electorate do not have meaningful beliefs, even on issues that have formed the basis for intense political controversy among elites for substantial periods of time."[4]

Many subsequent assessments of Americans' political preferences have been only slightly more hopeful. After examining hundreds of survey measures of political information, for example, Michael Delli Carpini and Scott Keeter conclude that

> More than a small fraction of the public is reasonably well informed about politics—informed enough to meet high standards of good citizenship. Many of the basic institutions and procedures of government are known to half or more of the public, as are the relative positions of the parties on many major issues of the day.[5]

But the flip side of this coin is that a large proportion of the public does not rise to this level. "[L]arge numbers of Americans citizens are woefully underinformed," Delli Carpini and Keeter write, and "overall levels of knowledge are modest at best."[6]

These two analyses address the two most troubling aspects of public opinion casting doubt on the feasibility of meaningful democratic government: the public's lack of knowledge about political affairs and the seeming randomness of policy preferences expressed on surveys as reflected in their lack of stability over time, and the weakness of associations between related issues or across similar formulations of the same policy issue.

Scholars who take a more sanguine view of the quality of citizens' policy preferences point to three aspects of mass political attitudes to explain how a public with minimal political information can nevertheless form meaningful issue preferences. First, citizens with modest levels of information might turn to more knowledgeable others for "cues" about the desirability of alternative policies or politicians. Second, individual citizens are not equally interested in the full range of political issues in play at any given time but tend to "specialize" in a subset of issues about which they are more knowledgeable and have more stable and well thought out preferences. The division of citizens into these "issue publics" means that the ability of any individual citizen to meaningfully participate in shaping government policy should be judged relative to the set of issues that that individual cares about; all citizens need not hold equally well developed preferences on all issues for the public to fulfill its role in democratic governance. Finally, the fickle element of individual citizens' policy preferences will, to some degree at least, tend to cancel out when preferences are aggregated across the public as a whole (or across distinctive subgroups of the public). Aggregate opinion, by this reckoning, will typically be more stable, with a higher "signal to noise ratio" than the individual opinions that make it up.

Cue Taking as a Basis for Political Preferences

Given the stringent standards for "the ideal democratic citizen" noted above, it is not surprising that these authors view the American public as falling short. Political opinions, they write, are more frequently "matters of sentiment and disposition rather than 'reasoned preferences' … characterized more by faith than by conviction and by wishful expectation rather than careful prediction of consequences."[7] Yet Berelson and his coauthors believed that despite the public's general lack of politically relevant information and poor quality of reasoning about policy matters, the ignorant many are able to leverage the expertise of the well-informed few who are politically knowledgeable and engaged. If most citizens are indifferent to and uninformed about public affairs, it is nevertheless true that some are absorbed in the world of politics and policy. Moreover, social networks, they maintain, allow for a division of labor in which more informed "opinion leaders" provide policy insights and endorsements to their less informed friends and acquaintances.

"The political genius of the citizenry," they conclude, "may reside less in how well they can judge public policy than in how well they can judge the people who advise them how to judge public policy."[8]

Taking cues from more knowledgeable elites or acquaintances is a sensible strategy for citizens who lack the ability or inclination to gather the information needed to formulate a preference on a given policy issue. Anthony Downs, writing shortly after Berelson et al., notes that the average citizen "cannot be expert in all the fields of policy that are relevant to his decision. Therefore, he will seek assistance from men who are experts in those fields, have the same political goals he does, and have good judgment."[9]

A substantial literature has developed over the past decades which identifies the wide range of cue givers that citizens can rely on in forming political judgments.[10] Most cue taking models posit that citizens adopt the policy positions expressed by "like minded" elites (judged on the basis of partisan or ideological compatibility, or the more specific affinities associated, for example, with a citizen's religious, union, or professional organization) and either ignore those of the "non-like minded" or adopt the opposite position from the one that they espouse.[11] Cue givers of this sort can be either social leaders whose views are transmitted through the media, or individual acquaintances who are perceived as comparatively well informed on the issue at hand.

The strategy of turning to those with greater knowledge when faced with a challenging decision is hardly limited to political novices. Even citizens who follow politics closely will inevitably lack sufficient information (or technical expertise) to form opinions "from scratch" on many issues. In a modern nation, there are simply too many detailed and technical issues for even the most motivated members of the public to possibly keep abreast of. Indeed, even elected representatives who have abundant informational resources and who "follow politics" for a living turn to experts in specific issue areas for advice and take cues from other representatives in their own party who "specialize" in particular issue domains.[12]

Issue Publics

Cue taking is one mechanism by which citizens may be able to form meaningful preferences on issues despite a lack of knowledge and expertise, and the relationship between cue taker and cue giver highlights the large differences in political knowledge held by different members of the public. At the same time, however, any given individual's knowledge may differ greatly from one policy issue to another. Among the many enduring contributions of Converse's seminal paper was the concept of issue publics—the obvious but often overlooked fact that different people care about different political issues. In order to participate in democratic governance, citizens must be able to form meaningful preferences on the policy issues that government addresses.

But that does not mean that every citizen must have a preference on every issue. Given the broad range of backgrounds, interests, and situations that citizens in a large and diverse society face, it would be surprising if there were not substantial variations in the specific political issues that different citizens care about and attend to.

Converse based his negative assessment of the mass public's political preferences in part on the substantially stronger inter-correlations of preferences on related issues among the political elites he surveyed. (Converse's sample of political elites consisted of candidates for the U.S. Congress, arguably an unrealistically sophisticated comparison group.) Nevertheless, when Converse restricted his analysis of the public's policy positions in a given issue domain like foreign aid or racial policy to those respondents who he judged to be members of a given issue public,[13] he found that the inter-correlations among ordinary Americans resembled those among his political elites. "[R]emoval from analysis of individuals who, through indifference or ignorance, lie outside the issue publics in question serves to close much of the gap in constraint levels between mass and elite publics."[14]

Subsequent analyses confirm Converse's insight regarding issue publics.[15] Jon Krosnick, for example, sorted survey respondents into issue publics on the basis of the level of importance they attached to a dozen different political issues.[16] Krosnick reported that the greater the importance a respondent attached to a given policy issue, the more likely they were to mention that issue as a reason for liking or disliking the presidential candidates, the less likely they were to change their issue preference in response to persuasive communications, and the more stable their reported issue preference was over time.

Another technique for identifying issue publics is to rely on demographic group membership on the assumption that members of particular groups are, at least on average, more interested in some issues than others. Vincent Hutchings, for example, identifies union members and people living in union households as more likely to have an interest in labor issues while abortion policy is likely to be of greater interest to women and religious conservatives.[17] Consistent with these expectations, he finds that members of these groups are more attentive to Senate and gubernatorial campaigns when "their" issues were raised and more likely to base their Senate votes on their senator's record on the particular issues associated with their group.

Research on issue publics suggests that assessments of the quality of public preferences that look only at the average level of knowledge, preference stability, or other measures across the public as a whole may strongly understate the degree to which a typical citizen holds meaningful policy preferences. True, the typical citizen may attend to only a few of the many issues facing the country at any point in time. But if citizens have sensible, stable, and reasonably informed preferences on the subset of issues that they care most about, and if they use those issues disproportionately as a basis for choosing among parties and candidates, then the public can fulfill its assigned role in democratic governance, even if most citizens lack meaningful opinions on most issues.

The "Magic of Aggregation" and the Quality of Public Preferences

Cue taking suggests that even citizens with minimal information may be able to form meaningful preferences by relying on others who share their general outlooks or political orientations, and the division of the citizenry into issue publics suggests that meaningful participation in democratic governance does not require all citizens to hold meaningful preferences on all issues. A third factor relevant to the assessment of the public's role in democracy is that the aggregate preferences of the public as a whole have different characteristics than the individual preferences that make them up.

The eighteenth century French philosopher and mathematician Condorcet explained in his famous "jury theorem" that if each individual in a group has even a modest tendency to be correct, the group as an aggregate can have a very high probability of reaching the correct decision (and the larger the aggregate, the higher the probability that the collective judgment will be correct). This insight has been applied to the political attitudes expressed on surveys to suggest that the "errors" in respondents' reports of their own preferences will, at least under some circumstances, tend to cancel out, resulting in a measure of aggregate opinion that is more stable and more reliable than the individual opinions that make it up.[18]

But how can respondents be "wrong" about their own preferences? Two different kinds of "errors" in survey-based measures of policy preferences can be distinguished. First, even if respondents had perfectly fixed and certain views on a particular policy option, the reports of those views as captured on surveys would contain some degree of error. The ambiguities of question wording, the difficulty in matching a specific sentiment to the available response options, and mistakes in reading or hearing the survey question or recording the respondent's answer will all introduce some degree of "measurement error" (see Chapter 2 of this volume).

Second, most respondents are not likely to have perfectly fixed and certain views on most political issues. Current understandings of political attitudes suggest that citizens typically hold a variety of considerations relevant to a given policy issue and use those considerations to construct a position on a policy question when asked by a survey interviewer.[19] For example, if asked whether they favor cutting government spending on foreign aid, a survey respondent might consider his or her views about taxes and government spending, about humanitarian needs in developing countries, about waste and corruption in those countries, about competing domestic needs, and so on. This process of canvassing considerations and constructing positions is an imperfect one, however. Given the time and motivational constraints typical of a survey interview, only a subset of all possible considerations bearing on a particular question are likely to be brought to mind. Moreover, this subset of considerations may be biased toward those that are at the "top of the head" as a result of earlier questions in the survey, stories that have been in the news, recent experiences the respondent may have had, specific aspects of the question wording, or any number of other reasons.

From this perspective, most citizens cannot be said to "have attitudes" corresponding to a particular survey question on a political issue, in the sense that those attitudes existed in a crystallized form before the question was asked.[20] But individual citizens can be said to have "response tendencies" or "long term preferences" which represents their (hypothetical) average opinion if it were to be ascertained repeatedly over time.[21] This Platonic "true attitude" is nothing more than the imperfectly revealed average of these hypothetical repeated preference constructions (in the same way that a "true circle" is a hypothetical shape that can only be approximated by any actual circle in the real world).

It is impractical, of course, to measure citizens' "long term preferences" by repeatedly surveying the same individuals. But aggregating survey responses across many individuals will produce much the same result (without the problem of dealing with new information or changed circumstances which might alter the set of relevant considerations). To the extent that the biases in formulating a preference from a given set of considerations are randomly distributed across individuals they will balance out, just as the errors in individuals' judgments in a jury context cancel each other out. If randomly distributed idiosyncratic factors lead individual citizens to report preferences that differ from their "true" or "long term" preferences, those errors will lead some citizens to under-report support for a policy while leading others to over-report support. With a large enough sample of citizens, these errors will cancel out resulting in aggregate preferences that closely match the average of the individuals' long-term preferences. Of course, not all factors that lead citizens to wrongly report their issue preferences will be random and therefore offsetting, a concern I'll return to below.

The most thorough examination of aggregate opinion toward public policy is Benjamin Page and Robert Shapiro's influential book *The Rational Public.*[22] Page and Shapiro do not view aggregation as a cure for all of the shortcomings of public opinion. But they argue that collective preferences display a degree of stability and cogency that far exceeds the typical individual level preferences that make them up.

> While we grant the rational ignorance of most individuals, and the possibility that their policy preferences are shallow and unstable, we maintain that public opinion as a *collective* phenomenon is nonetheless stable (though not immovable), meaningful, and indeed rational … it is able to make distinctions; it is organized in coherent patterns; it is reasonable,

based on the best available information; and it is adaptive to new information or changed circumstances.[23]

Moreover, they maintain, "surveys accurately measure this stable, meaningful, and reasonable collective public opinion."[24] The collective rationality of public opinion stems, Page and Shapiro argue, from the aggregation of individual opinions which cancel out both random measurement errors in surveys and temporary fluctuations in individuals' opinions. The aggregate preferences that result from this process tend to be quite stable, but also exhibit sensible responsiveness to changing conditions. For example, public support for unemployment assistance increases as unemployment rates rise, public support for defense spending increases when the threat of war goes up, public support for tax cuts declines when tax rates are lowered, and so on.

Two principal objections have been raised about the "miracle of aggregation." The first, which Page and Shapiro discuss at some length, is that "errors" in individuals' policy preferences will not always be randomly distributed. One source of non-random "error" in preference formation is misinformation that leads most or all members of the public to shift their policy preferences in the same direction. For example, John F. Kennedy and others claimed during the late 1950s that the United States was facing a nuclear "missile gap" with the Soviet Union. In retrospect it is clear that not only was there no missile gap (the United States had and maintained a considerable advantage in nuclear missiles) but that good evidence was available at the time demonstrating the absence of such a gap. This sort of misinformation will inevitably "pervert" the preferences that the public would otherwise hold on related policy issues (in this case, defense spending and foreign policy).

Shared misinformation need not result from purposeful attempts to mislead the public. Sizeable misperceptions of changes in the crime rate, spending levels on foreign aid, the racial composition of the poor, and the typical length of time beneficiaries receive welfare have all been widespread among the American public at various points in time.[25] The extent of collectively held misinformation among the public is difficult to assess, in part because the truth about many politically relevant facts may not become known until later (if ever). After canvassing some of the sources and content of misinformation held by Americans, Page and Shapiro conclude

> we cannot hope to offer a precise or definitive account of the extent (or, for that matter, the nature) of information biases in the United States. But if we are on track concerning important instances of opinion manipulation and general patterns of biased and misleading information, these pose troubling implications for the workings of democracy.[26]

Just how troubled we should be about biased or misleading information is difficult to judge. To the extent that misinformation is universal (or nearly universal) among elites and the public at large, it is hard to see how any form of government could make optimal decisions. The consequences of misinformation that are unique to democracy, on the other hand, are those in which large numbers of citizens fall prey to *avoidable* misperceptions or biases. For example, if the preferences of the majority of citizens were influenced by misinformation that the best informed citizens knew to be untrue, then a democratic government that reflected the public's collective preference might do a poor job of serving the public's true interests. Misinformation always has the potential to bias preferences under any form of government, but the special challenge to democracy arises from situations in which the collective preferences of the public would look different if the public had the same level of relevant information that the most politically knowledgeable and engaged members of society hold.

In the following section, I will discuss the degree to which this sort of misinformation appears to bias public preferences and undermine democratic governance. But there is a second principled objection to the optimistic account of aggregate opinion that we must consider as well. As Scott Althaus explains, the notion that "errors" in the individual preferences reported on surveys will cancel out when those individual reports are aggregated rests on the assumption that preferences are measured in such a manner that errors in one direction and errors in the other direction are equally likely.[27] But this is not always the case. For example, consider a question with only two response options (in addition to "don't know"), such as those gauging support or opposition to some proposed policy change. Among citizens who "really" favor the proposed change, some proportion will mistakenly be recorded as opposing the change, because they misunderstood the question, because they were misinformed about the policy, or simply because the interviewer entered the wrong code. But if these sources of error are randomly distributed across the survey respondents, then (approximately) the same proportion of citizens who "really" oppose the policy will be recorded as favoring the policy.

It might appear that this balancing out of opposite errors will leave the aggregate preference on this policy as measured by this hypothetical survey question unchanged. But that is only the case if equal numbers of citizens support and oppose the policy. If "true" supporters outnumber opponents by say, three to one, then the number of survey respondents erroneously counted as opponents will be three times as great as the number erroneously counted as supporters. In this example, if 20 percent of all respondents are misclassified then 15 percent of the respondents will be "erroneously" shifted from supporters to opponents (20 percent of 75) while 5 percent will be erroneously shifted from opponents to supporters (20 percent of 25). As a result, it will appear that 65 percent rather than 75 percent of respondents favor the proposed policy and 35 rather than 25 percent oppose it.[28]

More generally, random errors will shift the apparent distribution of preferences on questions with only two valid responses toward 50 percent. (If the true distribution of preferences on such an item is 50 percent, then random errors will in fact be equal and offsetting.) The same logic applies to survey questions with more than two valid response categories to the extent that the preferences of respondents who belong in the highest category can only be moved downward while those in the lowest category can only be moved upward. If the true distribution of long term preferences is asymmetrical then random errors will not cancel out but will tend to move the recorded mean toward the center of the scale.

These sorts of non-offsetting errors on policy issues with asymmetric distributions of preferences will dampen the apparent extremity of preferences for the public as a whole. But the distortion of public opinion that results will be only one of degree, not of kind. The distribution of policy preferences will appear to be somewhat more "centrist" and less "extremist" than is really the case. Consequently the amount of opinion difference associated with a given change in the probability of a proposed policy change being adopted will appear somewhat smaller than it should (and the strength of the preference/policy link somewhat stronger than is really the case). In sum, the "magic of aggregation" cannot be assumed to cancel out all of the random error inherent in measures of political preferences. Highly popular policies will appear somewhat less popular and highly unpopular policies somewhat less unpopular than is really the case. But this "moderating bias" will have only a modest impact in strengthening the apparent association of government policy and public preferences.

How Well Does Cue Taking and Aggregation Work?

To what extent do cue taking, preference aggregation, and issue publics ameliorate concerns about low levels of political information and the low quality of public preferences on political issues? No actual public in a large society is likely to meet the classical expectations of the well-informed citizen. But does the existing public display enough "wisdom" in its political preferences to recommend a system of governance that strongly reflects the preferences of the public?

We know that cue taking *can* be an effective strategy for forming policy preferences on complex issues. In one study, for example, respondents who were poorly informed about the details of five competing insurance-reform initiatives on a California ballot, but who knew where the insurance industry stood on each initiative, were able to closely emulate the voting behavior of their better-informed peers.[29] But just because cues *can* serve as effective shortcuts doesn't mean the necessary cues are always available or that citizens will make use of them when they are. One way to assess the quality of public preferences that emerge from the processes described above is to compare the actual preferences expressed on surveys to some hypothetical standard of "well-informed preferences" that citizens would hold if they had the ability, time, and inclination to gather the relevant information on a given set of policy issues.

The most straightforward way to assess how far actual preferences diverge from hypothetical well-informed preferences is to inform a representative group of citizens about some set of policy issues and see how their preferences shift as a result. James Fishkin and Robert Luskin have done just this in a series of "deliberative polls."[30] For example, the 1996 National Issues Convention brought 466 participants, selected at random from the U.S. population, to Austin, Texas, for four days, during which time they read briefing materials on various economic, foreign policy, and family issues, discussed those issues in small groups, and participated in question-and-answer sessions with experts. When initially contacted, and once again at the end of their stay in Austin, participants answered identical questions concerning their policy preferences in these three issue areas. To provide a comparison group, members of the initial sample who elected not to come to Austin completed the same surveys.

The participants in the National Issues Convection did shift their preferences somewhat on many of the 48 political attitude questions they were asked. But the average change in aggregate preferences was not large and barely exceeded the aggregate change of preferences expressed by the control group which was not provided with the information or opportunity to deliberate. On a 100-point scale, the average net (i.e., aggregate) difference in pre-post preferences across these 48 issue questions was about five points for the deliberation group and about three points for the control group.[31] The four days of focused study and deliberation, it appears, resulted in a two percentage point greater aggregate change in policy preferences than would otherwise be expected by simply resurveying the same respondents with no intervening activity.

The results of the National Issues Convention study suggest that on the topics addressed, participants' pre-existing aggregate preferences closely resembled the "well-informed preferences" they expressed after four days of education and deliberation. But these conclusions hinge on the specific information provided to the deliberating respondents. If the information provided was not new to the participants, or was not different enough from what they already knew, or was not relevant enough to the policy judgments they were asked to make, then the possibility remains that different information might have shifted aggregate preferences to a greater degree. Nevertheless, since the organizers' goal was to provide just the sort of educational experience that critics of the quality of public opinion view as lacking, these results do lend some credibility to the notion that cue taking and aggregation result in collective judgments that differ little from what a well-informed and engaged citizenry would express.

A very different way to compare actual to hypothetical "well-informed" preferences is to use statistical tools to simulate a well-informed citizenry.

This approach takes advantage of the fact that, as Philip Converse observed, the mean level of political knowledge among the electorate is very low, but the variation in knowledge is very high.[32] By modeling the vote choices or policy preferences of the most well-informed segment of the electorate, one can impute preferences for citizens who share a given set of characteristics but have lower levels of political information.

Larry Bartels, for example, compared the presidential votes of the most well-informed respondents with those of less-informed respondents of the same age, education, income, race, sex, occupational status, region, religion, union membership, urban residence, homeowner status, and labor force participation.[33] Bartels found an average individual deviation of about ten percentage points between actual and "well-informed" votes for the six presidential elections between 1972 and 1992. Many of these deviations were off-setting, however—some poorly informed citizens reported casting a Republican vote when they would have been predicted to vote Democratic if well informed, but other poorly informed citizens "mistakenly" voted Democratic when they would have been predicted to vote Republican. The more relevant *aggregate* deviation between actual and well-informed presidential votes was only three percentage points.[34]

In an even more directly relevant study that used a similar methodology, Scott Althaus compared respondents' expressed preferences on 235 political opinion questions with imputed preferences calculated by assigning to each respondent the predicted preference of someone with the maximum level of political knowledge but otherwise identical in terms of education, income, age, partisan identification, race, sex, marital status, religion, region, labor force participation, occupational category, union membership, and homeownership.[35] Althaus found that in the aggregate, imputed "fully informed preferences" differed from expressed preferences by an average of about 6.5 percentage points. Not a trivial amount, but hardly enough to dismiss existing preferences as an unsuitable guide to government decision making.

Two lessons can be drawn from the research on "enlightened preferences." First, while heuristics or informational shortcuts might, in theory, be extremely effective at allowing citizens to reach the same preferences they would if they were more fully informed, in practice a gap remains between actual and hypothetical "well-informed" preferences, whether those preferences are statistically imputed or arrived at after exposure to new information and deliberation. Second, the size of the aggregate gap is rather modest. The two most directly relevant analyses that focus on policy preferences find gaps of two and 6.5 percentage points, with a three percentage point gap in presidential voting. Differences of this size might be enough to swing a close election or to shift aggregate preferences from slightly favorable toward some policy option to slightly opposed. But the policy proposals I examine below range widely from strong opposition to strong support (about two-thirds of the proposed policy changes in my dataset were favored by under

40 or over 60 percent of the respondents). Thus, the relatively small differences in favorability that might be expected from a better informed, more "enlightened" citizenry, would be unlikely to lead to substantially different conclusions.

Question Wording and Framing Effects

Even casual consumers of survey data are aware that subtle differences in how a question is worded can sometimes produce large differences in responses. Advocacy groups sometimes take advantage of this phenomenon by asking "loaded" or "biased" questions which are designed to portray public sentiment as highly favorable toward the group's preferred policies. But many observers are skeptical that even careful and well-crafted surveys can avoid this problem. One popular book aimed at explaining surveys and their use in American politics claims:

> Even when the sponsor has no obvious ax to grind, question wording choices greatly influence the results obtained. In many instances, highly reputable polling organizations have arrived at divergent conclusions simply because they employed different (although well-constructed) questions on a particular topic.[36]

But just how ubiquitous and how consequential are such question wording effects? This is a difficult question to answer because there is no clear way to define the range of plausible question wordings on a given topic or the set of topics that should be considered. Some of the most frequently cited examples of question wording effects do raise doubts about the ability of survey measures to accurately capture the public's policy preferences. For example, Tom Smith reports that 64 percent of Americans thought the government was spending too little on "assistance to the poor" but only 22 percent thought too little was being spent on "welfare."[37] Howard Schuman and Stanley Presser found that in the 1970s two in five Americans felt that the United States should "not allow" public speeches against democracy, but only half that number felt that the United States should "forbid" public speeches against democracy.[38] Finally, George Quattrone and Amos Tversky found that 64 percent of their respondents preferred a program that would increase inflation somewhat while *reducing unemployment* from 10 percent to 5 percent, but only 46 percent made the same choice when the program was described as *increasing employment* from 90 percent to 95 percent.[39]

Each of these examples reveals substantial effects from apparently minor changes in the words used to describe a policy choice and each has been replicated numerous times, so we cannot dismiss them as statistical flukes. Yet their implications for how we understand citizens' policy preferences (or their lack of preferences) and our ability to gauge those preferences is far from clear. For example, the greater appeal of "assisting the poor" over "welfare" has often been interpreted as indicating the sensitivity of the public to particular positively or negatively loaded terms. If the preferences expressed toward the same policy can be shifted so dramatically by calling it one thing rather than another, can we even say the public has a "real" and discernable preference toward that policy? Yet this example can be viewed another way entirely. There are many different government programs that assist the poor by providing medical care, housing subsidies, legal aid, child care, job training, and so on. For some respondents, all of these programs might be included under the rubric "welfare" but for many Americans, welfare is understood as cash assistance to the able-bodied working-age unemployed poor. The public tends to be strongly supportive of these other anti-poverty programs, so the lesser appeal of "welfare" in comparison to "assisting the poor" can be understood not as a superficial response to an emotionally laden term, but a sophisticated differentiation between different sorts of government anti-poverty programs.[40]

The broader lesson from this alternative perspective on the "welfare" question wording experiment is that much of what passes for question wording effects are in actuality differences in responses resulting from differences in the policy that respondents are asked to respond to. The same survey that showed more support for "assisting the poor" than for "welfare" also found greater support for "halting the rising crime rate" than for "law enforcement" and greater support for "dealing with drug addiction" than for "drug rehabilitation" (General Social Survey). But these alternative question wordings are not simply different formulations of the identical policies; they are references to different aspects of their respective issues.

In the second example above, which contrasts "forbid" and "not allow," the alternative wordings do appear to have identical meanings. The substantial differences in responses to these two formulations are a bit of a mystery, especially since the alternate question wordings sometimes produce dramatically different responses (like the case of "speeches against democracy" described above), sometimes modest differences (e.g., in a parallel experiment focused on "speeches in favor of communism"), and sometimes no differences at all (e.g., in questions about "showing x-rated movies" or "cigarette advertisements on television").[41] Sometimes respondents seem to react differently to "forbid" and "not allow" but at other times these alternative wordings seem to make no difference.

The third example above revealed different evaluations if a policy choice was presented in terms of its effect on the percent of the workforce that would be *employed* or on the percent of the workforce that would be *unemployed*. These sorts of mathematically equivalent alternative descriptions have been labeled "equivalency frames."[42] This example is explained by recognizing that people tend to evaluate differences in magnitude (like the employment or unemployment rates) at least partly in terms of ratios. The difference between

10 percent and 5 percent unemployment appears large because the former is twice as big as the latter. In contrast, the difference between 90 percent employment and 95 percent employment appears small because their ratio is close to one.[43]

These sorts of framing effects have led many scholars to doubt whether the public can plausibly be said to have preferences on the underlying policies. But other scholars point out that such framing effects in survey experiments take place under highly artificial conditions. In the real world alternative ways of characterizing a policy choice are typically encountered not in isolation (as in survey experiments) but simultaneously as part of the political debate. The availability of competing frames, and the give and take of political debate have been shown to undermine framing effects, reducing or eliminating differences in responses.[44]

Question wording and framing effects potentially challenge the notion that the public holds meaningful preferences and that we can use survey interviews to discern what those preferences are. Yet the real world impact of these problems may be small, as two recent examples suggest. In the first example, opponents of the inheritance tax were said to have boosted their cause by relabeling it the "death tax."[45] But the best evidence suggests that the label made little difference. In a survey experiment using two alternative wordings administered to randomly selected halves of the sample, 69 percent of respondents favored doing away with the "estate tax" while 73 percent favored doing away with the "death tax."[46]

In a parallel example, observers have claimed that the label "climate change" generates greater concern among the public than "global warming."[47] But the only randomized survey experiment to pit these two formulations against each other found little difference: 57 percent of Americans believed that "global warming" would become a "very serious" or "extremely serious" problem if nothing was done, compared with 60 percent who felt that way about "climate change" and 58 percent about "global climate change."[48]

In sum, we cannot dismiss concerns about question wording and framing effects entirely. The evidence is strong that how a policy is described can have an impact on the level of support or opposition expressed toward that policy. These effects, however, do not imply that the public has no "real" attitudes toward these policies, or that we cannot know (at least approximately) what those attitudes are. As one expert who has himself conducted numerous studies of framing effects concludes "framing effects appear to be neither robust nor particularly pervasive. Elite competition and heterogeneous discussion limit and often eliminate framing effects."[49]

Feigned Attitudes and Feigned Non-Attitudes

Two additional problems are sometimes viewed as affecting survey measures of political attitudes. First, respondents who lack opinions may be reluctant to say "don't know" either out of embarrassment or in an effort to be "helpful" to the interviewer. In such cases, claims to support or oppose some policy represent "non-attitudes" which distort the observed measure of public preferences. In other cases, respondents who in fact do have relevant opinions nevertheless may answer "don't know" perhaps because they think their true preference is embarrassing or out of step with perceived social norms. In either situation, respondents who engage in these behaviors may be distinctive in ways that result in a misleading assessment of what the true distribution of preferences in the population looks like.

Scholars have examined both of these kinds of "mis-reported" attitudes. Respondents' tendency to feign preferences on issues on which they lack opinions has been assessed by asking respondents about wholly fictitious issues. For example, 24 percent of respondents in one survey expressed a preference on whether the "1975 Public Affairs Act" should be repealed and 39 percent offered an opinion on the "Agricultural Trade Act of 1984" despite the fact that neither of these supposed pieces of legislation existed.[50] This suggests that some of the opinion preferences collected by survey interviewers about policies (or potential policy changes) that really do exist are in fact "non-attitudes" reported by respondents who are reluctant to say "don't know." These sorts of findings are often seen as embarrassments undermining the notion the surveys reveal meaningful preferences. Yet the 76 percent and 61 percent of respondents who did say "don't know" in response to these two questions about fictitious legislation is far higher than the percentage of respondents saying "don't know" to any of the real issues represented in the data I analyze below.

Since most respondents do seem able to resist the pressure to express a preference on an issue they have never heard of, most of the preferences that are expressed in response to the questions I examine in this study are likely real preferences, even if the respondents offering those preferences are only vaguely familiar with some of the issues they were asked about. Taking the "worst case scenario" above as a guide, if only 61 percent of those who really don't have an opinion on an issue say "don't know" and the rest offer a substantive preference anyway, the observed proportion of "don't knows" will be an underestimate of the true proportion. Thus if we observed that 5 percent of respondents said "don't know" (about the average for my data) we could infer that the real percentage of respondents who lack an opinion is about 8.2 percent (since 61 percent of 8.2 is 5.0).

The "hidden" non-attitudes in the example above consist of the 3.2 percent of respondents who gave a substantive answer despite having no real opinion. Of course, if the question concerned a more obscure policy on which a larger percentage of the respondents in fact had no opinion, the size of the hidden non-attitudes group would be proportionately larger. Since few of the policy questions in my data set produce observed "don't know" rates of greater than 10 percent, the extent of such hidden non-attitudes is simply too small to seriously distort the real information contained in the substantive survey responses that form the basis of my analyses.[51]

The second threat to the validity of survey data mentioned above is the opposite of hidden non-attitudes. In this second scenario, respondents who in fact hold opinions nevertheless give "don't know" responses. Adam Berinsky offers the most extensive analysis of this phenomenon. Berinsky hypothesizes that survey questions on political attitudes are most likely to elicit "don't know" responses from people who in fact do have opinions if the issue being discussed is either complex or if the respondent's views run counter to perceived social norms.[52] In the former case, for example, a question about tax policy might require considerable effort from respondents to connect the proposed policy to their own interests and preferences on taxes. Rather than engage in this effortful processing, respondents may simply say "don't know." In the latter case, a respondent who opposes laws protecting homosexuals from discrimination may prefer to avoid the risk of embarrassment or social sanction by saying "don't know" instead.

Berinsky tests this theory with a series of questions about race, social welfare policy, and the Vietnam war. Of concern here is the extent to which observed measures of policy preferences are distorted by respondents with real attitudes saying "don't know." Using a sophisticated statistical model to impute preferences to respondents who said "don't know," Berinsky finds virtually no such distortion for questions that lack complexity and have no clear socially normative answer. In contrast, he does find distortions on questions with one or the other of these qualities. But like the impact of hidden non-attitudes, the size of the distortions uncovered in Berinsky's analysis is quite small. The largest distortions occur on racial policy questions asked during the 1990s for which he estimates that opposition to school integration would appear 3 to 5 percent higher if the hidden attitudes of respondents saying "don't know" were statistically taken into account. The distortions on the other questions hypothesized to produce hidden attitudes are even smaller: observed preferences on social welfare policy in the 1990s and on the Vietnam war in the 1960s never differ from the estimated true preferences by more than two percentage points.

Survey questions are imperfect measures of public preferences in many ways. The question for scholars and others interested in what the public thinks is whether the distortions inherent in survey data are small enough that such data can be relied on to gauge public sentiments. With regard to both of the potential threats to validity examined above, it appears that these distortions are minor. Neither hidden attitudes nor hidden non-attitudes appear to be substantial enough to significantly impact the value of survey-based preference measures for analyzing Americans' preferences on matters of public policy.

Public Preferences and Government Responsiveness

If the policy preferences expressed by the mass public are meaningful (at least in the aggregate) and reflective of Americans' genuine attitudes toward alternative government actions, then one criterion for assessing the degree of democratic legitimacy is the strength of the association between public preferences and policy outcomes. Of course we would not expect or desire a perfect match between majority preferences and government policy. First, there are issues of minority rights to be considered. Second, the public is not capable of guiding policy on all questions that come before the government. Issues like alternative high-definition TV standards, or which government regulatory agency should be responsible for agricultural futures trading, are simply too obscure for most citizens to have meaningful preferences on. Finally, one subset of the public might care intensely about a particular issue another is fairly indifferent. If I care deeply about foreign policy and am indifferent to education, and you care strongly about education and not foreign policy, a government that responds to my preferences on foreign policy and yours on education would make us both happier than one that took each of our views equally into consideration in both issue domains.

These considerations notwithstanding, it remains true that a government that responds only weakly or not at all to the preferences of the governed, or that systematically responds to some citizens but ignores others, has but a weak claim to being considered a democracy. The association of government policy with public preferences measured by surveys is only one basis for judging government responsiveness, but it is a useful starting point for assessing the nature and degree of representation.

To estimate the association between public preferences and government policy I make use of the dataset mentioned briefly above. These data consist of 2,245 survey questions asked between 1964 and 2006.[53] Each question asked whether respondents favored or opposed some specific change in federal government policy. In my dataset, I collected the responses to these questions separately for respondents at different income levels in order to compare the strength of the preference/policy link for more and less well-off Americans.

As we would expect, the more support a given policy has among the public, the more likely it is that that policy will be adopted, and this pattern holds true for respondents at all income levels. Figure 3.1 shows this relationship separately for respondents at the 10th, 50th, and 90th income percentiles.[54] The far left side of the figure shows that policies with strong public opposition (with fewer than 20 percent favoring the proposed change), have a low probability of being adopted, with the probability of adoption increasing as support increases. However, the far right side of the figure shows that even policies with strong public support (at least 80 percent of the public favoring the proposed change) have a less than even chance of being adopted. This

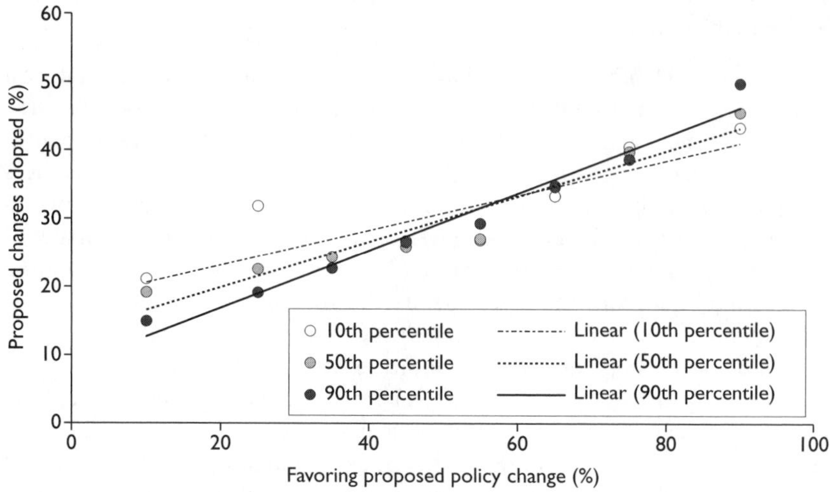

Figure 3.1 The Preference/Policy Link for Respondents at the 10th, 50th, and 90th Income Percentiles.

Note
Based on 2,245 survey questions concerning proposed policy changes asked between 1964 and 2006.

pattern suggests that the political system is responsive to public preferences, but with a strong status quo bias. Given that our federal government was designed by its framers to inhibit as much as facilitate lawmaking (with its separation of powers, multiple veto points within congress, supermajority requirements in the Senate, and so on), this status quo bias should not be surprising.

Figure 3.1 also shows that the probability of a policy being adopted is somewhat more strongly related to the preferences of the affluent than those of the middle class or the poor: the solid line, representing respondents at the 90th income percentile, is somewhat steeper than the lines for the 50th and 10th income percentiles. But the differences among income groups are modest, and at every level of income, favored policies are substantially more likely to be adopted than unfavored policies.

To better gauge the true influence over policy making of Americans at different income levels, we need to take into account the fact that poor and well-off Americans agree on many policy questions. If affluent Americans are better able to influence policy outcomes that the less well-off, the association of policy outcomes with the preferences of the poor or the middle class shown in Figure 3.1 may simply reflect those proposed changes on which Americans at all income levels agree.

Figure 3.2 shows the same relationships shown in Figure 3.1, but restricted to proposed policy changes for which low and high income

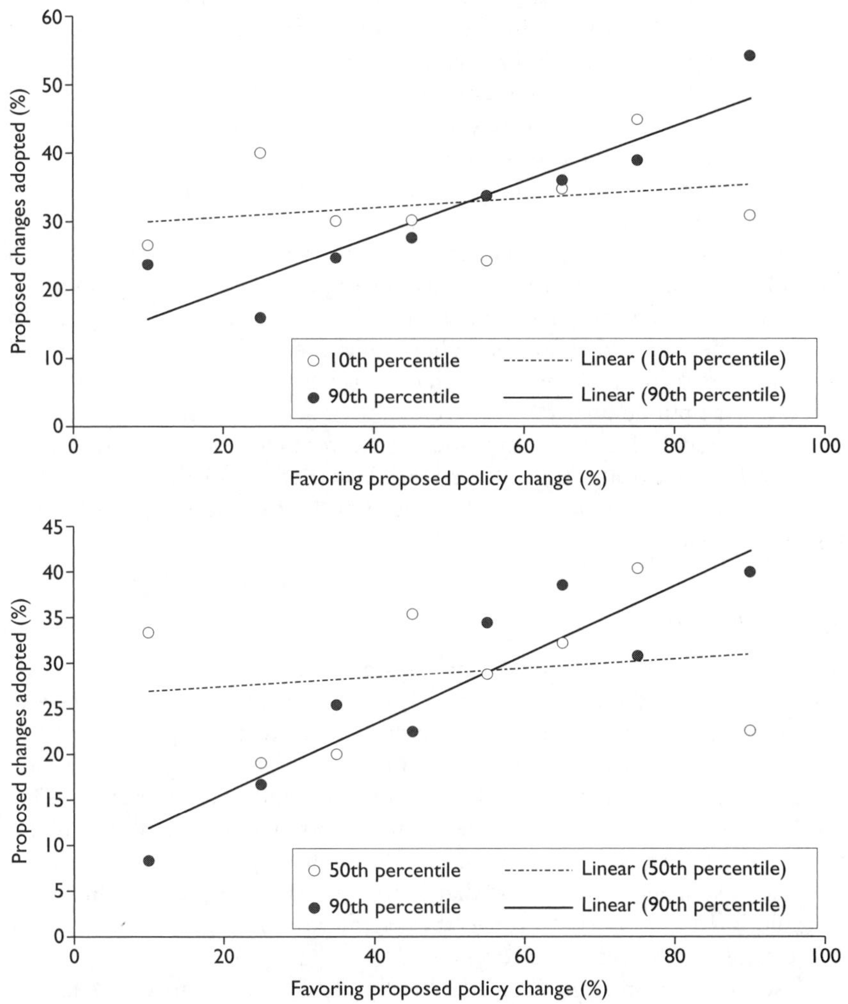

Figure 3.2 The Preference/Policy Link when Preferences at the 10th or 50th Income Percentiles diverge from the 90th Income Percentile.

Note

Based on the 932 and 414 survey questions on which the preferences of people at the 10th and 90th and 50th and 90th income percentiles diverged by at least ten percentage points.

Americans' preferences, or middle and high income Americans' preferences, diverge by at least ten percentage points. Here we see a very different picture: the preference/policy link for the affluent remains strong, but when the preferences of less well-off Americans diverge from those at the top of the income distribution, the preferences of the less well-off appear to have virtually no relationship with policy outcomes. In other publications I explore these relationships in greater detail. I find that the basic pattern shown in Figure 3.2 is similar with regard to foreign policy, economic policy, social welfare, and moral or religious issues and cannot be explained by the higher levels of voting among the affluent, or a lack of strong preferences among the middle class or the poor.[55]

A number of different factors may contribute to the influence over policy exerted by affluent Americans and the lack of influence among the less well-off, but they all relate directly or indirectly to the importance of money in the political system. The well-off contribute to parties, candidates, and interest organizations at far higher rates than the middle class or the poor. In addition, they tend to share the policy preferences of an even smaller and more powerful group of truly rich Americans who help determine who runs for and wins public office (and therefore what sorts of policies they subsequently pursue). Finally, government policy makers are themselves far better off economically than the average American, and their own policy preferences are more likely to reflect those of their economic peers than of less well-off citizens.

Conclusions

The American public's knowledge of political issues and understanding of the policy choices government faces is clearly limited. And studies of framing and question wording show the potential difficulties of measuring public preferences. Yet, on balance, the evidence indicates that framing and question wording effects in the real world are infrequent, and that aggregate preferences as measured by surveys reflect much the same set of attitudes that a more fully informed and engaged public would express. This evidence, I suggest, is sufficient to conclude that survey measures of public opinion are sensible bases on which to judge the extent to which government policy reflects the preferences of the governed.

Based on the findings described briefly above, American democracy is found wanting. The problem lies not in the failure of the public to form meaningful policy preferences, but in the failure of policy makers to respond to the public. Affluent Americans appear to have substantial influence over policy outcomes, but when less well-off Americans' preferences diverge from those of the affluent, government policy makers appear to take into account only the desires of the most economically advantaged.

In every society the well-off have more influence over government than the less economically advantaged. But the degree of inequality in how government responds to its citizens is a fundamental gauge of how truly democratic a society is. In this regard, we have a long way to go before we can claim to be a democracy characterized by "the continuing responsiveness of the government to the preferences of its citizens, considered as political equals."[56]

Notes

1. Robert A. Dahl, *Polyarchy: Participation and Opposition* (New Haven, CT: Yale University Press, 1971), p. 1.
2. Bernard R. Berelson, Paul F. Lazarsfeld, and William N. McPhee, *Voting: A Study of Opinion Formation in a Presidential Campaign* (Chicago, IL: University of Chicago Press, 1954), p. 308.
3. Philip E. Converse, "The Nature of Belief Systems in Mass Publics," in *Ideology and Discontent*, ed. David E. Apter (New York: Free Press, 1964).
4. Ibid., p. 245.
5. Michael X. Delli Carpini and Scott Keeter, *What Americans Know About Politics and Why It Matters* (New Haven, CT: Yale University Press, 1996), p. 269
6. Ibid., p. 270.
7. Berelson et al., *Voting: A Study of Opinion Formation in a Presidential Campaign*, p. 311.
8. Ibid., p. 109.
9. Anthony Downs, *An Economic Theory of Democracy* (New York: Harper Collins, 1957), p. 233.
10. Samuel L. Popkin, *The Reasoning Voter: Communication and Persuasion in Presidential Campaigns* (Chicago, IL: University of Chicago Press, 1991); Paul M. Sniderman, Richard A. Brody, and Philip E. Tetlock, *Reasoning and Choice: Explorations in Political Psychology* (Cambridge: Cambridge University Press, 1991); Arthur Lupia, "Shortcuts Versus Encyclopedias—Information and Voting-Behavior in California Insurance Reform Elections," *American Political Science Review* 88, no. 1 (1994); Arthur Lupia and Mathew D. McCubbins, *The Democratic Dilemma: Can Citizens Learn What They Need to Know?* (Cambridge: Cambridge University Press, 1998); Martin Gilens and Naomi Murakawa, "Elite Cues and Political Decision-Making," in *Research in Micropolitics*, eds. Michael X. Delli Carpini, Leonie Huddy, and Roberty Y. Shapiro (Oxford: Elsevier, 2002); Richard R. Lau and David P. Redlawsk, "Voting Correctly," *American Political Science Review* 91, no. 3 (1997); Richard R. Lau and David P. Redlawsk, *How Voters Decide: Information Processing During Election Campaigns*, Cambridge Studies in Public Opinion and Political Psychology (Cambridge/New York: Cambridge University Press, 2006); John R. Zaller, *The Nature and Origins of Mass Opinion* (Cambridge: Cambridge University Press, 1992); Edward G. Carmines and James H. Kuklinski, "Incentives, Opportunities, and the Logic of Public Opinion in American Political Representation," in *Information and Democratic Processes*, eds. John A. Ferejohn and James H. Kuklinski (Urbana, IL: University of Illinois Press, 1990).
11. Arthur Lupia, 1995. "Who Can Persuade? A Formal Theory, a Survey and Implications for Democracy." Paper presented at the annual meeting of the Midwest Political Science Association, Chicago, IL, April 6–8.
12. E.g., John W. Kingdon, *Congressmen's Voting Decisions*, 3rd ed. (Ann Arbor: University of Michigan Press, 1989).
13. Converse assessed issue public membership by dint of the consistency of responses to the same questions over time.
14. Converse, "The Nature of Belief Systems in Mass Publics," p. 246.
15. Shanto Iyengar, Kyu S. Hahn, Jon A. Krosnick, and John Walker, "Selective Exposure to Campaign Communication: The Role of Anticipated Agreement and Issue Public Membership," *Journal of Politics* 70, no. 1 (2008); Amy R. Gershkoff, "How Issue Interest Can Rescue the American Public" (Doctoral dissertation, Department of Politics, Princeton University, 2006); Jon A. Krosnick, "Government Policy and Citizen Passion: A Study of Issue Publics in Contemporary America," *Political Behavior* 12, no. 1 (1990).

16. Krosnick, "Government Policy and Citizen Passion: A Study of Issue Publics in Contemporary America."
17. Vincent L. Hutchings, *Public Opinion and Democratic Accountability: How Citizens Learn About Politics* (Princeton, NJ: Princeton University Press, 2003).
18. Nicholas R. Miller, "Information, Electorates, and Democracy: Some Extensions and Interpretations of the Condorcet Jury Theorem," in *Information Pooling and Group Decision Making*, eds. Bernard Grofman and Guillermo Owen (Greenwich, CT: JAI, 1986); Benjamin I. Page and Robert Y. Shapiro, *The Rational Public: Fifty Years of Trends in Americans' Policy Preferences* (Chicago, IL: University of Chicago Press, 1992); Philip E. Converse, "Popular Representation and the Distribution of Information," in *Information and Democratic Processes*, eds. John A. Ferejohn and James H. Kuklinski (Urbana, IL: University of Illinois Press, 1990); Christopher H. Achen, "Mass Political Attitudes and the Survey Response," *American Political Science Review* 69, no. 4 (1975).
19. Zaller, *The Nature and Origins of Mass Opinion*; John Zaller and Stanley Feldman, "A Simple Theory of the Survey Response: Answering Questions Versus Revealing Preferences," *American Journal of Political Science* 36 no. 3 (1992).
20. Larry M. Bartels, "Democracy with Attitudes" (New York, May 9, 1998).
21. Page and Shapiro, *The Rational Public: Fifty Years of Trends in Americans' Policy Preferences*.
22. Ibid.
23. Ibid., p. 14.
24. Ibid., p. 14.
25. Martin Gilens, "Political Ignorance and Collective Policy Preferences," *American Political Science Review* 95, no. 2 (2001); J.H. Kuklinski, P.J. Quirk, J. Jerit, D. Schwieder, and R.F. Rich, "Misinformation and the Currency of Democratic Citizenship," *Journal of Politics* 62, no. 3 (2000); Martin Gilens, *Why Americans Hate Welfare: Race, Media, and the Politics of Antipoverty Policy* (Chicago, IL: University of Chicago Press, 1999).
26. Page and Shapiro, *The Rational Public: Fifty Years of Trends in Americans' Policy Preferences*, p. 381.
27. Scott L. Althaus, *Collective Preferences in Democratic Politics: Opinion Surveys and the Will of the People* (New York: Cambridge University Press, 2003).
28. With 20 percent of respondents reporting the "wrong" preference, the true 75 percent favoring is reduced by 15 percentage points (75×0.20) who are recorded instead as opposing. The true 25 percent who oppose is reduced by five percentage points (25×0.20) who are recorded instead as favoring. Thus the total percentage recorded as favoring is $75 - 15 + 5 = 65$ and the total percentage recorded as opposing is $25 - 5 + 15 = 35$.
29. Lupia, "Shortcuts Versus Encyclopedias—Information and Voting-Behavior in California Insurance Reform Elections."
30. Robert C. Luskin and James S. Fishkin (1998) "Deliberative Polling, Public Opinion, and Democracy: The Case of the National Issues Convention." Paper presented at the annual meeting of the American Political Science Association, Boston, MA, September 2–6; James S. Fishkin and Robert C. Luskin, "Bringing Deliberation to the Democratic Dialogue," in *A Poll with a Human Face*, eds. Max McCombs and Amy Reynolds (London: Lawrence Erlbaum Associates,1999); James S. Fishkin and Robert C. Luskin, "Experimenting with a Democratic Ideal: Deliberative Polling and Public Opinion," *Acta Politica* 40, no. 3 (2005).
31. See Gilens and Murakawa, "Elite Cues and Political Decision-Making" for an analysis of these results.
32. Philip E. Converse, "Assessing the Capacity of Mass Electorates," *Annual Review of Political Science* 3 (2000).

33. L.M. Bartels, "Uninformed Votes: Information Effects in Presidential Elections," *American Journal of Political Science* 40, no. 1 (1996).
34. Ibid., Table 3.
35. Althaus, *Collective Preferences in Democratic Politics: Opinion Surveys and the Will of the People.*
36. Herbert B. Asher, *Polling and the Public: What Every Citizen Should Know*, 7th ed. (Washington, DC: CQ Press, 2007), p. 56.
37. Tom W. Smith, "That Which We Call Welfare by Any Other Name Would Smell Sweeter: An Analysis of the Impact of Question Wording on Response Patterns," *Public Opinion Quarterly* 51 (1987).
38. Howard Schuman and Stanley Presser, *Questions and Answers in Attitude Surveys* (San Diego, CA: Academic Press, 1981), p. 277.
39. George A. Quattrone and Amos Tversky, "Contrasting Rational and Psychological Analyses of Political Choice," *American Political Science Review* 82, no. 3 (1988).
40. Gilens, *Why Americans Hate Welfare: Race, Media, and the Politics of Antipoverty Policy.*
41. Schuman and Presser, *Questions and Answers in Attitude Surveys*, pp. 281–83.
42. James N. Druckman, "The Implications of Framing Effects for Citizen Competence," *Political Behavior* 23, no. 3 (2001).
43. Quattrone and Tversky, "Contrasting Rational and Psychological Analyses of Political Choice," p. 728.
44. James N. Druckman, "Political Preference Formation: Competition, Deliberation, and the (Ir)Relevance of Framing Effects," *American Political Science Review* 98, no. 4 (2004); Paul M. Sniderman and Sean M. Theriault (1999) "The Dynamics of Political Argument and the Logic of Issue Framing." Presented at the annual meeting of the Midwest Political Science Association, Chicago, IL.
45. Michael J. Graetz and Ian Shapiro, *Death by a Thousand Cuts: The Fight over Taxing Inherited Wealth*, 1st ed. (Princeton, NJ: Princeton University Press, 2005).
46. Larry M. Bartels, *Unequal Democracy: The Political Economy of the New Gilded Age* (Princeton, NJ: Princeton University Press, 2008).
47. Katy Butler, "George Lakoff Says Environmentalists Need to Watch Their Language," *Sierra Magazine* 89, July/August (2004).
48. Ana Villar and Jon A. Krosnick, "Global Warming vs. Climate Change, Taxes vs. Prices: Does Word Choice Matter?" *Climate Change* 105, nos. 1–2 (2010).
49. Druckman, "Political Preference Formation: Competition, Deliberation, and the (Ir)Relevance of Framing Effects," p. 683.
50. George F. Bishop, Alfred J. Tuchfarber, and Robert W. Oldendick, "Opinions on Fictitious Issues—The Pressure to Answer Survey Questions," *Public Opinion Quarterly* 50, no. 2 (1986).
51. Ninety-one percent of the proposed policy change questions in my dataset elicited no more than 10 percent "don't know" responses; 97 percent of the questions elicited no more than 15 percent "don't know" responses.
52. Adam J. Berinsky, *Silent Voices: Public Opinion and Political Participation in America* (Princeton, NJ: Princeton University Press, 2004).
53. For reasons explained in Martin Gilens, "Paying the Piper: Economic Inequality and Democratic Responsiveness in the United States" (unpublished book manuscript, Princeton University, n.d.), only survey questions asked during 1964–1968, 1981–2002, and 2005–2006 were included.
54. Figures 3.1 and 3.2 show the mean proportion adopted for policies favored by less than 20 percent, 20–30, 30–40, 40–50, 50–60, 60–70, 70–80, and 80 percent of respondents or more (for respondents at the 10th, 50th, and 90th income percentiles). See Martin Gilens, "Inequality and Democratic Responsiveness," *Public*

Opinion Quarterly 69, no. 5 (2005) for an explanation of how preferences at different income percentiles are calculated.

55. Gilens, "Inequality and Democratic Responsiveness"; Martin Gilens, "Preference Gaps and Inequality in Representation," *PS: Political Science and Politics* 42, no. 2 (2009); Martin Gilens, "Policy Outcomes and Representational Inequality," in *Who Gets Represented?* ed. Peter K. Enns and Christopher Wlezien (New York: Russell Sage Foundation, 2011); Gilens, "Paying the Piper: Economic Inequality and Democratic Responsiveness in the United States."
56. Dahl, *Polyarchy: Participation and Opposition*, p. 1.

Part II

The Foundations of Political Preferences

Chapter 4

Ideology and Public Opinion

Christopher M. Federico[1]

Few concepts in the study of public opinion have attracted as much attention as that of ideology. While social scientists have always shown a keen interest in the nuts and bolts of belief systems, the resurgence of bitter divisions between the left and right has brought the topic back to the forefront of scholarship and lay discussion alike. In this chapter, I review past and present work on the nature of ideology and its consequences for public opinion. I begin by addressing the definitional question of *what* ideology actually is. Next, I provide an overview of several decades' worth of research on *what attracts* individuals to different ideological postures like liberalism and conservatism and *when* individuals think and make judgments about issues and candidates in ways that reflect ideology. As we shall see, these two aspects of ideology do not always go hand-in-hand. While most citizens willingly identify themselves as "liberals" or "conservatives," only those who have absorbed a great deal of information from political leaders think about politics in terms of these ideological categories and express opinions that are consistently liberal or conservative. Finally, I expand on the question of when citizens rely on ideology by suggesting that information is not the whole story. To this end, I review evidence suggesting that citizens must possess both political information and a strong desire to appraise things as "good" or "bad" in order to think ideologically and express ideologically consistent opinions.

What is Ideology?

While the concept of ideology has a familiar ring to it, students of public opinion—including political scientists, sociologists, and psychologists—have struggled to settle on a common definition of what it is.[2] As a result, those who dive into the topic may find themselves adrift on a sea of competing interpretations. Nevertheless, in public opinion research, the most important working definitions of ideology do repeatedly converge on a number of crucial claims.[3] First, ideologies are *belief systems* or frameworks of interrelated ideas. That is, they consist of opinions, values, and beliefs about the nature of social reality that can be grouped together under some common social theme, e.g., moving society in the direction of greater justice and equality. In the language of psychology, this claim suggests that ideologies are *schemas*—i.e., organized clusters of ideas about social and political life that have been stored away in long-term memory.[4] Second, ideologies are shared by and reflect the life situations of groups of individuals. In this respect, a given ideology is typically not idiosyncratic; it is held in common by a group of people living in a particular social and historical context and it expresses the opinions, values, and concerns they have developed as a result of the challenges and opportunities present in that context. Third, ideologies are both descriptive and prescriptive in nature. That is, they both provide an interpretation of society as it currently exists and offer normative guidelines about how society should ideally be organized and the acceptable means for attaining political goals.

Thus, ideologies can be thought of as shared belief systems that reflect some group's understanding of the social world and its vision of what that world should ideally look like. However, this definition tells us very little about how ideological belief systems are organized. On this point, there has also been a good bit of debate among scholars about the nature of the ideological beast. On one hand, the standard assumption is that ideological positions can be ordered according to the familiar "left–right" spectrum. This perspective suggests that ideological phenomena can be boiled down to a single belief dimension anchored by preferences for equality and openness to social change on the left end of the spectrum and by preferences for hierarchy and preservation of the status quo on the right end.[5] In this usage, the terms "left" and "right" date back to seating arrangements in the French National Assembly during the revolutionary era, which placed the more conservative factions on the right side of the hall and the more radical factions on the left.[6]

This understanding of the structure of ideology continues to inform current scholarship, and it receives support from a number of sources. To begin with, use of a single left–right spectrum is clearly the norm among those most involved in political action and political decision making, i.e., "political elites" in government, party and activist organizations, the media, and academia.[7] Similarly, the most well-informed and politically active members of the general public also rely strongly on the basic left–right dimension in their thinking and political judgments.[8] Finally, a great deal of evidence suggests that individuals who place themselves at different positions on the left–right spectrum tend to adopt correspondingly different opinions about issues connected with the core distinctions of equality versus inequality and openness to change versus the status quo, especially if they are politically well informed.[9] That is, self-described liberals are more likely to take liberal positions on specific issues, whereas self-described conservatives are more likely to take conservative stances on the same issues.

Of course, ideological self-placement and the general liberalism or conservatism of one's issue preferences rarely align in a simple one-to-one fashion. In this regard, researchers have been careful to distinguish between *symbolic* (or *philosophical*) ideology and *operational* ideology.[10] Symbolic ideology refers to whether one generally identifies oneself as a "liberal," "conservative," or some moderate position in between; while operational ideology refers to one's average left–right position across issues, especially those relevant to government spending. Importantly, evidence suggests that these two types of ideology do not coincide for many citizens. An example of this is Free and Cantril's classic finding that many Americans living in the middle of the twentieth century were simultaneously "philosophical conservatives" and "operational liberals," opposing "big government" in the abstract but offering strong support for the individual programs that made up "big government."[11] More recently, Stimson has noted that over two-thirds of those who identify as symbolic conservatives are operational liberals on the issues.[12] Thus, even in situations where citizens do appear to rely on a single left–right spectrum, their belief profiles may differ at the levels of general identification and actual judgments about issues. We return to this point about the lack of concordance between left–right self-placement and issue opinions below.

While the notion of a single ideological dimension is simple and consistent with a great deal of evidence, other scholars have argued that citizens' ideological views may have more than one dimension. "Multidimensional" approaches of this sort come in a number of forms, but the most common variant argues that ideology can be characterized in terms of two different content dimensions.[13] Broadly speaking, the first dimension reflects one's preference for equality versus inequality in social life, while the second dimension reflects one's preference for openness versus social order. These "dual process" models suggest that the two dimensions are governed by distinct but related sets of psychological processes.[14] Importantly, this postulate suggests that the dimensions may operate somewhat independently. Thus, while the notion of a single left–right spectrum implies that a "right-wing" orientation on one dimension (e.g., a preference for inequality) should be accompanied by a right-wing orientation on the other (e.g., support for social order), the dual-process approach suggests that one's views on the two dimensions need not be perfectly congruent with one another.

Indeed, two dimensions of this sort appear to recur repeatedly in analyses of various kinds of social and political beliefs. For example, researchers interested in *human values*—abstract beliefs about desirable social goals or modes of conduct—suggest that the former can be arrayed according to two such dimensions.[15] The first dimension deals with "self-transcendence versus self-enhancement," and it reflects one's concern for power and rank. This dimension is anchored by values like benevolence and universal concern for others at one end and values like power and achievement at the other. The second deals with "openness versus conservation," and it reflects one's concern for security and order. This dimension is anchored by values like self-direction at one end and tradition and conformity at the other. Similar dual dimensions have been identified in studies of political extremism, which suggest that ideologies can be distinguished in terms of their level of support for equality versus inequality, on one hand, and their level of intolerance for alternative points of view, on the other.[16] The dual-process approach also finds an echo in public-opinion research suggesting that there are distinct dimensions corresponding to attitudes about "economic" issues (e.g., regulation of business, social spending) and "social" issues (e.g., gay rights, abortion).[17] A similar dichotomy manifests itself at the level of differences between political parties across nations, with research suggesting that parties compete with one another for votes along two dimensions corresponding to concern for equality and preferences regarding tradition versus change.[18]

So, which of these perspectives is correct? Is ideology best thought in terms of a single left–right dimension, or multiple dimensions corresponding to preferences regarding equality and social openness? While the bulk of the data suggests that two dimensions of ideology are in fact present, it is also clear that these dimensions are not completely independent of one another and that they may be very highly aligned among the politically engaged.[19] In this vein, a number of theorists have suggested that having multiple dimensions of political evaluation makes many political decisions more difficult.[20] Many common political choices—such as who to vote for or which party to affiliate with—are dichotomous in nature: there is a left-wing option and a right-wing option. If one's preferences on the two dimensions are not aligned, political choices become more fraught with conflicts and tradeoffs. This implies that individuals who are most involved in political decision making—including not just political professionals, but also the most informed and politically involved segments of the mass public—would benefit most from a belief system in which the two dimensions of ideology overlap with one another to form a single left–right axis.

Consistent with this argument, attitudes associated with the equality and openness dimensions are more likely to be aligned with one another among the highly informed and involved and among elected officials.[21] Research also suggests that intensified political competition may lead multiple ideological dimensions to collapse more cleanly into a single left–right dimension. For example, cross-national comparisons reveal that the equality and openness dimensions are more likely to be positively correlated in countries with established systems of party competition with distinct left-wing and right-wing options.[22] Moreover, once a second dimension of ideological competition arises in a political system, it tends to become aligned with the existing dimension, such that parties and politicians that support equality also tend to support openness and freedom.[23] Thus, while there may be multiple dimensions of ideology, they are seldom fully independent of one another—and the need to effectively organize political competition and decision making may lead to considerable overlap between the dimensions among those most engaged in politics.

What Attracts People to Different Ideological Positions?

Having discussed the issue of what ideology is, I turn to the question of what attracts people to various ideological positions. Working from a variety of theoretical perspectives, political scientists, psychologists, and sociologists have brought a great deal of data to bear on this question. From this welter of research a number of answers have emerged. While some of these answers have a decidedly "social" feel and center on features of an individual's social environment, such as his or her social position and group memberships, others focus more on processes within individuals, such as their psychological needs, personality traits, and even their genetic make-up. At a glance, Figure 4.1 summarizes some of the most important factors that attract people to particular ideological positions. Below, I review these factors in more detail.

Identifications and Relationships

As one might expect, social relationships—both with other individuals and with groups—are a major influence on citizens' ideological inclinations. In general, we tend to adopt the views of those we like, identify with, or otherwise have some social connection to. For example, psychological research suggests that activating a desire for closeness to a significant other leads individuals to align their own social and political opinions more closely

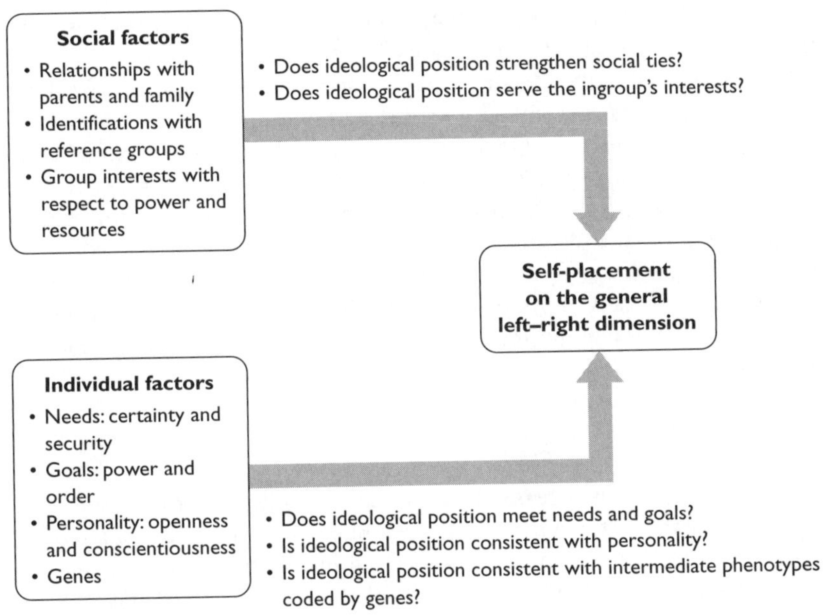

Figure 4.1 What Attracts People to Different Ideological Positions?

with the perceived views of the other. In turn, this increased similarity in opinions produces a "shared reality" that helps solidify the relationship in question.[24]

Research on political socialization—the process by which individuals learn about the political world and acquire their opinions and views from others—also illustrates the role of relational influences on the acquisition of ideological positions.[25] In this vein, decades of research suggest that ideological positions are likely to be transmitted from parents to children, especially if both parents have similar beliefs and discuss politics frequently and if bonds within the family are close.[26] Similarly, reference groups—groups that people use as a standard for evaluating themselves and their behavior—also have a strong influence on ideological affinity.[27] That is, we tend to adopt the views of groups we relate to in some way. This was famously demonstrated by Theodore Newcomb in his study of female undergraduates at Bennington College.[28] Newcomb's undergraduates were largely conservative in their views when they first arrived at Bennington, having come from fairly well-off Eastern families. However, the Bennington environment itself—consisting of faculty and older students—was largely liberal. Accordingly, Newcomb's undergraduate subjects moved further and further to left the longer they were at Bennington, as they came to identify more with the campus social environment; the only exceptions were undergraduates who remained unusually close to their families while at college. Naturally, these reference-group effects are not limited to one's college environment. They are also quite evident with respect to a number of more politically relevant group identities, such as one's religion, region, or occupational category.[29]

These relational influences on ideology also appear to be stronger at some times than at others. In general, parents, peers, and reference groups have their strongest effects on ideological affinity during late adolescence and early adulthood, before a person's identity is fully fleshed out.[30] Moreover, the resulting identifications tend to persist as long as a person's pattern of relationships with other individuals and groups does not change markedly. For example, this pattern was notably evident in Newcomb's Bennington study: while Newcomb observed profound changes in his subjects' attitudes over the course of college, follow-up interviews later in their adult lives revealed little additional change.

Group Interests

Another relational influence on ideological affinity follows from identification with groups, namely, the pursuit of those groups' collective political interests. In general, a long line of theorizing—derived mainly from economics—suggests that individuals should make political choices that reflect self-interest. However, a wide variety of research suggests that personal self-interest has only minor effects on what people believe ideologically; that is, calculations about one's own economic interests or the interests of one's family have little influence on political attitudes.[31]

Nevertheless, the perceived collective interests of the social groups one identifies with do tend to influence ideology, especially when people are highly aware of their identity as a member of a particular group. Generally speaking, members of groups with low social status, less power, and/or fewer resources tend to be more egalitarian and left-wing in their political outlook, while members of more privileged groups gravitate toward the right.[32] However, this effect is not a simple "reflective" one: not all individuals who identify with a group adopt group-interested ideological positions. In fact, for some members of less well-off groups, the group-interest motive may be countered by other motives, such as the need to avoid the uncertainty or insecurity that might come from challenging the political status quo.[33] Thus, the effect of group interest—while often present—is rarely total.

Psychological Needs

Moving away from the level of broader social influences on ideological affinity, a great deal of research suggests that one's preference for the left versus the right may be heavily shaped by various psychological needs. In particular, attraction to different positions on the left–right spectrum is not random but systematically rooted in one's underlying level of comfort with uncertainty and threat. This body of work finds that strong needs for certainty and security correlate with greater conservatism—as support for the status quo allows individuals to stick with what is known, familiar, and safe—whereas weaker needs for certainty and security are associated with greater liberalism. This argument was first and perhaps most famously made by the authors of *The Authoritarian Personality*, who suggested that attraction to far-right ideological positions (as opposed to liberal or left-leaning positions) was driven by an "authoritarian personality" type consisting of nine interrelated tendencies, such as rigid moral conventionalism, aggressiveness, submission to idealized leaders, and a preoccupation with power and toughness.[34] In turn, this intolerant type was explained using some of Sigmund Freud's ideas about the management of anxiety. Specifically, Adorno and his colleagues argued that harsh childrearing led authoritarians to "repress" hostility toward their parents and other traditional authorities and "project" it outward onto the scapegoats and outsiders often targeted by right-wing political ideologies (e.g., minorities, those who desire social change). This need-based perspective was echoed by other early theorists as well.[35]

While these models—and the Adorno et al. model in particular—were later the subject of numerous theoretical and methodological criticisms,[36] the notion that ideological affinity may be rooted in some underlying feature of psychological functioning has persisted. In this vein, psychologist Bob Altemeyer has updated the authoritarianism construct, relabeling it *right-wing authoritarianism* and characterizing it more simply as a learned constellation of three attitudes: conventionalism, "authoritarian submission" to traditional social authorities, and "authoritarian aggression" toward disliked out-groups.[37] More recently, John Jost and his colleagues—echoing the scholars mentioned above—have reiterated and provided much new evidence for the view that support for the right is associated with need for certainty and security, whereas support for the left is associated with greater tolerance for uncertainty and potential social danger.[38]

Other psychological approaches have suggested that different sets of needs may account for preferences in different domains of political belief. As noted above, many researchers have suggested that ideology may consist of two dimensions—one corresponding to one's preference for equality versus inequality and the other corresponding to one's preference for openness versus order. In turn, these two dimensions may each be related to a distinct set of psychological needs. For example, Duckitt and Sibley argue that the equality dimension reflects one's orientation toward social hierarchy and depends on the value one places on superiority, achievement, and power, while the openness dimension reflects one's orientation toward traditional morality and social conformity and depends on the value one places on order and security in social life.[39] Moreover, each dimension may be connected with a distinct worldview—either the extent to which one believes that the world is a competitive, violent place, in the case of the equality dimension, or the extent to which one believes that it is a dangerous place, in the case of the openness dimension. People who see the world as a dangerous place tend to prefer order, conformity, and security, which attracts them to conservative positions on social issues related to religion, gender, and social convention. In comparison, people who see the world as highly competitive place a premium on social hierarchy and social dominance, which attracts them to those aspects of conservatism which favor inequality, particularly in the economic realm. Thus, the needs for certainty and security highlighted by the "classic" models of ideological affinity reviewed earlier may actually be pertinent to only some of the political concerns that distinguish the left from the right—namely, those dealing with openness and freedom versus tradition and order.

PERSONALITY CHARACTERISTICS

Another set of psychological approaches to ideology has focused on how individual differences in personality might account for variation in ideological sympathies. By "personality," these approaches refer to set of characteristics possessed by a person that uniquely shape his or her thoughts, feelings, and behaviors across various situations.[40] Speculation about links between personality traits and politics has long been a preoccupation among psychologists. For example, several of the scholars discussed earlier—including the authors of *The Authoritarian Personality*—were interested not only in how needs for certainty and security might shape political sympathies, but also in how these needs might be shaped by enduring personality differences between individuals.[41] However, the dominant framework for examining the relationship between personality and ideology in recent years has been the "Big Five" model of personality traits.[42] Using analyses of personality adjectives found in everyday language, this model boils variation in personality down to five key dimensions. These include *extroversion*, one's level of sociability and assertiveness; *agreeableness*, one's level of altruism and concern for others; *conscientiousness*, one's level of concern for social duty, responsibility, and impulse control; *emotional stability*, one's level of even-temperedness or freedom from negative emotion; and *openness to experience*, one's level of interest in novelty, complexity, and originality.

Numerous studies by psychologists and political scientists alike have examined relationships between these five dimensions and support for the left versus the right. This impressive body of work is reviewed in detail elsewhere in this volume,[43] so I will touch only on its key findings. In this regard, the Big Five dimensions that have the most consistent relationships with ideological affinity are openness to experience and conscientiousness. While openness is typically associated with greater support for the left, conscientiousness is usually associated with greater support for the right.[44] The relationships between each of these dimensions and ideology are not negligible in size; indeed, they are similar in magnitude to the relationships between ideology and key demographic variables like education and income. In contrast, the relationships between the other three Big Five dimensions and ideology are far less consistent across studies, and they also tend to vary across issue domains (i.e., economic issues versus social issues) and social groups (e.g., blacks versus whites).[45]

The Role of Genetics

Finally, researchers in a number of disciplines have begun to explore the possibility that ideological sympathies may at least in part be genetically shaped and transmitted.[46] This view is a sharp departure from most work on ideology in public-opinion research, which has traditionally assumed that ideological affinity is socially learned from parents, peers, and important social groups. This line of work generally relies on what is known as the "classic twin design" in order to estimate what proportions of the variation among individuals in political opinion is due to genes, common environmental influences (i.e., those shared by members of a family), and unique environmental influences (i.e., those not shared by family members).[47] The method does this by comparing the attitudes of identical twins, who effectively share 100 percent of their genetic makeup; and fraternal twins, who share roughly 50 percent of one another's genetic heritage. This fixed difference between identical and fraternal twins in genetic relatedness, along with the assumption that a given pair of twins—whether identical or fraternal—is subject to the same level of environmental influence, allows the researcher to tease apart the relative impact of genes and environment.

Studies using this and other related methods have found strikingly large effects of genes on ideological opinions. Specifically, some 40 percent to 50 percent of the variability in left–right political opinions among individuals appears to be attributable to genetic differences as opposed to differences in social environment.[48] Interestingly, however, genetics does not appear to contribute to differences in partisanship, although it may have an influence on the strength of people's partisan identifications.[49] Although much work remains to be done, research does not suggest that the influence of genes on political attitudes is direct; rather, genes are believed to influence intermediate phenotypes or observable traits related to social behavior (e.g., orientations toward threat or social order), which then affects specific attitudes in the domain of politics (e.g., social conservatism). Thus, while social influences on ideological affinity are undoubtedly important, at least some portion of what people believe politically may in fact be linked to their genetic makeup. Future work will need to build on this promising new perspective on the origins of ideological affinity, particularly with respect to the question of exactly which intermediate characteristics account for the relationship between genetic differences and differences in ideology.

When Do People "Use" Ideology?

Thus far, I have discussed ideology primarily in terms of attraction to particular ideological identities or positions along the left–right spectrum. However, as noted at the outset, ideologies are belief systems. Besides some crowning posture or identity—like liberalism or conservatism—they consist of an interlocking web of opinions, values, and interpretations of existing social reality that go along with that posture. For example, an identification with the political left implies a wide range of issue opinions across a variety of domains—support for welfare spending, support for gay rights, support for diplomacy over the use of force in international relations, and so on. Moreover, it implies support for general value postures (e.g., preferences for equality and self-direction) as well as certain beliefs about the nature of the social world (e.g., inequality stems from structural factors like discrimination as opposed to an individual lack of ability or effort). Indeed, as we have seen, the general ideological label a person adopts typically has consequences for their opinions about specific issues: those who identify themselves conservatives tend to adopt conservative issue positions, while those who identify themselves as liberals tend to adopt liberal issue positions.

But where do these broader belief packages come from? Public opinion researchers have long noted that the sheer force of logic is not sufficient to explain why certain issue positions get linked together as part of an ideological whole; as just one example, there is no apparent reason why opposition to legal abortion should go together with support for lower taxes as part of the contemporary "conservative" belief package. As such, most scholars have come to regard ideologies as products of convention—or more specifically, the culture of the groups that share the ideology.[50] Nevertheless, most perspectives on ideology suggest that the social activities which give rise to ideological content are disproportionately the province of narrow elites within the groups that share different ideologies—usually powerful and unrepresentative ones. This emphasis is perhaps most evident in the classical sociological tradition and in Marxist approaches to social science, both of which have argued—albeit with different evaluative implications, depending on the writer—that the discursive content of ideologies should disproportionately represent the interests of powerful groups and justify states of affairs the latter benefit from. Other approaches have placed a similar emphasis on the construction of belief packages by small, highly involved segments of the population. However, in these models, the focus is less on the role of dominant groups whose interests color the content of ideologies and more on the role of the "political elites" discussed earlier—the politicians, activists, and media figures whose activity develops the constellations of positions, values, and interpretations of reality that make up different ideological positions.[51] From this perspective, groups of political elites in competing political parties coalesce around particular interests and values and construct belief packages reflecting those interests and values.[52] These opposed packages of opinions and positions then serve to psychologically "anchor" the ends of the left–right spectrum in a particular context; they make up the ideological "menu" from which members of the mass public typically make their political choices (e.g., votes).

The flip side of this notion of "elite opinion leadership" is that the beliefs held by citizens at the mass level are typically not constructed by the citizens themselves. Rather, the content associated with different ideological positions is acquired by members of the mass public when they "take cues" about what to believe from political figures who share their basic partisan or ideological identifications.[53] Thus, for most people, the packages of issue opinions, values, and views associated with a particular ideological posture are learned from those more highly involved in politics. This raises an important question: to what extent does the content associated with particular ideological positions fully diffuse to the broader public? By and large, decades of research suggest that most citizens do not learn the full set of "correct" opinions and views associated with the ideological identity they claim, even when they do claim a left–right position.[54] On one hand, at least 66 percent of individuals are willing to place themselves on the left–right spectrum and label themselves as liberals, conservatives, or something in between.[55] On the other hand, most citizens—even if they do adopt an ideological position—fail to pick up the broader systems of opinions and views associated with particular ideological positions in elite discussion.[56]

Perhaps the most important demonstration of this incomplete learning of ideology was provided by Philip Converse in a famous essay on "The Nature of Belief Systems in Mass Publics."[57] In this essay, Converse reviewed findings taken from large surveys of American political elites and everyday citizens conducted during the 1950s. To begin with, Converse demonstrated that most members of the general public showed what political scientists refer to as a low "level of conceptualization"—that is, only a minority typically characterized political parties and candidates in terms of ideological categories like liberalism and conservatism. Similarly, most people were not able to explain the philosophical differences between conservatism and liberalism, and they were not able to accurately indicate which issue positions "go along" with each of these two ideological categories. Moreover, most citizens showed relatively low levels of *ideological constraint*, i.e., they did not take consistently liberal or consistently conservative positions across different issues. Finally, the issue opinions of most citizens showed little stability over time—that is, they tended to fluctuate randomly over time, which is not what we would expect if opinions were more deeply anchored in an overarching ideological posture like liberalism or conservatism. Importantly, in each of these cases, Converse found that his samples of political leaders showed far more ideological sophistication: on average, they revealed a higher level of conceptualization, they understood the meaning of ideological labels better, and their issue opinions showed greater constraint and stability over time.

To Converse, this suggested that the issue opinions of a large portion of the general public were effectively "non-attitudes." That is, in most cases, survey respondents were neither interested in nor informed about the issues they were queried on, and they definitely did not use a common left–right standard when making judgments about them. Accordingly, they offered off-the-cuff, "doorstep" opinions that showed little structure, ideological or otherwise. Although there has been some debate about whether the public's apparent ideological innocence is really an artifact of imperfect measurement[58] and about the extent to which the average citizen makes greater use of ideology than in the past,[59] much of the research in this area has followed Converse in concluding that most citizens' political preferences are not structured by ideology.[60] Other lines of work have demonstrated a similar lack of ideological structure in citizens' opinions. For instance, to refer back to an example from earlier, recall that several researchers have noted a lack of concordance between symbolic and operational ideology—that is, there are many citizens who label themselves as "conservatives" while taking issue positions that lean toward the left.[61]

Naturally, the conclusions reached by Converse and others have somewhat negative implications for democracy, as they suggest that much of the citizenry is too disengaged from politics to form "real" opinions about crucial issues and organize their opinions in an ideological fashion. This has led many scholars to ask what factors allow citizens to think in ideological terms and adopt opinions that are consistent with the ideological positions they claim. At the mass level, the main factor governing the acquisition of ideological content is exposure to flows of information from leading political figures, which is highest among those with a strong interest in politics, the highly educated, those who see themselves as politically competent, and members of relatively privileged social groups.[62]

Individuals who receive a good deal of political information over time eventually build up elaborate political knowledge structures in long-term memory, leading to the development of *political expertise*.[63] As a result, highly informed citizens are more likely to have learned what goes with what politically, i.e., the specific issue positions and views about the world that go along with being a liberal, a conservative, or something in between. In turn, this knowledge results in patterns of thinking and opinion which more closely resemble those of political leaders. So, for example, well-informed citizens are more likely to make active use of concepts like liberalism and conservatism in explaining differences between parties and candidates,[64] and they show higher levels of ideological constraint in their opinions toward different issues.[65] They are also more likely to possess operational issue positions that match their symbolic ideological identifications.[66] Moreover, it even appears to be the case that the psychological needs commonly linked to ideology—such as needs for certainty and security—predict differences in ideological sympathies only among those who possess a great deal of political information.[67] Thus, information appears to be central not only to the learning of the full range of content associated with particular ideological positions, but also to the ability to "choose" the ideological position that best satisfies underlying psychological needs.

On the whole, the sheer volume of data suggesting that the well informed are more likely to think and make judgments in ways that reflect a mastery of ideological content has had a profound effect on how public opinion researchers understand the phenomenon of ideology. Indeed, even a brief look at the literature on the topic makes it clear that researchers have adopted a largely information-based perspective on the use of ideology: the consensus view is that a given citizen will think about political actors in an ideological way and adopt an ideologically consistent set of opinions to the extent that he or she has successfully received political information and stored it away in long-term memory in the form of an organized knowledge structure. While this focus on information has greatly improved our understanding of when ideology becomes relevant to the political behavior of the average citizen, it is not without its hazards. In particular, it sidesteps the question of whether citizens also have to be motivated to use political information in certain ways in order for that information to result in "ideological" patterns of thought and judgment.

I return to this key point below. At this juncture, though, it should be noted that the poor mastery of ideological content that follows from a lack of information does not make citizens incapable of being political. In this respect, other orientations that are not strictly ideological but which have some political content or relevance—like values and social group memberships—may serve many of the same functions as the more complex ideological belief systems discussed above: they provide cues about what positions to take on various political issues, justify one state of affairs over another, and so on.[68] Among others, these "proxies for ideology" include *core political values* such as egalitarianism, moral traditionalism, and self-reliance, which even information-poor citizens may be able to use in making political judgments.[69] Similarly, much evidence suggests that reference groups—like one's social class, racial or ethnic group, or religious affiliation—can be used as cues about what positions to take or how to vote by individuals at all levels of information.[70] Finally, standard surveys may not be able to detect discursive frameworks that differ from the ones offered by political leaders. Since these techniques are best used to detect "ideology" in the conventional left–right sense, they may miss idiosyncratic belief systems that are as elaborate and internally consistent as those offered by elites and which serve all of the important functions of ideology (e.g., organizing different opinions together under common themes, justifying political action, explaining the world). Indeed, in-depth interviews of citizens with low-to-average levels of political information have shown that normal conversation can reveal coherent "ideological" understandings of political reality that nevertheless depart from the left–right framework used by political elites.[71]

Information, Motivation, and the Use of Ideology

As noted above, public-opinion researchers generally regard the use of ideology as being an informational problem. As a wide range of research has shown, citizens are more likely to think about politics in ideological terms and express ideologically consistent opinions about issues if they possess larger stores of political information. To the extent that citizens possess enough information to understand what goes with what ideologically, they are assumed to use that information. However, in psychology, a growing body of work suggests that key needs, goals, and wants determine if and how prior information is used to make judgments.[72] This trend suggests that public opinion research on ideology might benefit from a closer look at the role of *motivation*—that is, a closer look at how people's needs or goals shape their use of political information pertinent to the content of ideology. In a series of recent studies, I have attempted to fill this gap by proposing that information is more likely to predict ideologically guided thinking and judgment when citizens are motivated to use political information in certain ways.

But what motives lead citizens to use information in an ideological way? My studies suggest that the critical motive is the need to use information for *evaluative* purposes. Specifically, I argue that the relationship between information and reliance on ideology should depend on factors that strengthen people's tendency to evaluate people and things as "good" or "bad." Since ideology provides an overarching framework for the evaluation of many different objects, information about the content of various ideological positions should be of greater importance to those motivated to make evaluative judgments about the things they encounter—regardless of whether this motivation comes from personality traits, characteristics of the situation the individual finds himself or herself in, or a general interest in politics.[73]

This point leads to a simple hypothesis: citizens who possess large stores of political information will be particularly likely to think about politics in ideological terms and express ideologically consistent issue positions when they also approach politics with a high level of evaluative motivation. The necessary "motive to evaluate" may come from a number of sources. For example, these include individual differences in personality like the *need to evaluate*, i.e., the extent to which an individual is motivated to spontaneously form evaluations of experiences, ideas, and social objects as either "good" or "bad."[74] While the need to evaluate is a very general motivation that encourages people to form more opinions—and stronger opinions—across a variety of domains, individuals with a high need to evaluate are particularly likely to be politically opinionated.[75] Other potential sources of evaluative motivation are more specific to politics, such as the extent to which the political domain itself is seen as important and relevant to the self (i.e., personal involvement).[76]

Regardless of its source, a motive to evaluate things should have important effects on how individuals think about politics and make judgments about political issues. As we have seen, ideology provides a common reference point that helps citizens reach a consistent set of conclusions about the nature of the social world and how to confront various political issues. Moreover, having a clear ideological position may simplify important political choices that are fundamentally evaluative in nature, like which party is the best one to join or which candidate is the best to vote for. This suggests that the understanding of ideology provided by political information may be more useful to those who feel the need to have opinions about the things they encounter. Since ideology offers a handy mental rubric for the evaluation of multiple issues, candidates, and political questions, information about the content of the left–right distinction should be more useful to people who want to form opinions. Consequently, well-informed citizens who are also high in evaluative motivation may be particularly inclined to rely on ideology, increasing the extent to which their political thinking is colored by ideological categories and the degree to which their issue opinions are ideologically consistent with one another.

In contrast, information may make little difference among citizens who lack a strong evaluative motive. Instead of relying on their knowledge of the content of ideology, these individuals may make political judgments in a more fragmented, episodic way. As such, their thinking and opinions may be influenced less by a common ideological reference point than by whatever is salient at the time. An overall representation of this model can be found in Figure 4.2; the dashed arrow pointing from evaluative motivation to the connection between information and the use of ideology indicates the aforementioned role of evaluative motivation in turning the influence of information on ideological thinking and judgment "on" and "off."

Using data from four large surveys of American adults, I have provided a consistent body of evidence for this hypothesis. In particular, in several studies, I have used a short measure of the need to evaluate to assess evaluative motivation in terms of individual personality differences. Analyses using this measure have repeatedly shown that politically well-informed survey respondents are more likely to think about politics in ideological terms and express ideologically consistent issue opinions when they are also high in the need to evaluate. For example, using data from the 1998 and 2000 American National Election Studies (ANES), I found that information more strongly predicted ideological constraint—the degree to which one expresses consistently liberal or consist-

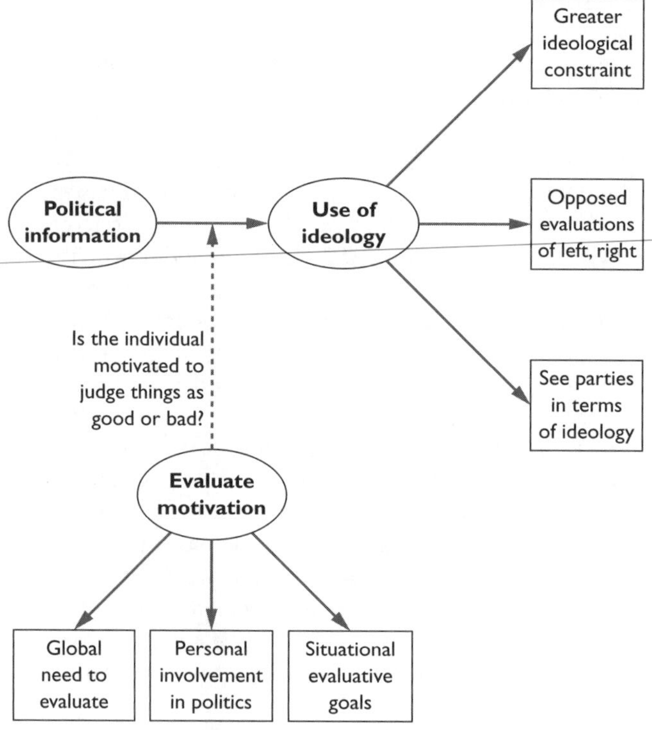

Figure 4.2 Information, Motivation, and the Use of Ideology: A General Model.

ent conservative issue positions—among those high in the need to evaluate.[77] Figure 4.3 presents the results of this analysis for the 1998 ANES Pilot.

Moreover, in the 2000 and 2004 ANES, I have shown that expertise is more strongly associated with a tendency to evaluate ideologically antagonistic groups, candidates, and parties in opposite ways among those with a high need to evaluate.[78] That is, the well informed are more "consistent" in their evaluations of competing actors—for example, evaluating conservatives and Republicans positively if they evaluated liberals and Democrats negatively—if they are also high in the need to evaluate. I have found similar patterns with respect to other outcomes indicative of a strong reliance on ideology. For instance, in another set of analyses using the 2000 ANES, I demonstrated that well-informed survey respondents are more likely to explain the differences between the Democratic and Republican parties in ideological terms when they are also high in the need to evaluate.[79]

In a more recent study, I have found similar results using other variables that should encourage individuals to form opinions.[80] As noted earlier, factors specific to the political domain—such as personal involvement in politics—should also strengthen the relationship between information and reliance on ideology. Accordingly, using data from the 2004 ANES and a national survey of my own construction, I found that political information more strongly predicted ideological constraint among respondents who were highly interested in politics and who indicated that their political attitudes were central to their sense of who they are. Similarly, a second indicator of personal involvement in politics—strength of partisanship—had a similar effect: information more strongly predicted constraint among those who identified as "strong" Democrats or Republicans.

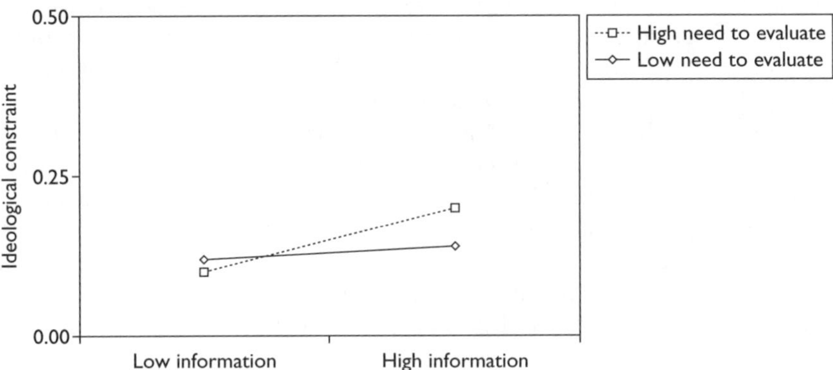

Figure 4.3 Information and the Need to Evaluate as Predictors of Ideological Constraint (source: based on Christopher M. Federico and Monica Schneider, "Political Expertise and the Use of Ideology: Moderating Effects of Evaluative Motivation," *Public Opinion Quarterly* 71 (2007): 221–252. Data for the graph are from the 1998 ANES Pilot).

Conclusion

As Philip Converse noted almost a half-century ago, ideologies have often "served as primary exhibits for the doctrine that what is important to study cannot be measured and that what can be measured is not important to study."[81] Since then, public-opinion research has made considerable progress not only in overcoming the difficulties inherent in studying ideology, but also in reinforcing the importance of ideology as an explanatory concept. In this chapter, I have attempted to provide the reader with an overview of this body of work. Specifically, I have tried to address the questions of what ideology is, which social and psychological factors attracts citizens to one ideological posture rather than another, and when citizens use the full range of content associated with various ideological postures in order to think about the political world and form opinions about major political topics.

As we have seen, ideologies—defined here as belief systems that reflect some group's understanding of the social world and its preferences about how that world should be ordered—are clearly relevant to mass opinion in certain respects. Ideologies of the left and right play a key role in the organization of opinion-holding and debate among political leaders and other elites. Moreover, under the influence of various identifications and interests, psychological needs and traits, and perhaps even their genetic inheritance, most members of the general public are sufficiently attracted to one ideological posture or another to place themselves on the left–right spectrum as liberals, conservatives, or something in between. However, at the mass level, far fewer citizens actually adopt the full range of views and opinions that "go along" with these postures. In an effort to explain this state of relative ideological innocence, researchers have focused in particular on the role of information received from political leaders, repeatedly observing that well-informed citizens are more likely to think about politics in ideological terms and express opinions that are ideologically consistent with one another. Building on this perspective, my own work suggests that the motivation to use information in a specifically evaluative way may also matter, such that well-informed citizens are more likely to think about politics ideologically and express ideologically consistent issue opinions when they are also strongly driven to form opinions of things as good or bad. Thus, while ideology plays a key role in the organization of political discussion in the political system as a whole, its influence in the political lives of individual citizens depends heavily on how much they know about politics and how they are motivated to use that knowledge.

Notes

1. The author would like to thank Adam Berinsky, John Jost, and Jaime Napier for their comments and suggestions.
2. Philip Converse, "The Nature of Belief Systems in Mass Publics," in *Ideology and Discontent*, ed. D. Apter (New York: Free Press, 1964); John T. Jost, Christopher

M. Federico, and Jaime L. Napier, "Political Ideology: Its Structure, Functions, and Elective Affinities," *Annual Review of Psychology* 60 (2009): 307–337.

3. Arthur D. Denzau and Douglass C. North, "Shared Mental Models: Ideologies and Institutions," in *Elements of Reason: Cognition, Choice, and the Bounds of Rationality*, eds. Arthur Lupia, Matthew McCubbins, and Samuel L. Popkin (New York: Cambridge University Press, 2000).
4. Susan T. Fiske, Richard R. Lau, and Richard A. Smith, "On the Varieties and Utilities of Political Expertise," *Social Cognition* 8 (1990): 31–48; Charles M. Judd and Jon A. Krosnick, "The Structural Bases of Consistency Among Political Attitudes: Effects of Expertise and Attitude Importance," in *Attitude Structure and Function*, eds. Anthony Pratkanis, Steven Breckler, and Anthony Greenwald (Hillsdale, NJ: Erlbaum, 1989).
5. R.S. Erikson and K.L.Tedin, *American Public Opinion* (6th ed.) (New York: Longman, 2003); Jost et al., "Political Ideology"; Seymour M. Lipset, *Political Man* (New York: Doubleday, 1960).
6. N. Bobbio, *Left and Right* (Cambridge, UK: Polity Press, 1996).
7. Angus Campbell, Philip E. Converse, Warren E. Miller, and Donald E. Stokes, *The American Voter* (New York: Wiley, 1960); Converse, "The Nature of Belief Systems"; Nolan McCarty, Keith T. Poole, and Howard Rosenthal, *Polarized America: The Dance of Ideology and Unequal Riches* (Cambridge, MA: MIT Press, 2006).
8. John Zaller, *The Nature and Origins of Mass Opinion* (New York: Cambridge University Press, 1992).
9. Erikson and Tedin, *American Public Opinion.*
10. Lloyd A. Free and Hadley Cantril, *The Political Beliefs of Americans* (New Brunswick, NJ: Rutgers University Press, 1967); James A. Stimson, *Tides of Consent: How Public Opinion Shapes American Politics* (New York: Cambridge University Press, 2004).
11. Free and Cantril, *The Political Beliefs of Americans.*
12. Stimson, *Tides of Consent.*
13. Stanley Feldman, "Values, Ideology, and the Structure of Political Attitudes," in *The Oxford Handbook of Political Psychology*, eds. David O. Sears, Leonie Huddy, and Robert Jervis (New York: Oxford University Press, 2003).
14. John Duckitt and Christopher G. Sibley, "A Dual Process Model of Ideological Attitudes and System Justification," in *Social and Psychological Bases of Ideology and System Justification*, eds. John T. Jost, Aaron C. Kay, and Hulda Thorisdottir (New York: Oxford University Press, 2009).
15. Shalom H. Schwartz, "Universals in the Content and Structure of Values: Theoretical Advances and Empirical Tests in 20 Countries," *Advances in Experimental Social Psychology* 25 (1992): 1–65; Milton Rokeach, *The Nature of Human Values* (New York: Free Press, 1973).
16. Hans J. Eysenck, *The Psychology of Politics* (New York: Praeger, 1954); Rokeach, *The Nature of Human Values.*
17. E.g., Geoffrey Evans, A. Heath, and M. Lalljee, "Measuring Left-Right and Libertarian-Conservative Attitudes in the British Electorate," *British Journal of Sociology* 47 (1996): 93–112.
18. E.g., Seymour M. Lipset and S. Rokkan, *Party Systems and Voter Alignment* (New York: Free Press, 1967).
19. Jost et al., "Political Ideology."
20. Anthony Downs, *An Economic Theory of Democracy* (New York: Harper and Row, 1967); Paul M. Sniderman and John Bullock, "A Consistency Theory of Public Opinion and Political Choice: The Hypothesis of Menu Dependence," in *Studies in Public Opinion: Attitudes, Nonattitudes, Measurement Error, and Change*, eds. Willem E. Saris and Paul M. Sniderman (Princeton, NJ: Princeton University Press, 2004).

21. On the informed and involved, see Judd and Krosnick, "The Structural Bases of Consistency"; on elected officials, see Converse, "The Nature of Belief Systems" and McCarty et al., *Polarized America.*
22. Duckitt and Sibley, "A Dual Process Model."
23. Stimson, *Tides of Consent.*
24. For a discussion, see Jost et al., "Political Ideology," p. 322.
25. For a review, see David O. Sears and S. Levy, "Childhood and Adult Political Development," in *The Oxford Handbook of Political Psychology*, eds. David O. Sears, Leonie Huddy, and Robert Jervis (New York: Oxford University Press, 2003).
26. M. Kent Jennings and Richard G. Niemi, *Generations and Politics: A Panel Study of Adults and their Parents* (Princeton, NJ: Princeton University Press, 1981).
27. Duane F. Alwin, R.L. Cohen, and Theodore Newcomb, *Political Attitudes Over the Life Span* (Madison, WI: University of Wisconsin Press, 1991).
28. Theodore M. Newcomb, *Personality and Social Change: Attitude Formation in a Student Community* (New York: John Wiley and Sons, 1943).
29. B.R. Berelson, Paul F. Lazarsfeld, and W.N. McPhee, *Voting: A Study of Opinion Formation in a Presidential Campaign* (Chicago, IL: University of Chicago Press, 1954); Campbell et al., *The American Voter.*
30. Alwin et al., *Political Attitudes Over the Lifespan*; Sears and Levy, "Childhood and Adult Political Development."
31. David O. Sears and Cary L. Funk, "The Role of Self-Interest in Social and Political Attitudes," *Advances in Experimental Social Psychology* 24 (1991): 1–91.
32. James R. Kluegel and Eliot R. Smith, *Beliefs about Inequality: Americans' Views of What Is and What Ought to Be* (New York: Aldine de Gruyter, 1986); Sears and Funk, "The Role of Self-Interest."
33. Jost et al., "Political Ideology."
34. Theodor W. Adorno, Else Frenkel-Brunswik, D.J. Levison, and R.N. Sanford, *The Authoritarian Personality* (New York: Harper and Row, 1950).
35. For reviews, see John T. Jost, Jack Glaser, Arie W. Kruglanski, and Frank J. Sulloway, "Political Conservatism as Motivated Social Cognition," *Psychological Bulletin* 129 (2003): 339–375; and Jost et al., "Political Ideology."
36. For a discussion of these criticisms, see Robert A. Altemeyer, *The Authoritarian Specter* (Cambridge, MA: Harvard University Press, 1996), 45–47.
37. Ibid.
38. Jost et al., "Political Conservatism as Motivated Social Cognition."
39. Duckitt and Sibley, "A Dual Process Model."
40. See Mondak and Hibbing, "Personality and Public Opinion," this volume (Chapter 10).
41. Jost et al., "Political Conservatism as Motivated Social Cognition."
42. Mondak and Hibbing, this volume.
43. Ibid.
44. Alan S. Gerber, Gregory A. Huber, David Doherty, Conor M. Dowling, and Shang E. Ha, "Personality and Political Attitudes: Relationships Across Issue Domains and Political Contexts," *American Political Science Review* 104 (2010): 111–133; Mondak and Hibbing, this volume.
45. Gerber et al., "Personality and Political Attitudes."
46. For additional review, see Mondak and Hibbing, this volume.
47. John R. Alford, Carolyn L. Funk, and John R. Hibbing, "Are Political Orientations Genetically Transmitted?" *American Political Science Review* 99 (2005): 153–167.
48. Ibid.
49. Peter Hatemi, John Alford, John Hibbing, and Lindon Eaves, "Is There a 'Party' in Your Genes?" *Political Research Quarterly* 62 (2009): 584–600.

50. Converse, "The Nature of Belief Systems."
51. Ibid.; Zaller, *The Nature and Origins of Mass Opinion.*
52. Sniderman and Bullock, "A Consistency Theory of Public Opinion."
53. Zaller, *The Nature and Origins of Mass Opinion.*
54. Converse, "The Nature of Belief Systems."
55. Erikson and Tedin, *American Public Opinion*; Stimson, *Tides of Consent.*
56. Zaller, *The Nature and Origins of Mass Opinion.*
57. Converse, "The Nature of Belief Systems."
58. Christopher H. Achen, "Mass Political Attitudes and the Survey Response," *American Political Science Review* 69 (1975): 1218–1223.
59. E.g., Norman H. Nie, Sidney Verba, and John Petrocik, *The Changing American Voter* (Cambridge, MA: Harvard University Press, 1976).
60. Michael X. Delli Carpini and Scott Keeter, *What Americans Know About Politics and Why it Matters* (New Haven, CT: Yale University Press, 1996); Judd and Krosnick, "The Structural Bases of Consistency"; Zaller, *The Nature and Origins of Mass Opinion.*
61. Stimson, *Tides of Consent.*
62. Delli Carpini and Keeter, *What Americans Know About Politics*; Martin Gilens, "Two-thirds Full? Citizen Competence and Democratic Governance," this volume (Chapter 3).
63. Fiske et al., "On the Varieties and Utilities of Political Expertise."
64. Converse, "The Nature of Belief Systems."
65. See Delli Carpini and Keeter, *What Americans Know About Politics.* While these results suggest that most citizens do not learn the content of various ideologies in all their glorious detail, they should not be taken as a sign that the poorly informed are utterly devoid of ideological understanding. Rather, it is merely the case that those less exposed to political information flows understand and use the content of ideology less competently and with less elaboration than those who receive more information; on this point, see Jost et al., "Political Ideology."
66. Stimson, *Tides of Consent.*
67. Christopher M. Federico and Paul Goren, "Motivated Social Cognition and Ideology: Is Attention to Elite Discourse a Prerequisite for Epistemically Motivated Political Affinities?" in *Social and Psychological Bases of Ideology and System Justification*, eds. John T. Jost, Aaron C. Kay, and Hulda Thorisdottir (New York: Oxford University Press, 2009).
68. Jost et al., "Political Ideology."
69. See Feldman, "Values, Ideology, and the Structure of Political Attitudes." Here, "values" should be distinguished from ideologies in that the latter are usually more abstract and encompassing. In this respect, ideologies are usually thought of as tying together multiple values into a larger posture.
70. Berelson et al., *Voting*; Campbell et al., *The American Voter.*
71. Robert E. Lane, *Political Ideology* (New York: Free Press, 1962). There is one caveat worth mentioning in the context of this argument: it is not clear that all individuals who fail to show an understanding of the discursive content associated with the left–right distinction are in fact using their "own" ideologies. If this were the case, we would observe substantial attitude stability even in the absence of left–right understanding. However, such stability is rarely observed, and it tends to be higher among those who are politically well informed; on this point, see Converse, "The Nature of Belief Systems," and Zaller, *The Nature and Origins of Mass Opinion.*
72. Howard Lavine, "Online versus Memory-Based Process Models of Political Evaluation," in *Political Psychology*, ed. Kristen R. Monroe (Mahwah, NJ: LEA, 2002).
73. W. Blair, G. Jarvis, and Richard E. Petty, "The Need to Evaluate," *Journal of Personality and Social Psychology* 70 (1996): 172–194.

74. Ibid.
75. Christopher M. Federico, "Predicting Attitude Extremity: The Interactive Effects of Schema Development and the Need to Evaluate—and Their Mediation by Evaluative Integration," *Personality and Social Psychology Bulletin* 30 (2004): 1281–1294.
76. Christopher M. Federico and Corrie V. Hunt, "Political Expertise, Political Interest, and Reliance on Ideology in Political Evaluation" (paper presented at the annual meeting of the American Political Science Association, Washington, DC, September 3–5, 2010).
77. Christopher M. Federico and Monica Schneider, "Political Expertise and the Use of Ideology: Moderating Effects of Evaluative Motivation," *Public Opinion Quarterly* 71 (2007): 221–252.
78. Federico, "Predicting Attitude Extremity"; Christopher M. Federico, "Expertise, Evaluative Motivation, and the Structure of Citizens' Ideological Commitments," *Political Psychology* 28 (2007): 535–562.
79. Federico and Schneider, "Political Expertise and the Use of Ideology."
80. Federico and Hunt, "Political Expertise, Political Interest, and Reliance on Ideology."
81. Converse, "The Nature of Belief Systems," p. 206.

Chapter 5

Partisanship and Polarization

Marc Hetherington

Believing that American political parties, always weaker than their European counterparts, had become so ineffectual as to render them all but meaningless, a group of political scientists penned a document entitled "Toward a More Responsible Two Party System" in 1950. They argued that steps needed to be taken to strengthen American parties, so they could do what parties do well, namely, play a meaningful role in structuring political conflict in government and, in turn, provide ordinary Americans with meaningful choices. American parties only grew weaker in the succeeding decades. In fact, newspaper columnist David Broder even suggested in the early 1970s that American parties had died.[1]

Compare that situation with today. According to data collected by Keith Poole and Howard Rosenthal every Democrat in the U.S. House of Representatives is more liberal than every Republican, a stark departure from the past when liberal northeastern Republicans and conservative southern Democrats roamed the political world. And, those divisions in Washington are starting to spill over more into the electorate with voters supporting their party elites much more loyally than in the past. Sometimes the partisan heat seems to be boiling over. In the 2010 midterm election campaign, for example, fisticuffs broke out twice, once in the state of Washington and once in Kentucky, between Republican and Democratic candidate supporters. So much for the idea that ordinary Americans do not care much about party politics. More and more of them care and care a lot.

With concerns about weak parties replaced by concerns of hyper partisanship, worries that parties are too weak seem almost quaint. Indeed, political scientists might be careful what they wish for. Political commentators now fret about the pernicious effects of party polarization.

Increased party strength is evident at all levels of American politics. The national party organizations are in better financial shape than ever. The parties in Congress pursue ideologically distinct policies, making it easier for the electorate to distinguish between them. And, as a consequence of this resurgence of parties among political elites, ordinary Americans now identify more closely with parties than they have for decades. In fact, in the 2004 and 

2008 presidential elections, partisans were more faithful to their party's candidates than any election in the history of polling.

In this chapter, I make sense of these profound changes in the American political universe, with a focus on the role that parties play for ordinary people. I start by explaining what scholars mean by party identification. In providing this conceptual sketch, I trace the development of the concept as well as detail the arguments that critics have leveled against its central importance. I then turn to an explanation of why partisanship is so important to understand. Finally, I trace the historical arc that has led us from party decline to party polarization, with a particular emphasis on the contemporary scholarly debate on party polarization.

What is Partisanship and Where Does it Come From?

The scholars who pioneered the concept of party identification hailed from the University of Michigan. Thus, those who understand party identification as the central variable in most people's political calculus are often said to follow the Michigan Model. The Michigan scholars thought of party identification in social psychological terms, defining it as an intense attachment to a political group.[2] As evidence of its centrality to people's political life, the authors of *The American Voter* asked the same people about their party identification at two year intervals, finding that very few people went from thinking about themselves as Democrats one year and Republicans two years later, or vice versa. Of all the political attitudes they studied, it was by far the most stable.

Most research suggests that party identification is learned early in life, with parents playing an influential role in its formation. If a child grows up in a household where Republicans are held in high esteem and Democrats are not, the child will typically grow up to be a Republican and vice versa. In that sense, people are born into a party, much as they are born into a religion. Like rooting for a sports team, this association tends to grow stronger through the life cycle. Once someone has decided that he roots for the Red Sox and not the Yankees, he does not easily change sides and, in fact, usually becomes a more intense fan. Similarly, once someone decides that he is a Republican, he usually remains a Republican, and his identification tends to grow stronger over time.

Although parental party identification is important in understanding a person's party identification, it is not the only factor.[3] In fact, a fair number of people grow up in families where parents' party identification is not clear because politics is simply not an important part of family life. Other cues can be helpful for people in developing bonds with a political party. Over the last several decades, people have connected the two major parties with a remarkably consistent set of social groups. Americans tend to connect the Republicans with business interests and those higher in socio-economic status, and Democrats with labor unions and the working class.[4] More recently, other group attachments have developed as well. For example, people increasingly connect the Republicans with social conservatism and religious groups and the Democrats with racial minorities and ethnic diversity.

These connections are important because people tend to identify themselves with different social groups as well. As a result, people can use the groups they identify with to deduce which party they ought to identify with. The connections developed from being part of such groups can also allow people to acquire significant information about politics, which most often serves to reinforce group identifications with parties. For example, when a labor union member goes to a union meeting, leaders tell members who their political friends and enemies are. When union members socialize with other members of the group, shared views are likely to be reinforced rather than challenged. Similarly, when someone regularly attends an Evangelical Christian church, it brings that person together with people who are sympathetic to the Republican party and the policies it supports. Informal encounters with people connected with the church will have a reinforcing effect. For example, people who are opposed to abortion rights will most often find themselves sharing a meal or an evening with others who share that opinion.

Although stable influences like parental partisanship and social group identification are clearly important, there have been too many shifts in party identification over the last 40 years to think that it is only the result of stable long term forces. Scholars have shown that early political experiences bear on party identification as well. Figure 5.1 helps make the point.

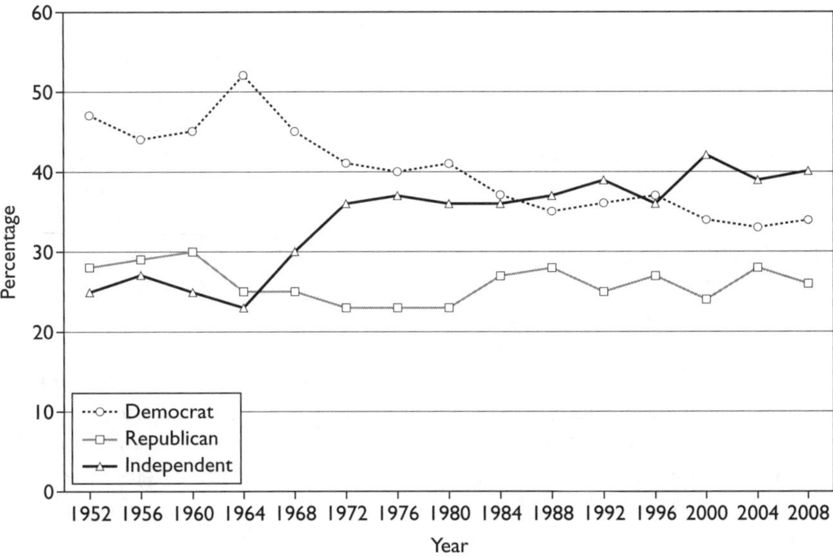

Figure 5.1 The Distribution of Party Identification in the Electorate, 1952–2008.

In the 1950s, when academic political surveys first became available, Democrats outnumbered Republicans by about 20 percentage points. This was in large measure because of the Great Depression of the 1930s. People who grew up in its shadow, which was blamed on Republican president Herbert Hoover and the Republican majorities in Congress who presided over the economic collapse, tended to be less Republican than the population as a whole. Since Franklin Roosevelt and a series of Democratic Congresses were credited with lifting the country out of the Depression, the Democrats developed a huge identification advantage that was still obvious in 1952.

Note, however, that the Democrats' identification advantage narrowed dramatically in the 1980s. In fact, if one examines only voters, the difference in party identification then was even narrower. The reason for the change is that those who came of age politically during what many perceived as Democratic president Jimmy Carter's failures in the late 1970s came to identify with the Democrats much less than the population as a whole. Instead they became more likely to adopt the Republican label, due in large part to Republican Ronald Reagan's economic and foreign policy successes in the eight years after the Carter presidency. In that sense, to predict people's party identification, it is helpful to know when they were young.

That youth of the 1980s identified more as Republicans may seem strange given that young people today tend to identify themselves more as Democrats, which fits the popular belief that young people are always liberals and Democrats, and older people always conservatives and Republicans. In fact, young people do not always identify disproportionately with the more liberal party. Rather, young people today are more likely Democrats than Republicans because of the Great Recession that took hold late in George W. Bush's presidency combined with a decreasingly popular war in Iraq that Bush initiated.

In fact, some scholars have argued that people's party identification is nowhere near as stable as the Michigan scholars originally argued in *The American Voter*. For example, Morris Fiorina argued that party identification was not an intense psychological attachment but rather just a running tally of recent political outcomes.[5] If people perceived that the economy was getting better under a Republican president, then they shifted their party identification toward the Republicans. If they perceived the economy was getting worse under a Republican president, they shifted their party identification in a Democratic direction. In a similar vein, Charles Franklin and John Jackson argued that people's vote choices affected their party identification, in addition to party identification affecting their vote choices.[6] So, someone who might have identified himself an independent going into an election might start to identify himself as a Republican if he really liked the Republican presidential candidate. Surely most young people today know someone who did not seem particularly interested in politics before 2008 but came to identify as a Democrat because of very positive feelings about Barack Obama during his successful run.

Scholars have identified a number of other reasons that individuals might change their party identification as well. One is issues. Someone who grew up in a Republican household but developed an intense pro-choice position on abortion may shift to the Democratic party or become an independent. A person's personal circumstances could also change. For example, an irreligious Democrat might come to identify with a conservative church. This new religious identification might cause a Republican turn for this person. Or, a person from a lower social class might move up the economic ladder, causing movement from Democrat to Republican, especially in the south.[7]

It is also possible for the social group identifications of the parties to change. Since the states of the former Confederacy regularly vote for Republicans for president and Congress today, it is easy to forget that the Republican party—the party of Lincoln—barely existed in the region until the 1960s. Whereas older southerners grew up being represented by very conservative southern Democrats, younger southerners have been represented by very conservative southern Republican leaders like Newt Gingrich of Georgia (House Speaker), Tom DeLay of Texas (House Majority Leader), and Haley Barbour (head of the Republican National Committee) and Trent Lott (Senate Majority Leader) of Mississippi. As a result, young southern whites are much more likely than their parents to identify with the Republican party.[8]

Although party is not immutable and these critiques have been very thoughtful over the years, the fact remains that party identification is generally stable for most people. Moreover, it appears that it has become even more stable recently. In analyzing data collected in the 1950s and 1970s, Fiorina showed that about 15 percent of people changed from one party to the other, changed to being an independent, or changed from being an independent over the course of only two short years, which was part of the evidence he used to argue against the Michigan Model. These results were based on panel data, which is data about the same individuals collected at several different points in time. The American National Election Study's (NES) most recent panel survey occurred from 2000–2004. In it, changes in party identification were much less common than before. In fact, only about 10 percent of Americans moved between party categories between 2002 and 2004, much less than what Fiorina found in the 1970s. In fact, only 5 percent of panel respondents switched from identifying with one party in 2002 to the other in 2004. This suggests that party identification might be an even more important concept to understand now than it was when the authors of *The American Voter* identified it 50 years ago.

What Party Affects

For most people, party identification provides the most useful shortcut, or heuristic, for understanding a complicated political world. People have neither the time nor the desire to learn everything they should know about politics; party identification helps them navigate a complicated and often confusing political world with less than perfect information about all its nuances. The best way to evaluate the importance of party identification is to consider the way the authors of *The American Voter* thought of it, as a "perceptual screen." All incoming information about politics that people receive goes through this screen. As a result, Democrats will tend to take away certain bits of information from a given news report, conversation, or political advertisement while Republicans might be inclined to take away different bits of information from the same piece of news.

John Zaller makes the most complete statement about the importance of party identification in processing political information.[9] He advances his RAS model, which stands for Receive, Accept, and Sample. People first *Receive* information, whether from the news media, a friend, or some personal experience. Some people, of course, take in more information than others. The key point is that no one bothers to evaluate all information about anything because there is simply too much of it, so shortcuts are necessary to survive.

Next, people decide whether to *Accept* the information that they just received. This is where a person's party identification plays the most critical role. When information runs counter to their partisan predispositions, people are more likely to reject it than accept it. For example, a Democrat who hears that Barack Obama is really a Muslim is much more likely than a Republican to reject such information than accept it. Similarly, when information is presented by a source that someone perceives to be of the opposite party of the person receiving the information, that person will be more likely to reject the information than if it came from someone with the same party affiliation of the person. So, Democrats will be more likely than Republicans to reject information heard on *Fox News* and Republicans will be more likely than Democrats to reject information heard on *MSNBC*. In the end, these filters mean that the information people have in their memories will be biased by their party affiliation.

What information is accepted and what information is rejected has important implications for the last stage in Zaller's model. When ordinary people are asked about their opinions in a survey, they *Sample* from all the pieces of information that have remained in their memories about a particular subject. This is important because their partisanship has caused them to reject a lot of information that ran counter to their partisanship. As a result, Democrats will, when asked about politics, tend to express pro-Democratic positions on the issues and Republicans will tend to express pro-Republican positions because they have rejected much of the information they received that didn't jibe with their partisanship.

It is worth exploring just how powerful this partisan filter can be, especially in the present day where partisanship seems to be playing an increasingly outsized role. In his treatment of the polarizing presidency of George W. Bush,

Jacobson shows that Republicans and Democrats developed much different beliefs about factual information. For example, even though Saddam Hussein was not involved in the September 11 terrorist attacks, 44 percent of Republicans thought he was as late as October 2005. This is likely because Bush administration officials found that support for invading Iraq, a policy they pursued, increased when they connected Hussein and 9/11 indirectly. Importantly, partisanship profoundly affected whether or not people believed the Hussein connection, with only 25 percent of Democrats expressing belief.[10] It is not just Republicans who are prone to misperceiving the political world. Bartels showed that Democrats were much more likely to think that inflation and unemployment had gotten worse when Republican Ronald Reagan was president even though both had gotten much better under Reagan.[11] Republicans, on the other hand, tended to get these questions right. One set of partisans filtered out the correct information because it ran counter to their view of Reagan while the other set of partisans embraced it.

Not surprisingly, this perceptual screen has an enormous impact on how well people think specific politicians are doing their jobs. In fact, since the scientific use of public opinion polling got its start in the 1930s, Republicans and Democrats in the electorate have never perceived a president's job performance more differently than they did George W. Bush's. According to a poll by *USA Today*–Gallup taken as Bush left office in January 2009, 78 percent of Republicans approved of his job performance compared with only 6 percent of Democrats, a 72 percentage point difference. Things have not changed much under President Obama. In a November 2010 poll from Gallup, 81 percent of Democrats thought he was doing a good job while only 11 percent of Republicans did. Just two years into his presidency, Obama's job approval numbers were as polarized by party as Bush's were by the end of his run in office.

In addition to acting as a perceptual screen, party can help people make sense of the complicated nuances of politics. Since many know little about politics, they can use their attachment to a party to decide where they stand on issues or how they should identify themselves ideologically. A surprisingly large percentage of Americans do not understand the words "liberal" and "conservative." In fact when asked to place themselves on a scale from extremely liberal to extremely conservative with moderate or middle of the road in between, fully 20 percent of people fail to even answer. Yet Americans are pretty good at knowing what goes with what. Based on data from the 2008 NES, for example, only 3 percent of Republicans classified themselves as liberal, while fully 74 percent identified themselves as conservative (the other 23 percent either identified themselves as moderates or said they did not know).

Party also predicts a range of issue preferences. Democrats are much more likely than Republicans to take the liberal position on the degree to which government ought to provide aid to minority groups, provide Americans with a guaranteed job and standard of living, take a more active role in the health insurance system, be pro-choice on abortion and in favor of more rights for gays and lesbians. Indeed, Abramowitz and Saunders show that over the last three decades party identifiers have become much better at matching their parties with their issue preferences.[12]

It is important to note, too, that people are much more likely to use their party identification to inform their issue preferences rather than the other way around.[13] That is, most people do not decide first they are pro-life on abortion, favor lower taxes on the wealthy, and fewer government programs for the poor and, as a result, choose to be Republicans. Rather, most identify with a party first and then choose their issue preferences accordingly, based on information that they get from the news media or from friends and relatives about where most partisans tend to stand on these issues. Sometimes issues cause people to update their party identification. But it requires that people care a lot about the issue, and know where the parties stand on it to bring about such a change in party.[14]

Party identification affects an impressive array of things. When there is a Republican president, Democratic partisans always view the economy as worse than their Republican counterparts do, and vice versa. In evaluating the personal characteristics of political candidates, Republican partisans always rate the competence, character, and attractiveness of Republican candidates more favorably than do Democrats, and vice versa. Moreover, attitudes that were once somewhat immune to party differences, such as support for foreign wars, now show massive differences by party, indicating that partisanship in the electorate is stronger than in decades past.[15] In short, party identification structures the political world of partisans more thoroughly than any other attitude or set of attitudes.

The choice that scholars have most often focused on in assessing the central importance of party identification is the voting decision. This was the end point in *The American Voter*'s famous "funnel of causality," for which party identification acted as the filter. Party identification profoundly affects the choices people make. For instance, in the 2008 presidential election, exit polls revealed that over 90 percent of self-identified Democrats voted for Barack Obama and about the same percentage of Republicans voted for John McCain. Although the effect of party identification is somewhat weaker in structuring vote choice for other federal and state level offices, it is still very strong and growing increasingly so at least as it relates to congressional voting.[16]

Are Ordinary Americans Polarized?

While scholars expressed concern about party weakness in the 1950s, they are now concerned that parties are too polarized. By polarization, people mean that Democrats and Republicans are so far apart on the issues and their outlook on the world that they cannot agree on much of anything or find compromises when compromises are necessary and possible. In that sense, polarization has a negative connotation, suggesting that parties have exactly the opposite problem from before. They are viewed by some as too strong now.

Little doubt remains that political elites—partisans who serve in government and in party organizations—are polarized today. A host of scholars over the last several decades identify marked increases in party line voting in both the House and Senate.[17] Figure 5.2 depicts the ideology of members who served in the 109th Congress (2005–2006) using a measure developed by Keith Poole and Howard Rosenthal called DW-NOMINATE scores. It uses the voting records of Members of Congress to tap their ideology. Note that only a small handful of members grade out as moderates and the major parties have no members who would be better ideological fits in the other party. Data like these are often used to argue that Congress is polarized by party.

It remains unresolved whether ordinary people are polarized in their political outlooks. Whereas politics is a life and death struggle for party activists and representatives, it is simply not that important to most people. Can people be polarized about something that they have only a passing interest in?

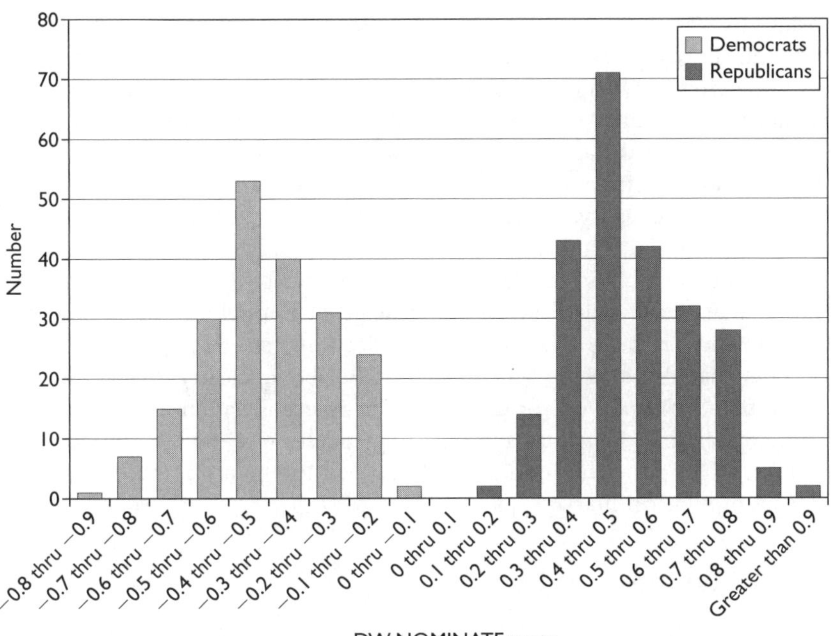

Figure 5.2 Ideology of Members of House of Representatives, 109th Congress, DW-NOMINATE scores.

Those who argue that the electorate is polarized usually point to recent election results as evidence. As I noted above, it is quite remarkable how loyal people are to their party's presidential candidate. In fact, partisans are now more loyal to both their party's presidential and congressional candidates than at any time that we have survey data.[18] Moreover, the Electoral College map has been very resistant to change lately. Concerns about polarization picked up steam after the 2004 election when 47 of the 50 states voted the same way that they did in the 2000 election, with only New Mexico, Iowa, and New Hampshire switching sides. In fact, fully 32 states have voted for the same party's presidential candidate in every election between 1992 and 2008. This is true despite the fact that there have been Republican incumbents, Democratic incumbents, no incumbents, white candidates, black candidates, male candidates, and female (Vice Presidential) candidates. Nothing seems to disrupt the general behavior of most states.

Although true, states do not vote. People do. And Morris Fiorina argues that people aren't polarized. They only appear to be polarized because their choices are. Even moderate Democrats and Republicans have to choose between very liberal and very conservative candidates like John Kerry and George W. Bush.[19] And even when candidates with a reputation for moderation run, as was the case with John McCain in 2008, they tend to run as more ideologically extreme in an effort to secure their party's nomination. Fiorina brings to bear an impressive amount of evidence to suggest that: (1) people in Republican red states are not much different in their political thinking from people living in Democratic blue states; (2) Democrats and Republicans are somewhat more divided than they used to be, but the differences are not huge; (3) attitudes toward abortion, supposedly one of the most polarizing issues, have remained fairly constant; and (4) that Americans are much less hostile toward homosexuality, which suggests moderation rather than polarization on another hot button social issue.

In that sense, Fiorina argues that the political world is closely divided rather than deeply divided. The percentage of Republican and Democratic voters tends to be almost equal most elections, so, to Fiorinia, it is little wonder that elections are generally close. But being closely divided does not mean that people are deeply divided on the issues. Even on the most contentious issues, like abortion, Fiorina suggests the electorate is moderate by nature, looking for common ground between the polarized choices that the parties provide ordinary people.

Little Evidence of Polarization

If one is looking for a picture of the electorate like the one above of Congress, with Republican and Democratic preferences clustering at opposite poles, there is little evidence of polarization. Consider the NES's ideological self-placement question. The survey asks people to place themselves on a seven point scale from extremely liberal to extremely conservative with moderate, middle of the road at the midpoint. About 50 percent of Americans either call themselves moderate or are unable to place themselves on the scale. Figure 5.3 shows responses in 2008 broken down by party.

The most common response among Democrats is "moderate" or "haven't thought enough about it." In fact, fewer than 40 percent of Democrats label themselves as liberals of any sort. Republicans embrace the conservative label more easily than Democrats do the liberal label. Still, fully 30 percent of Republicans consider themselves moderate or say they haven't thought enough about it to have an opinion.

It would be easy to conclude from these results that the American public is not polarized. Perhaps, though, this definition of polarization is too limited to apply to ordinary people. In surveys, many like the safety of the midpoint because moderation carries a positive connotation and, if people are not sure, the middle is an attractive place to choose. In fact, a relatively small percentage of Americans have the cognitive ability and the political certainty to choose responses toward the poles. Even during the Civil War, surely the most polarized time in the nation's history, many southerners sympathized with the north and many northerners sympathized with the south. Indeed, Dahl notes that less than a year before secession, "abolitionist" was not a word used by ordinary citizens.[20]

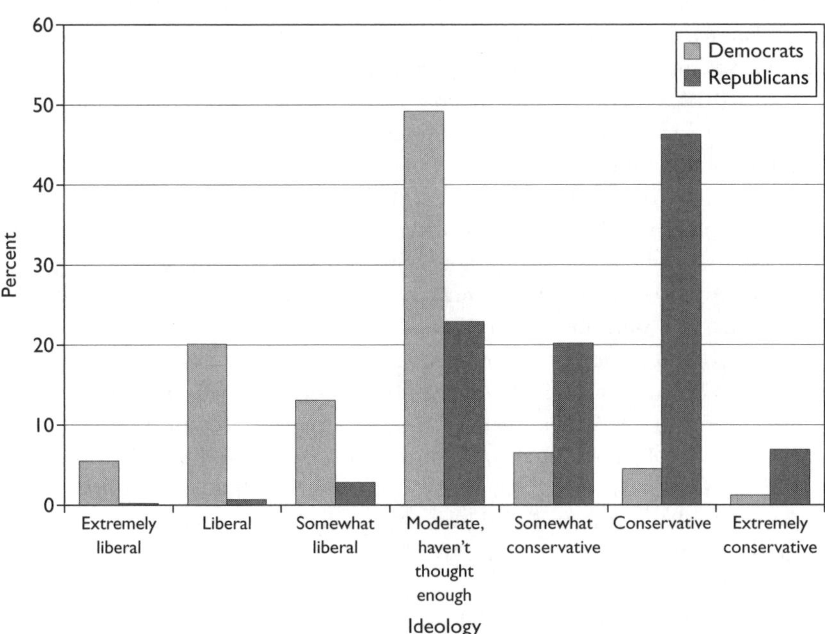

Figure 5.3 Ideological Self-Placement by Party Identification, Leaners Not Treated as Partisans 2008.

Strong Indication of Partisan Sorting

Scholars who see polarization in the electorate think about what it means differently from Fiorina. For them, the most important feature is that the distance between average Republicans and Democrats has increased even if their opinions are not getting more extreme.[21] How can this be? People are "sorting" themselves more "correctly," matching their party and issue preferences more often. They are better able to do this because of the polarization among political elites.[22] It is easy to tell where congressional Republicans and Democrats stand, making it easier for ordinary Republicans and Democrats to parrot these positions. This process decreases the heterogeneity within the parties, because there are now fewer conservative Democrats and liberal Republicans. It also increases the average distance between them.

With sorting, differences between partisans in the electorate can increase, even if the public remains relatively moderate, as Fiorina argues. For example, opinions about abortion might not have become more extreme, but the average Democrat and Republican could be farther apart if formerly Democratic pro-lifers changed their party affiliation, realizing their old party was not an appropriate home (and vice versa). This is the process by which Democratic partisans have become more homogeneously liberal and Republican partisans more homogeneously conservative, creating a larger average difference between them. Sorting of this type has definitely occurred. For example, the distance between where the average Democrat and Republican place themselves on the ideology scale described above data has increased dramatically. In 1972, a mere 0.66 points separated Republicans and Democrats in the electorate on the seven point scale, but, by 2008, the mean distance had nearly tripled to 1.80 points.

In addition, Americans are better sorted by party now on things that might cause people to feel like the political system is polarized.[23] If Republicans and Democrats are increasingly far apart on values—and they are—it might be what contributes to the widespread sense that the differences between the parties feel irreconcilable. Since 1986, the NES has asked several questions to measure what it terms "moral traditionalism." Respondents are asked to agree or disagree with several statements, including "the newer lifestyles are contributing to the breakdown of our society," "the country would have many fewer problems if there were more emphasis on traditional family ties," and "the world is always changing and we should adjust our view of moral behavior to those changes." The items are designed to provide a fundamental understanding of how the world works, whether people are "orthodox" or "relativistic."

Figure 5.4 shows how wide the gap between partisans has grown since the 1980s. In 1986, the first year the items were asked, the average difference was a miniscule four percentage points. By the mid-1990s, the difference had increased to 15 percentage points. And the year Bush faced Kerry in the

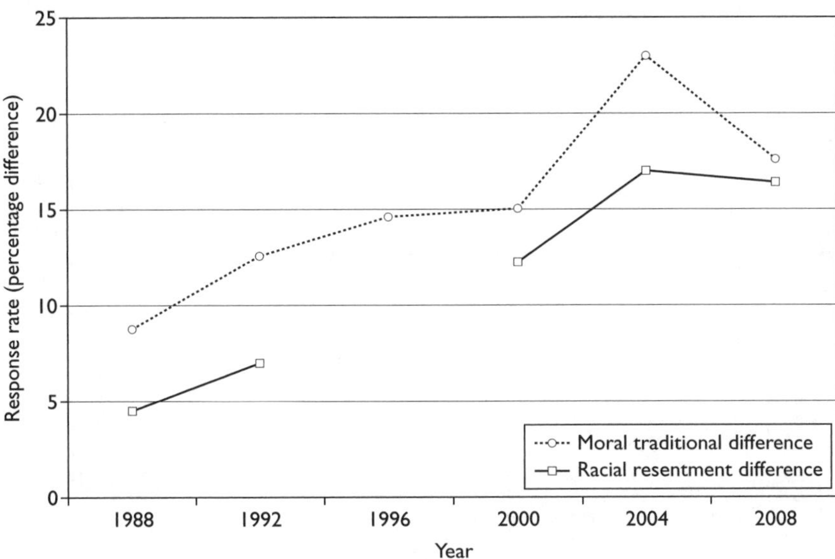

Figure 5.4 Changes in the Differences Between Mass Partisans on Values Batteries, 1988–2008.

presidential election, the difference had increased further to 23 points. This is a large difference by public opinion standards.

The figure also shows the parties are further apart on another deeply felt value, namely racial resentment. Developed by Donald Kinder and David Sears and extended by Kinder and Lynn Sanders to tap symbolic racism, the concept has replaced measures of overt racism from years past.[24] The difference between the average white Republican and average white Democrat in racial resentment was only about five percentage points in 1988, and it increased very gradually through the late twentieth century. The difference then surged to about 20 percentage points in 2004. Race is what Edward Carmines and James Stimson term an "easy issue," one that is experienced more in their guts than their brains.[25] Differences in racial attitudes might also cause Americans to feel like the parties are polarized as well.

What Has Caused the Sorting?

The most likely reason that the public has gotten better at matching their party and their issue preferences is because elites are now polarized. The data provide strong evidence. Figure 5.5 tracks the average distance between the parties in Congress in the session before survey data about ordinary Americans was gathered and the average distance between Republicans and Democrats on the NES's ideology question.

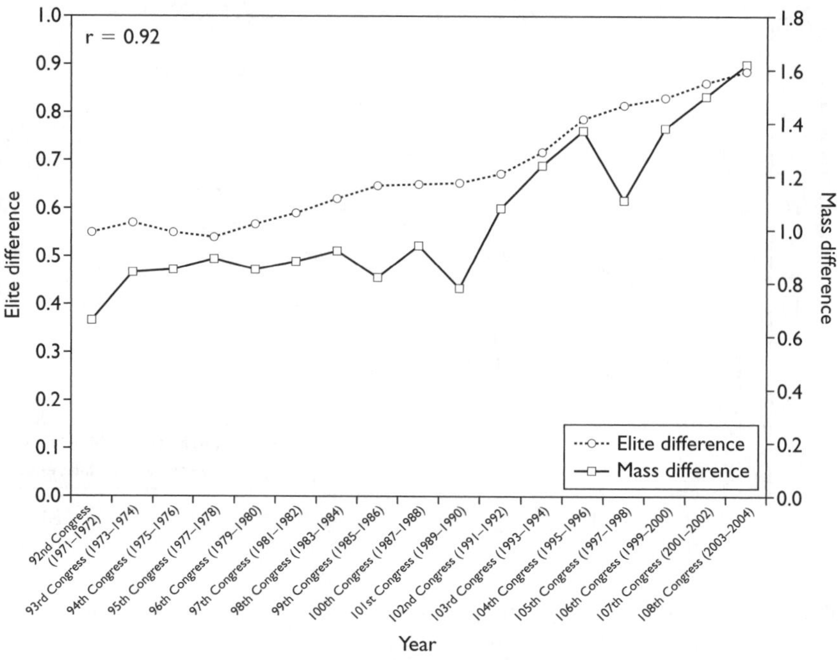

Figure 5.5 Mean Ideological Distance Between Congressional and Mass Partisans, DW-NOMINATE Scores and NES Ideological Self-Placement, 1971–2006.

The correlation over the years 1972–2006 is 0.92. If I examine only presidential election years, when Americans are paying closer attention, the correlation is even higher.

In addition, some argue that hot button issues like morality and race have become more prominent lately. Although the popular conception is that issues like these are designed to fire up a party's base, Hillygus and Shields also show that they are used to winning over what they call cross-pressured voters.[26] These are people who do not agree with their party on certain issues. This is more likely to happen on hot button issues. Specifically, there is a relatively high proportion of pro-school prayer Democrats, pro-choice Republicans, and anti-gay marriage Democrats. These issues excite the party base, but it is also an effective strategy for attracting a fair number of cross-pressured voters at the same time.

Changes in the mass media might also provide an engine for party sorting. Patterson argues the media today are more adversarial and interpretive in their reporting than they were in the 1950s and 1960s.[27] Such changing conventions could encourage people to think more negatively about those in the other party because journalists are more likely to suggest nefarious motives to politicians. In addition, cable news is now full of ideological programming rather than the straight news of decades past. Glenn Beck, Bill O'Reilly, and Sean Hannity on *Fox News* are unabashed conservative voices while Keith Olbermann and Rachel Maddow on *MSNBC* provide their liberal counterparts. The format of these shows, and many other cable news offerings before them, facilitate party sorting in the electorate. Most often they invite guests from the far left of the Democratic party and far right of the Republican party and let them have it. Mutz and Reeves argue that such reporting, along with the close up camera angles employed on these shows, violate social norms of civility and proximity, causing people to ignore counter arguments thereby intensifying their own opinions.[28]

Before blaming cable news as the main villain, however, keep in mind that fewer people watch these shows than might be popularly believed. Prior notes that fewer than five million people tune in for even the highest rated cable news shows whereas popular non-news shows garner an audience of more than 20 million on a weekly basis.[29] It is also important to remember that most cable news viewers are probably pretty well sorted to begin with. Figures like Beck and Maddow probably do more to reinforce already strong feelings rather than creating them.

Talk radio and the Internet blogosphere also probably contribute to the sense that the differences between Democrats and Republicans are irreconcilable. Conservatives who want the conservative spin on the day's events can listen to Rush Limbaugh or peruse the Drudge Report on line, while liberals might log onto the *Daily Kos*, *Huffington Post*, or *Talking Points Memo* for their preferred spin. Both types of consumers will hear only their party's side of things, decreasing the number of counter arguments that they might carry in their heads. This is in stark contrast to the 1960s and 1970s when everyone got their TV news from one of three major network sources and people read newspapers with roughly the same news norms that favored objectivity over ideology.

Conclusion

Whether or not the electorate is polarized, it is still the case that party identification is the most important political attitude. Knowing one's party identification provides more information than any other single source about a person's political behaviors, positions on issues, or feelings about groups. Political commentators often suggest that people start with preferences about political issues, weigh the parties' positions on these issues carefully, and decide whether they are Democrats or Republicans. Decades of research suggest the process does not usually work this way because most Americans do not follow politics particularly closely. Instead people usually develop their partisanship first and match it with where office holders and other elites in their parties stand on the issues. In that sense, people use their party identification as a shortcut, or heuristic, to help inform their opinion and behaviors. More generally, party identification provides a guide to how people process information, make decisions, and come to conclusions. Indeed making sense of politics for many, perhaps most, people would be all but impossible if not for the identification that they develop with one of the major political parties.

Although scholars still have not resolved the question of polarization in the electorate, perhaps the best way to make sense of the debate is in the following manner. Partisans are not, nor will they likely ever be, polar opposites. There is no doubt that they are more divided about things that people care about deeply. Things like morality, race, and maintaining safety and security are all things about which people have strong feelings. With the parties more deeply divided along these lines, the intensity generated by politics has increased. Certain things are easier to disagree about civilly—such as how high taxes ought to be or how much money we ought to spend on education. Other things are harder, such as when fundamental conceptions of right and wrong enter the fray. We are experiencing more of the latter today. And, given that political parties are structuring this conflict, they are now even more relevant to us than they have been in many decades.

It also might be worth noting that difference between Republicans and Democrats today extend well beyond politics. Consider sports. You will find significantly more Republicans among professional football, college football, and especially NASCAR fans. Democrats like certain sports more than Republicans, particularly soccer and a range of sports played by women.[30] The same is true of television shows. Republicans are significantly more likely than Democrats to prefer reality shows like *Survivor* and *Amazing Race*. Democrats are more likely than Republicans to like critically acclaimed shows about quirky people like *Mad Men*, *Dexter*, and *30 Rock*.[31]

That said, it is important to keep in mind that most Americans still call themselves moderate or are non-ideological and many do not identify strongly with either party, and that makes a difference. If all voters were seriously polarized into one camp or another, rapid turns in party electoral fortunes would be unlikely. But that is what we have seen lately. In 2004, Republicans won a decisive victory with George Bush re-elected and Republicans maintaining congressional majorities. In 2006 and 2008, however, Democrats won big victories, first taking back control of the House and Senate and then the presidency. Then, in 2010, voters handed control of the House back to the Republicans in the biggest seat swing since the 1940s. It is surely true that a substantial percentage of Americans, probably a majority, could not conceive of voting for candidates of the party they do not identify with. But there are still plenty of swing voters who are not so tightly tied to a party to cause these kinds of changes. In that sense, some Americans are polarized in their thinking, but not all of them are.

Consider what might happen if a self-professed moderate, with a strong record of governance either in politics, the military, or business, not to mention a willingness to spend a few hundred million dollars, decided to run in the next election as a third party presidential candidate. Let's further assume that the major parties continued their trend of nominating a liberal Democrat and a conservative Republican. The evidence seems to suggest that someone like New York City Mayor Michael Bloomberg, General David Petreaus, or Bill Gates might do quite well with the American voter simply by virtue of not being a partisan. In that sense, while partisanship is increasingly strong for some people, there are enough for whom it is not that the present trend toward polarization in Washington could be a liability to the future success of the parties.

Notes

1. David S. Broder, *The Party's Over: The Failure of Politics in America* (New York: Harper and Row, 1972).
2. Angus Campbell, Philip Converse, Warren Miller, and Donald Stokes, *The American Voter* (New York: Wiley, 1960).
3. M. Kent Jennings and Richard G. Niemi, "The Transmission of Political Values from Parent to Child," *American Political Science Review* 62 (March 1968): 169–184.
4. Donald Green, Bradley Palmquist, and Eric Schickler, *Partisan Hearts and Minds: Political Parties and the Social Identities of Voters* (New Haven, CT: Yale University Press, 2002).
5. Morris P. Fiorina, *Retrospective Voting in American National Elections* (New Haven, CT: Yale University Press, 1981).
6. Charles H. Franklin and John E. Jackson, "The Dynamics of Party Identification," *American Political Science Review* 85 (December 1983): 957–973.
7. Andrew Gelman, *Red State, Blue State, Rich State, Poor State: Why Americans Vote the Way They Do* (Princeton, NJ: Princeton University Press, 2008).
8. Green et al., *Partisan Hearts and Minds.*
9. John Zaller, *The Nature and Origins of Mass Opinion* (New York: Cambridge University Press, 1992).
10. Gary C. Jacobson, *A Divider, Not a Uniter: George W. Bush and the American People* (New York: Pearson Longman, 2007).
11. Larry M. Bartels, "Beyond the Running Tally: Partisan Bias in Political Perceptions," *Political Behavior* 24 (2002): 117–150.
12. Alan Abramowitz and Kyle Saunders. "Is Polarization a Myth?" *Journal of Politics*, 70 (2008): 542–555.
13. Thomas M. Carsey and Geoffrey C. Layman, "Changing Sides or Changing Minds? Party Identification and Policy Preferences in the American Electorate," *American Journal of Political Science* 50 (2006): 464–477.
14. Thomas M. Carsey and Geoffrey C. Layman, "Changing Sides or Changing Minds?
15. Jacobson, *Divider Not a Uniter*, and Adam J. Berinsky, *In Time of War: Understanding Public Opinion from World War II to Iraq* (Chicago, IL: University of Chicago Press, 2009).
16. Larry M. Bartels, "Partisanship and Voting Behavior, 1952–1996," *American Journal of Political Science* 44 (January 2000): 35–50.
17. Joseph A. Schlesinger, "The New American Political Party," *American Political Science Review* 79 (1985), 1152–1169; David W. Rohde, *Parties and Leaders in Postreform House* (Chicago, IL: University of Chicago Press, 1991); Keith T. Poole and

Howard Rosenthal, "The Polarization of American Politics," *Journal of Politics* 46 (1984): 1061–1079.

18. Bartels, "Partisanship and Voting Behavior."
19. Morris Fiorina with Samuel J. Abrams, and Jeremy C. Pope, *Culture War? The Myth of Polarized America* (1st ed.) (New York: Pearson Longman, 2004).
20. Robert A. Dahl, *Democracy in the United States: Promise and Performance* (3rd ed.) (New York: Rand McNally, 1976), pp. 420–433.
21. Abramowitz and Saunders, "Is Polarization a Myth?"
22. Marc J. Hetherington, "Resurgent Mass Partisanship: The Role of Elite Polarization," *American Political Science Review* 95 (2001): 619–631.
23. Marc J. Hetherington and Jonathan Weiler, *Authoritarianism and Polarization in American Politics* (Cambridge: Cambridge University Press, 2009).
24. Donald R. Kinder and David O. Sears, "Prejudice and Politics: Symbolic Racism versus Racial Threats to the Good Life," *Journal of Personality and Social Psychology* 40 (1981): 414–431, and Donald R. Kinder and Lynn M. Sanders, *Divided By Color: Racial Politics and Democratic Ideals* (Chicago, IL: University of Chicago Press, 1996).
25. Edward Carmines and James Stimson, *Issue Evolution* (Princeton, NJ: Princeton University Press, 1989).
26. D. Sunshine Hillygus and Todd Shields, *The Persuadable Voter: Strategic Candidates and Wedge Issues in Presidential Campaigns* (Princeton, NJ: Princeton University Press, 2008).
27. Thomas Patterson, *Out of Order* (New York: Knopf, 1993).
28. Diana C. Mutz and Byron Reeves, "The New Videomalaise: Effects of Televised Incivility on Political Trust," *American Political Science Review* 99 (2005): 1–15.
29. Markus Prior, *Post-Broadcast Democracy: How Media Choice Increases Inequality in Political Involvement and Polarizes Elections* (New York: Cambridge University Press, 2007).
30. These data were drawn from an NMRPP analysis of Scarborough USA+ surveys from August 2008 and September 2009.
31. James Hibberd, "The Reign of Right-Wing Primetime." Retrieved from http://www.hollywoodreporter.com/blogs/live-feed/right-wing-tv-43558, December 17, 2010.

Chapter 6

Race and the Group Bases of Public Opinion

Jane Junn, Tali Mendelberg, and Erica Czaja

Scholarship in political science on race and its impact on political preferences has undergone substantial transformation in the last quarter century. Once defined racially by black and white, today the U.S. population is characterized by a multiplicity of racial and ethnic group divisions. Hispanics are now the largest minority population in the United States, followed by African Americans and then Asian Americans and Native Americans. The "multi-racial" population—a category formed by counting more than one racial group and allowed by the census since 2000—is among the fastest-growing groups.[1] The United States is in the midst of the most significant wave of immigration in a century, and the vast majority of the newest Americans are no longer from Europe as they once were in the nineteenth century. Instead, more than half of today's immigrants are from Latin America and another quarter come from Asia. While black migrants from Africa and the Caribbean constitute a much smaller share of new immigrants, their presence creates important diversity within the racial category of black.[2]

In this chapter we take the increased racial and ethnic diversity of the United States as a starting point, and analyze the significance of race and the group bases of political preferences. We begin with a discussion of categories of race and ethnicity in the United States and argue that these divisions are based not in "objective" biological difference, but rather in social constructions formed through the institutions and practices of U.S. government and society.[3] Next we focus on individual-level measurements of psychological attachment to groups—group identity and consciousness—as critical intervening variables between racial group classification and the formation of political preferences. The contours of the relationships between racial group identity, racial group consciousness, and public opinion, particularly for Latinos and Asian Americans, are especially challenging for scholars because these populations and their politics are in flux. Finally, we proceed to analyze additional factors that may differentially influence the political opinions of individuals, depending in part on their racial group classifications and attachments, including party identification and mobilization, interpersonal contact and the racial and economic context, and perceptions of and experiences with discrimination.

Categorizing Race and Ethnicity

The practice of official racial classification in the United States dates to the nation's founding. Information on racial categorization was vital to the apportionment of legislative seats in the federal government. The now-infamous "Three-Fifths" compromise found in Article I Section 2 of the U.S. Constitution specifies that both taxes and the number of elected representatives be calculated by adding the number of free persons and three-fifths of all other persons, "excluding Indians not taxed." The enslaved population was black, and, hence, the enumeration by slave status was also an enumeration by race.

In every decennial census since the first in 1790, race has been recorded for each person counted. Political scientist Melissa Nobles demonstrates how government agencies such as the U.S. Bureau of the Census constructed categories of race in order to meet social and political goals of the time.[4] It would take almost 100 years and a bloody civil war for the United States to abolish slavery, but, by then, race was embedded in the fabric of the polity, and the practice of recording race has continued unabated. Throughout the vast majority of the nation's history, racial categorization went hand in hand with preferential treatment—from citizenship and property rights to eligibility to vote—for those recognized as white. Political scientists have documented clear patterns of the role of the American state in the maintenance and definition of both racial categories and unequal treatment by race.[5] These scholars argue that racial discrimination is deeply embedded in American political institutions and culture. Even when discrimination on the basis of racial categories was prohibited by law, as in the Fourteenth Amendment, state and local governments as well as private individuals found creative ways to use ostensibly race-neutral practices and rules to virtually eliminate racial minorities from public life from the 1860s until today. Some scholars draw an important distinction between systemic structures of discrimination, such as election rules that prevented African Americans from voting, and individuals' feelings of racial antipathy, arguing both that the former do not necessarily lead to the latter and that institutionalized racism is what matters for political outcomes.[6]

The long-standing patterns of racial categorization and white privilege in the United States have persisted at the same time that the categories themselves have undergone change. Individuals at any point in time may be designated as part of a racial group not because they are objectively Latino or black but instead because of a combination of social and political constructions that work together to ascribe a specific category of race to the person. Especially relevant is the move among "white ethnics" during the period of mass immigration in the late-nineteenth and early-twentieth centuries to be classified by the government as white.[7] Some groups such as the Irish, Italians, and Jews were successful, while others including Asian Americans, were not able to get the courts to recognize them as white and thus eligible for the full privileges of U.S. citizenship.[8] Federal law prohibited Asian immigrants from naturalization until 1952, breaking more than 70 years of explicit Asian exclusion from the United States.[9] From the 1860s, local, state, as well as the national government of the United States enacted laws targeting Asian Americans that barred property ownership, levied additional race-based taxes, and forcibly interned Americans of Japanese descent during World War II.[10]

Going beyond the traditional black–white racial binary, political scientist Claire Kim shows how Asian Americans have been placed in a "triangulated" position between blacks and whites.[11] Complicating matters further is the introduction by the federal government of a fourth major category, Hispanic or Latino. While developed decades earlier, the requirement of reporting Hispanic/Latino ethnicity along with other racial categories was implemented by the federal Office of Management and Budget in the 1970s. The complexity, multiplicity and fluidity of racial categories suggest that the study of race and groups should utilize categories of white, black, Latino, and Asian American carefully and with an awareness of their contingent nature and the role that cultural norms and politics play in shaping our perceptions of race.

Key Concepts, Measurement, and Methodology

Key Concepts in the Study of Race and Groups

A central challenge facing researchers of race and groups is the clear, consistent conceptualization of variables within and across studies. Researchers are concerned with three key concepts: *racial group membership*, or what we have referred to above as racial categorization, *racial group identity*, and *racial group consciousness*. According to McClain et al. and to a long tradition of research, simply membership does not tell us how strongly a person identifies with the group or whether they view politics as relevant to the group.[12] "Group identification refers to an individual's awareness of belonging to a certain group and having a psychological attachment to that group based on a perception of shared beliefs, feelings, interests, and ideas with other group members"; whereas

> [g]roup consciousness is in-group identification *politicized* by a set of ideological beliefs about one's group's social standing, as well as a view that collective action is the best means by which the group can improve its status and realize its interests.[13]

The more strongly that society and politics define group members by their racial category, and the more isolated and discriminated against people are because of their assigned group membership, the more likely they are to identify with their assigned racial group, and the higher the potential for group members to view their unequal treatment as a condition created by politics and to organize for political change. Paradoxically, then, the very conditions that stifle individuals can facilitate their political mobilization.

The interaction between the structure imposed by the state and society and the agency non-white minorities exercise within the limited choices available to them is well illustrated by another set of key concepts in the study of racial groups developed in the study of African American politics by Michael Dawson: *linked fate*, the *black counterpublic*, and the *black utility heuristic*.[14] Linked fate is the idea among individual blacks that their fates are inextricably linked with the fate of the race as a whole; essentially, they believe that their success depends on the success of the group, so what is good for the race is good for the individual. According to Dawson, African Americans' unique history of racial subjugation and forced segregation has led to the transmission of notions of linked fate across generations, so that still today African Americans continue to receive messages that reinforce their sense of shared racial group interests through the black counterpublic—mainly, black media, predominantly black organizations, and, the mainstay of black public life, the black church. Information shared in these segregated spaces, Dawson argues, enables and encourages African Americans to evaluate politics using a rational, mental shortcut that he calls the "black utility heuristic." That is, African Americans form their political opinions about political parties, candidates, and public policies by using their perceptions of what is best for the entire racial group instead of what they think is best for them individually. The sense of linked fate is so strong that it overcomes the force of class interests for the large black middle class and the lure of cultural conservatism, which resonates with many African Americans; it is the reason why African Americans vote nearly unanimously for the Democratic party in presidential and many lower-level electoral contests.

Researchers of Asian American and Latino politics are beginning to use both sets of concepts, but, we argue, should do so with care because of the different historical and contemporary experiences of racial groups. Today, for example, Asian Americans and Latinos are typically much closer to the immigration experience that helps shape political incorporation. Michael Jones-Correa's study of first-generation Latino immigrants in Queens, New York, suggests that there are important psychological and material costs in renouncing homeland citizenship that prevent some immigrants from becoming citizens.[15] He argues that Latinos practice a "politics of in-between," being torn between two nations, neither fully politically engaged in their new homes nor in their homelands. However, beyond such individual factors, he as well as others also identified a lack of institutional mechanisms to aid in the incorporation of immigrants, including exclusive local party machines.[16] Latino organizations such as churches may be evolving to play an increasingly political role that could strengthen Latinos' identification with all Latinos rather than merely their national origin as, say, Mexicans, and enhance their sense of linked fate and group consciousness.

Measurement of Key Concepts

There are a number of important challenges in the measurement of racial group membership, identity, and consciousness, and we highlight two of the primary challenges here. The first emanates from the flexibility and contingent nature of racial identities among individuals, particularly those whose racial and ethnic backgrounds do not fit neatly into one of the four categories. In-person and telephone survey interviews are the most common ways to measure these concepts in the study of public opinion, but different individuals understand questions about race and ethnicity differently.[17] In addition, as we have seen above, racial and ethnic groups have systematically varying levels of group identification and consciousness as a function of the way that politics and society shape the experience of what it means to be a group member.

Second, the survey questions that attempt to measure group-based identities vary widely in their wording, making it difficult to compare the specific type of psychological attachment being measured across measurements. Furthermore, racial identification and consciousness may vary depending on the context in which the survey is administered. Given the range of ethnic and national origin groups that make up the pan-ethnic categories of both Latino and Asian American, what it means to identify with a group depends upon the racial category posed to the respondent in a survey question. While Mexican Americans make up the largest share of the Latino population in the United States, the category of Hispanic or Latino also includes Cubans, Caribbeans, Puerto Ricans, and people from other Latin American countries. Similarly, there are as many national origin and ethnicity groups within the pan-ethnic racial category of Asian American, with the six largest groups being Chinese, Asian Indian, Filipino, Vietnamese, Korean, and Japanese. Finally, while blacks demonstrate the highest degree of racial group consciousness, the internal diversity of this group is also in flux, with native-born African Americans included in the same racial category as new arrivals from the African continent as well as large numbers of Afro-Caribbeans.

Thus, differences in the ways in which individuals understand the same questions, differences in the ways that survey questions are worded, and the contexts in which these questions are administered complicate the measurement and comparison of group membership, identity, and consciousness across racial groups.

Methodological Challenges in Survey Research

There are also methodological challenges in collecting data on racial groups in the United States, particularly those heavily comprising immigrants. Geographic concentration and dispersion and the prevalence of speaking a language other than English characterize Latino and Asian American populations today, and reaching individuals for interviews requires innovative methods of survey research designed specifically for these respondents.

Asian Americans and Latinos, and immigrant groups more generally, have increasingly complex patterns of geographic mobility. Once heavily concentrated in the southwestern United States and large urban metropolitan areas such as Los Angeles and New York City, Latinos are moving in increasing numbers to the south, mid-Atlantic, and the plains states.[18] At the same time, Asian Americans, while once heavily concentrated in a handful of states, are beginning to disperse as well, with sizeable populations in states such as Virginia, Florida, and Nevada. Sampling these populations for survey interviews is challenging, but making sure that subjects are not drawn only from high-density locations is critical for obtaining survey samples that are representative of the population.

Similarly, because eight in ten adult Asian Americans and nearly half of Latinos are foreign born, writing surveys in languages other than English and hiring interviewers who can speak in the respondent's native language greatly increase the likelihood of acquiring both a good sample and good data. While many immigrants speak English, it is a second language for many, and answering survey questions in their native language is preferable.[19]

Finally, given the high degree of internal heterogeneity within each of these groups, the size of the sample must be large enough to include sufficient numbers of respondents from specific national origin groups. For example, Mexican Americans and Cuban Americans not only have different migration histories to the United States, but they are also distinctive in their political beliefs.[20] National origin groups within the pan-ethnic rubric of Asian Americans demonstrate similar differences.[21]

Racial Group Identity and Racial Group Consciousness

There is no simple way to characterize the multiplicity of identities of Americans classified as racial minorities today. Moreover, the political influence of group identity and group consciousness may differ across racial categories and individuals. In this section, we examine the individual and contextual antecedents that impact racial group identity and consciousness as well as the ways in which racial identity and consciousness affect political attitudes.

Explaining Group Identity and Consciousness

Several recent studies demonstrate the contextual nature both of group identity and group consciousness and the ways in which they operate differently for different groups. First, with respect to racial identity, Pei-te Lien and colleagues illustrate that racial identification among Asian Americans is a complex choice for group members, not a fixed, objective membership classification.[22] They found that just one-sixth of all respondents identified with this pan-ethnic term. Identifying as Asian American also varied by national origin group, ranging from 23 percent of South Asians to 12 percent of Chinese respondents. In contrast, 34 percent of all respondents reported generally identifying as ethnic American (e.g., Chinese American) and 30 percent reported a general identification with solely their ethnicity of origin (e.g., Chinese).

These results might suggest that ethnicity is more central to the group identities of Asians living in the United States than the pan-ethnic identifier of Asian American. However, when respondents who did not immediately self-identify as Asian American were asked the follow-up question, "Have you ever thought of yourself as an Asian American?" approximately 50 percent of respondents provided an affirmative response.[23] Combining the results of both the first and the second questions, Lien et al. found that "[t]ogether, close to six in ten respondents (57 percent) would consider themselves panethnic American ("Asian American") at some point in time; that percentage ranges from 50 percent for Chinese and Korean to 66 percent among Filipino respondents."[24] These results highlight the multiple identity options for Asian Americans, as well as the possibility of adopting different identities at different times. Ethno-racial identity among Asian Americans is influenced by context, including both the immediate survey context and the diverse experiences of different Asian American descent groups.

Second, with respect to racial group consciousness, the evidence suggests that environmental cues can play a role in whether one's racial group identity becomes politicized. Jane Junn and Natalie Masuoka conducted a survey experiment intended to uncover the potential effects of descriptive representation—that is, representation by an elected official who shares a particular demographic characteristic, in this case race—on African American and Asian American racial group consciousness.[25] In the experiment, half of the participants in each racial group were randomly assigned to a treatment condition in which they were exposed to photographs and brief biographies of U.S. presidential cabinet members who shared their race while the remaining participants in each racial group were not.

Junn and Masuoka hypothesized that African Americans' typically high levels of group consciousness would be unlikely to increase much further as a result of cuing descriptive representation in the treatment condition. However, they expected Asian Americans' group consciousness, though lower than that of African Americans' overall, to be more malleable in response to contextual cues that remind them of "the political consequences of being Asian American," such as exposure to same-race political actors. They found Asian Americans who received the descriptive representation treatment scored significantly higher on measures of racial group consciousness than the control group of Asian Americans. People who were exposed to the treatment were more likely than control subjects to agree that their individual fates are linked to those of Asian Americans as a group and to say that being Asian/Asian American is at least "somewhat important" to their political identity and "ideas about politics."[26] The treatment condition resulted in similar but weaker effects among African Americans, confirming Junn and Masuoka's expectations that a ceiling effect would be in operation among this already highly race conscious group. These results support their contention that racial groups have very different levels of racial group consciousness and, as a result, that they are also not influenced by the political environment to the same degree.

In his study of mayoral elections in five major U.S. cities, Matt Barreto provides evidence that a similar latent group consciousness may operate among Latinos.[27] He compared consecutive mayoral elections in Houston, Los Angeles, San Francisco, Denver, and New York—one in which a competitive Latino candidate was on the ballot and one in which a Latino candidate was not—in order to test whether Latino candidates would be more likely than non-Latino candidates to mobilize Latinos. He finds that "[p]recincts with larger proportions of Latino registrants were more likely to evidence high rates of turnout when a Latino candidate was running for office."[28] Ethnic and racial identity may be a critical factor enabling racial minorities to overcome their relative disadvantage in resources such as education, employment, and interest in politics, which have proven crucial for participating in politics.[29] Descriptive representation may activate and politicize these identities and help to level the political playing field.

Beyond candidate co-ethnicity, numerous other features of contemporary campaigns heighten Latino voters' awareness of their ethnic identity "in a way that directly connects Latino identity with politics."[30] Personalized mobilization of Spanish-surname voters, targeted ads stressing the immigrant experience, Spanish-language campaign materials, and candidate endorsements by well-known Latinos may all serve to mobilize and engage Latinos.[31] In addition, Barreto and Pedraza argue that a steady stream of immigration from Latin America anchors Latino identities in the immigrant experience and garners popular attention for Latinos, including negative attention in the form of discriminatory public discourse and policies.[32] All of this serves to further politicize Latino identity and elevate Latino group consciousness, an effect we noted earlier with regard to African Americans experiences of racial discrimination.

At the same time, Cristina Beltrán argues for greater scrutiny of the conventional wisdom of the existence of a coherent Latino political agenda in *The Trouble with Unity: Latino Politics and the Creation of Identity*.[33] Taking an historical and theoretical approach to the question of Latino political identity, Beltrán documents the distinctive ways Latinos have forged both shared similarities and distinctive perspectives in U.S. politics.

Finally, the socioeconomic context in which African Americans live matters. Cohen and Dawson found that poor and isolated black neighborhoods generate more hopelessness.[34] Gay found that the lower the quality of one's neighborhood in terms of the maintenance and value of homes, cleanliness and safety of streets, and accessibility of public and private services like reliable trash removal and grocery stores, the higher was African Americans' sense of linked fate.[35]

Diversity vs. Solidarity in Group Identity and Consciousness

Beginning with Michael Dawson's seminal work, *Behind the Mule*, the political impact of racial group consciousness, usually measured with questions about racial linked fate, has primarily been studied within the African American population.[36] Dawson's work has been used to explain the apparent homogeneity in political opinions within the black community across other lines of difference, such as class, and to explain African Americans' near universal support for the Democratic Party since the mid-1960s.

However, Cathy Cohen argues the notion of linked fate itself is limited and that

> a more accurate characterization of the political positioning of most black Americans is that of a *qualified linked fate*, whereby not every black person in crisis is seen as equally essential to the survival of the community, as an equally representative proxy of our own individual interests, and thus as equally worthy of political support by other African Americans.[37]

Cohen demonstrates the consequences of this qualified linked fate through her in-depth study of the African American political response to the HIV/AIDS crisis in the 1980s and early 1990s. She focuses on the actions of black media, organizations, and leaders in New York City, and finds that, despite eventually acknowledging that AIDS severely affects many in the black community and attempting to provide services for afflicted individuals, these black elites ultimately failed to transform most African Americans' thinking about the disease. African Americans do not view AIDS as an issue of primary importance to the black community nor are those living with AIDS in the black community "embraced and 'owned' as essential members of the group."[38]

Generalizing beyond the HIV/AIDS case, Cohen contends that black politics has historically been focused on "consensus issues construed as having an equal impact on all those sharing a primary identity based on race";[39] but increasingly, cross-cutting issues relating to the particular concerns of vulnerable or stigmatized subpopulations within the black community—usually along the lines of class, gender, and sexuality—are competing for a place on the black political agenda.

> Further, these issues bring into question and cast doubt on the idea that a shared group identity and feelings of linked fate can lead to the unified group resistance or mobilization that has proved so essential to the survival and progress of black and other marginal people.[40]

Cohen's study challenges us to think more carefully about how racial minority groups address internal heterogeneity, highlighting the complexities of group consciousness and its dependency both on context for activation or development and on the subpopulation and issue area to which it is applied.

Building on Dawson's historical account of the heterogeneity of black ideological traditions,[41] Melissa Harris-Lacewell examines the adult socialization processes that occur in the contemporary black counterpublic—including social spaces like barbershops, churches, and media outlets. She demonstrates that ordinary African American citizens make sense of the world and form "identifiable patterns of public opinion that can be understood as ideologies" through processes of "everyday talk."[42] In the segregated spaces of the black counterpublic, African Americans can feel free to candidly talk to each other "beyond the gaze of racial others," particularly whites, and this conversation serves to socially (re)construct a variety of unique black worldviews.[43] Harris-Lacewell identifies four black political ideologies that continue to operate today: Black Conservatism, Liberal Integrationism, Black Feminism, and Black Nationalism. While there are similarities between these ideologies and the traditional liberal–conservative spectrum used in survey research (developed to understand white ideology), the relevant difference between the two overall frameworks is in whether there is a deliberate recognition of race as politically salient. Whereas the white ideological spectrum is, on its face, race neutral, Harris-Lacewell argues that all of the black political ideologies are built upon a kind of black race consciousness that she calls "black common sense."[44] Exactly *how* one believes that being black matters is proscribed by one's ideology.

Work on other racial groups also emphasizes the important types of diversity within each group. Abrajano, for example, argues that Latinos who speak English orient more toward the substance of issues in political campaigns, while Latinos who speak only Spanish are more oriented toward easily digestible cues to their ethnic identity and language.[45] More generally, some scholars raise questions about the downside of group solidarity and political unanimity. Blacks have been called a "captured" group with the Democratic Party, and thus they lack the influence that comes with the credible threat of defecting to the other party.[46] Latinos vote Democratic but in less consistent and uniform numbers, and this may give them leverage to get more of what they want from politics.[47] In addition, when group membership becomes a simplistic cue, it can produce support for co-ethnic leaders or for parties at odds with what fully informed voters would choose.[48]

Taken together, these studies of minority group identity and racial consciousness illustrate the complexity of conceptualizing and measuring how Asian Americans, Latinos, and African Americans understand their relationships to one another, and how these factors are related to public opinion.

What Influences Public Opinion?

Among the multiple facets of public opinion and factors influencing political attitudes, we focus on: (1) party identification and mobilization, (2) interpersonal contact and the racial and economic context, and (3) perceptions of and experiences with discrimination. It is crucial to consider how and why the same antecedents might work in distinctive ways for different groups.

Partisan Identification

Scholars have consistently identified partisanship as the most enduring, stable, and powerful of all political predispositions.[49] For white Americans, party identification amounts to an early emotional attachment to one party or the other, often learned through socialization in the home or other institutions. The available evidence indicates that (overwhelmingly Democratic) partisanship is acquired through similar processes of institutional socialization for African Americans, though for this group, partisanship appears to be more instrumental and group-interested than affective.

It is unclear how immigrant-based racial groups acquire partisanship when often their early and even adult political socialization does not occur in the United States and, as demonstrated by the work of Rogers[50] and Jones-Correa,[51] they encounter numerous barriers to institutional incorporation once in the United States. Wong argues that the longer an immigrant resides in the U.S.,[52] the greater political exposure she will have, the more likely she is to become a citizen, and the more likely she is to learn English proficiently; thus, the more likely she will be to identify with one of the political parties.

Wong and her colleagues also examined partisan *choice* among the Asian American respondents interviewed in the 2008 National Asian American Survey and found that, overall, 48 percent of Asian Americans identify as Democrats, 31 percent as independent, and 22 percent as Republicans.[53] There was internal variation among Asian Americans by national origin group, with Japanese, Koreans, Asian Indians, and Filipinos being the most Democratic (50 percent or more), Chinese being most likely to call themselves independents (46 percent) or Democrats (41 percent), and Vietnamese being most likely to identify as Republican (45 percent).

Party mobilization (or lack of it) also seems to be a pivotal factor in whether and how immigrant groups are incorporated into the American polity. Being ignored or excluded by local political parties discourages naturalization,[54] which in turn depresses the acquisition of partisanship, while becoming a citizen and being brought into the fold by the political parties encourages immigrants to adopt a partisan identification, likely that of whichever party is most welcoming.[55]

Race Relations

Developed under the black–white paradigm, two primary hypotheses have been advanced relative to the impact of cross-racial exposure: the *threat hypothesis* and the *contact hypothesis*. Most basically, greater exposure between members of different races will worsen race relations according to the threat hypothesis but improve race relations under the contact hypothesis. Classical formulations of the threat hypothesis predict that dominant groups will perceive increasing threats to their political and economic privileges as the population of subordinate group members in the immediate environment increases; then, as threats to resources increase so do dominant group hostilities toward subordinate groups.[56] The contact hypothesis, on the other hand, predicts improved racial relations and cooperation through interpersonal contact under certain ideal conditions of equal status and shared objectives.[57] Because of the different ways in which Asian Americans and Latinos have been incorporated into and racialized within U.S. society, it is unclear whether and how these hypotheses may apply to whites' attitudes toward these non-black groups. Locations with larger populations of Latinos and African Americans show systematic differences in opinion and behavior.[58] Similarly, how these frameworks might operate among racial minorities to inform their attitudes toward other minority groups and whites remains to be seen.

Several recent studies help to remedy these uncertainties by taking a closer look at environmental particulars and extending research to a multiethnic context. Welch et al. provide support for the contact hypothesis in their finding that integrated neighborhoods actually reduce racial hostilities by promoting interactions between members of different racial groups.[59] At the same time, the prevalence of racially segregated neighborhoods noted by Massey and Denton[60] calls the primary mechanism of the racial threat hypothesis in question; that is, whites are unlikely to live in neighborhoods with African Americans, so observing the size of the black population and thus perceiving a threat to one's resources and privileges would appear to be an unlikely source of white hostility (note that by this same logic, interracial contact also seems unlikely to occur).[61] Accordingly, Oliver and Mendelberg emphasize the importance of analyzing environmental factors at both the smaller neighborhood level and the larger metropolitan level.

Oliver and Mendelberg find that the size of the African American population is unrelated to white racial attitudes at the neighborhood level, though it is moderately related to whites' anti-black stereotypes at the metropolitan level. However, the strongest contextual effects come from neighborhood educational composition, a measure of white economic vulnerability, not racial composition. Furthermore, whites living in low-education contexts are not only more racially prejudiced but also more anti-Semitic and authoritarian than whites living in higher education contexts. They attribute this generalized out-group hostility to the psychological stresses of living in economically vulnerable environments and suggest that in the specific racial context of the United States, such generalized out-group hostility is perhaps most often directed at African Americans. Considering the rapidly changing racial topography of the United States, future research should explore the impact of these psychological stresses on attitudes toward other racial minorities as well.

Contrary to Oliver and Mendelberg's findings in the case of whites and African Americans, Claudine Gay finds that the *overall* economic conditions of a neighborhood do not influence African Americans' expressions of anti-Latino prejudice.[62] Instead, it is the *relative* economic positions of the two racial groups that matter. That is, African Americans who shared neighborhoods with economically advantaged Latinos exhibited more prejudice against Latinos, were less supportive of "special preferences in hiring and promotion" for Latinos than they were for themselves, and agreed more with the statement "more good jobs for Latinos means fewer good jobs for Blacks."[63] Both racial prejudice and unsupportive policy attitudes intensified somewhat as the size of the Latino population increased but only in contexts of Latino economic advantage. When African Americans are better off than or economically equal to their Latino neighbors, the groups' relative positions have no impact on blacks' attitudes toward Latinos. These results lend partial support to the threat hypotheses and suggest that interpersonal contact may only be effective under conditions of economic equality.

Oliver and Wong take the research that can be used to adjudicate between the threat and contact hypotheses several steps further by using interview data taken from all four of the primary racial groups while analytically distinguishing between smaller neighborhood and larger metropolitan contexts.[64] They examined racial prejudices among these groups and found that among whites, African Americans, and Latinos the more integrated the neighborhood the less hostility they expressed toward racial out-groups. Asian Americans who were interviewed in English followed a similar pattern; however, Chinese and Korean respondents who were interviewed in their native languages reported greater prejudice when living in more integrated neighborhoods. The authors speculate that these findings may be related to the lower level of incorporation that non-English-speaking Asian Americans experience, or possibly to the violence in Los Angeles against Asian American small businesses that occurred shortly before the survey was administered. Overall, these neighborhood-level findings provide support in favor of the contact hypothesis but against the threat hypothesis.

Oliver and Wong's key finding, however, is that these effects were most apparent in metropolitan areas in which there were large populations of racial out-groups—a central tenet of the threat hypothesis. For example, African Americans and whites living in racially homogeneous neighborhoods in Los Angeles displayed much higher rates of anti-Latino sentiment than their counterparts in Atlanta because the size of the Latino population in the Los Angeles metropolis is much greater than in Atlanta.[65] Their different findings relative to minority group size depending upon whether the analysis was conducted using the neighborhood or the city as the unit of analysis helps to explain why previous research on the threat and contact hypotheses has been so mixed: researchers were using different units of analysis. Moreover, as Oliver and Wong conclude, their "findings strongly suggest that it is not only critical to consider the effects of local context on racial attitudes, but also how these attitudes depend to some degree on the relationship between neighborhood and larger metropolitan contexts."[66]

Discrimination

Dennis Chong and Dukhong Kim's "theory of opportunities" echoes our theme, that "[t]he assimilation of a minority group into American society depends not only on the actions of group members but also on the reception accorded that group by the majority population."[67] Specifically, they ask why members with higher economic status sometimes continue to have strong racial group consciousness. They find that the effects of class will depend upon racial group members' perceptions of opportunities for social mobility—beliefs about their chances of moving up in the world.

At the group level—that is, looking at between-group differences among African Americans, Asian Americans, and Latinos—Chong and Kim find that economic status has the smallest effect on African Americans' levels of group consciousness. They find that support for policies that benefit the group is least affected by improved economic fortunes for African Americans, relative to other racial groups, because of frequent experiences with discrimination and perceptions that blacks have fewer opportunities relative to whites. In contrast, improved economic status for Asian Americans and Latinos is often accompanied by fewer experiences with discrimination and a more positive outlook on U.S. society, making increased economic status for these groups a significant predictor of diminished support for racial group interests.

Chong and Kim find the same dynamic at work at the individual level. In other words, when they focus on the between-person differences within each racial minority group, they find that economic status has no effect on group consciousness for minority individuals, including Asian Americans and Latinos, who frequently experience discrimination and perceive unequal opportunities. In contrast, high economic status reduces support for group interests among individuals from all racial minority groups who have few experiences with discrimination and believe that U.S. society offers equal opportunities for all.

Importantly, Chong and Kim's research contradicts earlier scholarship on black public opinion. Sigelman and Welch found that African Americans' perceptions of group discrimination influenced their views about the sources of racial disparities, and both these perceptions and explanations influenced the policy solutions that African Americans preferred to remedy racial inequality.[68] Furthermore, they found that African Americans perceived much higher levels of discrimination against blacks as a group than they reported experiencing personally, and, as such, personal experiences with discrimination had little effect on their attitudes.

But why do personal experiences with discrimination impact African Americans' opinions in Chong and Kim's 2006 study but not in that of Sigelman and Welch in 1991? In answering this question, it is critical to look at the ways in which the different pairs of researchers measured their personal discrimination variables. Chong and Kim used a combination of seven wide-ranging questions to measure respondents' levels of perceived discrimination, including questions that ask whether respondents have experienced discrimination in the past ten years or have ever been "physically threatened or attacked" or "unfairly stopped by police."[69] Respondents in Chong and Kim's 2006 study were also asked about the frequency with which they have been given "less respect" and "poorer service" (while shopping or dining) than others, as well as about how often people insult or call them names or seem fearful of them because of their race. In contrast, Sigelman and Welch used four questions about basic "quality of life" issues, which they acknowledged were "fairly crude," including whether respondents had ever been discriminated against in getting "quality education" and "decent" housing, jobs, and wages.[70] Sigelman and Welch astutely note that their measurements "ignore possible discrimination in the daily routines of life," like shopping, eating at restaurants, and interacting with others in the community.[71] As Chong and Kim's measures highlight, Sigelman and Welch's research also fails to capture discrimination at the hands of state actors like the police.

The causes of others' perceptions of discrimination against out-group members are also important to understand because of the consequences these perceptions have for public opinion about policies intended to benefit racial minority groups. Whites' belief that blacks are discriminated against is positively correlated with white support for a range of policies that serve to ameliorate racial inequality, like affirmative action, as well as less race conscious policies.[72] Believing that African Americans, Latinos, and Asian Americans continue to be discriminated against is positively related to support for policies intended to benefit all racial minorities, including job training, educational assistance, and preferential hiring and promotion programs, among white, African American, Latino, and Asian American respondents.[73]

Concluding Remarks

We began our review of research in political science on race and the group bases of public opinion by describing the complexity and the socially constructed nature of racial categories in the United States. Despite the inherent difficulties in measuring these concepts, race and ethnicity remain among the most important divisions in political attitudes among Americans. To better understand the group bases of public opinion, researchers have attempted to define, measure, and examine the three key concepts of *racial group membership* (what we have referred to as racial categorization), *racial group identity*, and *racial group consciousness*. Most scholarship has focused on one of the four primary racial groups: whites, African Americans, Latinos, and Asian Americans. Michael Dawson developed the concept of *linked fate* from the experiences of African Americans in U.S. politics. This idea has been influential in scholarship in racial and ethnic politics; however, the extent to which the concept is applicable to other minority populations facing different political circumstances, including Asian Americans and Latinos, is not clear. Differences in the ways in which individuals understand the same questions on surveys, and the distinctive contexts in which surveys are administered, complicate the measurement and comparison of group membership, identity, and consciousness across groups.

We conclude that the contours of the relationships between racial group identity, racial group consciousness, and public opinion, particularly for Latinos and Asian Americans, are not well understood because of the dynamic nature of these populations and the still-early stage of systematic research. For members of these pan-ethnic racial groups, identification is a complex choice. For all racial and ethnic groups, membership and identity are fluid and primarily based on the forces of politics and the circumstances of society. They are not fixed or objective. Within all groups, there are important tensions between unity and difference, favored status and marginalization.

Finally, we reviewed three widely studied causes of public opinion, including party identification, race relations, and perceptions of discrimination. In terms of race relations, the contextual interaction between neighborhood and metropolis and the mixture of the resident groups is key to understanding public opinion. In terms of discrimination, it is crucial to understand how the discriminatory treatment directed at a group member, and her interaction with society, vary systematically as a function of her group membership. The different historical and current circumstances of groups explain the varied outlooks their members adopt on individual opportunity.

Notes

1. Masuoka, Natalie. 2008. "Political Attitudes and Ideologies of Multiracial Americans: The Implications of Mixed Race in the United States." *Political Research Quarterly*, 61 (June): 253–267; Williams, Kim M. 2006. *Mark One or More: Civil Rights in Multiracial America*. Ann Arbor, MI: University of Michigan Press.

2. Rogers, Reuel. 2006. *Afro-Caribbean Immigrants and the Politics of Incorporation: Ethnicity, Exception or Exit.* Cambridge, MA: Cambridge University Press; Alex-Assensoh, Yvette. 2009. "African Immigrants and African-Americans: An Analysis of Voluntary African Immigration and the Evolution of Black Ethnic Politics in America." *African and Asian Studies*, 8: 89–124.
3. Omi, Michael and Howard Winant. 1994. *Racial Formation in the United States: From the 1960s to the 1990s.* New York: Routledge; Marx, Anthony W. 1998. *Making Race and Nation: A Comparison of the U.S., South Africa, and Brazil.* New York: Cambridge University Press; Roediger, David. 1999. *The Wages of Whiteness: Race and the Making of the American Working Class.* New York: Verso Books.
4. Nobles, Melissa. 2000. *Shades of Citizenship: Race and the Census in Modern Politics.* Stanford, CA: Stanford University Press.
5. Katznelson, Ira. 2005. *When Affirmative Action Was White: An Untold History of Racial Inequality in Twentieth-Century America.* New York: W.W. Norton & Company; Smith, Rogers. 1997. *Civic Ideals: Conflicting Visions of Citizenship in U.S. History.* New Haven, CT: Yale University Press; Tichenor, Daniel J. 2002. *Dividing Lines: The Politics of Immigration Control in America.* Princeton, NJ: Princeton University Press.
6. Frymer, Paul. 2008. *Black and Blue: African Americans, the Labor Movement, and the Decline of the Democratic Party.* Princeton, NJ: Princeton University Press.
7. Hattam, Victoria. 2007. *In the Shadow of Race: Jews, Latinos, and Immigrant Politics in the United States.* Chicago, IL: University of Chicago Press; Ignatiev, Noel. 1995. *How the Irish Became White.* New York: Routledge; Jacobson, Matthew Frye. 1999. *Whiteness of a Different Color: European Immigrants and the Alchemy of Race.* Cambridge, MA: Harvard University Press; Gross, Ariela. 2008. *What Blood Won't Tell: A History of Race on Trial in America.* Cambridge, MA: Harvard University Press.
8. Lopez, Ian Haney. 2006. *White by Law: The Legal Construction of Race*, revised and expanded edition. New York: New York University Press.
9. Daniels, Roger. 2004. *Guarding the Golden Door: American Immigration Policy and Immigrants since 1882.* New York: Hill and Wang.
10. Ngai, Mae. 2004. *Impossible Subjects: Illegal Aliens and the Making of Modern America.* Princeton, NJ: Princeton University Press.
11. Kim, Claire. 1999. "The Racial Triangulation of Asian Americans." *Politics and Society* 27 (March): 105–138.
12. McClain, Paula, Jessica D. Johnson Carew, Eugene Walton, Jr., and Candis S. Watts. 2009. "Group Membership, Group Identity, and Group Consciousness: Measures of Racial Identity in American Politics?" *Annual Review of Political Science*, 12: 471–485.
13. McClain et al. 2009: 474, 476, emphasis in original.
14. Dawson, Michael. 1994. *Behind the Mule: Race and Class in African American Politics.* Princeton, NJ: Princeton University Press.
15. Jones-Correa, Michael. 1998. *Between Two Nations: The Political Predicament of Latinos in New York City.* Ithaca, NY: Cornell University Press.
16. Jones-Correa 1998; Rogers 2006.
17. Lee, Taeku. 2008. "Race, Immigration, and the Identity-to-Politics Link." *Annual Review of Political Science*, 11 (June): 457–478; Chong, Dennis and Reuel Rogers. 2005. "Racial Solidarity and Political Participation." *Political Behavior*, 27 (December): 347–374.
18. McClain, P.D., N.M. Carter, V.M. DeFrancesco Soto, M.L. Lyle, J.D. Grynaviski, S.C. Nunnally, T.J. Scotto, J.A. Kendrick, G.F. Lackey, and K.D. Cotton. 2006. "Racial Distancing in a Southern City: Latino Immigrants' Views of Black Americans." *Journal of Politics*, 68: 571–584. Saenz, Rogelio. 2005. "Latinos and the

Changing Face of America," in *The American People: Census 2000*, Eds., Reynolds Farley and John Haaga. New York: Russell Sage Foundation, 352–379.
19. Barreto, Matt and Francisco Pedraza. 2009. "The Renewal and Persistence of Group Identification in American Politics." *Electoral Studies*, 28: 595–605.
20. Barreto and Pedraza 2009; Fraga, Luis Ricardo, John A. Garcia, Rodney E. Hero, Michael Jones-Correa, Valerie Martinez-Ebers, and Gary M. Segura. 2010. *Latino Lives in America: Making it Home*. Philadelphia, PA: Temple University Press.
21. Lien, Pei-te, M. Margaret Conway, and Janelle Wong. 2003. "The Contours and Sources of Ethnic Identity Choices Among Asian Americans." *Social Science Quarterly*, 84 (June): 461–481; Ramakrishnan, S. Karthick, Janelle Wong, Taeku Lee, and Jane Junn. 2009. "Race-Based Considerations and the Obama Vote." *DuBois Review*, 6: 219–238.
22. Lien et al. 2003.
23. Ibid., p. 465.
24. Ibid., p. 466.
25. Junn, Jane and Natalie Masuoka. 2008. "Asian American Identity: Shared Racial Status and Political Context." *Perspectives on Politics*, 6 (December): 729–740.
26. Ibid., p. 737.
27. Barreto, Matt. 2007. "Si Se Puede! Latino Candidates and the Mobilization of Latino Voters." *American Political Science Review*, 101 (August): 425–441.
28. Ibid., p. 438.
29. Tate, Katherine. 1993. *From Protest to Politics: The New Black Voters in American Elections*. New York: Russell Sage Foundation.
30. Barreto and Pedraza 2009, p. 599.
31. Abrajano, Marisa A. and R. Michael Alvarez. 2010. *New Faces New Voices: The Hispanic Electorate in America*. Princeton, NJ: Princeton University Press.
32. Barreto and Pedraza 2009.
33. Beltrán, Cristina. 2010. *The Trouble with Unity: Latino Politics and the Creation of Identity*. New York: Oxford University Press.
34. Cohen, Cathy and Michael Dawson. 1993. "Neighborhood Poverty and African American Politics." *American Political Science Review*, 87 (June): 286–302.
35. Gay, Claudine. 2004. "Putting Race in Context: Identifying the Environmental Determinants of Black Racial Attitudes." *American Political Science Review*, 98 (November): 547–562.
36. Dawson 1994.
37. Cohen, Cathy. 1999. *The Boundaries of Blackness: AIDS and the Breakdown of Black Politics*. Chicago, IL: University of Chicago Press, pp. x–xi, emphasis added.
38. Cohen 1999, p. 118.
39. Cohen 1999, p. 8.
40. Cohen 1999, p. 13.
41. Dawson, Michael. 2001. *Black Visions: The Roots of Contemporary African-American Political Ideologies*. Chicago, IL: University of Chicago Press.
42. Harris-Lacewell, Melissa. 2004. *Barbershops, Bibles, and BET: Everyday Talk and Black Political Thought*. Princeton, NJ: Princeton University Press, p. xxiii.
43. Ibid., p. 9.
44. Ibid., p. 23.
45. Abrajano and Alvarez 2010.
46. Frymer, Paul. 1999. *Uneasy Alliances: Race and Party Competition in America*. Princeton, NJ: Princeton University Press.
47. Pantoja, Adrian D., Ricardo Ramirez, and Gary M. Segura. 2001. "Citizens by Choice, Voters by Necessity: Patterns of Political Mobilization by Naturalized Latinos." *Political Research Quarterly*, 54: 729–750.
48. Kuklinski, James H. and Norman L. Hurley. 1994. "On Hearing and Interpreting

Political Messages: A Cautionary Tale of Citizen Cue-Taking." *Journal of Politics*, 56: 729–751; Philpot, Tasha. 2007. *Race, Republicans, and the Return of the Party of Lincoln*. Ann Arbor, MI: University of Michigan Press; Mansbridge, Jane and Katherine Tate. 1992. "Race Trumps Gender: The Thomas Nomination in the Black Community." *PS: Political Science and Politics*, 25: 488–492.

49. Campbell, Angus, Philip Converse, Warren Miller, and Donald Stokes. 1960. *The American Voter*. Chicago, IL: University of Chicago Press.
50. Rogers 2006.
51. Jones-Correa 1998.
52. Wong, Janelle. 2000. "The Effects of Age and Political Exposure on the Development of Party Identification among Asian American and Latino Immigrants in the United States." *Political Behavior*, 22: 341–371.
53. Wong, Janelle, S. Karthick Ramakrishnan, Taeku Lee, and Jane Junn. 2011. *Asian American Political Participation: Emerging Constituents and their Political Identities*. New York: Russell Sage Foundation.
54. Rogers 2006; Jones-Correa 1998.
55. Wong 2000; Lien, Pei-te, Christian Collet, Janelle Wong, and S. Kathick Ramakrishnan. 2001. "Asian Pacific-American Public Opinion and Political Participation." *PS: Political Science and Politics*, 34 (September): 625–630.
56. Key, V.O. 1984 [1949]. *Southern Politics in State and Nation*. New York: Knopf; Blalock, Hubert M. 1967. *Toward a Theory of Minority-Group Relations*. New York: Wiley.
57. Allport, Gordon. 1954. *The Nature of Prejudice*. Cambridge: Addison-Wesley Publishing Company.
58. Hajnal, Zoltan. 2007. *Changing White Attitudes toward Black Political Leadership*. New York: Cambridge University Press; Hero, Rodney E. and Caroline Tolbert. 2005. "Exploring Minority Political Efficacy: Considering the Impact of Social and Institutional Context," in *Diversity and Democracy: Minority Representation in the United States*, Eds., Gary Segura and Shaun Bowler. Charlottesville, VA: University of Virginia Press, pp. 170–189.
59. Welch, Susan, Lee Sigelman, Timothy Bledsoe, and Michael Combs. 2001. *Race & Place: Race Relations in an American City*. Cambridge: Cambridge University Press.
60. Massey, Douglas and Nancy Denton. 1993. *American Apartheid: Segregation and the Making of the Underclass*. Cambridge, MA: Harvard University Press.
61. Oliver, Eric J. and Tali Mendelberg. 2000. "Reconsidering the Environmental Determinants of White Racial Attitudes." *American Journal of Political Science*, 44 (July): 574–589.
62. Gay, Claudine. 2006. "Seeing Difference: The Effects of Economic Disparity on Black Attitudes toward Latinos." *American Journal of Political Science*, 50 (October): 982–997.
63. Ibid., p. 990.
64. Oliver, Eric J. and Janelle Wong. 2003. "Intergroup Prejudice in Multiethnic Settings." *American Journal of Political Science*, 47 (October): 567–582.
65. Ibid.
66. Ibid., p. 575.
67. Chong, Dennis and Dukhong Kim. 2006. "The Experiences and Effects of Economic Status among Racial and Ethnic Minorities." *American Political Science Review*, 100 (August): 336–337.
68. Sigelman, Lee and Susan Welch. 1991. *Black Americans Views of Racial Inequality: The Dream Deferred*. Cambridge: Cambridge University Press.
69. Chong and Kim 2006, p. 350.
70. Sigelman and Welch 1991, pp. 55, 59.

71. Ibid., p. 59.
72. Kinder, Donald and Lynn Sanders. 1996. *Divide By Color: Racial Politics and Democratic Ideals.* Chicago, IL: University of Chicago Press; Sears, David O., Jim Sidanius, and Lawrence Bobo (Eds.). 2000. *Racialized Politics: The Debate About Racism in America.* Chicago, IL: University of Chicago Press.
73. Lopez, Linda and Adrian D. Pantoja. 2004. "Beyond Black and White: General Support for Race-Conscious Policies among African Americans, Latinos, Asian Americans and Whites." *Political Research Quarterly*, 57 (December): 633–642.

Chapter 7

Categorical Politics

Gender, Race, and Public Opinion

Nancy Burns and Donald Kinder

Research on public opinion is booming, and this holds particularly for investigations that center on gender or on race. For those of us trying to keep up, it is downright alarming. Every time we turn around, there are more papers to read, more books to review, more conferences to attend, and more findings to assimilate. Our purpose here is to bring some order and coherence to this lively and rapidly expanding field of scholarship.

We begin by enumerating important features that gender and race share in common and then point out one major difference. This one difference, which has to do with how gender and race are organized in society, has far-reaching ramifications for the distinct roles that gender and race play in public opinion. Or so we try to show here, as we take up a series of consequential political puzzles: the changing relationship between gender and race and the American party system; gender gaps and racial divides in public opinion on policy; gender and race as sources of group solidarity; gender and race as objects of attitude; and, finally, the activation of gender and race in politics. In the conclusion, we speculate, cautiously, on the future.[1]

Important Similarities between Gender and Race—And One Big Difference

Gender and race are alike in several important respects. Both are socially constructed; both are central to how we think about ourselves and about others; and both represent relationships of ongoing inequality. Gender and race also differ from one another—most notably, in the way that men and women, on the one hand, and blacks and whites, on the other, are distributed in everyday life. Understanding the parts played by gender and by race in public opinion begins with an appreciation of these factors.

Gender and Race as Social Constructions

Sex is a biological concept. It has to do with genetic structure, with physiology, and anatomy. Women give birth, breast-feed infants, and menstruate;

men do not. On average, men are larger and stronger. These physical facts of life are real—but they are trivial compared to the extraordinary and far-reaching arrangements and practices that constitute relations between men and women in modern society. This is gender. Gender is what society makes of sex.[2]

Much the same can be said about race. If, as the *Oxford English Dictionary* asserts, race is "One of the great divisions of mankind, having certain physical properties in common," then, according to modern biology, no such thing exists. The idea that all of human diversity can be reduced to a small number of pure races is nonsense.[3] And yet our social beliefs and practices are organized as if race were real.

Gender and Race as Mental Categories

Categories are essential to human thinking. In their absence, mental life would be overwhelmed by detail, language staggeringly complex, and communication virtually impossible.[4] As far as experiencing and understanding social life are concerned, no categories are more important than gender and race. The capacity for classifying the social world in these terms emerges very early. Before children have command of language, they are able to make gender and race distinctions. By age three, children "know" whether they are a boy or a girl and whether they are white or black. Around the time they enter kindergarten, they have come to believe that gender and race are fixed and immutable. They understand differences between men and women and between whites and blacks as natural. Gender and race are now central to their sense of personal identity and central as well to how they think about others, tendencies they carry with them through the rest of their lives.[5]

Gender and Race as Sites of Durable Inequality

In the United States, as in other advanced industrial societies, individuals vary tremendously in wealth, power, and status. Inequality is generated in part by individual differences in talent and enterprise. It is generated in part by luck, good and bad. And it is generated in part by recurrent social processes, whereby different social groups are subject, again and again, over time and across situations, to systematically different treatment.

Over the course of American history, men and women and blacks and whites have often been singled out in this way. Indeed, gender and race are exemplary instances of what Charles Tilly calls "durable inequalities." Tilly argues that differences in advantage that pivot on categorical opposites—male versus female, black versus white, Muslim versus Jew, citizen versus foreigner, Catholic versus Protestant—tend to be persistent. Durable inequality—inequality that lasts—depends heavily on the institutionalization of categorical pairs.[6]

In Tilly's theory, systems of enduring categorical inequality are established by two general processes. The first of these is *exploitation*, whereby members of a categorically bounded network command resources from which they draw significantly increased returns, accomplished by denying outsiders the full value of their efforts. Slavery provides an extreme example.[7]

Complementing exploitation is a second mechanism, *opportunity hoarding*, whereby members of a categorically bounded network gain control over a valued resource from which outsiders are excluded. Depending on time and place, hoarding might encompass high-paying jobs, good education, desirable neighborhoods, or any other valued resource.

Once established, categorical inequality is generalized by a process of *emulation*, whereby existing inequalities are transplanted from one setting to another. This can take place in labor markets when firms copy categorical inequalities established in other settings. Some firms assign certain jobs—high paying, promising advancement—to one group (say, whites), and assign other kinds of jobs—low paying, dead end—to another group (say, blacks). Other firms follow suit. Eventually the practice generates pools of workers with different experiences and different capabilities defined along group lines. Firms hire and promote accordingly. The result is categorical inequality entrenched within an entire industry.[8]

Inequality is locked into place through *adaptation*, whereby daily routines are organized around categorical distinctions. One variety is the invention of norms governing day-to-day interaction between members of categorically unequal groups, as in the extensive and intricate system of deference that grew up between blacks and whites in the Jim Crow south. Racial "etiquette" guided every detail of every encounter—forms of address, topics of conversation, appropriate demeanor, and more—thereby providing blacks and whites a regular reminder of the unbridgeable gulf that separated them.[9]

As categorical inequality spreads, participants invent stories about social group differences. Such stories are first and foremost boundary maintaining: they "embody shared understandings of who we are, who they are, what divides us, and what connects us." Members of advantaged groups create what Elizabeth Anderson calls "stigmatizing stories." Their purpose is to explain and rationalize inequality. In such stories, glaring differences between groups in wealth, power, and status are accounted for by corresponding differences between groups in talent, virtue, or culture.[10]

Today, of course, slavery is gone. The Jim Crow regime of racial oppression that followed emancipation has been dismantled. The 1964 Civil Rights Act made discrimination by race illegal, and surely it is neither as flagrant nor as pervasive today as it once was. But this does *not* mean that exploitation and opportunity hoarding along racial lines have disappeared. Evidence to the contrary is overwhelming.

African Americans still face discrimination in the labor market. African Americans looking to purchase homes are still steered away from white neighborhoods and still subject to racial bias in mortgage lending. African Americans still endure racist epithets on the streets, harassment by police officers in public spaces, rudeness, excessive surveillance, and price discrimination while they shop, coolness from their teachers and bosses, and racist jokes from their co-workers.[11]

More generally, in American society today, race and disadvantage remain closely inter-connected. Take the basic matter of health. Black women who bear children today are much less likely to lose an infant than were their parents and grandparents before them, but the infant mortality rate remains more than twice as high among blacks than among whites. Moreover, black children who survive their first year can look forward to poorer health, more illness, and a substantially shorter life, on average, than white children.[12]

Likewise, while African Americans made significant inroads into the middle class over the last fifty years, sharing in the economic prosperity that came to all of American society following World War II, racial differences remain and they are imposing. Blacks are twice as likely to be unemployed; they are substantially over-represented among "discouraged workers," those who have given up looking for work and so do not appear in official unemployment figures; and when blacks are employed, they earn less. These differences are large, but they are nothing compared to racial differences in wealth. According to recent figures, the average white household commands more than *ten* times the financial assets of the average black household.[13]

Progress and inequality also characterize the domain of politics. Thanks to the heroic efforts of the Civil Rights Movement, black participation in political life towers over what it was a generation or two ago. And as a consequence of *that*, many blacks now hold positions of political authority.[14] In 1965, the year of the Voting Rights Act, of the 435 elected officials serving in the U.S. House of Representatives, just four were black. Not a single black served in the Senate. Just three were mayors of American cities. In the entire country, fewer than 300 blacks held elected office, most as members of school boards, city councils, or state houses. A decade later the number of blacks holding elective office across the nation had increased more than tenfold. This sharp upward trend continued through the 1970s, but now is leveling off—and leveling off well below strict proportionality. African Americans make up roughly 13 percent of the voting age population in the United States, but they comprise less than 2 percent of elected officials. Blacks have made impressive gains in politics—illustrated most dramatically by Barack Obama's election in 2008—but taken all around, black Americans remain substantially underrepresented.[15]

In Tilly's theory, remember, differences in advantage that pivot on categorical opposites are especially likely to endure. According to Tilly, "paired and unequal categories do crucial organizational work, producing marked, durable differences in access to valued resources. Durable inequality depends heavily on the institutionalization of categorical pairs."[16] Race qualifies in this respect, but so, too, does gender. Indeed, the categorical distinction between men and women is no doubt the oldest and most durable of social distinctions. All human societies engender the social world. Everywhere, women do more of the "tending, cooking, cleaning, clothing, washing, nurturing, and otherwise caring for people." Societies vary tremendously in how sharply they are stratified by gender, of course. In the contemporary United States, men generally amass more wealth, exercise greater power, and enjoy higher status than women.[17]

Parallels between gender and race in this respect are striking. In the first place, for most of American history, women were denied first-class citizenship. Full voting rights did not come to American women until 1920 with ratification of the 19th Amendment. In the 1930s about one half the states still denied married women ownership of their wages. Not until 1979 did sexual harassment became a serious legal concept. And not until 1984 did courts find it possible for rape to take place within marriage. Domestic violence, sexual abuse, rape, prostitution, and pornography remain commonplace features of contemporary American life. All this can be read as evidence of women's subordinate place.[18]

Economic inequality in gender relations in the United States has been generated and maintained principally by separating men and women into distinctive occupational structures. Over most of American history, this separation was accomplished by assigning women to work inside the household and men to work outside the household. After the turn of the twentieth century, increasing numbers of women entered the paid labor force, but as they did so they were steered away from positions of influence and authority. Stenographer, typist, secretary, and filing clerk became women's jobs; supervisor, manager, partner, and professional were reserved for men.[19]

Over the last thirty years, gender's role in the structure, organization, and operation of the labor market has diminished. Women now constitute nearly one-half of the U.S. labor force. The gap in earnings between men and women is narrowing. Educational and employment opportunities for women are opening up. But economic inequalities between men and women still exist. Under current trajectories, they will not disappear anytime soon.[20]

A final parallel we will draw between race and gender has to do with politics. We've already noted that full voting rights were not extended to American women until 1920. In the immediate aftermath of the 19th Amendment's ratification, differences in participation between men and women were enormous. Now they are negligible. Today, on such matters as turning out to vote, working on a campaign, serving on a local governing board, or attending a public meeting, women take part nearly as often, and sometimes more often, than men.[21]

With increases in political participation have come increases in political power. In 1974, Jeane Kirkpatrick began her groundbreaking study of female state legislators with this crisp assertion:

> Half a century after the ratification of the nineteenth amendment, no woman has been nominated to be president or vice president, no woman has served on the Supreme Court. Today, there is no woman in the cabinet, no woman serving as governor of a major state, no woman mayor of a major city, no woman in the top leadership of either major party.[22]

Things have changed. Over the last thirty years, women have made dramatic progress in securing positions of political authority. But, as in the case of race, so, too, for gender, progress toward full equality on this front has recently slowed. Despite impressive gains, women—like African Americans—remain substantially underrepresented in the halls of power.[23]

Gender and Race in Society

As norms and practices, gender and race are made by society. As mental categories, gender and race are important and consequential features of how we think about ourselves and others. As sites for discrimination and exclusion, gender and race remain prime examples of durable inequality. In all these important respects, gender and race are alike.

Gender and race are not alike in all respects, however. Most significantly for our purposes here, gender and race differ from one another in their social organization. Gender and race are "made" by society, but they are made in very different ways. The social organization of gender emphasizes intimacy; the social organization of race emphasizes separation.

For analytic purposes, it is useful, as Goffman points out, to distinguish between two kinds of disadvantaged groups: "those that can and tend to be sequestered off into entire families and neighborhoods and those that do not." Women belong to the latter category. Women are not segregated into enclaves—but neither are they scattered haphazardly through the social structure. On the contrary, women "are allocated distributively to households in the form of female children, and then later, but still distributively, to other households in the form of wives." Women spend much of their lives in intimate relationships with men: with fathers, husbands, brothers, and sons.[24]

Things are very different for race. A persistent feature of race relations in the United States is spatial segregation. Despite federal fair housing legislation passed in 1968, the United States remains today, in many respects, a segregated society. In neighborhoods across the country, blacks and whites are separated more completely now than they were 100 years ago. In a typical major American city at the close of the twentieth century, nearly 80 percent of the black population would need to pick up and move into new neighborhoods in order to achieve racial balance in the city as a whole. And if neighborhoods continue, by and large, to reflect the color-line, then so do other important American institutions: schools, churches, work, and marriage.[25]

Because gender and race are central to how Americans think about social life, and because gender and race are sites of persistent and serious inequality in America, we expect both to figure importantly into public opinion. Because gender and race—men and women, whites and blacks—are organized so differently in American society, we expect gender and race to figure differently into public opinion. Let's see.

Gender, Race, and Political Parties

At the center of American politics are political parties, long-lasting coalitions among politicians, interest groups, activists, and donors. Through elections, parties seek control of government in order to further coalition goals: to extend affirmative action, say, or to end it; to legalize abortion or to prohibit it. With such goals in mind, parties recruit candidates and supply them with the money, expertise, and labor they need to win public office.[26]

As parties are central to American politics, party identification is central to how ordinary citizens think about political life. Most Americans identify themselves as Democrats or as Republicans, and this is not a casual thing. Party identification is a standing decision, a "durable attachment, not readily disturbed by passing events and personalities." Nor is party identification inconsequential:

> To the average person, the affairs of government are remote and complex, and yet the average citizen is asked periodically to formulate opinions about these affairs.... In this dilemma, having the party symbol stamped on certain candidates, certain issue positions, certain interpretations of reality is of great psychological convenience.[27]

Our first question for public opinion, then, is what do gender and race have to do with party identification? A general analysis of the relationship between social groups and political parties is set out by Lipset and Rokkan in *Party Systems and Voter Alignments* (1967). There, Lipset and Rokkan trace the origins of social groups relevant to politics back to the "two revolutions"—the national and the industrial—that mark the onset of modernity. The rise of the nation state, Lipset and Rokkan argue, generated a pair of conflicts of continuing relevance to politics: one that opposed the nation-building center against the ethnically, linguistically, and religiously diverse subject populations in the provinces; the other that set the state against the church. According to Lipset and Rokkan, the conflicts arising from the national revolution primarily concerned moral values and cultural identities. The industrial revolution gave rise to conflict between economic interests. The expansion of markets and the rapid spread of new technologies opened up new and enduring cleavages: first between landed interests and the rising class of industrial entrepreneurs; and later between owners and employers on the one side and tenants and workers on the other.

The generation of distinctive interests associated with particular social groups encourages alignments to form between those groups and the political parties. A key point here is that once established, such alignments persist. The party system tends to "lock in" conflict between groups.[28]

The alignment between social groups and political parties is durable, as Lipset and Rokkan say, but it is not permanent. There is perhaps no clearer illustration of this point than that provided by race in the United States.

We pick up this story with the rising of the Civil Rights Movement, which became visible nationally for the first time through simple acts of civil disobedience carried out as protest against segregation in a handful of southern towns. Marches, demonstrations, "freedom rides," and voter registration efforts soon followed, eventually triggering massive resistance in the Deep South and, finally, action from the federal government. In July of 1964, after the longest legislative debate in the history of the U.S. Congress, President Johnson signed the Civil Rights Act into law. Arguably the greatest legislative achievement of the Civil Rights Movement and the most important domestic legislation of the postwar era, the Civil Rights Act made possible rapid and dramatic declines in racial segregation of public places, opened up employment opportunities for black Americans, and laid the groundwork for enforcement of the Supreme Court's historic 1954 decision on school desegregation.[29]

The Civil Rights Act also became part of the 1964 presidential campaign, thanks in no small measure to Senator Goldwater's success in capturing the Republican Party's presidential nomination. In his campaign, Goldwater argued against the encroachments of the federal government in general and against the civil rights legislation sponsored by the Johnson administration in particular. As he made his case, Goldwater moved the Republican Party decisively to the right on matters of race, just as Johnson hauled the Democratic Party to the left. The result, in the short run, was a Republican catastrophe. Outside the Deep South, Goldwater carried only his home state of Arizona and was buried under a landslide of historic proportions.

As is often the case, the long run was a different and more complicated affair. After his lop-sided victory, Johnson created a flurry of new programs as part of a War on Poverty. He engineered passage of the Voting Rights Act. He established the Department of Housing and Urban Development, putting in place for the first time the capacity to develop and carry out an urban policy, and appointed Robert Weaver as its secretary, the first black cabinet member in United States history. Johnson pressed for and eventually obtained legislation to prohibit discrimination in the housing market, through the Fair Housing Act of 1968. And he appointed Thurgood Marshall to the Supreme Court, the ninety-sixth Justice and the first black, some twenty-five years after Marshall had argued the Brown school desegregation case.

Here (finally), is the relevant point: the Johnson–Goldwater contest and the liberal initiatives that shortly followed precipitated a massive and rapid shift in party allegiances. African Americans moved almost unanimously into the Democratic Party, while white southerners began to move out. The net result, shown in Figure 7.1, was the emergence of a huge racial divide in partisanship.

A huge and *persistent* racial divide: since Johnson's presidency, party differences over matters of race—over school desegregation, anti-poverty programs, crime, welfare reform, and affirmative action—have remained. Black Americans have continued to vote in overwhelming numbers for Democratic candidates. Southern whites have continued to vote for Republican candidates. And the south, for 100 years solidly Democratic, is now a Republican stronghold.[30]

The story of gender and the party system is similar in some respects, but, as we'll see, comes to a much less dramatic conclusion. In the first decades of the twentieth century, the prospect of extending the franchise to women generated a lively debate over the possibility of a "women's vote." Feminists hoped that newly enfranchised women voters would support candidates promoting "maternalist" social policies: protective labor laws or government subsidy of health and housing. For their part, professional politicians doubted that women would coalesce behind one of the parties—and they turned out to be right. Ratification of the 19th Amendment gave women the vote, but the parties undertook only modest and probably off-setting measures to appeal to women, and no distinctive women's vote materialized.[31]

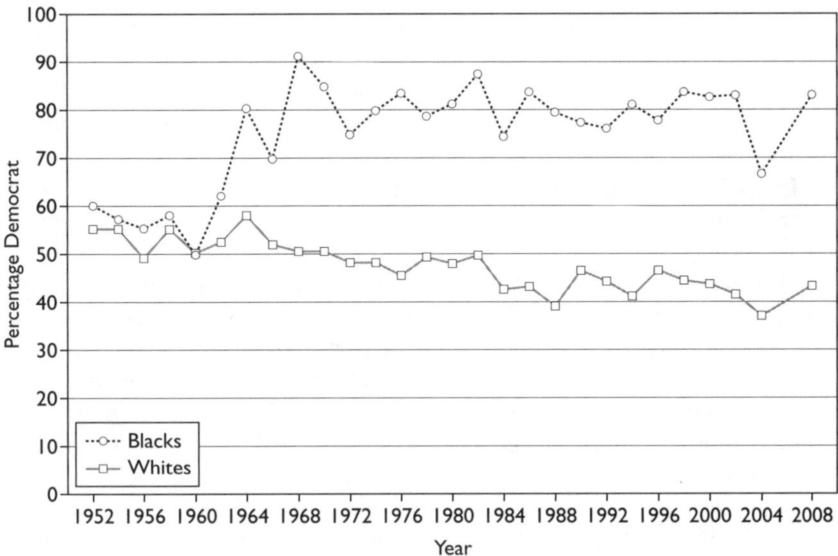

Figure 7.1 The Racial Divide in Partisanship 1952–2008 (source: American National Election Studies).

Not until the rising of the modern women's movement—the second wave of feminism—were gender issues again pushed onto the national agenda. In 1963, the President's Commission on the Status of Women issued its report documenting serious inequalities at work and before the law. In the same year Congress passed the Equal Pay Act, outlawing different pay for women and men doing the same work. Betty Friedan's *Feminine Mystique*, urging women into careers and public life, also appeared in 1963. The following year passage of the Civil Rights Act prohibited discrimination on the grounds of race, religion, or (as an afterthought) sex. In 1966, the National Organization for Women came into being, providing women with organizational representation in Washington and some assurance that the new laws would be enforced.[32]

Suddenly there were press conferences, meetings, protests, marches, and demonstrations. More and more women declared themselves sympathetic to feminism, enlisted in feminist organizations, and ran for public office. Hearings on women's rights became commonplace in Congress. Women's rights became a salient subject in national party platforms and conventions. Bills representing various aspects of the women's rights agenda were routinely introduced and very often passed. The Equal Rights Amendment (ERA), promising that "Equality of rights under the law shall not be denied or abridged by the United States or by any State on account of sex," sailed through both houses of Congress. This (apparent) triumph was followed in short order by *Roe* v. *Wade* (1973), the Supreme Court's ruling that efforts to regulate abortion by the states were unconstitutional.[33]

For many socially conservative Americans, "the ERA and abortion symbolized everything about feminism worth opposing." Conservatives organized, entered the political fray, and often won. They blocked state ratification of the ERA, and through persuasion, pressure, litigation, and in some cases intimidation, placed restrictions on abortion.[34]

The political struggle over women's rights and roles is ongoing. The point we wish to emphasize here is that, increasingly, the fight takes place *between* the political parties. Over the last forty years or so, the two parties have staked out distinctive positions on gender. The Democratic Party has embraced feminist ideas. In turn, the Republican Party has welcomed the conservative reaction to feminism. This polarization of the parties over gender is apparent in all sorts of ways: in party platforms, roll-call votes in the House and in the Senate, in sponsorship of legislation, in ratings of Members of Congress by relevant interest groups, in the views expressed by delegates to the national party conventions, in presidential campaigns, and in State of the Union addresses. The polarization is especially pronounced on abortion. In the early 1970s, the Democratic and Republican congressional delegations were more or less indistinguishable on abortion. No longer. The typical Democratic Member of Congress now takes a strong pro-choice position; the typical Republican Member of Congress is now ardently pro-life.[35]

In short, over the course of the last several decades, the Democratic and Republican parties have shifted their positions on gender, just as they have on race. The Democratic Party moved to the left; the Republican Party moved to the right. The question then is this: in response to these changes in what the parties were offering, did men move to the Republican Party while women moved to the Democratic Party, in effect retracing the steps taken by whites and blacks over matters of race? And the answer, shown in Figure 7.2, is: not really.

As Figure 7.2 reveals, men's and women's partisan movement over matters of gender is nowhere near as clear and decisive as blacks' and whites' partisan movement over matters of race. There is evidence in Figure 7.2 of an emerging gender gap in partisanship, but a modest one. During the Eisenhower administration, women were actually slightly more likely than men, not less, to identify with the Republican Party. By the early 1970s this difference was reversed. For some time now, women have been some eight to ten percentage points more likely than men to identify as Democrats.[36]

The contrast between gender and race here is dramatic. This is surprising. We expected that the relationship between gender and party, on the one side, and race and party, on the other, would be the same. Both, we thought, would be governed by the same principle: namely, that when the political parties change position on an important issue decisively, and maintain that change persistently, ordinary citizens will adjust their partisan allegiances accordingly. In the case of race, we expected African Americans would move in one

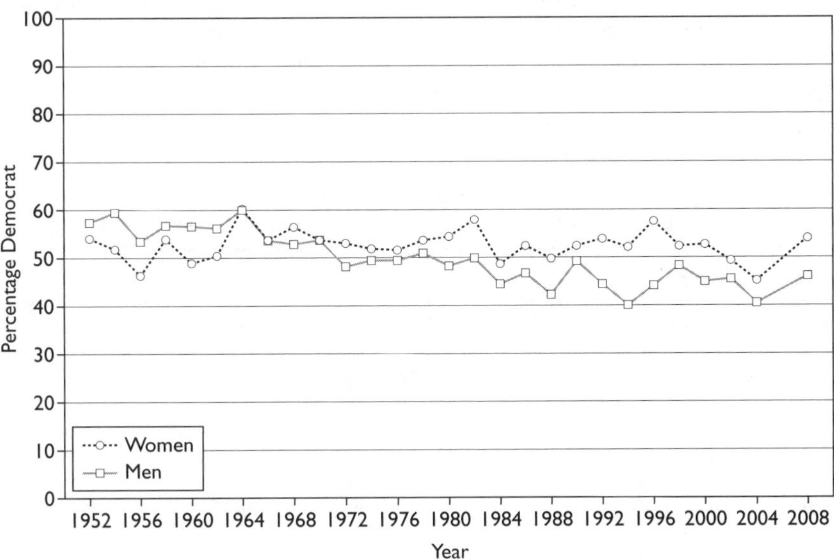

Figure 7.2 The Gender Gap in Partisanship 1952–2008 (source: American National Election Studies).

direction and white Americans would move in the opposite direction. Likewise, in the case of gender, we expected that men would go one way while women went the other. This is not what we find.

Our expectation, notice, was based on two parallel assumptions: first, that blacks and whites differ in their interests, opinions, and aspirations on matters of race, and so will gravitate naturally to one party or the other when the parties offer a real choice; and second, that men and women differ in their interests, opinions, and aspirations over gender, and so will gravitate naturally to one party or the other when presented with a real choice. As we'll see next, the first assumption is (more or less) right, but the second is not.

Gender Gap, Racial Divide

In this section we focus on public opinion on matters of policy: what Americans say that the government should do about pressing national problems. Here we are especially interested in the possibility of differences between men and women on issues of gender, and differences between blacks and whites on issues of race.

Table 7.1 presents a small but representative sampling of findings, taken from the 2008 American National Election Study. The results shown there are about as clear as public opinion findings get. Differences between men and women on policy in the domain of gender are tiny. Women are a bit more likely to support abortion rights than men, and a bit more likely to support increased federal spending on childcare. The overwhelming pattern is similarity. In contrast, differences between African Americans and whites on policy in the domain of race are enormous. Blacks are much more likely to support government prohibiting racial discrimination than whites, and much more likely to support affirmative action in hiring and promotion. What stands out in the case of race is difference.

Table 7.1 Opinion of Men and Women on Gender versus Opinion of Whites and Blacks on Race (percentage supporting the liberal option)

Gender			
Abortion rights		*Childcare spending*	
Women	Men	Women	Men
62	59	75	72
Race			
Fair employment		*Affirmative action*	
White	Blacks	Whites	Blacks
47	76	17	57

Source: 2008 American National Election Study.

The pattern shown in Table 7.1 is utterly general. Whatever the exact policy, differences between men and women on policy in the domain of gender are negligible, while differences between blacks and whites on policy in the domain of race are enormous. Tiny gender gaps and huge racial divides on matters of gender and race are the rule.[37]

Why are differences between men and women in politics so muted? The principal cause, we think, goes back to social organization. In the typical case, women spend much of their lives in intimate relationships with men: with fathers, husbands, brothers, and sons. This means both that women are cut off from their own kind in significant ways, and that they acquire interests and values in common with the men whose lives they share. Women, as Simone de Beauvoir once put it,

> have no past, no history, no religion of their own; and they have no such solidarity of work and interest as that of the proletariat. They are not even promiscuously herded together in the way that creates community feeling among the American Negroes, the ghetto Jews, the workers of Saint-Denis, or the factory hands of Renault. They live dispersed among the males, attached through residence, housework, economic conditions and social standing to certain men—fathers or husbands—more firmly than they are attached to other women.[38]

Women and African Americans as Objects of Identification

If mere membership in social groups is sometimes sufficient to generate differences of opinion on matters of policy, the political consequences of group membership are typically accentuated among those who belong to the group psychologically, or, as we will say, who *identify* with their group. Group identification comes in two main varieties. Common fate refers to the extent to which individuals believe that their life chances and outcomes are intertwined with the opportunities and experiences of their group, that what happens to their group, will happen to them. Those highly identified with their group on grounds of common fate will come to a political choice with their group's interests prominently in mind. A second variety of group identification is grounded in emotional interdependence, occurring when individuals feel close to their group, experiencing pride when other group members do well and anger when they are treated unfairly. Emotional interdependence reflects the expressive side of politics. To the degree Americans derive their sense of self from their membership in social groups, political choices become acts of affirmation and solidarity.[39]

People vary in the degree to which they identify with a group. For some group members, attachment is effectively zero; for others, identification with a social group constitutes a central aspect of identity; and there exist all shades in between. Strength of identification is a sign of a person's priorities. The stronger the identification, the more powerful the political consequences of group membership will be.[40]

This is an altogether general claim, and as you might expect by now, it applies more readily to race than to gender. Our findings on this point come from a pair of surveys undertaken in the fall of 2000, one in Atlanta, the other in Detroit. In each city, we questioned equal numbers of whites and blacks and equal numbers of women and men, more than 2,000 people in all. We assessed group identification with a series of standard questions, tapping both forms of identification (common fate and emotional interdependence). Women were asked how much they thought their own fate was tied up with the fate of women in general; whether they felt close to women; how often they felt pride over the accomplishments of women; and how often they felt angry about the way women were treated. A parallel series of questions was posed to African Americans about their group.

On each of these measures, African Americans were much more likely to identify with their race than women were with their gender. For example, 40 percent of African Americans reported that they often felt angry over how blacks were treated in American society, compared to just 21 percent of women saying the same about society's treatment of women. Furthermore, racial group identification turned out to be a more powerful force influencing opinions on matters of race policy among African Americans than was gender group identification as a force influencing opinions on matters of gender among women. African Americans who strongly identified with their race were more likely to push for integration of the public schools, for affirmative action in the workplace, and for increased foreign aid to African nations, compared to African Americans who claimed no such identification. In contrast, women who strongly identified with their gender were sometimes more likely to support women's issues but sometimes not. They were more likely to favor equal pay for equal work but no more likely to endorse the pro-choice position on abortion than were women who were psychologically less attached to their gender.[41]

In sum, group identification appears to be both more prevalent among African Americans *and* more potent. Why? The social organization of gender emphasizes intimacy between men and women; the social organization of race emphasizes separation between whites and blacks. Separation fosters solidarity among African Americans. Integration impairs solidarity among women.

Women and African Americans as Objects of Attitude

Now we turn from in-group to out-group, from feelings of solidarity among one's own kind to attitudes of resentment or condescension directed at others.

We have known for some time that attitudes toward out-groups can powerfully influence the views Americans take on particular matters of public policy. The argument behind this empirical regularity is straightforward. It goes like this. Policy is complicated. The arguments are hard to follow. It is unclear what will really work. Under these conditions, many Americans may happily forego careful analysis of a policy's merits and instead decide what their opinion is according to how they feel about the groups implicated in the policy. According to this logic, support for tightening welfare benefits derives from hostility toward the poor; opposition to government action against AIDS turns on contempt for homosexuals; resistance to immigration reflects suspicions that the new immigrants are somehow un-American. Attitude toward out-groups is not the only force driving opinion in these various policy disputes, but it is always present, and of all the forces that shape opinion, it is often the most powerful.[42]

Does this argument apply to opinion in the domains of gender and race? Yes—though successful application requires taking into account, once again, differences in how gender and race are organized in society.

By attitude toward women we mean this: belief about the proper place of women in contemporary society—where women belong, and where they do not. For at least 100 years, public discussions over gender have been preoccupied with this one overriding question: whether women's primary, or even exclusive, responsibilities should lie in the private sphere of home and family. Politicians, activists, intellectuals, and religious leaders have all had something to say about women's place. The traditional position holds that women belong, properly and naturally, to the private sphere of home and family; that their fragile and delicate natures must be protected from the heat and grime and rough and tumble world of work; that their mission, ordained by biology if not by God, is to support their husbands and nurture their children.

This view came under intense and public challenge by the modern women's movement. For the first time, Americans in visible numbers began to question the notion that men and women were essentially and fundamentally different, and that society must be organized to the last detail to harmonize with this fundamental fact of nature. Perhaps women were equal in talent and ambition to men and could make significant contributions outside the home.

To capture differences over women's place, we have drawn upon research done by Janet Spence and her Attitude toward Women Scale (AWS), developed in the early 1970s. AWS is a measure of beliefs about women's roles, rights, and responsibilities. The scale puts front and center the traditional view of the family, in which the husband works in the world and the wife maintains the home. The particular questions we use to measure beliefs about women's proper place are presented in Table 7.2. As shown there, some of the questions are about where women and men belong (e.g., "It is much better for everyone involved if the man is the achiever outside the home and the woman takes care of the home and family"). Some, going further, propose that the traditional division of labor between men and women is a direct reflection of differences in their underlying essences ("Men are naturally better-suited to the world of work than women are").[43]

Table 7.2 suggests that the traditional notion of women's place is no longer taken for granted. The traditional position has many defenders, but at least as many opponents. Notice also that the questions displayed in Table 7.2 make no attempt to directly assess hostility toward women. To do so would be a mistake from our perspective, for it would ignore the distinctive social arrangement of gender. Gender is characterized by intimacy and interdependence. Intimacy and interdependence generate complicated feelings. Men depend on women for affection, pleasure, and descendants. Women are revered for their role as mothers and counted on for their kindness. Resistance to change in the status quo in gender relations is expressed not through resentful feelings and denigrating stereotypes, but through beliefs aimed at keeping women in their (natural) place.[44]

If we are trying to understand opposition to women's issues, outright hostility toward women should play a minor part. More important in fueling opposition to family leave or abortion rights should be a conviction about social order, a conviction that women's proper place is the home. This turns out to be so. Men who subscribe to the traditional view of women's place tend to oppose a wide range of progressive initiatives in the domain of gender. These effects are especially strong for policies that entail changes in roles: for example, on whether women in the military should be permitted to serve in combat.[45]

The social organization of race is characterized by separation. Separation, in the presence of inequality, is a breeding ground for stereotyping and denigration. The particular variety of racial stereotyping and denigration prominent in American society today emerged out of the post-Civil Rights era. Its principal theme is that blacks fail to take advantage of the ample opportunities provided them in a society that is now blind to color. Freed from discrimination and segregation, African Americans choose idleness over work, crime over honest labor, promiscuity over restraint and responsibility, and alcohol and drugs over sobriety.[46]

A measure of racial resentment (as we will call it) is presented in Table 7.3, taken from the January 2008 component of the Cooperative Campaign Analysis Project (CCAP). As the table reveals, substantial numbers of whites agree that if blacks would only try harder they could be just as well off as whites or that the best way for blacks to solve their problems is to stop complaining and get to work. Likewise, many whites reject the proposition that blacks must settle for jobs below what they deserve or that blacks still face substantial discrimination on account of their race. Taken together, responses to these

Table 7.2 Men's View of Women's Place (%)

A working mother can establish just as warm and secure a relationship with her children as a mother who does not work.	
Agree strongly	15.6
Agree	20.2
Neither agree nor disagree	11.9
Disagree	36.0
Disagree strongly	16.3
It is much better for everyone involved if the man is the achiever outside the home and the woman takes care of the home and family.	
Agree strongly	10.9
Agree	22.6
Neither agree nor disagree	29.7
Disagree	19.6
Disagree strongly	17.3
As a general rule, when a couple gets divorced, their children should go live with their mother.	
Agree strongly	5.3
Agree	11.1
Neither agree nor disagree	36.6
Disagree	25.2
Disagree strongly	21.8
Men are naturally better suited to the world of work than women are.	
Agree strongly	7.3
Agree	20.3
Neither agree nor disagree	27.5
Disagree	24.3
Disagree strongly	20.6
When it comes to the care of children, women are just naturally better than men.	
Agree strongly	13.4
Agree	40.2
Neither agree nor disagree	19.9
Disagree	14.8
Disagree strongly	11.8
It's fine for a husband to stay home to take care of home and family instead of working outside the home.	
Agree strongly	6.5
Agree	5.2
Neither agree nor disagree	18.4
Disagree	43.1
Disagree strongly	26.8

Source: 2007–2008 CCAP.

Note
Number of cases: 512.

Table 7.3 White Attitudes toward Blacks (%)

Irish, Italians, Jews, and many other minorities overcame prejudice and worked their way up. Blacks should do the same without any special favors.	
Agree strongly	42.4
Agree	28.1
Neither agree nor disagree	14.5
Disagree	10.2
Disagree strongly	4.7
Even today, government officials usually pay more attention to a complaint from a white person than from a black person.	
Agree strongly	7.9
Agree	21.9
Neither agree nor disagree	19.0
Disagree	27.4
Disagree strongly	23.8
If blacks would only try harder they could be just as well off as whites.	
Agree strongly	17.0
Agree	28.3
Neither agree nor disagree	27.0
Disagree	17.0
Disagree strongly	10.7
When it comes to good jobs and decent salaries, most blacks still end up with less than they deserve.	
Agree strongly	6.1
Agree	27.0
Neither agree nor disagree	25.8
Disagree	25.3
Disagree strongly	15.8
In America today, blacks still face plenty of discrimination because of their race.	
Agree strongly	15.4
Agree	40.4
Neither agree nor disagree	15.5
Disagree	17.9
Disagree strongly	10.7
Blacks face real problems, but the way to solve these problems is to stop complaining and get to work.	
Agree strongly	30.7
Agree	35.4
Neither agree nor disagree	16.8
Disagree	11.7
Disagree strongly	5.5

Source: CCAP 2007–2008.

Note
Number of cases: 865.

various propositions allow us to distinguish between those whites who are generally sympathetic toward blacks from those who are generally unsympathetic, who resent the failure of blacks, as they see it, to demonstrate the virtues of self-reliance and hard work.

Such differences turn out to be politically consequential. Racial resentment strongly predicts white opinion on school integration, fair employment, foreign aid to Africa, federal support for Head Start, affirmative action in hiring and promotion decisions, and much more. Of course, opinion on such matters is not a reflection of racial resentment alone. But among the standard explanations of public opinion—party identification, several varieties of contemporary conservatism, age and education—none is more important than racial resentment.[47]

Political Activation of Gender and Race

Americans belong to many social groups at once. They are simultaneously black or white or brown; Catholic, Protestant, Jewish, or atheist; male or female; bankers or carpenters; urbanites or suburbanites; Southerners or Yankees; and so on. This means that Americans have available, in principle at least, an extensive repertoire out of which to create an identity. In parallel fashion, Americans possess attitudes toward many social groups—towards Catholics, women, bankers, and more—any number of which could be relevant to their political opinions.

Which aspects of identity and attitude become important—which are *activated*—depends on political circumstances. More precisely, activation depends on the clarity of group cues. Some issues clearly evoke social group memberships and attitudes (e.g., affirmative action in college admissions); others do not (e.g., rebuilding infrastructure).

To illustrate this point, consider public opinion on federal support for early education. Respondents to a national survey were asked for their opinions on "spending more money on the schools in *black* neighborhoods, especially for pre-school and early education programs" or they were asked for their opinions on "spending more money on the schools in *poor* neighborhoods, especially for pre-school and early education programs." The proposal is identical in each case but for the intended beneficiaries: black children in the first case, poor children in the second. This one difference has major consequences. When government policy is targeted on black children, the racial divide in opinion doubles in size (compared to opinion on early education for poor children); black support increases slightly; white support declines dramatically; and the effect of racial resentment on white opposition to federal support of early education increases substantially. When policies and programs explicitly designed to provide assistance to black Americans are put before the public, racial considerations are activated.[48]

Clarity of group cues depends not only on the issue itself, but on how the issue is framed. The issues that government take up are always complex; they are always subject to alternative interpretations. For example, what exactly is affirmative action? Who is it for? Is it quotas or outreach? Is it reverse discrimination? Is it compensation for the injustices of the past? Activists and partisans are constantly trying to frame issues in ways that will advance their cause, hoping that others, including the general public, will find their framings persuasive. Which frames prevail among elites affect how citizens understand the issue, and, in the end, what their opinions on the issue turn out to be.[49]

The importance of frames for activation is illustrated in an experiment on public opinion on affirmative action. In a national survey, Americans were asked for their views on affirmative action in college admissions, posed in one of two ways. For half the sample, affirmative action was framed this way: "Some people say that because of past discrimination, it is sometimes necessary for colleges and universities to reserve openings for black students. Others oppose quotas because they say quotas *discriminate against whites.*" The other half of the sample was presented with affirmative action framed this way: "Some people say that because of past discrimination, it is sometimes necessary for colleges and universities to reserve openings for black students. Others oppose quotas because they say quotas *give blacks advantages they haven't earned.*" All respondents were then asked whether they were for or against quotas to admit black students.

In both versions of the question, it is suggested affirmative action might be supported on the grounds that such policies are necessary to overcome past discrimination. The questions differ in that one version suggests that affirmative action might be opposed because such policies constitute discrimination against whites (the reverse discrimination frame), while the other version suggests that affirmative action might be opposed because such policies give to blacks advantages they have not earned (the unfair advantage frame).

It turns out that framing opposition to affirmative action in terms of advantages to blacks that they do not deserve evokes white Americans' racial feelings powerfully. Racial resentment is a much more powerful factor in white opinion on affirmative action when the issue is framed in this way. Put the other way around, the impact of racial resentment diminishes dramatically when affirmative action is framed as reverse discrimination. This is an important result. It suggests that even on controversial issues that are transparently and obviously about race, racial resentment need not play a dominant role in white public opinion. It depends on how the issue is framed.[50]

Implications

Gender and race are central to how people think about social life; both are "made" by society; and as sites for discrimination and exclusion, both have been and continue to be good illustrations of durable inequality. In all these important respects, gender and race are alike. They differ in social organization—in the characteristic ways that men and women, on the one hand, and blacks and whites, on the other, experience one another. The social organization of gender emphasizes intimacy, the social organization of race emphasizes separation, and this difference, we have argued, has important implications for the roles that gender and race play in American public opinion. Intimacy impairs group solidarity among women and interferes with hostility between men and women. Separation encourages group solidarity among African Americans and encourages hostility between whites and blacks.

Shortly before we began to work on this chapter, a quite remarkable natural experiment was coming to a close. In the contest for the 2008 Democratic Party's presidential nomination, the two principal rivals were, of course, Hillary Clinton and Barack Obama. Heading into the race, Senator Clinton was the odds-on favorite. She enjoyed the backing of her party, endorsements from prominent African Americans, money to burn, and what appeared to be a commanding lead over all rivals. But, as we know, in a tight and fiercely contested race, Obama eventually secured the nomination, and then went on in the fall to be elected president of the United States.

If, as we say, the activation of identity and attitude depends on the clarity of group cues, then the 2008 contest for the Democratic Party's presidential nomination offers up a tantalizing and important additional test of the findings we have presented here. Senator Clinton made gender salient in exactly the same unequivocal way that Barack Obama made race salient—by embodying it.

As it happens, analysis of voters' reactions to Clinton and Obama yield the familiar results. Obama's campaign elicited a huge racial divide; Clinton's campaign produced a modest gender gap. African Americans expressed more solidarity with their group than women did with theirs. Racial solidarity was more powerful in building support for Obama than gender solidarity was in building support for Clinton. Traditional notions of women's proper place made some trouble for Clinton. Racial resentment among whites undermined support for Obama. In short, the claims we have made about gender and race seem to have been borne out in a most consequential practical case.[51]

A broader lesson of our chapter is the reminder that public opinion is a reflection, in part, of historical processes. Social movements come onto the political scene, new groups of voters are enfranchised, political parties modify their platforms in order to win elections, new candidates, with visible connections to certain social groups, are nominated. In the face of such changes, voters alter their views and adjust their political loyalties. Relations that we may think of as fixed—African Americans are Democrats, Republicans are anti-abortion—are not. Things change. Social movements, new voters, political parties, and fresh candidates are significant participants in the "dance" of public opinion.

This makes forecasting difficult. It would be foolish to predict the future course of gender and race and public opinion—and we won't try. But we will suggest, by way of closing, two factors that any sensible forecast should take into account.

The first is inequality. As pointed out in the first part of the chapter, the quality of life experienced by black Americans has improved notably over the last fifty years, but racial inequalities persist in many important domains of life. In some instances, the differences are actually increasing. The corresponding story for gender is quite different. By comparison to race, inequalities between men and women are less extreme and they appear to be narrowing relatively rapidly. Should this pattern continue into the future, the conclusion we have drawn here—that in the contemporary United States, race plays a more prominent role in public opinion than gender—is likely to continue to hold.

A second factor to consider concerns social organization. A central feature of American race relations is separation. Despite the efforts of the Civil Rights Movement and the intent of national legislation, the United States remains today, in many respects, a segregated society. We see this in neighborhoods, schools, workplaces, churches, and marriages. All true. But what is also true is that segregation is declining, if slowly and fitfully. Neighborhoods are less segregated than they were thirty years ago. Marrying across racial lines is still rare, but less rare than it was a generation ago. Insofar as these trends continue, the power of race to organize political conflict should diminish.[52]

One last point to keep in mind: inequality and segregation have something in common. Both are products, in part, of decisions made in politics. As such, inequality and segregation illustrate well the general doctrine that politics matters: that policies have material consequences for the lives its citizens lead. In a democratic political system, what the future brings for gender and race depends in an important way on what we decide to do.

Notes

1. As we say, research on public opinion that centers on gender *or* on race is booming, but research that takes up gender *and* race together is quite rare. Throughout our chapter, we compare the role of gender and the role of race in contemporary American public opinion, motivated by the intuition that a systematic comparison between the two will turn out to be informative about both. By race we mean the distinction between white (non-Hispanic white) and black (non-Hispanic black). Things are more complicated than that, of course. The chapter by Junn, Mendelberg, and Czaja in this volume takes up the increasingly multi-racial character of American society.
2. Goffman, Erving. 1977. The arrangement between the sexes. *Theory and Society* 4(3): 301–331.
3. Lewontin, Richard. 1995. *Human Diversity*. New York: Scientific American Library.
4. On the indispensability of categories, see Margolis, Eric, and Stephen Laurence.

1999. *Concepts: Core Readings*. Cambridge: MIT Press; Smith, Edward E., and Douglas Medin. 1981. *Categories and Concepts*. Cambridge: Harvard University Press.

5. See, for example Gelman, Susan A. 2003. *The Essential Child: Origins of Essentialism in Everyday Thought*. New York: Oxford University Press; Hirschfeld, Lawrence A. 1996. *Race in the Making: Cognition, Culture, and the Child's Construction of Human Kinds*. Cambridge: MIT Press; Maccoby, Eleanor E. 1998. *The Two Sexes: Growing Up Apart. Coming Together*. Cambridge, MA: Harvard University Press; and Ruble, D.N., and C.L. Martin. 2000. Gender development. In *Handbook of Child Psychology*, W. Damon and N. Eisenberg (editors). New York: Wiley. Pp. 933–1016.
6. Tilly, Charles. 1998. *Durable Inequality*. Berkeley, CA: University of California Press.
7. Beginning in the early part of the seventeenth century, West Africans were taken forcibly from their homelands and shipped under nightmarish conditions to the southern colonies. They came first in a trickle and then in a flood. By the time of the first U.S. Census in 1790, African Americans—nearly all slave—made up roughly 20 percent of the national population and more than one-third of the population of the south. Slavery, imposed and maintained by violence, was at the center of the new American economic order (Berlin, Ira. 1998. *Many Thousands Gone: The First Two Centuries of Slavery in North America*. Cambridge: Belknap Press; Farley, Reynolds, and Walter R. Allen. 1987. *The Color Line and the Quality of Life in America*. New York: Russell Sage Foundation).
8. This example comes from Anderson, Elizabeth, 2010. *The Imperative of Integration*. Princeton, NJ: Princeton University Press, p. 9.
9. See Dollard, John. 1937. *Caste and Class in a Southern Town*. New Haven, CT: Yale University Press; Myrdal, Gunnar. 1944. *An American Dilemma: The Negro Problem and Modern Democracy*. New York: Harper and Row, pp. 606–618; and Litwack, Leon F. 1961. *North of Slavery: The Negro in the Free States, 1790–1860*. Chicago, IL: University of Chicago Press.
10. Quotation is from Tilly (1998, p. 63). Anderson (2010, pp. 19–20). According to Tilly, exploitation, opportunity hoarding, emulation, and adaptation are responsible for establishing and then maintaining *all* the multifarious varieties of durable inequalities that modern societies display. Tilly goes too far, and on three fronts. He claims to explain *all* durable inequalities. He insists that *most* of differences in advantage are due to categorical inequalities. And, most important from our point of view, he fails to appreciate the direct role stigmatizing stories can play in the generation and maintenance of inequality through democratic processes—through public pressure and fair elections.
11. See Ayres, Ian. 2001. *Pervasive Prejudice? Unconventional Evidence of Race and Gender Discrimination*. Chicago, IL: University of Chicago Press; Kirschenman, Joleen, and Kathryn M. Neckerman. 1991; "We'd love to hire them, but...": The meaning of race for employers. In *The Urban Underclass*, Christopher Jencks and Paul E. Peterson (editors). Washington, DC: Brookings; and Ross, Steven L., and John Yinger. 2002. *The Color of Credit*. Cambridge, MA: MIT Press. Furthermore, Quillian, Lincoln. 2006. New approaches to understanding racial prejudice and discrimination. *Annual Review of Sociology* 32(1): 299–328 provides an excellent review of studies of racial discrimination.
12. As of 2007, the average white person could expect to live 78.4 years while the average black person could expect to live 73.6 years (Xu, J., K. Kochanek, S. Murphy, and B. Tejada-Vera. 2010. Deaths: Final data for 2007. Retrieved from http://www.cdc.gov/nchs/data/nvsr/nvsr58/nvsr58_19.pdf). On race and health and well-being more generally, see Farley, Reynolds. 2008. The Kerner Commission plus four

decades: What has changed? What has not? Unpublished paper, Center for Population Research, Institute for Social Research, University of Michigan; Farley and Allen (1987); Sandefur, Gary D., Molly Martin, Jennifer Eggerling-Boeck, Susan E. Mannon, and Ann M. Meir. 2001. An overview of racial and ethnic demographic trends. In *America Becoming: Racial Trends and Their Consequences*, Volume I, Neil J. Smelser, William Julius Wilson, and Faith Mitchell (editors). Washington, DC: National Academy Press; and Williams, David R. 2001. Racial variation in adult health status: Patterns, paradoxes, and prospects. In *America Becoming: Racial Trends and Their Consequences*, Volume II, Neil J. Smelser, William Julius Wilson, and Faith Mitchell (editors). Washington, DC: National Academy Press.

13. The literature on racial differences in economic status is enormous. For an introduction, see Blank, Rebecca M. 2001. An overview of trends in social and economic well-being, by race. In *America Becoming: Racial Trends and Their Consequences*, Volume I, Neil J. Smelser, William Julius Wilson, and Faith Mitchell (editors). Washington, DC: National Academy Press; Farley, Reynolds. 1996. *The New American Reality*. New York: Russell Sage Foundation; Farley, (2008); Farley and Allen (1987); Heckman, James J., and Paul A. LaFontaine. 2010. The American high school graduation rate: Trends and levels. *Review of Economics and Statistics* 92(2): 244–262; Jaynes, Gerald David, and Robin Murphy Williams. 1989. *A Common Destiny: Blacks and American Society*. Washington, DC: National Academy Press; Oliver, Melvin L., and Shapiro, Thomas M. 1997. *Black Wealth/White Wealth*. New York/London: Routledge; and Sandefur et al. (2001).
14. Formal obstacles to black participation in politics are gone now, swept away by hundreds of local struggles, Supreme Court decisions, the Voting Rights Act of 1965, and the threat of federal intervention (Valelly, Richard M. 2004. *The Two Reconstructions: The Struggle for Black Enfranchisement*. Chicago, IL: University of Chicago Press). Mostly gone, we should say. Criminal offenders typically forfeit voting rights following felony convictions. Because black Americans are much more likely to be arrested, convicted, and incarcerated than whites are, blacks are also much more likely to have their voting rights revoked on this ground. Many of the governing statutes were passed in the late 1860s and 1870s, at a time when the question of voting rights for black Americans was central to the national political debate. Restrictive laws were most common in states with large non-white prison populations (Behrens, Angela, Christopher Uggen, and Jeff Manza. 2003. Ballot manipulation and the "menace of Negro domination": Racial threat and felon disenfranchisement in the United States, 1850–2002. *American Journal of Sociology* 109(3): 559–605; Uggen, Christopher, and Jeff Manza. 2004. Lost voices: The civic and political views of disenfranchised felons. In *Imprisoning America: The Social Effects of Mass Incarceration*, Mary Patillo, David Weiman, and Bruce Western (editors). New York: Russell Sage Foundation).
15. The relevant evidence is reported in Bositis, D.A. 2001. *Black Elected Officials: A Statistical Summary 2001*. Washington, DC: Joint Center for Political and Economic Studies; Jaynes and Williams (1989); and Farley (2008).
16. Tilly (1998, p. 8).
17. Massey, Douglas S. 2007. *Categorically Unequal*. New York: Russell Sage Foundation; and Ortner, Sherry B. 1996. *Making Gender: The Politics and Erotics of Culture*. Boston, MA: Beacon Press.
18. On ratification of the 19th Amendment, see McConnaughy, Corrine M. 2010. The politics of suffrage extension in the American states: Party, race, and the pursuit of women's voting rights. Unpublished manuscript, Department of Political Science, Ohio State University. On ownership of women's wages and on marriage entailing women's sexual consent, see Cott, Nancy F. 2000. *Public Vows: A History of Mar-*

riage and the Nation. Cambridge, MA: Harvard University Press. And on sexual harassment as a legal concept, see MacKinnon, Catherine A. 1987. *Feminism Unmodified: Discourses on Life and Law*. Cambridge, MA: Harvard University Press.

19. Goldin, Claudia. 2006. The quiet revolution that transformed women's employment, education, and family. *American Economic Review, Papers and Proceedings* 96(May): 1–21. According to Goldin, "gender distinctions in work, job, and promotion were extended and solidified in the early twentieth century and became long-lived. These gender distinctions emanated from the treatment of individuals as members of a group, rather than as separate individuals."
20. For an introduction to this literature, see Blau, F.D., M.C. Brinton, and D.B. Grusky. Eds. 2006. *The Declining Significance of Gender?* New York: Russell Sage Foundation; Charles, Maria, and David B. Grusky. 2004. *Occupational Ghettos: The Worldwide Segregation of Women and Men*. Stanford, CA: Stanford University Press; Goldin, Claudia D. 1990. *Understanding the Gender Gap: An Economic History of American Women*. New York: Oxford University Press; Goldin (2006); Goldin, Claudia D., and Cecilia Rouse. 2000. Orchestrating impartiality: The impact of blind auditions on female musicians. *American Economic Review* 90(4): 715–741; MacKinnon (1987); Massey (2007); and Reskin, Barbara F., and Patricia A. Roos. 1990. *Job Queues, Gender Queues: Explaining Women's Inroads into Male Occupations*. Philadelphia, PA: Temple University Press.
21. Burns, Nancy, Kay Lehman Schlozman, and Sidney Verba. 2001. *The Private Roots of Public Action: Gender, Equality, and Political Participation*. Cambridge, MA: Harvard University Press. An exception to gender equality in participation shows up on what Doug McAdam (1986. Recruitment to high risk activism: The case of Freedom Summer. *American Journal of Sociology* 92(1): 64–90) calls "high-risk activism." Looting, arson, rock-throwing, and the other illegal and often violent activities that were part of the great urban eruptions of the 1960s were undertaken much more often by men than by women (e.g. Sears, David O., and McConahay, John B. 1973. *The Politics of Violence: The New Urban Blacks and the Watts Riot*. Boston, MA: Houghton Mifflin). Likewise, women were less apt to take part in Freedom Summer, the dangerous voting-registration project carried out in the summer of 1964 in Mississippi (McAdam 1986).
22. Kirkpatrick, Jeane J. 1974. *Political Woman*. New York: Basic Books.
23. As of 2010, seventeen women were serving in the U.S. Senate; seventy-three served in the House (16.8 percent); only six held governorships; and just seven occupied the mayor's office in a major U.S. city. These figures are based on information compiled by the Center for American Women and Politics (CAWP), Eagleton Institute of Politics, Rutgers University (2010).
24. On the spatial distribution of men and women in society, see Goffman (1977); Maccoby (1998).
25. On racial segregation, see Clotfelter, C.T. 2004. *After Brown: The Rise and Retreat of School Desegregation*. Princeton, NJ: Princeton University Press; Farley (2008); Farley and Allen (1987); Massey (2007); and Massey, Douglas S., and Nancy A. Denton. 1993. *American Apartheid: Segregation and the Making of the Underclass*. Cambridge, MA: Harvard University Press; and Wilson, W.J., and R.P. Taub. 2006. *There Goes the Neighborhood: Racial, Ethnic, and Class Tensions in Four Chicago Neighborhoods and their Meaning for America*. New York: Knopf.
26. On the nature of political parties, see Aldrich, J.H. 1995. *Why Parties? The Origin and Transformation of Political Parties in America*. Chicago, IL: University of Chicago Press; Cohen, Marty, David Carol, Hans Noel, and John Zaller. 2008. *The Party Decides: Presidential Nominations Before and After Reform*. Chicago, IL: Uni-

versity of Chicago Press; and Karol, David. 2009. *Party Position Change in American Politics*. Cambridge, UK: Cambridge University Press.

27. The first quotation is from Campbell, Angus, Philip E. Converse, Warren E. Miller, and Donald E. Stokes. 1960. *The American Voter*. New York: Wiley, p. 151; the second is from Stokes, Donald E. 1966. Party loyalty and the likelihood of deviating elections. In *Elections and the Political Order*, Angus Campbell, Philip E. Converse, Warren E. Miller, and Donald E. Stokes (editors). New York: Wiley. Pp. 126–127. On partisanship, also see Bartels, L.M. 2000. Partisanship and voting behavior, 1952–1996. *American Journal of Political Science* 44(1): 35–50; Bartels, L.M. 2002. Beyond the running tally: Partisan bias in political perceptions. *Political Behavior* 24(2): 117–150; Converse, Philip E. 1966. The Normal Vote: The 1960 election. In *Elections and the Political Order*, Angus Campbell, Philip E. Converse, Warren E. Miller, Donald E. Stokes (editors). New York: Wiley; and Green, D.P., B. Palmquist, and E. Schickler. 2002. *Partisan Hearts and Minds: Political Parties and the Social Identities of Voters*. New Haven: Yale University Press.
28. "The party systems of the 1960s," Lipset and Rokkan concluded, "reflect, with but few significant exceptions, the cleavage structure of the 1920s." Lipset, S.M., and S. Rokkan. 1967. Cleavage structures, party systems, and voter alignments: An introduction. In *Party Systems and Voter Alignments*, S.M. Lipset and S. Rokkan (editors). New York: Free Press (p. 50).
29. For a detailed accounting of this remarkable period in American history, see Branch, T. 1988. *Parting the Waters: America in the King Years 1954–1963*. New York: Simon and Schuster; and Branch, Taylor. 1998. *Pillar of Fire: America in the King Years 1963–65*. New York: Simon & Schuster.
30. For more on the shift in party positions on race and the consequences for partisanship in the American public, see Carmines, E.G., and J.A. Stimson. 1989. *Issue Evolution*. Princeton, NJ: Princeton University Press; Green et al., (2002); Karol (2009); Kinder, D.R., and L.M. Sanders. 1996. *Divided by Color: Racial Politics and Democratic Ideals*. Chicago, IL: University of Chicago Press; and Valentino, Nicholas A., and David O. Sears. 2005. Old times they are not forgotten: Race and partisan realignment in the contemporary south. *American Journal of Political Science* 49(3): 672–688. On the development of the Republican Party in the American South in the post-civil rights period, see Black, Earl, and Merle Black. 2002. *The Rise of Southern Republicans*. Cambridge, MA: Harvard University Press.
31. Harvey, Anna L. 1998. *Votes without Leverage: Women in American Electoral Politics, 1920–1970*. Cambridge, UK: Cambridge University Press; Manza, J., and C. Brooks. 1999. *Social Cleavages and Political Change: Voter Alignments and US Party Coalitions*. New York: Oxford University Press; McConnaughy (2010); and Skocpol, Theda. 1992. *Protecting Soldiers and Mothers: The Political Origins of Social Policy in the United States*. Cambridge, MA: Harvard University Press.
32. On this period, see Evans, Sara M. 1989. *Born for Liberty: A History of Women in America*. New York: The Free Press; and Freeman, J. 1975. *The Politics of Women's Liberation: A Case Study of an Emerging Social Movement and its Relation to the Policy Process*. New York: McKay.
33. Freeman (1975); Mansbridge, J.J. 1986. *Why We Lost the ERA*. Chicago, IL: University of Chicago Press; and Wolbrecht, C. 2000. *The Politics of Women's Rights: Parties, Positions, and Change*. Princeton, NJ: Princeton University Press.
34. Wolbrecht (2000, p. 40).
35. This evidence is presented in Adams, Greg D. 1997. Abortion: Evidence of an issue evolution. *American Journal of Political Science* 41(3): 718–737; Sanbonmatsu, Kira. 2002. *Democrats, Republicans, and the Politics of Women's Place*. Ann Arbor, MI: University of Michigan Press; and in Wolbrecht (2000).

36. Attempts to explain the gender gap in partisanship include Anderson, Kristi. 1975. Working women and political participation, 1952–1972. *American Journal of Political Science* 19(3): 439–453; Box-Steffensmeier, J.M., S. De Boef, and T.M. Lin. 2004. The dynamics of the partisan gender gap. *American Political Science Review* 98(3): 515–528; Hutchings, Vincent, L. Nicholas Valentino, Tasha S. Philpot, and Ismail K. White. 2004. The compassion strategy: Race and the gender gap in campaign 2000. *Public Opinion Quarterly* 68(4): 512–541; Iverson, Torben, and Frances Rosenbluth. 2006. The political economy of gender: Explaining cross-national variation in the gender division of labor and the gender voting gap. *American Journal of Political Science* 50(1): 1–19; Kaufmann, Karen M., and John R. Petrocik. 1999. The changing politics of American men: Understanding the sources of the gender gap. *American Journal of Political Science* 43(3): 864–887; Kellstedt, Paul M., David A.M. Peterson, and Mark D. Ramirez. 2010. The macro politics of a gender gap. *Public Opinion Quarterly* 74(3): 477–498; Manza and Brooks (1999); and Stoker, Laura, and M. Kent Jennings. 2005. Political similarity and influence between husbands and wives. In *The Social Logic of Politics*, Alan S. Zuckerman (editor). Philadelphia, PA: Temple University Press. Pp. 31–74.
37. Kinder and Sanders (1996); Kinder, D.R., and N. Winter. 2001. Exploring the racial divide: Blacks, whites, and opinion on national policy. *American Journal of Political Science* 45(2): 439–456; Sapiro, V. 2003. Theorizing gender in political psychology research. In *Oxford Handbook of Political Psychology*, David O. Sears, L. Huddy, and R. Jervis (editors). New York: Oxford University Press. Reliable differences between men and women in opinion do appear, but not on such matters as family leave or reproductive rights. The clearest case of difference shows up on violence and the use of force. Women are consistently less likely to support U.S. military action than men (by roughly ten percentage points). Men and women also differ over the provision of social welfare, with women a bit more likely to support such programs as Aid to Families with Dependent Children (AFDC), Medicare, and federal assistance to education (Sapiro 2003).
38. De Beauvoir, Simone. 1989. *The Second Sex*. New York: Vintage Books, p. XXV. On this point, also see Jackman, Mary R. 1994. *The Velvet Glove*. Berkeley, CA: University of California Press; and Gurin, P. 1985. Women's gender consciousness. *Public Opinion Quarterly* 49(2): 143–163.
39. On common fate, see Campbell, Donald T. 1958. Common fate, similarity, and other indices of the status of aggregates of persons as social entities. *Behavioral Science* 3(1): 14–25; and Dawson, Michael C. 1994. *Behind the Mule*. Princeton, NJ: Princeton University Press; on emotional interdependence, see Abelson, Robert P. 1995. The secret existence of expressive behavior. *Critical Review* 9(1/2): 25–36 and Tajfel, H. 1981. *Human Groups and Social Categories: Studies in Social Psychology*. Cambridge, UK: Cambridge University Press.
40. This point is amply documented, in many settings and for many social groups, including class (Centers, Richard. 1949. *The Psychology of Social Classes*. Princeton, NJ: Princeton University Press; Converse, Philip E. 1958. The shifting role of class in political attitudes and behavior. In *Readings in Social Psychology*, E.E. Maccoby, T.M. Newcomb, and E.L. Hartley (editors). New York: Holt, Rinehart, and Winston. Pp. 388–399), religion (Converse, Philip E. 1966. Religion and Politics. In *Elections and the Political Order*, Angus Campbell, Philip E. Converse, Warren E. Miller, and Donald E. Stokes (editors). New York: Wiley.), race (Dawson, Michael C. 1995. *Behind the Mule: Race and Class in African-American Politics*. Princeton, NJ: Princeton University Press), and gender (Conover, P.J., and V. Sapiro. 1993. Gender, feminist consciousness, and war. *American Journal of Political Science* 37(4): 1079–1099. For a good review of the literature on racial group identification

specifically, see McClain, Paula D., Jessica D. Johnson Carew, Eugene Walton, Jr., and Candis S. Watts. 2009. Group membership, group identity, and group consciousness: Measures of racial identity in American politics? *Annual Review of Political Science* 12(June): 471–485.

41. Burns, Nancy, and Donald R. Kinder. 2004. Social identity and political opposition. Paper delivered at the Annual Meeting of the American Political Science Association.
42. On the general argument, see Converse, P.E. 1964. The nature of belief systems in mass politics. In *Ideology and Discontent*, David Apter (editor). New York: The Free Press. Pp. 206–261; Nelson, Thomas E., and Donald R. Kinder. 1996. Issue framing and group-centrism in American public opinion. *Journal of Politics* 58(4): 1055–1078; and Sniderman, P.M., R.A. Brody, and P.E. Tetlock. 1991. *Reasoning and Choice: Explorations in Social Psychology*. Cambridge, UK: Cambridge University Press. On public opinion toward welfare, see Gilens, M. 1999. *Why Americans Hate Welfare*. Chicago, IL: University of Chicago Press. On AIDS, Price, V., and M.L. Hsu. 1992. Public opinion about AIDS policies: The role of misinformation and attitudes toward homosexuals. *Public Opinion Quarterly* 56(1): 29–52; and on immigration, see Citrin, Jack, Beth Reingold, and Donald Green. 1990. American identity and the politics of ethnic change. *Journal of Politics* 52(4): 1124–1154.
43. Spence, Janet T., and Robert L. Helmreich. 1972. *The Attitudes toward Women Scale: An Objective Instrument to Measure Attitudes toward the Rights and Roles of Women in Contemporary Society*. Washington, DC: American Psychological Association.
44. Glick, Peter, and Susan T. Fiske. 2001. Ambivalent sexism. *Advances in Experimental Social Psychology* 56(2): 109–118.
45. Burns, Nancy, and Donald R. Kinder. 2007. Public opinion on gender policy: The politics of rights and roles. Paper delivered at the Annual Meeting of the American Political Science Association. Society organizes gender with intimacy between women and men, and intimacy makes trouble for the development of the idea of the out-group. This means, perhaps surprisingly, that attitudes toward women's proper place are as available to women as to men. It turns out that women are just as likely as men to defend the traditional view of their place in society. Men who subscribe to the traditional view of women's place tend to oppose a wide range of progressive initiatives in the domain of gender. The same is true for women.
46. This argument is spelled out in Kinder and Sanders (1996).
47. See, for example, Hurwitz, Jon, and Mark Peffley. 2005. Playing the race card in the post-Willie Horton era. *Public Opinion Quarterly* 69(1): 99–112; Kinder, Donald R., and Katherine W. Drake. 2009. Myrdal's prediction. *Political Psychology* 30(4): 539–568; Kinder and Sanders (1996); Mendelberg, Tali. 2001. *The Race Card*. Princeton, NJ: Princeton University Press; Sears, David O., and P.J. Henry. 2005. Over thirty years later: A contemporary look at symbolic racism. *Advances in Experimental Social Psychology* 37: 98–150; Valentino, N.A., V.L. Hutchings, and I. White. 2002. Cues that matter: How political ads prime racial attitudes during campaigns. *American Political Science Review* 96(1): 75–90; Winter, Nicholas J.G. 2008. *Dangerous Frames: How Ideas about Race and Gender Shape Public Opinion*. Chicago, IL: University of Chicago Press.
48. Kinder and Sanders (1996).
49. On framing, see Kahneman, Daniel. 2003. A perspective on judgment and choice: Mapping bounded rationality. *American Psychologist* 58(9): 697–720; and Kahneman, Daniel, and Amos Tversky. 1981. The framing of decisions and the psychology of choice. *Science* 211(4481): 453–458. For reviews of the literature of framing

in politics, see Chong, Dennis, and Jamie N. Druckman. 2007. Framing public opinion in competitive democracies. *American Political Science Review* 101(4): 637–655; and Kinder, Donald R. 2003. Communication and politics in the age of information. In *Handbook of Political Psychology*, David O. Sears, Leonie Huddy, and Robert L. Jervis (editors). Oxford: Oxford University Press. Pp. 357–393.

50. Kinder and Sanders (1996).
51. Kinder, Donald R., and Allison Dale-Riddle. 2011. *The End of Race? Obama, 2008, and Racial Politics in America*. New Haven, CT: Yale University Press.
52. Sandefur et al. (2001) and Farley (2008).

Chapter 8

A Jump to the Right, A Step to the Left

Religion and Public Opinion

David E. Campbell, Geoffrey C. Layman, and John C. Green

On June 16, 2010, the Southern Baptist Convention (SBC) passed a resolution denouncing the massive oil spill in the Gulf of Mexico. The resolution called on the government

> to act determinatively and with undeterred resolve to end this crisis; to fortify our coastal defenses; to ensure full corporate accountability for damages, clean-up and restoration; to ensure that government and private industry are not again caught without planning for such possibilities; and to promote future energy policies based on prudence, conservation, accountability, and safety.

The SBC resolutions committee chairman told reporters "There is no Pharaoh-like dominion over the Earth … there is a Christ-like stewardship of the Earth."

Why was the largest evangelical Protestant denomination in the United States endorsing a liberal position on the environment—and justifying it on biblical grounds? Aren't evangelicals all extremely conservative and Republican?

As suggested by this one example, there is no iron law that links religion to the political right. It is true that on some issues many evangelicals, and religious Americans more generally, are highly conservative. But this is not true for all issues, nor for Americans of all religions. Neither has it been true over the nation's history. While religion today is most commonly associated with conservative positions like opposition to abortion and gay marriage, in the past, abolitionism, pacifism, and calls for the radical redistribution of wealth have all emanated from the pulpits of America's churches, synagogues, and other places of worship. And even in today's political environment, there are religious leaders trying to nudge their flocks to the left rather than the right. This is most obviously the case in black Protestant churches and Jewish synagogues—where there is a long tradition of political liberalism—but other religious voices advocate environmentalism, opposition to the death penalty, and amnesty for illegal immigrants. When put in that context, a pro-environmental resolution by the Southern Baptists should not be so surprising.

This chapter digs deep into the connections between public opinion and religion, to go beyond a simplistic description of religion-as-right wing. We will show evidence that, on some issues, religion can also move opinions to the left. More broadly, our point is simply that the connections between religion and public opinion are more complex than commonly realized.

What Do We Mean By Religion?

Studying religion's impact on public opinion is complicated by the fact that religion is multi-dimensional. Scholars of religion often refer to the three "Bs": belonging, behaving, and believing. These include the religious community or tradition to which someone belongs, the frequency of religious behavior (attendance at worship services, private prayer), and one's specific religious beliefs (Is there life after death? Should scripture be taken literally?). But even these three dimensions do not exhaust the many facets of religion, and therefore the ways that it might affect public opinion.

Given this complexity in the analysis of religion, a good place to start is with religious belonging—specifically, the *religious tradition* to which someone belongs. Social scientists have classified the myriad religions, and denominations within those religions, into a manageable set of religious families, or traditions. These include evangelical and mainline Protestants—the former being more theologically conservative than the latter. Owing to the unique history of the black church in America, black Protestants are considered distinct—agreeing with white evangelicals on many doctrines, but diverging in other important ways (e.g., their emphasis on liberation theology). Other religious traditions include Catholics, Jews, and Mormons. There are still more traditions, including Muslims, Buddhists, Sikhs and the like, but they are generally in such small numbers that most surveys of the national population have too few cases for reliable analysis. As the United States becomes more religiously diverse and these religious groups grow in numbers, scholars would be wise to learn more about the public opinion of members of these small-but-growing religions.

It is also important to pause and note that in speaking about how religion affects public opinion, we are implicitly acknowledging that public opinion can also be affected by the absence of religion in someone's worldview. While the United States remains a highly religious nation—especially when compared to other industrialized democracies—recent years have seen an increase in the percentage of Americans who report having no religious affiliation. Up until the late 1980s, roughly 7 percent of the population told pollsters they have no religion. By the mid-2000s that had more than doubled to 15 percent—and up to 25 percent among people under age thirty. Many of these "religious nones"[1] appear to be disassociated from organized religion but not from religious beliefs per se, as large numbers of them believe in God. One theory explaining the rise of the nones is that they are the product of a political environment where religion is intimately connected to politics, and to conservative politics at that. They believe that identifying with a religion implies that they are sympathetic to the religious right; thus, they choose to identify as a none. Whatever the explanation for their growth, roughly one-third of the nones are what Putnam and Campbell label "liminals"—half in a religion and half out—as they flit back and forth from reporting a religious affiliation to identifying as a none.[2] Also found among the ranks of the nones, though, is a group of ardent secularists. They are more than passively "non religious"; they have affirmatively rejected any religious influence on their lives. As their ranks grow, public opinion scholars will need to remember that studying "religion" also means studying the absence of, or even outright rejection of, religion. This chapter will take a step in that direction by examining how voters who have both high and low levels of personal religiosity react to religious cues by political candidates. Future research will profit from employing measures that differentiate between liminal, passive, and committed secularists.

Why Religion Might, or Might Not, Affect Public Opinion

To discuss *how* religion affects public opinion presupposes that it does, indeed, have such an effect. Not everyone agrees. Below we lay out the arguments for both points of view.

Why Religion Might Matter

Perhaps the primary reason why we might expect religion to shape public opinion is simply that religion is a source of values and beliefs. What other institution regularly offers instruction explicitly designed to inculcate a particular worldview, and has extensive terminology and symbology to do so? Religions are in the business of indoctrination. It seems reasonable to expect that at least some of those religious doctrines would have political relevance.

Previous research has provided evidence that various aspects of religion can have an effect on public opinion. The clearest evidence is that higher religiosity—no matter how measured—corresponds to conservative opinions on issues that relate to sex and the family, specifically abortion and gay marriage.[3] The fact that religious people have conservative opinions on issues related to sexuality is not new. For as far back as we have data, this has been the case.[4] However, the political salience of these issues is relatively new. In the current political environment, these issues are the glue uniting the "coalition of the religious" that votes predominantly Republican. Prior to the mid-1980s—

when the religious right emerged in American politics—these issues had little political relevance and, consequently, religion had little to do with how Americans voted.

There have also been a few studies that examine how religion affects opinion in domains other than social issues. For example, Barker and Carman provide a detailed analysis of how religious doctrine affects economic attitudes. Drawing on Max Weber's seminal *Spirit of Capitalism*, they find evidence that the beliefs of theologically conservative Protestants lead to economically conservative opinions.[5] Similarly, Wilson shows that economic attitudes have historically differed by religious tradition.[6] In an intriguing study, Guth et al. find a belief that the "end times" are coming soon correlates with opposition to environmentalism. According to this apocalyptic worldview, not only does the imminent end of the world make efforts toward environmental protection futile, environmental problems are themselves a sign that Christ will soon return (a doctrine known as "dispensationalism" or "premillennialism").[7] In a study of religion and opinion on international affairs, Barker et al. find that a belief in the authority of the Bible leads to greater support for a militaristic foreign policy, especially military support for Israel.[8] Guth also highlights how religious beliefs correspond to support for an aggressively interventionist foreign policy—again, with conservative beliefs corresponding to conservative political opinions.[9]

Layman and Green offer an explanation for why religion matters most for attitudes on social issues, and less so for issues like the economy and foreign policy.[10] They use Converse's famous distinction between various "sources of constraint" in public opinion to argue that the relationship between religious orientations and policy attitudes is likely to be strongest and most consistent across religious contexts when there is a logical connection between religious values and issue positions. For example, someone who views the Bible as the authoritative Word of God might be expected to oppose gay marriage. When the logic of how religious values relate to policy positions is less clear, the sources of constraint linking religion and issue attitudes have to be either individuals' psychological orientations or their social experiences—making the relevance of religion for these policy attitudes weaker overall and stronger in some religious groups than in others. Consider tax policy. It is not obvious what a belief in authoritative scripture means for one's opinion regarding the capital gains tax. Supporting this argument, Layman and Green find that religious commitment and the orthodoxy of religious beliefs are strongly related to conservative attitudes on moral and cultural issues such as abortion and gay rights across all of the major religious traditions. However, the effect of religious orientations on positions regarding social welfare, defense, and environmental attitudes is generally weaker and far more pronounced for evangelical Protestants than for mainline Protestants and Catholics. Consistent with Layman and Green, Putnam and Campbell show that, when controlling for other factors affecting public opinion, religious and secular Americans have sharply different opinions on abortion and gay marriage—with opposition to both concentrated among the highly religious. However, religious and secular Americans' opinions differ only modestly on social welfare, foreign aid, foreign policy, and civil liberties. They also find that, within the general population, religion has no connection to attitudes on immigration and the death penalty—two of the issues that we will examine in more detail below.[11]

The challenge in making sense out of this research literature is that scholars often conceptualize and measure "religion" in different ways. Some studies look at belonging, others examine behaving, and others focus on believing. Even when two studies are looking at the same dimension of religion, their precise measures often differ. Nonetheless, this small literature review has, collectively, begun to make the case that religion does have a causal effect on political attitudes.

Why Religion Might Not Matter

That case, though, is not yet closed. For all the reasons that the various dimensions of religion might affect public opinion, there are also plausible reasons to suspect that they do not actually have any effect. For example, while there is no doubt that religions are in the belief business, it is not always clear how a given religious belief translates into public policy. Virtually all religions teach of concern for the poor; but does that mean a believer should support a generous welfare state or favor private charities as a means to provide assistance to the disadvantaged?

Even when religious leaders do make explicit the connection between a religious belief and a political view, there is no guarantee that the "people in the pews" will adopt that political attitude. American Catholics are an excellent example. In spite of the Roman Catholic Church's long-standing opposition to abortion, a majority of Catholics nonetheless support a woman's right to choose an abortion in at least some circumstances. An even greater majority of Catholics support the death penalty, again in spite of the Church's teachings otherwise.

Even when the political beliefs held by members of a religious group correlate with the teachings within a religion, it is still not the "smoking gun" to establish a truly causal relationship. The fluid nature of American religion means that where and how one worships is typically a matter of individual choice. This is why in the United States religion is often referred to as a preference rather than an ascribed characteristic. People frequently switch religions and, even more frequently, move from one congregation to another. Roughly one-third of all Americans switch religious traditions over the course of their lifetimes, including switching to "no religion"; half have shopped for a new congregation.[12] With all of this fluidity, Americans sort themselves into like-minded religious groups—including when it comes to politics. Thus, for some people, it may not be that religion influences someone's political attitudes so much as those political attitudes influence someone's choice of religion. Or, as noted in the above discussion of the rise of the religious nones, a negative reaction to the mixture of religion and politics can lead people to disavow a religious identity at all. Similarly, politics can also influence religious behavior such that, over time, conservatives become more fervent and liberals less so. In other words, Americans are sorting themselves into "camps" defined both by their religion and their politics—religious conservatives in one and secular liberals in another.

Religion and Party Identification: The Indirect Effect Hypothesis

In between the contrasting arguments that religion either does, or does not, shape public opinion is still another possibility. It could be that religion affects public opinion through its impact on party identification. Party identification, in turn, shapes political attitudes. Call this the "indirect effect" hypothesis. It would still mean that religion matters, but is one step removed from having a direct effect on voters' opinions. Or, it could be that religion has a direct effect on some attitudes toward issues, and an indirect effect—through party identification—on others.

Religion, or more accurately "religious traditionalism," has become a major predictor of partisanship over roughly the last three decades. A number of studies have shown that, beginning in the 1980s and then accelerating through the 1990s, a so-called "God gap" has opened up in American politics, whereby highly religious voters are more likely to identify as Republicans than Democrats. Some have described this change as a "culture war" that divides the electorate between religiously orthodox and religiously progressive voters. Using more temperate language, Green refers to this change as the "old religion gap" between religious denominations—e.g., Catholic vs. Protestant—being replaced by a new "religion gap." This new gap is defined not by one's denomination, but instead one's level of religious devotion.[13]

One important reason for this shift has been the parties' differing positions on cultural issues like homosexual rights and—especially—abortion, which as noted above, are the two issues that have the strongest correlation with religiosity.  But in addition to the issues emphasized by candidates, the God gap has resulted from the religious "brand label" adopted by many Republican candidates. For at least a generation, Republicans running for office have been more likely to describe themselves in religious terms than their Democratic opponents. A particularly memorable example arose in the 2004 presidential election, when the Republican National Committee sent many thousands of glossy fliers to Ohio voters, complete with prominent images of churches and statements that the Republicans are the party "defending traditional marriage."[14]

We need not rely on anecdotal examples to see how religion has infused the Republican party's brand. When we examine systematic data, the Republican Party is more likely to be associated with religion than is the Democratic party. For example, when compared to the Democrats, more Americans say that the Republicans are friendly to religion.[15] And when we asked voters to list the groups that come to mind when they think of either party, only "conservatives" came out ahead of religious groups for the GOP. In sharp contrast, religious groups provide an infinitesimal share of the groups associated with the Democratic party.[16] The Republicans' religious brand label has meant that it is increasingly the home of religiously devout voters—with, however, the notable exception of African Americans, who as a group are highly religious but also predominantly Democratic (a hint that religion does not always move people rightward).

Thus far, we have proposed three alternatives for the potential influence of religion and public opinion. Perhaps it has no effect, in which case there is no point in studying religion and public opinion any further. Or maybe religion has an indirect effect, by influencing partisanship which, in turn, affects public opinion. If so, future research could be limited to understanding how religion affects party identification. Alternatively, there could be a direct, causal link between religion and public opinion, which would justify the further study of how, when, and why it has an effect.

Does Religious Always Mean Conservative?

Today, religion is routinely equated with political conservatism. But this has not always been the case. American history is replete with political mobilizers who have drawn on religion to inspire support for their cause. Some are easily categorized as conservatives, others as liberals, while still others do not map neatly onto a one-dimensional ideological map. Today, conservative opponents of abortion and gay marriage often use religiously grounded arguments. While these issues are, in historical terms, relatively new on the political agenda, the religious inflection of political rhetoric is not new at all. The American Revolution itself had religious underpinnings. Later on, abolitionism and, later still, the civil rights movement both had religious roots. Prohibition had a religious inflection, as did anti-communism in the Cold War. But so did opposition to the Vietnam War, and to war in general. In presidential politics, William Jennings Bryan—three-time Democratic nominee for the presidency—passionately defended the economic interests of laborers and farmers with fiery religious talk in the late nineteenth and early twentieth centuries. In perhaps the most famous speech ever delivered at a political convention, Bryan declared that the economic system of his day would "crucify mankind upon a cross of gold." Just to make his meaning clear, he then stood with his arms outstretched as though hanging on a cross.[17] More recently, while running for president in 1976 Jimmy Carter declared himself to be "born again," while—in probably the most cited example of presidential God talk—presidential candidate George W. Bush described "Christ" as his favorite political philosopher because "he changed my heart." Barack Obama is also no stranger to religious language; as a presidential candidate he spoke often of his conversion to Christianity.[18]

The fact that so many political candidates and activists use religious language suggests that religion can shape public opinion. These examples are hardly an exhaustive list of how religion has been woven into our national politics. Yet because they are all over the political map, collectively they suggest that religious framing of issues has not historically been limited to one side of the political spectrum.

Unfortunately, however, the scholarship on religion and public opinion might also lead one to the conclusion that religion nearly always pulls attitudes rightward. Since virtually all empirical research on religion and political attitudes has come during the era of the God gap, the great majority of it has focused on how religion and conservative ideology/Republican partisanship go together. Similarly, recall that the above examples of how religion affects attitudes on the environment, economic policy, and foreign policy all show how various religious beliefs drive conservative opinions. One intriguing exception is found in Barker et al.'s research on religion and militarism in foreign policy. They actually find that greater religious devotion leads to a liberal perspective on foreign policy—once they subtract out the influence of exposure to the religious right (what they refer to as "Christian culture").

When we direct our attention from political rhetoric to the substance of religious teachings, we see further reason to think that religion can buttress liberal, as well as conservative, attitudes. Many religions have doctrines that unambiguously align with the political left. In fact, there are notable examples of religious traditions whose adherents are predominantly political liberals rather than conservatives. Jews are one, while black Protestants are another.

Even religious traditions that are not known as bastions of liberal politics can have left-leaning teachings. Among Protestants there is a long tradition of the "social gospel," a belief that churches should be involved in eradicating poverty. In recent years, some evangelical pastors have publicly called for anti-poverty legislation, aid to Africa to fight AIDS, and greater environmental regulation. Do these appeals work? As evidence that they do, or at least that they *can*, Djupe and Gwiasda find that evangelicals—known for their political conservativism—become more liberal on environmental policy when they learn of a fellow evangelical having a religious "conversion experience" about the danger of global warming.[19] Catholicism also espouses teachings that align with the political left. Many Catholic theologians speak of a "preferential option for the poor"—which often translates into support for a generous welfare state. As we noted earlier, Catholic teaching also opposes the death penalty. While, as also noted, most Catholics actually favor capital punishment, this fact does not necessarily mean that the Church's teachings fall on deaf ears. Below we will test whether devout Catholics are more likely to oppose the death penalty than less-committed Catholics—which would suggest that they are absorbing their Church's teachings after all.

Even religious traditions known for their political conservatism occasionally take policy stands on the left. Consider, for example, the Church of Jesus Christ of Latter-day Saints, or the Mormon Church. Mormons are arguably the most politically conservative religious group in the country; certainly, they are the most heavily Republican. Typically, when the Mormon Church has been involved in politics it has been on the conservative side of social issues. Most recently, the Mormon Church has been a leading opponent of gay marriage. Indeed, in 2008 the Mormon Church took a high-profile position in support of California's Proposition 8, a state constitutional amendment to ban gay marriage. On immigration, though, Mormons are not nearly as conservative as on other issues. Immigration is an issue on which Mormon leaders have cut against the grain and sent signals favoring a liberal position, thus providing an important test for the influence of religion over political ideology. In the predominantly Mormon state of Utah, support for a bill that was punitive toward illegal immigrants (it would have denied them in-state tuition at Utah colleges) dropped over 20 points once a prominent Mormon leader spoke publicly of the need for compassion toward immigrants, and another signed a statement opposing the bill. As shown below, Mormons are also the religious group least likely to think that there should be a decrease in the percentage of "immigrants from foreign countries who are permitted to come to the United States to live."

In sum, while there is generally a correlation between religiosity and political conservatism, both historical and contemporary evidence indicates that religion has often been used in defense of positions on the ideological left rather than the right. However, it remains an open question whether, *in the current religious and political environment*, religion can actually move political attitudes to the left.

The Verdict

Having laid out the reasons why religion might—and might not—influence public opinion and, if so, why it might not always move attitudes rightward, we turn to some evidence to try and answer these questions.

We begin by comparing the attitudes of people in America's major religious traditions, including "none of the above." In addition to the nones, these include Catholics, mainline Protestants, evangelical Protestants, black Protestants, Jews, and Mormons.[20] The data we use comes from the Faith Matters survey, a nationally representative survey of 3,100 respondents.[21] Our comparisons are made by estimating a statistical model that holds constant an array of demographic factors that could both affect political attitudes and are potentially confounded with membership in a given religious tradition, including living in the south, education, age, race (African American), ethnicity (Hispanic), marital status, and gender. For example, the model controls for whether someone lives in the south because southerners are most likely to be evangelicals and to have conservative moral and cultural attitudes. We want to ensure that any impact we attribute to being an evangelical is not actually because someone lives in the South.

Figures 8.1–8.4 include one more control variable that, given our above discussion, is especially critical: party identification. We have accounted for any differences in partisanship across these religious traditions. In doing so, we are testing what we above labeled the "indirect effect" hypothesis: that religion's impact on public opinion works through partisanship. If there are no differences across religious traditions once we account for their differing partisan allegiances, then we can conclude that the indirect effect hypothesis is correct. On the other hand, if differences across religious traditions survive even when accounting for their adherents' party identification, that is evidence for a direct effect of religion on political attitudes. (Although there could still be indirect effects; it would only mean that they are not the whole story.)[22]

We focus on four issues: abortion, the death penalty, environmental policy, and immigration. These four issues are all politically salient, and have a plausible connection to religious doctrines. Abortion and capital punishment are often discussed in religious terms, while the environment has increasingly been given a religious frame (e.g., "creation care"). As the immigration debate

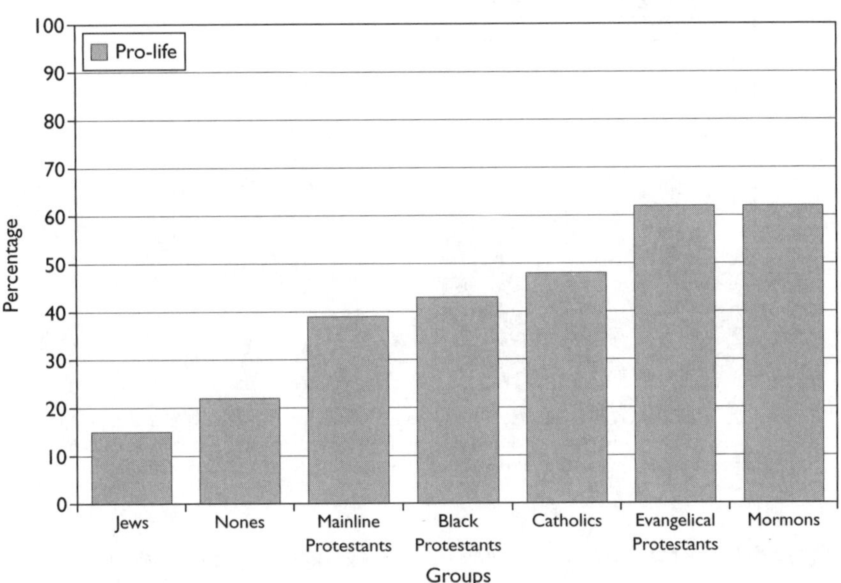

Figure 8.1 Abortion (controlling for demographics and party identification).

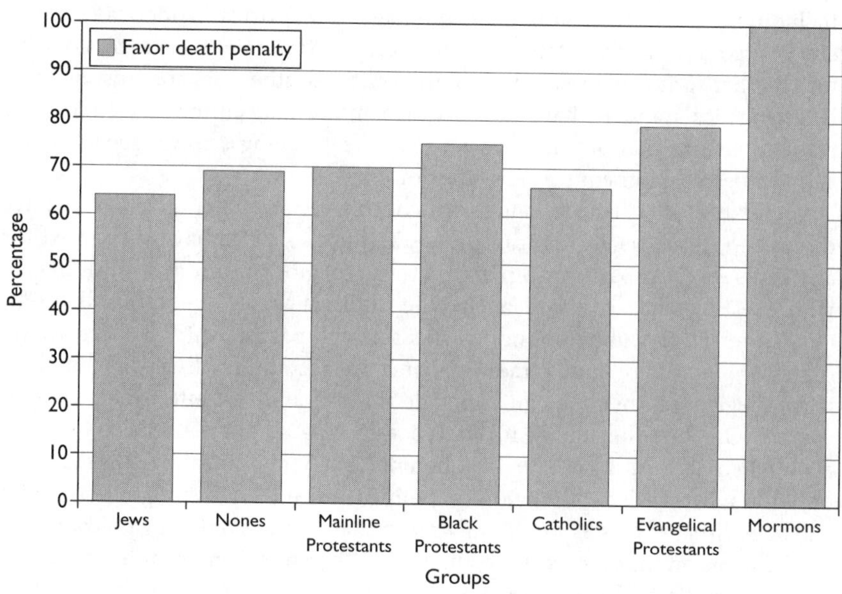

Figure 8.2 Death Penalty (controlling for demographics and party identification).

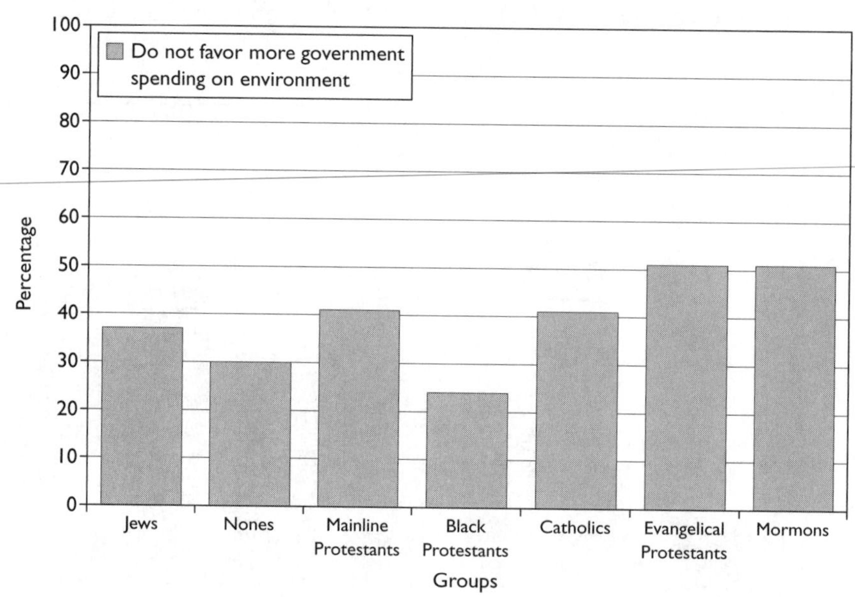

Figure 8.3 Environment (controlling for demographics and party identification).

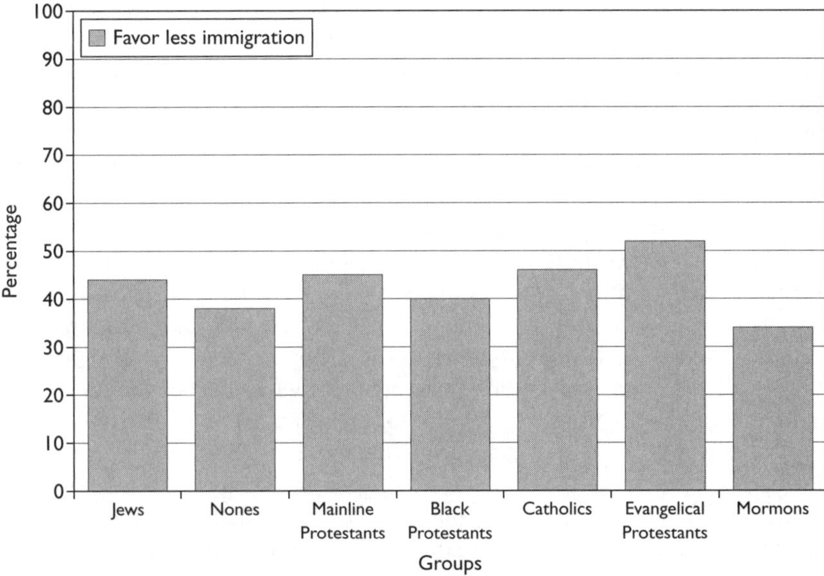

Figure 8.4 Immigration (controlling for demographics and party identification).

has heated up, many religious leaders have argued on behalf of compassion for undocumented workers over the strict enforcement of immigration laws.[23]

We calculate the mean opinion on each issue within each of America's major religious traditions, while also accounting for demographic and partisan differences across these groups. The results are displayed in Figures 8.1–8.4. The figures all display the percentage taking a conservative position on the issue in question: the percentage who are pro-life, favor the death penalty, oppose more government spending on the environment, and favor reducing immigration. Figure 8.1, for example, displays the results for abortion. Specifically, the figure shows the percentage in each religious tradition who oppose abortion in all circumstances, or only approve of it in cases of rape, incest, and when the life of the mother is in jeopardy. As you can see, attitudes on abortion vary dramatically across religious traditions. Only 15 percent of Jews oppose abortion, compared to 62 percent of both evangelicals and Mormons.

Differences are far more muted on the death penalty, however. Capital punishment has majority support across all religious traditions, although support among Jews and Catholics is a little lower. On the environment, there are again only modest differences, but this time because the conservative option is in the minority—except among evangelicals and Mormons, where opinion splits half-and-half. On this issue, black Protestants are the most liberal, with nones and Jews right behind.

Immigration is another story all together. Opinion on immigration does not vary much across religious traditions. Nones and black Protestants are among the most liberal, which is no surprise given their general liberal ideology. Only 38 percent of nones and 40 percent of black Protestants favor less immigration, compared to 52 percent of evangelicals. As alluded to earlier, Mormons are the group whose attitudes on immigration cut against their general ideological profile. Only 34 percent of Mormons favor less immigration—the lowest of any religious tradition.

What do we learn from these comparisons across religious traditions? First, we see that differences in opinion survive even when accounting for the partisan make up of each religious tradition. So, even though most Jews are Democrats, that alone does not explain their support for abortion rights. On the other side of that issue, evangelicals are heavily Republican, but their party affiliation does not completely account for their opposition to abortion.

Nor does religion's impact reduce to demography. Even when accounting for demographic differences across these groups, members of different religious traditions have widely varying opinions on some issues (most notably abortion). Nonetheless, the mere existence of these differences does not cinch the case that religion in and of itself shapes opinion. The very same results could follow from people sorting themselves into different religions on the basis of their political views, rather than the religions themselves influencing their politics.

Some of the specific differences we observe, however, are suggestive that perhaps the religions themselves influence opinion, rather than the other way around. Furthermore, they also provide some evidence that religion can move opinions to the left as well as the right. Catholics, for example, have a relatively low level of support for the death penalty, which is presumably because of the Catholic Church's opposition to capital punishment. While a majority of Catholics favor capital punishment (66 percent), it is quite a bit lower than evangelicals (79 percent) and black Protestants (75 percent), and a little lower than mainline Protestants (70 percent) and nones (69 percent). Only Jews (64 percent) are less likely than Catholics to favor the death penalty.

Modestly lower level of support for the death penalty among Catholics is hardly definitive evidence that church teachings have had a large effect on Catholics' attitudes. Still, the evidence is suggestive.

More convincing evidence of religion's impact on political attitudes—and in a leftward direction—can be seen among Mormons. This highly conservative group nonetheless has the most liberal attitudes on immigration, an outcome that is difficult to explain solely on the basis of self-selection. It seems more plausible that Mormons' relatively liberal perspective on immigration is a result of their religion. However, scratching below the surface of that conclusion only underscores the complexity of understanding religion's impact on attitudes. Are Mormons liberal on immigration because they are members of a religious minority, and thus empathize with immigrants?[24] Is it because so many Mormons do missionary work in foreign countries, often in Latin America?[25] Is it because the LDS Church accommodates illegal immigrants within its ranks?[26] Or, most likely, is it owing to some combination of these, and perhaps other, factors? These are the sorts of questions to which the public opinion literature has not yet provided definitive answers—whether for the specific case of Mormons, or for other religious traditions more generally.

Religiosity

Having seen some evidence of differences in public opinion across religious traditions, we turn next to a different aspect of religion: religious commitment, or religiosity. Think of religious tradition—Catholic, evangelical, etc.—as the "flavor" of one's religion, while religiosity is the intensity of that flavor. Our measure of religiosity is an index that includes six different measures of religious commitment: frequency of religious attendance, frequency of prayer, importance of religion in one's daily life, religion as a source of personal identity, being a strong believer in one's religion, and strength of belief in God. All of these go together, so that people who score high on one measure are likely to be high on another.

We examine how attitudes vary as religiosity increases in Figures 8.5–8.7. Each graph displays how attitudes in a given religious tradition change as religiosity moves from its lowest to highest levels, while also accounting for

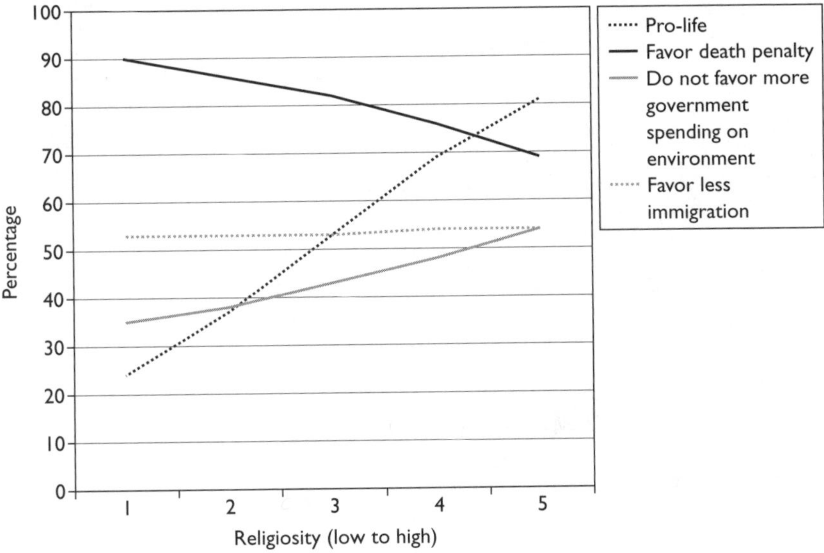

Figure 8.5 Evangelical Protestants.

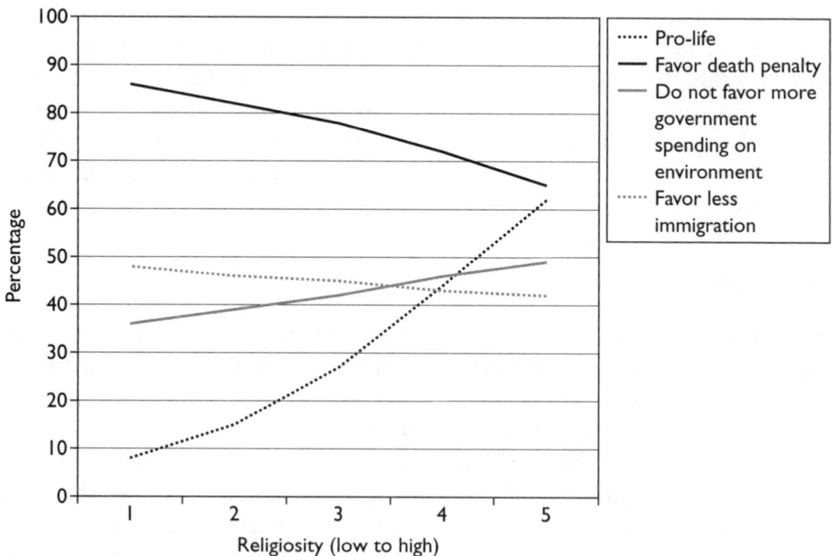

Figure 8.6 Mainline Protestants.

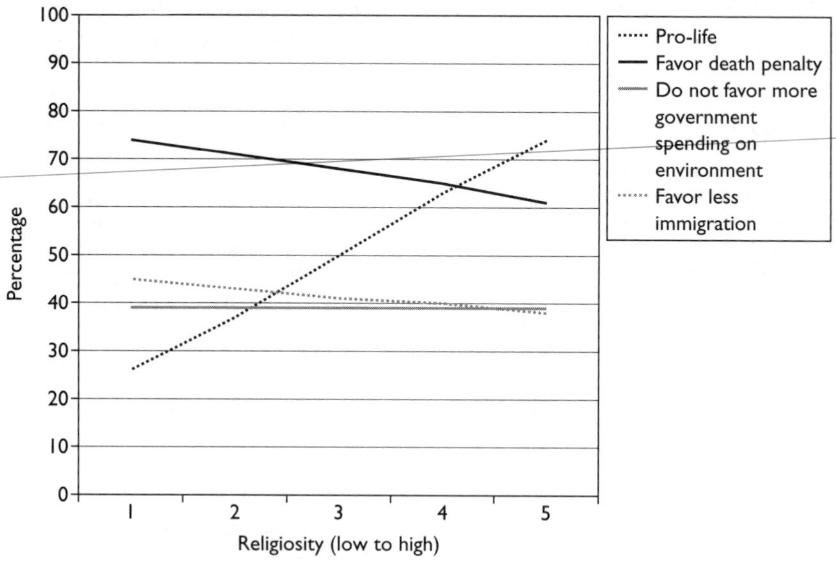

Figure 8.7 Catholics.

demographic characteristics.[27] For these figures, religiosity is divided into quintiles—that is, five equal-sized "bins" of religiosity. Each line in the graph represents a different issue: abortion, death penalty, environment, and immigration. We are only able to show results for the three largest religious traditions in the United States: evangelical Protestants, mainline Protestants, and Catholics. The other traditions have too few members, even in a large national survey, to produce reliable results in an analysis such as this.[28]

Across these three religious traditions, the results are strikingly similar. In each group, abortion has far and away the strongest relationship to religiosity—higher religiosity is associated with greater opposition to abortion. Among the two Protestant traditions, attitudes on the environment also shift rightward as religiosity increases; among Catholics, religiosity has no bearing on environmental attitudes. On immigration, there is essentially a flat line for all three traditions, meaning that opinion on immigration is unrelated to religiosity.

Opinion on the death penalty also shows a consistent pattern. Within each tradition, greater religiosity is associated with considerably less support for the death penalty. Majorities still support capital punishment, but the drop in support as religiosity rises from the bottom to the top quintile is nonetheless considerable. In other words, higher religiosity correlates with a liberal position on capital punishment.[29]

What conclusions can be drawn from this analysis of religiosity's impact on attitudes? For one, religiosity generally has a consistent relationship with opinions across the three largest religious traditions in the United States. That consistency includes one case where there is no connection between religiosity and opinion (immigration), one where religiosity moves opinion rightward (abortion), and another where it moves to the left (death penalty).

In the fourth case, environmental policy, rising religiosity moves attitudes to the right among evangelical and mainline Protestants, but not among Catholics. This difference in environmental attitudes among Protestants and Catholics could be related to Protestant beliefs about the "end times." As has been noted already, previous research has shown that those who believe that the world will end soon, a belief more commonly held by Protestants than Catholics—and highly religious Protestants at that—are less likely to support pro-environmental policies.

In sum, we have seen evidence that even in a political climate where religion is generally associated with conservative politics, religion can also serve to push public opinion to the left. No iron law links religion and political conservatism.

Religious Framing

As we have already mentioned, determining a causal relationship between any aspect of religion and public opinion is elusive. Causal inference is most convincing with a randomized experiment, but that proves difficult in the study of religion. It would require randomly assigning people to different religions, or different levels of personal religiosity.

However, it *is* possible to use experimental methods to test how voters of differing degrees of religiosity react when an issue is framed in religious vs. secular terms. Can candidates succeed in using a religious frame, thus winning the support of highly religious voters? And can they do so without losing the support of low-religiosity voters? We can test voters' reactions to religious frames by presenting hypothetical candidates to voters, some of whom use religious language to explain their rationale for a certain issue position and some who instead offer a secular rationale. In conducting such an experiment, we are able to test our two central questions from a new perspective: does religious framing influence voters' opinion, and can that influence be in a liberal direction?

The design of the experiment is simple. Respondents were given descriptions of two candidates, and asked whether they would be more likely to vote for one or the other. Each candidate had a party label, and was identified as having taken a conservative or liberal position on global warming, the death penalty, or immigration. In the results we display below, we examine what happens when a Republican candidate takes the liberal position on each of these three issues, in contrast to a conservative Democratic opponent. Half of the time the Republican candidate uses a religious frame for his liberal position, and the other half he uses a secular frame. The experiment thus enables us to see whether a candidate can earn greater support for a liberal policy position by framing it in religious terms.[30] (For the wording used in the experiment, see the Appendix to this chapter.)

In presenting the results, we divide respondents into three levels of religious commitment, as determined by an index similar to the one employed above.[31] This way, we can see how religious frames affect voters who have varying levels of personal religiosity.[32]

Figures 8.8 through 8.10 all have the same format. The darker bars show the percentage choosing the Republican candidate when he uses a secular frame; the lighter bars represent the Republican's support when using a religious frame. The difference between the bars, then, is the effect of a religious vs. a secular frame. For all three issues, we see that highly religious voters respond favorably to a religious frame, and thus are more likely to vote for the Republican candidate than when he uses a secular frame for the same issue position. For them, the religion effect is positive, statistically significant, and in a liberal direction.

Among voters with low religiosity, the story is more nuanced. On the environment, there is such a slight drop for the religious frame that it is statistically meaningless. On the death penalty, there is a more substantial drop in support for a God-talking candidate (from 44 to 29 percent, which is statistically significant). However, when the issue is immigration, the God-talking

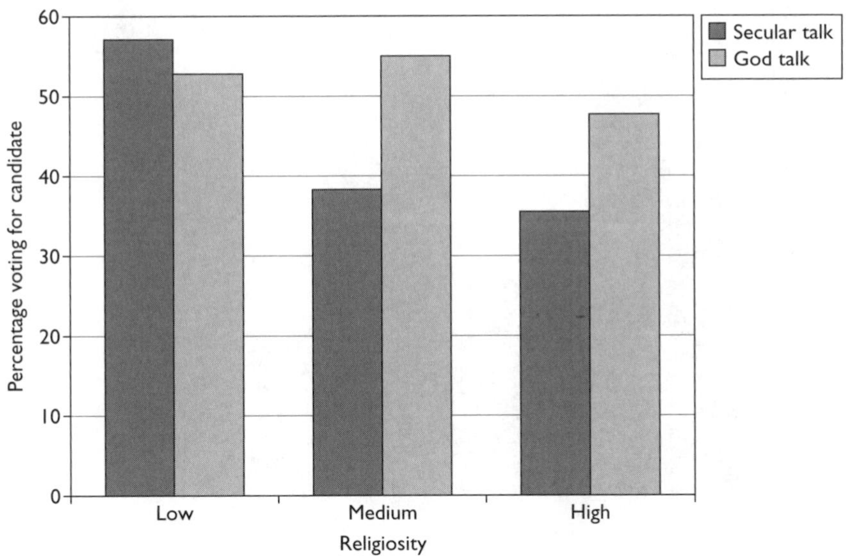

Figure 8.8 Secular vs. Religious Frame for the Environment.

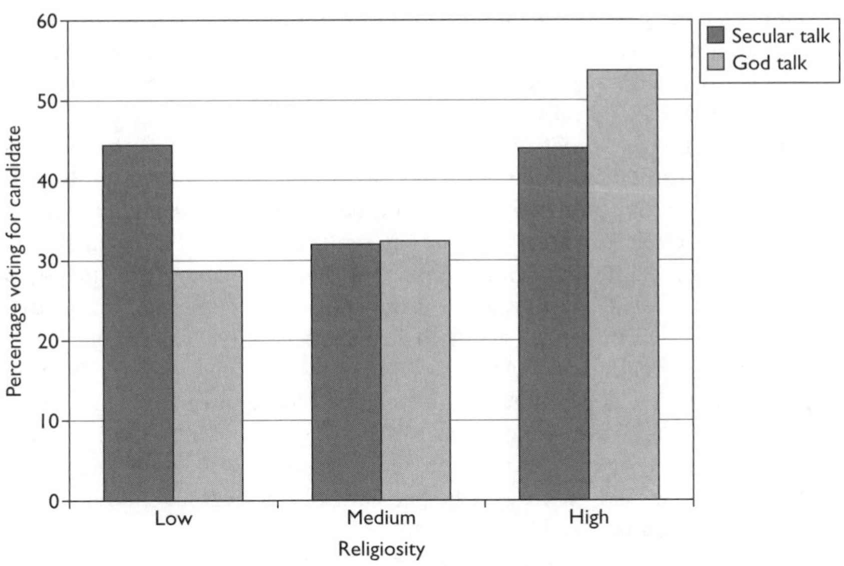

Figure 8.9 Secular vs. Religious Frame for the Death Penalty.

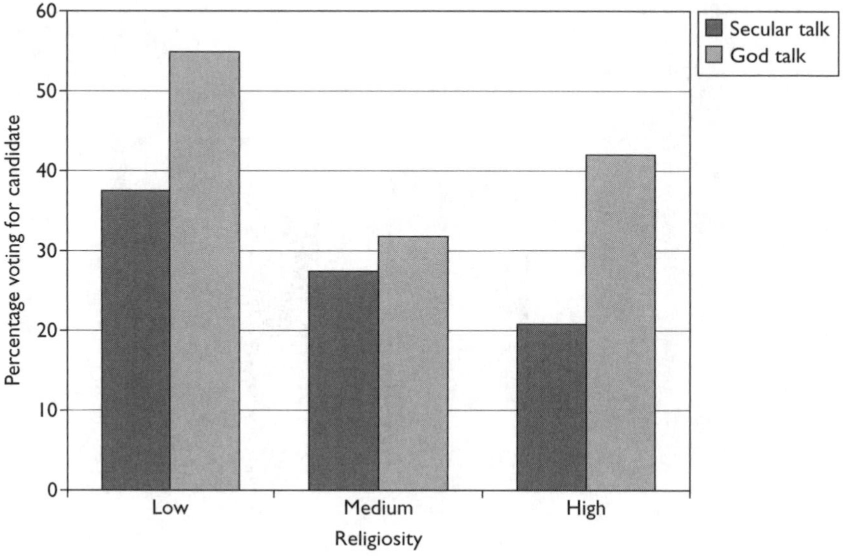

Figure 8.10 Secular vs. Religious Frame for Immigration.

candidate actually picks up support from low-religiosity voters.[33] This is the only issue for which God talk increases support across the religiosity spectrum. (Middle-religiosity voters increase their support, but the four-point rise does not achieve statistical significance.)

The overall story is that religious framing of issues can affect how voters respond to a candidate. For high-religiosity voters, this effect is most pronounced for the environment and immigration. The weaker effect for the death penalty may be related to the fact that high-religiosity voters are actually less likely to support capital punishment than more secular voters. Consequently, a religious cue to justify opposition to it may only be reinforcing a previously held opinion rather than successfully challenging voters' preconceptions.

Among low-religiosity voters, sometimes a religious frame decreases support for a liberal position (death penalty), sometimes it has no effect (environment), and sometimes it can increase support (immigration). The increased support for a liberal position on immigration is intriguing, as it suggests that even secular voters may be persuaded by a religious rationale for a controversial position.

Conclusion

The discussion of religion in contemporary politics typically assumes that religion is associated with conservatism, and support for the Republican party in particular. That assumption is not wholly unwarranted, as more-religious

Americans are generally more likely to identify as Republicans than the less religious. Yet, notwithstanding this general tendency, there are still important exceptions. Most notably, African Americans are simultaneously the most religious and the most Democratic group within the population. Historically, religion has also inspired many politically progressive causes. Even in today's political environment, religion is associated with liberal attitudes on at least one issue—the death penalty. Furthermore, our experimental evidence suggests that highly religious voters respond favorably to candidates who use religious frames for liberal positions on the environment, capital punishment, and immigration.

In showing that religion is not ineluctably associated with conservatism, our results also speak to the fundamental question of whether religion affects public opinion at all. Given that highly religious voters are *generally* conservative and Republican, to find a correlation between religion (and/or religiosity) and liberal attitudes strengthens the argument that it is religion driving opinion, and not opinion driving the choice of religion.

However, this chapter is merely a start to understanding the ways in which religion may—or may not—affect public opinion. Many more facets of religion in America are largely unexplored. Djupe and Gilbert, for example, stress the need for more attention to the political deliberation that takes place within congregations.[34] Other examples include the political implications of specific beliefs taught in various denominations, the growing ranks of the nones (who themselves are not monolithic), and the rising number of Americans who affiliate with Islam and other minority religions. But this list, too, is only a start, as there are myriad ways that the varied aspects of religion might move public opinion—both to the left and the right.

Appendix

Following are the questions used to gauge opinion on abortion, the death penalty, the environment, and immigration policy in the Faith Matters 2006 survey.

Abortion

Which one of these opinions best corresponds to your view?

1. By law, abortion should never be permitted.
2. The law should permit abortion only in cases of rape, incest, or when the woman's life is in danger.
3. The law should permit abortion for reasons other than rape, incest, or danger to the woman's life, but only after the need for the abortion has been clearly established.
4. By law, a woman should always be able to obtain an abortion as a matter of personal choice.

(Respondents were randomly assigned to receive the options in this or the reverse order.)

In the results shown, options 1 and 2 were combined into one pro-life category, and 3 and 4 into a pro-choice category.

Death Penalty

Do you favor or oppose the death penalty for persons convicted of murder?

1. Favor death penalty for persons convicted of murder.
2. Oppose death penalty for persons convicted of murder.

Environment

Next I am going to read you a list of federal programs. For each one, I would like you to tell me whether you would like to see spending increased, decreased, or kept about the same. The (first/next) program is Environmental Protection. Would you like to see spending for this increased, decreased, or kept about the same?

1. Spending increased.
2. Decreased.
3. Kept about the same.

Immigration

Do you think the number of immigrants from foreign countries who are permitted to come to the United States to live should be increased a lot, increased a little, left the same as it is now, decreased a little, or decreased a lot?

1. Increased a lot.
2. Increased a little.
3. Left the same as it is now.
4. Decreased a little.
5. Decreased a lot.

In the analysis, options 1–2 and 4–5 were each combined into one category, thus creating a tri-partite variable. The results show the percentage that favors less immigration (options 4 and 5).

Below are the frames used in the framing experiment in the 2008 Cooperative Campaign Analysis Project.

Environment

Please read the descriptions of the following two candidates for the U.S Congress and tell us who you would be more likely to vote for.

Robert Williams is age 48, married, and has three children. A Republican, he has served three terms in his state legislature. When asked in a debate about his position on the need to reduce global warming, he responded with enthusiasm:

> "Protecting the environment must be our top priority. I am in favor of working to reduce global warming." <Secular>

Or

> "God has given us this earth, and we must protect it. The Bible says we are to care for God's creation." <Religious>

Michael Clark is age 51, married, and also has three children. A Democrat, he has served for six years on his local school board. When asked in a debate about his position on the need to reduce global warming, he responded with skepticism:

> "I am in favor of putting jobs first, and oppose any so-called environmental bill that would hurt our economy." <Secular>

Based on the above information, would you be more likely to vote for Robert Williams or Michael Clark?

The frames for the death penalty used the same biographical information for the two candidates but varied the issue frames, as below.

Death Penalty

...When asked in a debate about his position on the death penalty, he indicated his opposition.

> "I am against the death penalty. It is too easy to convict the wrong person, as shown whenever DNA evidence frees an innocent man." <Secular>

Or

> "Only God should decide who lives and who dies. The Bible says 'thou shalt not kill,' which means even those who have committed terrible crimes." <Religious>

...When asked in a debate about his position on the death penalty, he indicated his support.

> "I favor capital punishment for the most violent criminals. The death penalty is the right punishment for those found guilty of first-degree murder." <Secular>

The immigration experiment was conducted on a separate survey than the previous two and thus used different hypothetical candidates, as described below.

Immigration

Please read the descriptions of the following two candidates for the U.S Senate and tell us who you would be more likely to vote for.

John Layman is a Democrat who wants to crack down on the problem of illegal immigration. He was recently quoted in the news as saying:

> "We are a nation that respects the law. Illegal aliens should not be rewarded for breaking the law."

David Green is a Republican who favors immigration reform so that people who have entered the United States illegally can stay in the country legally. In a recent news article, he said the following:

> "As a nation, we must show compassion to everyone. Undocumented workers in America should have a chance to become U.S. citizens." <Secular>

> "Jesus taught that we must show compassion to everyone. These hard-working people should have a chance to become U.S. citizens." <Religious>

Notes

1. Throughout this chapter, we will use the shorthand term "nones" to describe those who report no religious affiliation. Within the sociology of religion it has been used for decades and, more recently, has come into wider usage. See, for example, Joseph O. Baker and Buster G. Smith, "The Nones: Social Characteristics of the Religiously Unaffiliated," *Social Forces* 87, no. 3 (2009).
2. Robert D. Putnam and David E. Campbell, *American Grace: How Religion Divides and Unites Us* (New York: Simon and Schuster, 2010).
3. For a thorough discussion of religion and public opinion on social issues, see Ted G. Jelen, "Religion and American Public Opinion: Social Issues," in *The Oxford Handbook of Religion and American Politics*, eds. Corwin E. Smidt, Lyman A. Kellstedt, and James L. Guth (New York: Oxford University Press, 2009).
4. See Putnam and Campbell, *American Grace*, for evidence on this point.
5. David C. Barker and Christopher Jan Carman, "The Spirit of Capitalism? Religious

Doctrine, Values, and Economic Attitude Constructs," *Political Behavior* 22, no. 1 (2000).

6. J. Matthew Wilson, "Religion and American Public Opinion: Economic Issues," in *The Oxford Handbook of Religion and American Politics*, eds. Corwin E. Smidt, Lyman A. Kellstedt, and James L. Guth (New York: Oxford University Press, 2009).
7. James L. Guth, John C. Green, Lyman A. Kellstedt, and Corwin E. Smidt, "Faith and the Environment: Religious Beliefs and Attitudes on Environmental Policy," *American Journal of Political Science* 39, no. 2 (1995).
8. David C. Barker, Jon Hurwitz, and Traci L. Nelson, "Of Crusades and Culture Wars: 'Messianic' Militarism and Political Conflict in the United States," *Journal of Politics* 70, no. 2 (2008).
9. James L. Guth, "Religion and American Public Opinion: Foreign Policy," in *The Oxford Handbook of Religion and American Politics*, eds. Corwin E. Smidt, Lyman A. Kellstedt, and James L. Guth (New York: Oxford University Press, 2009).
10. Geoffrey C. Layman and John C. Green, "Wars and Rumours of Wars: The Contexts of Cultural Conflict in American Political Behavior," *British Journal of Political Science* 36, no. 1 (2006).
11. Putnam and Campbell, *American Grace.*
12. For more on religious switching, see Putnam and Campbell, *American Grace.*
13. John C. Green, *The Faith Factor: How Religion Influences American Elections* (Westport, CT: Praeger, 2007).
14. David E. Campbell and J. Quin Monson, "The Case of Bush's Re-Election: Did Gay Marriage Do It?" in *A Matter of Faith: Religion in the 2004 Presidential Election*, ed. David E. Campbell (Washington, DC: Brookings Institution Press, 2007).
15. For recent trends in the religious "brand labels" of the parties, see http://pewforum.org/Politics-and-Elections/Growing-Number-of-Americans-Say-Obama-is-a-Muslim.aspx#2.
16. David E. Campbell, John C. Green, and Geoffrey C. Layman "The Party Faithful: Partisan Images, Candidate Religion, and the Electoral Impact of Party Identification," *American Journal of Political Science* 55, no. 1 (2011).
17. Michael Kazin, *A Godly Hero: The Life of William Jennings Bryan* (New York: Alfred A. Knopf, 2006).
18. Eamon Javers, "Obama Invokes Jesus More Than Bush," *Politico*, June 9, 2009.
19. Paul Djupe and Gregory W. Gwiasda, "Evangelizing the Environment: Decision Process Effects in Political Persuasion," *Journal for the Scientific Study of Religion* 49, no. 1 (2010).
20. The number of respondents in other religious traditions (e.g., Muslims, Hindus) is too small to conduct a reliable analysis, so they have been omitted.
21. The survey was conducted in the summer of 2006. For more details on Faith Matters, see Putnam and Campbell, *American Grace.*
22. More technically, these results have been generated from logistic or ordered logistic regression models. All control variables were set to their means.
23. See the Appendix to the chapter for the exact wording of the questions.
24. Benjamin Knoll, "'And Who Is My Neighbor?' Religion and Immigration Policy Attitudes," *Journal for the Scientific Study of Religion* 48, no. 2 (2009).
25. David E. Campbell, Christopher Karpowitz, and J. Quin Monson, "A Politically Peculiar People: How Mormons Moved Into and then Out Of the Political Mainstream," (n.d.).
26. Daniel Gonzalez, "LDS Members Conflicted on Church's Illegal-Migrant Growth," *USA Today*, April 3, 2009.
27. These models mirror those used to create Figures 8.1–8.4, except that each one is limited to a single religious tradition and religiosity was included as an independent variable (along with all the same independent variables as before). The results

are generated by holding each control variable at its mean value, and varying religiosity.

28. The religious nones are actually a larger group than mainline Protestants, but it is nonsensical to examine the impact of religiosity on the attitudes of nones.
29. Even though they also analyze the Faith Matters data, these results for the death penalty are slightly different than those reported by Putnam and Campbell in *American Grace* for two reasons. First, Putnam and Campbell do not examine the impact of religiosity on attitudes toward the death penalty across religious traditions, but only for the population as a whole. Second, they do not control for party identification in their models.
30. These experiments were conducted as part of the 2008 Cooperative Campaign Analysis Project (CCAP), a large online panel survey that ran throughout 2008. CCAP was a collaborative effort by a consortium of universities; the surveys were administered by You Gov/Polimetrix to a sample of registered voters. The survey oversampled battleground states, such that voters in non-battleground and battleground states are represented in equal proportions. See Simon Jackman and Lynn Vavreck, "Primary Politics: Race, Gender, and Age in the 2008 Democratic Primary," *Journal of Elections, Public Opinion, and Policy* 20, no. 2 (2010). The experiments discussed in this chapter were administered in September (environment, death penalty) and October (immigration) of 2008. The average size for each cell of the experiment is roughly 200 cases.
31. The index has two components, religious attendance and the degree of guidance provided by religion. Frequency of attendance is measured with the following categories: never, less than once a year, once or twice a year, several times a year, once a month, two or three times a month, about once a week, once a week, more than once a week. Religious guidance has four categories: none, some, quite a bit, and a great deal. A principal factor of these items has an eigenvalue of 1.17.
32. Ideally, an experiment like this would also incorporate information about religious belonging. However, even with an experiment of this size, it still leaves too few members of any given religious tradition to conduct a reliable analysis. The general consistency in the relationship between religiosity and political attitudes shown in the previous section justifies our concentration on religiosity.
33. We do not have a ready explanation for why a God-talking liberal picks up support from low-religiosity voters, but one possibility may be that since the frame invokes compassion, it is more palatable to non-religious people than religious frames that appeal to authority. This is yet another example of where more research is needed to understand how religious language and framing is perceived within the population.
34. Paul Djupe and Christopher Gilbert, *The Political Influence of Churches* (New York: Cambridge University Press, 2009).

Chapter 9

The Emotional Foundations of Democratic Citizenship

Ted Brader

In a democracy, the people rule. Citizens exercise power over government by choosing leaders in elections and, on some occasions, expressing their preferences on matters of policy directly. The quality of democracy therefore depends not only on how well leaders and political institutions respond to the needs and desires of the people, but also how effectively citizens participate in the process of self-government. A growing body of evidence testifies to the important role emotions play in shaping the ability and motivation of citizens to take part in politics. Fear, anger, enthusiasm, and other emotions affect public opinion by altering whether and how citizens pay attention, learn, think through their decisions, and act on their opinions. This chapter surveys this new evidence on the emotional foundations of democratic citizenship.

Emotions and the Performance of Democratic Citizenship

What does democracy require of citizens? The ideal citizen has been variously envisioned as some combination of vigilant, active, independent, open-minded, informed, thoughtful, tolerant, loyal, and courageous.[1] A substantial portion of public opinion scholarship over the past seventy years has focused, implicitly or explicitly, on how well citizens live up to these expectations. The conclusions have been decidedly mixed, with enough evidence to sustain the views of both optimists and pessimists. The tone on balance tips toward the negative, ranging from alarm and disappointment, on one side, to contentment (things are "good enough") on the other side.

We see these mixed results across many aspects of democratic citizenship. Americans pay only scattered attention to politics, though they occasionally become much more engaged for a limited time or on a particular issue. Their knowledge about public affairs is spotty at best, but many seem capable of learning what they need to know under the right conditions. Opinions on political candidates and policy matters typically exhibit an extraordinary—to some observers, a disturbing—level of loyalty to one's social group, nationality, and especially political party. Yet this loyalty is tempered by some measure of responsiveness to changing circumstances, for example, when governance is lackluster or cherished policies are threatened. Where participation is concerned, some Americans are habitually active while others appear withdrawn from politics entirely, but these general tendencies obscure tremendous fluctuations in participation over time and across situations. All of these conclusions apply not just to Americans, but also to citizens of many democracies around the world.

Scholars, however, have not simply rested on the conclusion that the democratic glass is either half full or half empty. They instead have sought to identify features both of individuals and the political environment that help explain the best and worse in citizen performance. That said, we still know relatively little about the motivations that cause a person to react differently across situations or different people to respond differently to the same situation. Emotions turn out to be such key motivational forces, capable of shaping human decision making and behavior. Until recently, a long-running emphasis on "cognitive" processes in opinion formation meant that emotions received scant attention from public opinion scholars. But the past decade has witnessed a surge in research suggesting that emotions are indeed a potent force guiding both the formation of opinions and decisions to take political action. This chapter illustrates some of what we've learned about the role of emotions in recent years.

Emotional Foundations of Human Behavior

It may be helpful at the outset to define what is meant by "emotion." What we call emotions are, in fact, a complex set of interrelated reactions to our circumstances that can include electro-chemical processes in the brain, changes in autonomic and motor systems (e.g., breathing, heart rate, muscle tension), facial expressions, behavioral impulses, and conscious feelings. In our everyday lives, we often know emotions by our experience of the feeling states that accompany them. Therefore, an overly simplistic but sometimes helpful definition is that they are the processes that generate our feelings. However, it is important to recognize that people experience emotional responses all of the time without being aware of them, without *feeling* the emotional state. Scholars often use the term "affect" when discussing all emotional phenomena, including liking and disliking, pain and pleasure, moods, and emotions. For the remainder of this chapter, my discussion will focus primarily on discrete emotions such as anger, fear, hope, love, shame, sympathy, disgust, and so on.

So what is the function of emotions? What purpose do they serve? Emotions are motivational impulses. Our brains monitor the world around us for changes that have relevance for our goals and well-being.[2] These changes in our environment become signals that trigger an emotional reaction, each of which causes a distinct pattern of changes in our thinking and behavior. Scholars believe emotions evolved as a way to allow reasonably efficient, differentiated responses to the sorts of situations humans (and many other animals) tend to encounter repeatedly. Thus, emotions enable us to adapt our thinking and bodies rapidly to meet the needs of particular situations.

Consider examples for three emotions. When we make progress toward our goals, we feel enthusiastic and energized to keep doing what we've been doing. When something appears that threatens our well-being, we feel afraid, become more alert and focused on the danger, and shift from reliable habits to active reconsideration of our options. When someone puts obstacles between us and something we want (and feel entitled to), we feel angry and are emboldened to challenge and even punish those who stand in our way. Table 9.1 summarizes the circumstances that give rise to the emotions and their impact on thinking and behavior.

These three emotions, perhaps because they are such common parts of our experiences, have been studied the most, including by scholars of public opinion. The present chapter, therefore, also focuses most heavily on these emotions. These are not, however, the only emotions likely to hold relevance for public opinion, and other emotions have started to receive attention: sadness, shame, pride, and disgust. Sadness, for example, stems from our own failure to achieve goals and especially the loss of something (or someone) valued. It often causes us to withdraw and spend more time reflecting on the details of a situation. Disgust is a reaction to the presence of noxious conditions (e.g., rotting food, bodily excretions) and seems to have evolved to include both physical and moral impurities. It generates a strong desire to purge the offending substance and thereby purify one's environment. Pride and shame are social emotions that arise when we contemplate how others do or might judge us and how well we are living up to the standards of our community. Both emotions motivate us to conform better to the expectations of our group, though pride makes us want to put our behavior on display, while shame makes us want to hide ourselves away. Although these and other emotions have many potential implications for public opinion and political behavior, their political consequences have been the subject of very little research to date. The rest of the chapter thus considers primarily how enthusiasm, fear or anxiety (I will use those terms interchangeably in this chapter) and anger shape particular aspects of citizen performance.

Vigilance and (Selective) Learning about Politics

Emotions help explain why the public pays attention to some issues and events more than others. Because emotions arise from circumstances that are relevant to people, just about any emotion may predict *interest* in a subject. But we expect fear to trigger greater attentiveness beyond what routinely interests a person, because it signals the need to deal with a potential threat to the person's safety or well-being. Moreover, fear does not just make a person more attentive in general, but directs attention selectively toward the threat

Table 9.1 Some Causes and Consequences of Common Emotions

Emotion	*Causes*	*Consequences*
Enthusiasm	Progress toward desired goals Expectations for rewards met or exceeded	Motivated to continue pursuing goals Less likely to engage in effortful thinking Greater confidence in views
Fear/anxiety	Presence of threat to well-being Uncertainty about outcomes	Motivated to escape/remove danger Heightened alertness Attention focused on potential danger More likely to engage in effortful thinking Open to persuasion Less willing to avoid risks
Anger	Obstacles blocking path to goals Undeserved harm inflicted by others	Motivated to overcome/remove obstacle Motivated to punish More willing to take risks Less willing to compromise Less likely to engage in effortful thinking
Sadness	Failure to achieve own goals Loss of something valued	Motivated to withdraw More likely to engage in effortful thinking
Disgust	Presence of noxious contaminant Presence of physical/ moral impurity	Motivated to expel contaminant Motivated to avoid contact Inclined to harsh moral judgments
Pride	Recognition of achieving valued goal Recognition of meeting/ exceeding standards	Motivated to be expressive Motivated to achieve/enforce standards
Shame	Recognition of failing to meet standards	Motivated to hide (the failure) Motivated to achieve/enforce standards

and ways of removing it. This heightened attention, in turn, creates conditions favorable for increased learning by citizens.

The Influence of Emotions on Political Attention and Engagement

Citizens pay more attention to politics during election campaigns, though their attention waxes and wanes from one election to the next and even over the course of a single campaign. Emotions contribute to some of these short-term fluctuations. Drawing heavily on data from the American National Election Studies surveys, Marcus and colleagues have conducted extensive research into the impact of emotions on electoral behavior.[3] Even when controlling for citizens' long-term levels of engagement with politics, enthusiasm and anxiety about the presidential candidates are both associated with greater interest in the campaign, caring about the election outcome, and attention to the news media.[4] A more nuanced picture of the short-term effects of these emotions emerges, however, from "panel" surveys in which individuals are re-interviewed at multiple points during the campaign. Such surveys can help researchers isolate changes in emotions, opinions, and political behavior. In this case, Marcus and colleagues found that enthusiasm caused short-term boosts in citizens' expressed levels of interest in and caring about the election, while anxiety produced greater attention to all sources of campaign news coverage except television.[5]

Other survey studies also support the notion that negative emotions have a positive impact on interest and attention to politics. Anxiety, for example, seems to awaken greater interest in election campaigns particularly among citizens high in political efficacy—that is, those who feel competent to participate in politics.[6] This mirrors decades of research on the effectiveness of fear appeals in public health and safety campaigns, showing that fear appeals are more effective when people perceive the recommended actions as likely to work and themselves as capable of carrying out the recommendations.[7] In a study conducted during the build up to the 2003 Iraq War, Americans who felt anxiety and anger toward terrorists and Saddam Hussein spent more time thinking about the war, talking about the war, and consuming national news.[8] The impact of anxiety on thinking and talking, however, was much larger than the impact of anger.

In a departure from the results discussed so far, a study of the 1996 presidential election found that citizens who felt hopeful about the candidates were more likely to watch television coverage of the fall campaign and the summer political conventions of the two major parties.[9] The researchers in this study distinguished hopefulness from enthusiasm, as well as from anxiety and anger, in their analyses. Most researchers have found that individuals' self-reported feelings of hope and enthusiasm are so highly correlated as to be statistically indistinguishable. Nonetheless, Just and colleagues' decision to focus on hope is consistent with appraisal theories of emotion from social psychology. Appraisal theories emphasize hope's conceptual distinctiveness from enthusiasm: hope is oriented toward future and uncertain outcomes, something it shares with the negative emotion of anxiety.[10]

The emotions driving interest and attention in the preceding studies presumably are responses to events, messages, and other features of the political world, most of which citizens encounter through mass media. Scholars have made use of experiments to learn more about how such mass-mediated communications trigger emotions and in turn influence public opinion. For example, in two companion experiments carried out during a Democratic gubernatorial primary election, I examined how political ads use imagery and music to trigger emotions and thereby influence viewers.[11] Ads eliciting enthusiasm stoked viewer interest in the campaign, increasing expressed levels of interest by over twelve percentage points after exposure to a single ad embedded in a news program.[12] Ads eliciting fear increased the inclination to contact campaigns for more information and to watch television news about politics. As Figure 9.1 shows, fear cues caused the percentage of Democrats wanting to contact campaigns for information to rise from 3 percent to 17 percent and the percentage wishing to watch more political news from 41 percent to 60 percent.[13] Enthusiasm cues (not shown) did boost interest in the news, but had no effect on the desire to contact campaigns. Thus, the impact of emotional advertising appeals parallels the effects of feelings toward candidates as uncovered by Marcus and colleagues: enthusiasm boosts feelings of  interest, while fear stimulates attention to sources of new information.[14]

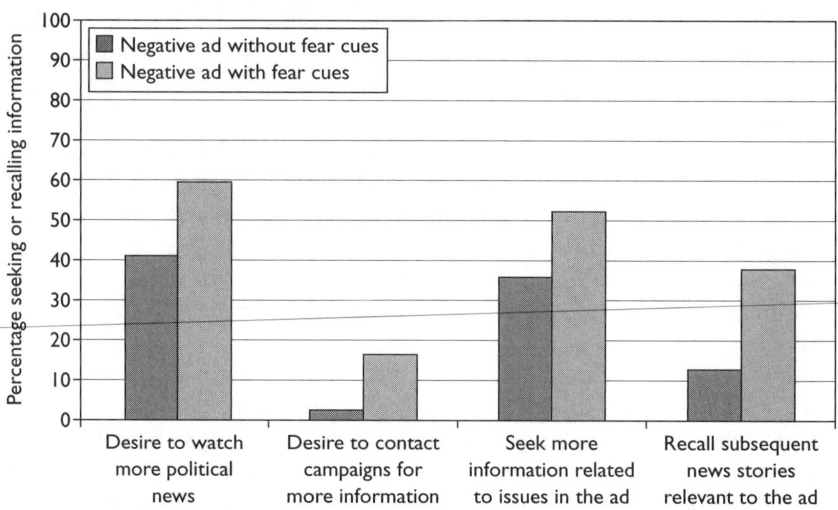

Figure 9.1 Fear Cues in Political Advertising Trigger Greater Attention and Information Seeking for Relevant Information.

Note

Data are drawn from experimental tests of the impact of emotional cues in political advertising during a Democratic gubernatorial primary campaign. Columns show the percentage of Democrats who, after seeing the ad, reported they were strongly ("quite," "very," or "completely") interested in watching more political news on television, were more likely than not to contact the campaigns to request more information, listed one or more topics in the political ad as something they would like to hear more about (in response to an open question), and recalled one or more news stories relevant to topics in the political ad that appeared in the news broadcast immediately after the ad itself. All differences between experimental conditions are statistically significant ($p < 0.05$).

It is well documented that news coverage affects which social problems and policy issues the public sees as most important.[15] The roots of this "agenda setting" effect are often thought to lie in the way news stories make some issues more cognitively accessible (i.e., more readily called to mind) than other issues.[16] Although beliefs about issue importance are not precisely the same as *individual attentiveness*, they are about what issues should receive *public attention*. Recent research argues that emotions play a key part in the agenda setting effect. Specifically, exposure to news stories alters perceptions of issue importance by either arousing or diminishing negative emotions, depending on whether the issue is portrayed as getting worse or better, respectively.[17] The experimental evidence confirms that, to change perceptions of importance, it is not enough for new stories to make the issue more accessible in minds of the audience, they must also influence emotions. Fear and sadness in particular—as opposed to anger or any of several positive emotions—mediate shifts in public priorities.

The Influence of Emotions on Political Information Seeking

Emotions influence not only citizens' attention and desire for information, but also their actual information seeking behavior. In the advertising study mentioned earlier, viewers exposed to fear-eliciting campaign ads more closely scrutinized and recalled information from subsequent news stories.[18] After watching the news broadcast in which the ad appeared, subjects had an opportunity to list as many topics from the news program as they could recall. Fear cues seemed to improve subjects' recall specifically of topics that aired after the political ad and were related to the themes contained in the ad. This suggests that fear cues caused subjects to keep their eyes out for relevant information even after the ad was finished; indeed, as Figure 9.1 indicates, recall of subsequent relevant news stories jumped from 13 percent to 38 percent in the fear-evoking version of the ad. In contrast to this, enthusiasm cues (not shown) actually produced a fifteen percentage point drop in Democrats' recall of those same news stories.

In another experimental study, anxiety aroused by news stories about immigration causes citizens to request additional information from the government and advocacy groups.[19] Researchers have turned recently to examining how people search for political information in an Internet environment. One such study finds that campaign related (and experimentally induced) anxiety consistently makes voters more inclined to pay attention to the candidates and debates, but that enthusiasm and anger also increase those inclinations at least some of the time.[20] When actual information seeking is monitored, however, anger causes voters to spend *less time* searching candidate websites and *less time* on each page clicked. In contrast to this, anxiety provoked by threatening election news stories causes voters to seek out a broader range of information by visiting more unique web pages.

Fear or anxiety therefore seems to play a strong role in motivating citizens to actively seek out more information. This inquisitiveness appears to be both broad and yet still selective or targeted in particular ways. Studies have long argued that people have a tendency to engage in selective exposure to information that confirms their existing point of view and, while this tendency does not always prevail, partisans often exhibit this sort of biased information search.[21] Studies of emotions and political information seeking, however, suggest that anxiety can disrupt this tendency while anger may reinforce it. Researchers compared the online behavior of individuals who got angry or anxious in response to threatening news stories about campus affirmative action policies.[22] Anxious individuals sought out more information that was challenging to their own views, but those who were angry avoided web pages that challenged their position. Another study found that experimentally induced anxiety made citizens more likely to visit an opposing candidate's website and indeed to visit the sites of both candidates in an election.[23] Anxiety generated such balanced information seeking, however, only when people were aware the information would be useful in the future (e.g., because they were told they would have to defend their views).

While anxiety tends to broaden the focus of citizens' attention in terms of agreement with a person's political views, it also narrows the focus of their attention to information relevant to the potential threat. In my own experimental studies, fear ads prompted viewers to request more information about the campaign and about the threatening issues raised in the ad.[24] After viewing the news and ads, subjects were invited to list issues they would like to hear more about from journalists and politicians. When Democrats saw a fairly unemotional negative ad, nearly 36 percent of them listed issues taken up in the political ads (e.g., education, crime, or the campaign more generally). This number jumped to over 52 percent among those who saw the identical messages except with fearful imagery and music (see Figure 9.1). Enthusiasm cues (not shown) had no discernable impact on these topical "wish lists." Similarly, in this same study, fear appeals increased the desire for political news, *as opposed to other news content*, and focused viewers' attention on subsequent news stories that were relevant to the issues raised in the ad, *but not on irrelevant news stories*.[25] Fears about increasing immigration caused citizens to request additional information from government and anti-immigrant organizations, more so than pro-immigrant or academic sources.[26] In a separate study that experimentally induced anxieties over immigration, anxious citizens were more likely to read online news stories about immigration, particularly negative stories, than about other topics.[27] Anxiety also caused them to remember better threatening news stories and to agree more with the arguments in threatening stories.

The Influence of Emotions on Political Learning

Does all of this increased interest, attention, and information seeking affect what citizens learn about candidates and issues? Few studies to date examine the ultimate impact of emotions on political learning. Evidence from electoral studies suggests that fear can precipitate increases in citizen knowledge. Citizens who are anxious (but not those who are enthusiastic) about presidential candidates possess more information or thoughts about the candidates and know better the relative policy positions of the candidates.[28] Panel studies further reveal that, over the course of a campaign, anxious citizens' knowledge of candidate positions improve much faster than that of either enthusiastic or unemotional citizens.[29] The study of political advertising contained only limited evidence on learning, confined to name recognition of the gubernatorial candidates. Neither enthusiasm appeals nor fear appeals led to higher name recognition in general, but fear appeals targeted at a person's preferred candidate improved name recognition of both candidates.[30] When threatening campaign information induced anxiety, as opposed to other emotions (i.e., anger, enthusiasm, disgust), citizens not only read a broader array of candidate web pages, they also demonstrated greater learning of information from these stories on a follow-up quiz.[31]

Some studies, however, arrive at more mixed conclusions about the relationship between anxiety and learning. One such study tracks subjects through a simulated, interactive campaign on computers. Anxious voters better learned their preferred candidate's policy views under highly threatening conditions (when subjects encountered lots of unexpected information), but this learning did not extend to learning other candidates' positions.[32] Feldman and Huddy also point to psychological studies suggesting that anxiety and stress can impair learning even as they cause people to devote more attention to what worries them.[33] Consistent with this, in surveys conducted between 2001 and 2003, they find that anxiety about terrorism, Saddam Hussein, and a possible war in Iraq led Americans to spend more time thinking about Iraq, yet worsened their knowledge of basic facts about the country.[34] These discrepancies suggest one should be cautious about assuming that fear-driven increases in attention and information seeking will lead automatically to gains in relevant public knowledge.

Emotions influence the political engagement and attentiveness of citizens. Fear or anxiety in particular powerfully shapes whether and when citizens adopt a more vigilant posture. Fear redirects the focus of citizens' own attention as well as their beliefs about which issues merit public attention more generally. Fear motivates citizens to seek out new information from a broader, more balanced array of political viewpoints, yet focused more narrowly on potential threats. This targeted vigilance can be beneficial, helping people to learn information that is useful in reassessing, reducing, or escaping a potential threat. But it can also produce distortions in public attention and knowledge, to the extent citizens focus *too much* on threatening issues and neglect non-threatening information that might ease their anxieties. Similarly, fear-induced vigilance will not give rise to better informed citizens, if citizens are largely exposed to information that is unhelpful, error-filled, or misleading.

Rigidity Versus Responsiveness in Opinion Formation

Emotions affect the way people make decisions and form opinions. Moreover, they do so in at least two ways. They can directly influence citizens' evaluations, with positive feelings leading to more positive judgments and negative feelings to negative judgments. Emotions can also influence opinions in a second, more indirect manner, by changing the *way* that citizens arrive at their views. Because such indirect effects reach to the very manner in which opinions are formed and because the implications are less obvious than in the case of direct effects, scholars tend to find the indirect effect of emotions on opinion formation more interesting. In that spirit, I too will devote more attention to indirect effects below.

The Direct Influence of Emotions on Opinions

Let us begin however by considering the direct impact of emotions on public opinion. That emotions exert such influence is not surprising since opinions usually involve affect—that is, liking or disliking—and affect of this sort is an emotional phenomenon much the same as the discrete emotions we've been discussing. Certainly, if a person makes me feel angry, afraid, sad, or disgusted, I will be inclined not to like that person as much. If a group or a policy makes me feel proud, hopeful, and enthusiastic, then I am more apt to like it. Many studies, including some of the earliest research on emotions and public opinion, indeed find that emotions have a strong impact on evaluations of government and political leaders, over and above any influence of cognitive beliefs or judgments.[35] For example, feelings of enthusiasm about a presidential candidate or even about the policies he champions feeds directly into greater support and likelihood of voting for the candidate.[36] Citizens may also draw, consciously or not, on their emotions about the country when expressing opinions: people who experience positive feelings about the United States express more trust in others, more trust in the government, and more support for policies like the North American Free Trade Agreement.[37] Even when unrelated events put people in a good or bad mood (e.g., a pleasurable smell, a sunny day), these feelings can cause more positive or negative evaluations of candidates, as long as the individual does not reflect on the true source of her feelings.[38]

The Influence of Emotions on Opinion Formation and Decision Making

Emotions also influence public opinion indirectly, altering the process by which citizens make decisions. People don't invest the same level of effort in making every decision. Sometimes they think through an issue carefully, taking the time and effort to sift through the available information and weigh arguments for or against each option. Other times they make a quick judgment based on simple cues or decision rules, such as a voter who decides just to mark the ballot for any candidates who are women or Republicans. The first mode of decision making is sometimes called "systematic," "central," or "effortful" processing, and the second is sometimes called "heuristic" or "peripheral" processing.[39] There is mounting evidence that a person's emotional state affects whether she engages in more or less effortful thinking and therefore what sorts of considerations play a role in decision making. Fear and sadness, for example, both appear to trigger more effortful thinking, while enthusiasm and anger encourage more peripheral or habitual thought processes.

Fear breaks citizens out of their habitual modes of thinking and gets them to reconsider their choices in light of the situation. As a result, it opens the door to persuasion. Fear does not guarantee a change of mind, but does prompt "second thoughts" about the decision. A number of studies find evidence consistent with these expectations. In elections over the past thirty years, voters anxious about presidential candidates have been less likely to rely on their partisan loyalties or ideological affinities, but more apt to make decisions on the basis of assessments of candidates' issue positions and leadership qualities.[40] Similarly, fear elicited by campaign ads causes voters to place greater weight on the advertising message; fearful ads are thus more persuasive.[41] Fear also increases the weight voters place on comparative evaluations of the candidates and decreases the weight on their initial preferences. Voters fearful about the threat of terrorism also cast votes less according to partisanship and more according to evaluations of the leadership qualities of candidates.[42]

Such findings are not confined to electoral settings, but rather extend to multiple domains of public opinion. For example, Americans anxious about the 1991 Gulf War were more likely to change their political judgments in light of their assessment of how well the war had gone.[43] Thus, *to the extent they felt anxiety*, Americans were more likely to set aside preconceptions and update their opinions about whether the United States did "the right thing" by going to war and to update their support for President George H.W. Bush more generally, based on the outcome of the war. Under more controlled experimental conditions, researchers found that anxious Republicans shed their party loyalties to express greater approval of the Democratic President Bill Clinton, even when the anxiety was induced subliminally with apolitical images (e.g., snakes, skulls).[44] In another study, anxiety influenced political tolerance judgments.[45] The judgments of anxious citizens were more responsive to persuasive arguments they had recently read that had been framed either in pro or anti free speech terms. These cases underscore anxiety's role in loosening the hold of predispositions, while facilitating the incorporation of new information and changes of opinion.

These sorts of indirect effects on opinion formation, however, are not confined to anxiety. A number of studies contrast the impact of two or more emotions. In the research on emotional advertising appeals, enthusiasm elicited by campaign ads, in contrast to fear, causes voters to place extra emphasis on their initial candidate preferences and to express greater certainty about their choice.[46] Figure 9.2 illustrates the contrasting ways that enthusiasm and fear affect the role of political predispositions in voter decision making.[47] In my experimental research on emotional advertising appeals, many subjects expressed a clear fondness for one candidate over the other when they began the study.[48] When asked near the end of the study which way they planned to vote, their original loyalties or "predispositions" predicted quite well their final voting decision. However, the strength of this relationship between predispositions and voting choice depends dramatically on which emotions, if any, had been elicited in the meantime by the political ad they saw. The correspondence between predispositions and voting decision is much

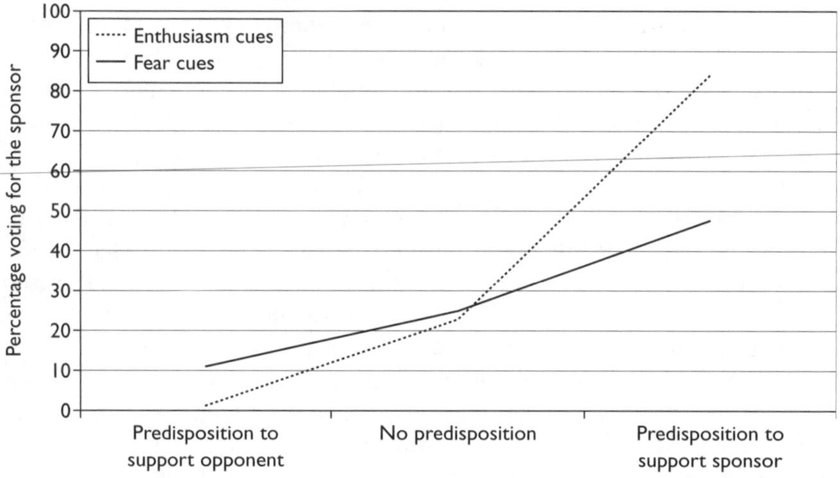

Figure 9.2 Fear Cues in Political Advertising Weaken the Impact of Predispositions on Voting Decisions, While Enthusiasm Cues Strengthen the Impact of Predispositions.

Note
Data are drawn from experimental tests of the impact of emotional cues in political advertising during a Democratic gubernatorial primary campaign. Results shown are averaged across experimental treatments that varied the sponsor and issue focus of the ad.

stronger following exposure to enthusiasm appeals, and notably weaker following exposure to fear appeals.

We encounter a similar pattern, pertaining to three emotions, in a study of how the framing of policy options affects individuals' preferences for risky policies. It is well established that people are more willing to undertake risks when information is framed in terms of potential losses, while they prefer less risky options when information is framed in terms of gains.[49] But responsiveness to these frames turns out to depend on an individual's emotional state.[50] Whereas anxiety increases individuals' responsiveness of opinions to the framing of options, both enthusiasm and anger decrease responsiveness. Another study highlights the contrasting effects of anger and sadness on opinion formation.[51] Sadness led citizens to engage in more effortful thinking when considering their preferences for providing public welfare assistance, while angry citizens did not engage in more effortful thinking. This resulted in divergent preferences, with sad citizens favoring more public assistance and angry citizens favoring less.

Emotions exert considerable influence over the opinions of citizens. In some cases, this impact is simple and direct. People who are in a bad mood or experiencing negative emotions such as anger, fear, or sadness, express more negative opinions (at times, regardless of whether their emotional state is substantively related to the opinion), and people experiencing positive emotions express more positive opinions. But the impact of emotions goes deeper to the very process of opinion formation. Some emotions, like fear and sadness, prompt citizens to reconsider their political predispositions, expend more effort thinking through the decision, and display greater responsiveness to new information and the details of the situation. Other emotions, like enthusiasm and anger, reinforce the automatic tendency of citizens to spend little time reflecting on their opinions and to stick more closely to their political habits and loyalties. Does this mean fear and sadness improve democratic citizenship, and anger and enthusiasm diminish it? Perhaps. Certainly many would consider it a good thing if public opinion were based on a more thoughtful review of the available information and arguments. But fear and sadness do not guarantee well-reasoned decisions or good outcomes. Indeed, as we have seen, the detachment from political habits and focus on present details can cause citizens to be more susceptible to persuasive advertising and framing effects, thus making political manipulation easier. Emotions clearly affect how people perform their functions as democratic citizens, but the normative desirability of the outcomes depends on more than the emotion or the thought process it provokes.

Turning Opinions into Political Action

Emotions motivate action and push it in particular directions. This doesn't mean people reflexively act on the emotional impulse, merely that action is more likely because the impulse exists. Emotions often elevate levels of physiological arousal and thus physically prepare people to take action, though there are also emotional states that reduce arousal and the inclination to act (e.g., sadness, serenity). Emotions also motivate people to act in ways that are specific to a particular emotion, what psychologists call the "action tendencies" of the emotion in question.[52] For example, anger creates an impulse to confront and fight, fear an impulse to escape, and disgust an impulse to avoid and purge.

In considering the political consequences of such heightened states of arousal and action tendencies, we must remember that democratic politics is primarily a realm of collective action. Citizens do not often take direct action to deal with social problems. They instead express preferences over (a) policy actions to be taken on their behalf by the government, (b) the selection of leaders entrusted to take these actions, and (c) policy actions determined directly from a collective voting process (e.g., ballot initiatives). Most forms of democratic political action thus occur through fairly institutionalized channels: voting, working on a campaign, donating money to a cause, contacting government officials. As a result, we expect emotions to affect overall levels of political participation, spurring citizens to greater political involvement or prompting them to withdraw from politics, commensurate with their level of physical arousal. However, direct personal action to satisfy more specific emotional impulses (to flee, fight, hide, help, etc.) is likely to be limited in the political realm by the lack of opportunities for meaningful actions of this sort. Nonetheless, these impulses may affect citizens' preferences for collective policy actions; the desire to fight, for example, may lead to greater support for aggressive policies. We therefore expect emotions to affect public opinion in distinct ways that reflect the action tendencies of the emotion in question.

The Influence of Emotions on Levels of Political Participation

The focus to date has been mostly on whether emotions trigger more or less action, and, not surprisingly, at that blunt level "high arousal" emotions tend to be associated with more political action. This general relationship between emotions and participation has illuminated both persistent differences among individuals and short-term reactions to specific situations. Recall that people respond emotionally when circumstances hold relevance for them or, in other words, when they care about what is happening. Some scholars, therefore, look to see if individuals report ever having emotional reactions—positive or negative—to a particular issue or cause and regard such emotions as indicators of those individuals' *conviction*.[53] The evidence shows that citizens who experience stronger feelings about policies indeed are more likely to take political action, above and beyond any intellectual investment reflected by their knowledge of the issue.

Other scholars are concerned with the participatory impact of short-term emotional reactions that can, from time to time, flare up and fade away for anyone regardless of the person's long-term interest in policies or politics. Citizens who both feel enthusiastic about presidential candidates and who feel anxious about the candidates are more likely to participate in election campaigns beyond simply voting.[54] Similarly, campaign ads that elicit enthusiasm and fear increase the desire to volunteer and vote during elections.[55] Similar effects occur outside of elections: for example, anxiety triggered by news stories on immigration provokes more citizens to contact their Members of Congress and express support for reducing the number of immigrants coming to the United States.[56] A recent study highlights the potential positive impact of three emotions—fear, anger, and enthusiasm—on political participation but notes important distinctions among them.[57] Fear has the most variable effects; in some cases it motivates voters, but other times has no effect or even suppresses their participation levels. Anger, in contrast, has an especially powerful impact of political mobilization, but its impact depends more heavily on the person possessing the sorts of resources (e.g., education, income, social ties, experience) that enable participation.[58] Absent such resources, citizens are less likely to act on their anger in politically consequential ways.

Data from the 2008 presidential election in the United States provide one example of the direct and distinctive impact of emotions on political participation. In a national survey, Nicholas Valentino and I asked Americans about their emotional reactions to the way things were going in the country. Given the unpopularity of the incumbent president and the onset of a global financial crisis, most Americans felt a good deal more fear and anger than enthusiasm in the fall of 2008. We also asked respondents during the campaign how likely they were to contact a government official and, right after the election, how often they had engaged in a range of different political activities. Table 9.2 shows how enthusiasm, fear, and anger about the way things are going in the country affected the propensity to participate in these various ways, controlling many of the social and political attributes known to predict participation.[59] Anger had the clearest, most consistent, and most powerful impact on political participation in 2008, exerting a strong positive effect for eight of the nine activities. In most cases, people who were extremely angry scored somewhere between ten and twenty-five percentage points higher on the frequency of participation scale. The impact of enthusiasm was considerably spottier: it appeared to exert a modest positive impact in several instances, though the "effects" fall shy of reaching conventional thresholds of statistical significance. The results for fear, in contrast, point rather consistently in a negative direction, though these too fall shy of significance in all but one case. While this general pattern is illustrative of the relative contributions of these emotions to political participation,[60] it is important to reiterate that other data have revealed some positive participatory effects of fear and especially enthusiasm.[61]

Table 9.2 The Impact of Emotions on Political Participation in the 2008 Election (%)

Political participation	*Emotional reactions to the way things are going in the country*		
	Enthusiasm	*Fear*	*Anger*
Contact government officials	+1.8	−22.8**	+24.3**
Discuss politics with friends and family	+10.6	+0.1	+17.4*
Argue about politics	−1.6	−4.4	+22.1*
Take part in a protest	0.0	−4.9	+7.0*
Attend political events for a candidate	−6.5	−3.0	+0.1
Display a campaign sign	+10.9	−7.6	+17.6*
Volunteer for a campaign	−5.5	−11.3	+12.1*
Donate money to a candidate or party	+8.3	−4.5	+14.2*
Sign a petition	+10.2	−10.2	+16.1*

Note
Table 9.2 shows the estimated effect of each emotion on political participation, expressed as a percentage point difference in the overall participation scale between those experiencing no emotion and those experiencing intense emotion (i.e., "not at all angry" vs. "extremely angry"). Participation questions asked respondents how likely they were to contact government officials or how often they had engaged in any of the other activities on a four, five, or eight point scale. Analyses are based on ordinary least squares regression and included statistical controls for gender, age, education, income, race, church attendance, residency, strength of partisanship, internal political efficacy, general interest in politics, and political knowledge. Data are from a representative national survey carried out in the United States during the 2008 presidential election. Asterisks indicate levels of statistical significance: ** $p < 0.01$, * $p < 0.05$.

Studies uncovering positive effects for fear and enthusiasm have tended to investigate emotions that are closely tied to specific candidates and issues, as opposed to the sort of broad emotions about the state of the country we solicited in the 2008 survey.[62]

The Influence of Emotions on the Proclivity for Specific Types of Action

Emotions don't just impel us to do "more" or "less," they also trigger the desire to act in some fairly specific ways. When people are afraid, the impulse they feel is not to do just anything, but specifically to hide, flee, or otherwise protect themselves from harm. In contrast, angry people feel inclined to confront and punish. But, where politics is concerned, citizens typically act through a limited set of institutional channels to influence the direction of government, while government itself takes more direct action to address the problems of society and pursue other collective goals. Thus, the distinctive action tendencies of fear, anger, enthusiasm, and other emotions may not be visible in standard forms of political participation like voting as much as in public preferences for what policies the government should pursue. Voting looks the same regardless of whether the voter is in the mood to protect, punish, help, or celebrate. However, those different motives may be readily distinguishable in the voter's policy priorities and positions, such as through preferences for heightened security, harsher criminal penalties, more aid to the poor, or simply maintaining the status quo.

Emotions indeed seem to influence the policy opinions of citizens in a way that parallels the immediate "action tendencies" generated by the emotional state. Most of the evidence to date comes from efforts to uncover the distinct effects of negative emotions. Anger and fear, for example, have opposite implications for risk taking. In the face of terrorism threats, fear decreases the willingness of citizens to engage in risky personal activities *and* the willingness to support policy actions that might put more Americans at risk.[63] Anger, meanwhile, increases support for taking both personal and policy risks. Faced with a potential public health threat, like the outbreak of a deadly disease, angry citizens prefer policy options that carry a risk of bigger losses or bigger gains over policy options with equivalent but more certain (known) outcomes.[64] But fearful citizens prefer certain results to actions that take a chance on bigger gains and bigger losses.

We can observe these distinct effects of fear and anger on risk preferences in the survey data from the 2008 election mentioned earlier. In light of the incipient economic meltdown and deep dissatisfaction about the direction of the country, we asked respondents their views on "the best way to deal with times of crisis and hardship": Do they prefer "taking bold action to solve a crisis more quickly, even if it comes with a risk of making our problems worse" or, instead, "acting with caution and avoiding big risks, even if it will likely take much longer to solve the crisis?" Figure 9.3 plots the relationship between preferences for bold, risky action and levels of fear and anger, controlling for other social and political attributes that may affect risk preferences. As fear became more intense, Americans shied away from a risky approach to crisis. Anger had the opposite effect, making Americans more likely to endorse risky action. Enthusiasm (not shown) had no effect on risk preferences.

Anger and fear also diverge by pushing citizens toward aggressive or defensive actions, respectively. This is again visible in responses to terrorism. When angry, Americans are more willing to expand U.S. military efforts in the war on terror within and beyond Afghanistan; when afraid, Americans more strongly prefer to deport Arab Americans, Muslims, or first-generation immigrants.[65] Similar tendencies appear for other issues. In the face of a potential viral pandemic threatening public health, anger increases the willingness of citizens to write letters urging prosecution of anyone found responsible, as well as support both for official investigations and for punishment of those at fault for the outbreak.[66] In this same situation, fear makes citizens more likely to undertake a variety of protective behaviors (e.g., learning more about the

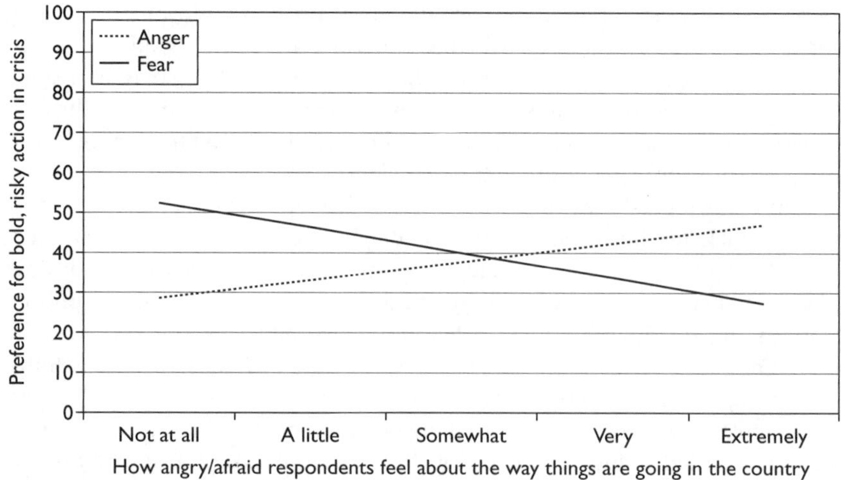

Figure 9.3 Anger Increases and Fear Decreases the Preference for Risky Action.

Note
The figure displays the expected preference for risky action at several levels of fear and anger, while holding all other factors, including emotions, constant at their mean levels. Higher values on the y-axis indicate a preference for "taking bold action to solve a crisis more quickly, even if it comes with a risk of making our problems worse," while lower values indicate a preference for "acting with caution and avoiding big risks, even if it will likely take much longer to solve the crisis." Fear and anger had statistically significant effects on preferences for risky action ($p < 0.01$), while enthusiasm (not shown) had no discernable relationship to these preferences. Analyses included statistical controls for gender, age, education, income, partisanship, unemployment status, and retirement status. Data are from a representative national survey carried out in the United States in the weeks prior to the 2008 presidential election.

illness, telling friends and family about the danger, washing hands). Fear does not generate greater interest in prosecutions or punishments, but it does strengthen the preference for greater government oversight and regulation aimed at preventing future outbreaks. Finally, citizens anxious about affirmative action policies show greater willingness to consider compromises, while citizens angry about the policy are less willing to compromise.[67]

Emotions prepare and push people to act. Many citizens hold opinions about political candidates and policy issues, but only sometimes do they act on these opinions. Emotional reactions often provide citizens with the motivation to turn opinions into political action. This is especially true for high arousal emotions like fear, anger, and enthusiasm; anger in particular is a powerful resource for political mobilization. Although more participation typically is regarded as desirable, the consequences of emotional arousal are not simply a matter of participating more or less. In addition to the implications for attention and thoughtfulness already discussed, emotions have action tendencies that impel citizens in specific directions. These tendencies become manifest in both personal behavior and public opinion about collective policy actions. Fear triggers behavior and opinions aimed at reducing risks, protecting against harm, and accepting compromises. In contrast, anger gives rise to behavior and opinions that are risky, aggressive, punitive, and uncompromising.

Conclusion

In sum, emotions serve as guides that adapt thinking and behavior to meet certain situational needs. They direct attention and learning selectively. They modulate how actively and broadly citizens think through the matter at hand. They prepare and motivate citizens to take appropriate actions, including no action at all.

Researchers have learned a good deal so far about the political implications of three commonplace emotions: enthusiasm, fear, and anger. Enthusiasm arises when things are going well, when people are achieving or exceeding their goals. It causes citizens to take a greater interest in politics, adhere to partisan or other political loyalties, feel more confident in their views, and participate more in campaigns and elections. Because it encourages more participation that hews more closely to partisan lines, the feel-good emotion of enthusiasm can ironically be the source of more intense political polarization.

Fear is a response to circumstances that are threatening or where the potential for danger is unknown. It causes citizens to pay greater attention to what is happening (especially as relates to possible danger), seek out more information, reconsider their options in light of available information, avoid risky courses of action, and prefer public policies focused on prevention and protection. As a result, fear may lead to an increase in learning, persuasion, and compromise.

Anger is triggered when someone intentionally threatens or stands in the way of a person's goals, especially if the situation is seen as unfair and controllable. It causes citizens to stick with their convictions, eschew compromise, spend less time thinking things through, embrace risks more readily, and prefer aggressive and punitive public policies. Anger is a consistently powerful source of political mobilization, motivating people to act on their opinions, particularly to the extent citizens feel they have the ability and resources to contribute effectively.

There are many emotional states beyond these three best understood emotions. Scholars are just beginning to explore the implications of these other emotions for public opinion and politics. For example, sadness, not unlike fear, prompts people to expend more effort on thinking through decisions. When sadness is elicited, citizens therefore are more likely to pay attention to the details of a situation and, as a result, take account of those situational details in deciding whether the government should provide welfare assistance to individuals.[68] Disgust triggers an inclination to purify one's environment. Accordingly, it seems to give rise to harsher moral judgments and moral conservativism such as disapproval of gays.[69] Pride and shame are "social emotions" that people experience when they realize that others may judge them as exemplifying or falling short of, respectively, the standards and values expected by their community or group. As a result, both emotions motivate citizens to adopt or apply more faithfully the values of their group.[70] While shame prompts a desire to hide one's transgressions, pride triggers a desire to display one's behavior and group membership proudly.[71]

Emotions, specifically their role in opinion formation and political behavior, can help us to understand more fully the vicissitudes of democratic citizenship. But they typically can't tell us whether a person is a good or bad citizen, nor whether Americans on average are better or worse citizens than we expected. Emotions are neither good nor bad in themselves, but simply useful for human reasoning and action. Moreover, though they collectively and individually serve useful functions, this does not mean emotions improve decisions and actions in every instance. They can distract attention needlessly, disrupt learning, give rise to wrong or bad decisions, and motivate harmful behaviors. As public opinion scholars and political observers begin to appreciate more and more the critical role emotions play, it is important to become neither overly sanguine nor overly discouraging about their implications for democratic citizenship.

Notes

1. Charles Bens, "What Does It Mean to Be a Good Citizen?" *National Civic Review* 90 (2001): 193–7; Michael Delli Carpini and Scott Keeter, *What Americans Know about Politics and Why It Matters* (New Haven, CT: Yale University Press, 1996); Will Kymlicka and Wayne Norman, "The Return of the Citizen," in *Democracy*, eds. Ricardo Blaug and John Schwarzmantel (New York: Columbia University Press, 2001), 220–7; Michael Schudson, *The Good Citizen: A History of American Civic Life* (New York: Free Press, 1998); and Michael Walzer, *What It Means to Be an American* (New York: Marsilio, 1992).
2. For example, see Richard S. Lazarus, *Emotion and Adaptation* (New York: Oxford University Press, 1991).
3. George E. Marcus, W. Russell Neuman, and Michael MacKuen, *Affective Intelligence and Political Judgment* (Chicago, IL: University of Chicago Press, 2000).
4. Ibid., 85–7.
5. Ibid., 91–2.
6. Thomas Rudolph, Amy Gangl, and Dan Stevens, "The Effects of Efficacy and Emotions on Campaign Involvement," *Journal of Politics* 62 (2000): 1189–97.
7. Kim Witte and Mike Allen, "A Meta-Analysis of Fear Appeals: Implications for Effective Public Health Campaigns," *Health Education Research* 27 (2000): 591–615.
8. Leonie Huddy, Stanley Feldman, and Erin Cassese, "On the Distinct Political Effects of Anxiety and Anger," in *The Affect Effect*, eds. W. Russell Neuman, George Marcus, Ann Crigler, and Michael MacKuen (Chicago, IL: University of Chicago Press, 2007), 202–30.

9. Marion Just, Ann Crigler, and Todd Belt, "Don't Give Up Hope: Emotions, Candidate Appraisals, and Votes," in *The Affect Effect*, eds. W. Russell Neuman, George Marcus, Ann Crigler, and Michael MacKuen (Chicago, IL: University of Chicago Press, 2007), 231–59.
10. Cf. Donald Kinder, "Reason and Emotion in American Political Life," in *Beliefs, Reasoning, and Decision Making*, eds. Roger Schank and Ellen Langer (Hillsdale, NJ: Lawrence Erlbaum, 1994), 277–314; and Lazarus, *Emotion and Adapation.*
11. Ted Brader, *Campaigning for Hearts and Minds* (Chicago, IL: University of Chicago Press, 2006).
12. Emotions often last for relatively short periods of time, unless they continue to be aroused by new or ongoing circumstances. There has been little research to date into the persistence of political emotions or their effects over time. Regardless of how long the emotions themselves last, some effects might be expected to fade with the emotion (e.g., effects on attention or inclinations to act in a certain way) and others to last beyond the life of the emotion (e.g., effects on thought processes that lead to lasting changes in opinions or knowledge).
13. For more details on the design of the study and analyses, see Ted Brader, "Striking a Responsive Chord: How Political Ads Motivate and Persuade Voters by Appealing to Emotions," *American Journal of Political Science* 49 (2005): 388–405; and Brader, *Campaigning for Hearts and Minds.*
14. Marcus et al., *Affective Intelligence and Political Judgment.*
15. Maxwell McCombs, *Setting the Agenda: The Mass Media and Public Opinion* (Cambridge: Polity, 2004).
16. Shanto Iyengar and Donald Kinder, *News That Matters* (Chicago, IL: University of Chicago Press, 1987).
17. Joanne Miller, "Examining the Mediators of Agenda Setting: A New Experimental Paradigm Reveals the Role of Emotions," *Political Psychology* 28 (2007): 689–717.
18. Brader, *Campaigning for Hearts and Minds.*
19. Ted Brader, Nicholas A. Valentino, and Elizabeth Suhay, "What Triggers Public Opposition to Immigration? Anxiety, Group Cues, and Immigration Threat," *American Journal of Political Science* 52 (2008): 959–78.
20. Nicholas Valentino, Vincent Hutchings, Antoine Banks, and Anne Davis, "Is a Worried Citizen a Good Citizen? Emotions, Political Information Seeking, and Learning via the Internet," *Political Psychology* 29 (2008): 247–73.
21. Shanto Iyengar, Kyu S. Hahn, Jon A. Krosnick, and John Walker, "Selective Exposure to Campaign Communication: The Role of Anticipated Agreement and Issue Public Membership," *Journal of Politics* 70 (2008): 186–200; and Natalie Jomini Stroud, "Media Use and Political Predispositions: Revisiting the Concept of Selective Exposure," *Political Behavior* 30 (2008): 341–66.
22. Michael MacKuen, Jennifer Wolak, Luke Keele, and George Marcus, "Civic Engagements: Resolute Partisanship or Reflective Deliberation," *American Journal of Political Science* 54 (2010): 440–58.
23. Nicholas Valentino, Antoine Banks, Vincent Hutchings, and Anne Davis, "Selective Exposure in the Internet Age: The Interaction Between Anxiety and Information Utility," *Political Psychology* 30 (2009): 591–613.
24. Brader, "Striking a Responsible Chord."
25. Brader, *Campaigning for Hearts and Minds*, 134–9.
26. Brader et al., "What Triggers Public Opposition to Immigration?"
27. Shana Kushner Gadarian and Bethany Albertson, "Fear and Learning in the Immigration Debate" (unpublished manuscript, University of California, Berkeley, 2010); see also Bethany Albertson and Shana Kushner Gadarian, "Is Lou Dobbs Frightening? The Effect of Threatening Advertisements on Black, White, and Latino Attitudes toward Immigration" (unpublished manuscript, University of Texas, Austin, 2010).

28. Marcus et al., *Affective Intelligence and Political Judgment*, 87–89.
29. Ibid., 93.
30. Brader, *Campaigning for Hearts and Minds*, 135.
31. Valentino et al., "Is a Worried Citizen a Good Citizen?"
32. David Redlawsk, Andrew Civettini, and Richard Lau, "Affective Intelligence and Voting," in *The Affect Effect*, eds. W. Russell Neuman, George Marcus, Ann Crigler, and Michael MacKuen (Chicago, IL: University of Chicago Press, 2007), 152–79.
33. Stanley Feldman and Leonie Huddy, "The Paradoxical Effects of Anxiety on Political Learning" (unpublished manuscript, Stony Brook University, New York, n.d.).
34. It remains unclear whether the discrepancy between these and other findings is due to the nature of the threat (e.g., fears about life and death), to anxiety shifting attention to other information in the environment at the expense of these sorts of factual details, or some other reason.
35. Robert Abelson, Donald Kinder, Mark Peters, and Susan Fiske, "Affective and Semantic Components in Political Personal Perception," *Journal of Personality and Social Psychology* 42 (1982): 619–30; Pamela Conover and Stanley Feldman, "Emotional Reactions to the Economy," *American Journal of Political Science* 30 (1986): 30–78; Kimberly Gross, "Framing Persuasive Appeals: Episodic and Thematic Framing, Emotional Response, and Policy Opinion," *Political Psychology* 29 (2008): 169–92; Kimberly Gross, Paul Brewer, and Sean Aday, "Confidence in Government and Emotional Responses to Terrorism After September 11, 2001," *American Politics Research* 37 (2009): 107–28; Just et al., "Don't Give Up Hope"; and Kinder, "Reason and Emotion in American Political Life."
36. Marcus et al., *Affective Intelligence and Political Judgment.*
37. Wendy M. Rahn, Brian Kroeger, and Cynthia M. Kite, "A Framework for the Study of Public Mood," *Political Psychology* 17 (1996): 29–58; and Wendy M. Rahn, "Affect as Information: The Role of Public Mood in Political Reasoning," in *Elements of Reason*, eds. Arthur Lupia, Mathew McCubbins, and Samuel Popkin (New York: Cambridge University Press, 2000), 135–50.
38. Linda Isbell and Victor Ottati, "The Emotional Voter," in *The Social Psychology of Politics*, eds. Victor C. Ottati, R. Scott Tindale, John Edwards, Fred B. Bryant, Linda Heath, Daniel C. O'Connell, Yolanda Suarez-Balcazar, and Emil J. Posavac (New York: Kluwer, 2002), 55–74.
39. Alice H. Eagly and Shelly Chaiken, "Attitude Structure and Function," in *Handbook of Social Psychology*, eds. Daniel Gilbert, Susan Fiske, and Gardner Lindzey, 4th ed., vol. 2 (Boston: McGraw-Hill, 1998), 269–322.
40. Marcus et al., *Affective Intelligence and Political Judgment.* Ladd and Lenz raise reasonable concerns that the emotions voters express toward candidates in surveys may partially or wholly be a consequence—rather than a cause—of the voting decision those voters have made. See Jonathan Ladd and Gabriel Lenz, "Reassessing the Role of Anxiety in Vote Choice," *Political Psychology* 29 (2008): 275–96; and cf. George E. Marcus, Michael MacKuen, and W. Russell Neuman, "Parsimony and Complexity: Developing and Testing Theories of Affective Intelligence," *Political Psychology* 32 (2011): 323–36. Fortunately, evidence on the indirect effects of emotions on opinion formation is now available from a diverse array of studies, some of which use methodological and measurement strategies where such concerns of reverse causation are minimized or eliminated. See Ted Brader, "The Political Relevance of Emotions: 'Reassessing' Revisited," *Political Psychology* 32 (2011): 337–46. Nonetheless, Ladd and Lenz's warning is an important reminder about interpreting and designing future studies.
41. Brader, *Campaigning for Hearts and Minds.*
42. Jennifer Merolla and Elizabeth Zechmeister, *Democracy at Risk: How Terrorist Threats Affect the Public* (Chicago, IL: University of Chicago Press, 2009).

43. Donald Kinder and Lisa D'Ambrosio, "War, Emotion, and Public Opinion" (unpublished manuscript, University of Michigan, Ann Arbor, 2000); see also Marcus et al., *Affective Intelligence and Political Judgment.*
44. Baldwin M. Way and Roger D. Masters, "Political Attitudes: Interactions of Cognition and Affect," *Motivation and Emotion* 20 (1996): 205–36.
45. George Marcus, John Sullivan, Elizabeth Theiss-Morse, and Daniel Stevens, "The Emotional Foundation of Political Cognition," *Political Psychology* 26 (2005): 949–63.
46. Brader, *Campaigning for Hearts and Minds.*
47. For more details regarding the design of the study and these findings see Brader, *Campaigning for Hearts and Minds*, especially tables 5.1 and B.3.
48. Brader, *Campaigning for Hearts and Minds.*
49. Daniel T. Kahneman and Amos Tversky, "Choices, Values, and Frames," *American Psychologist* 39 (1984): 341–50.
50. James Druckman and Rose McDermott, "Emotion and the Framing of Risky Choice," *Political Behavior* 30 (2008): 297–321.
51. Deboral Small and Jennifer Lerner, "Emotional Policy: Personal Sadness and Anger Shape Judgments About a Welfare Case," *Political Psychology* 29 (2008): 149–68.
52. Lazarus, *Emotion and Adaptation.*
53. Nancy Burns and Donald Kinder, "Conviction and Its Consequences" (unpublished manuscript, University of Michigan, Ann Arbor, 2003); and Kinder, "Reason and Emotion in American Political Life."
54. Marcus et al., *Affective Intelligence and Political Judgment.*
55. Brader, *Campaigning for Hearts and Minds.*
56. Brader et al., "What Triggers Public Opposition to Immigration?"
57. Nicholas Valentino, Ted Brader, Eric Groenendyk, Krysha Gregorowicz, and Vincent Hutchings, "Election Night's Alright for Fighting: The Role of Emotions in Political Participation," *Journal of Politics* 73 (2011): 156–70.
58. Nicholas Valentino, Krysha Gregorowicz, and Eric Groenendyk, "Efficacy, Emotions and the Habit of Participation," *Political Behavior* 31 (2009): 307–30.
59. For more details on the data and more extensive analyses of the impact of emotions on political participation, see Valentino et al., "Election Night's Alright for Fighting."
60. Cf. Valentino et al., "Election Night's Alright for Fighting."
61. Brader, *Campaigning for Hearts and Minds*; Brader et al., "What Triggers Public Opposition to Immigration?"; and Marcus et al., *Affective Intelligence and Political Judgment.*
62. Note also that statistical controls include respondents' general interest in politics, which is not only a powerful predictor of participation, but also an outcome that previous experimental research demonstrates can be *influenced by* emotions. See Brader, *Campaigning for Hearts and Minds.* Thus, to the extent emotions are elevating the public's interest in politics and thereby encouraging more participation, Table 9.2 is likely to underestimate the impact of the emotions on participation.
63. Huddy et al., "On the Distinct Political Effects of Anxiety and Anger"; and Jennifer Lerner, Roxana Gonzalez, Deborah Small, and Baruch Fischhoff, "Effects of Fear and Anger on Perceived Risks of Terrorism: A National Field Experiment," *Psychological Science* 14 (2003): 144–50.
64. Druckman and McDermott, "Emotion and the Framing of Risky Choice."
65. Linda Skitka, Christopher Bauman, Nicholas Aramovich, and G. Scott Morgan, "Confrontational and Preventative Policy Responses to Terrorism: Anger Wants a Fight and Fear Wants 'Them' to Go Away," *Basic and Applied Social Psychology* 28 (2006): 375–84; and cf. Leonie Huddy, Stanley Feldman, Charles Taber, and Gallya

Lahav, "Threat, Anxiety, and Support for Antiterrorism Policies," *American Journal of Political Science* 4 (2005): 593–608.

66. Ted Brader, Eric Groenendyk, and Nicholas Valentino, "Fight or Flight? When Political Threats Arouse Public Anger or Fear" (unpublished manuscript, University of Michigan, 2010).
67. MacKuen et al., "Civic Engagements."
68. Small and Lerner, "Emotional Policy."
69. Yoel Inbar, David A. Pizarro, and Paul Bloom, "Conservatives Are More Easily Disgusted than Liberals," *Cognition and Emotion* 23 (2009): 714–25; Yoel Inbar, David A. Pizarro, Joshua Knobe, and Paul Bloom, "Disgust Sensitivity Predicts Intuitive Disapproval of Gays," *Emotion* 9 (2009): 435–9; and Simone Schnall, Jonathan Haidt, Gerald L. Clore, and Alexander H. Jordan, "Disgust as Embodied Moral Judgment," *Personality and Social Psychology Bulletin* 34 (2008): 1096–109.
70. Elizabeth A. Suhay, "Group Influence and American Ideals: How Social Identity and Emotion Shape Our Political Values and Attitudes" (PhD dissertation, University of Michigan, 2008); and cf. Alan S. Gerber, Donald P. Green, and Christopher W. Larimer, "An Experiment Testing the Relative Effectiveness of Encouraging Voter Participation by Inducing Feelings of Pride or Shame," *Political Behavior* 32 (2010): 409–22; and Stephen Knack and Martha Kropf, "For Shame! The Effect of Community Cooperative Context on the Probability of Voting," *Political Psychology* 19 (1998): 585–600.
71. Bryce Corrigan and Ted Brader, "Campaign Advertising: Reassessing the Impact of Campaign Ads on Political Behavior," in *New Directions in Campaigns and Elections*, ed. Stephen Medvic (New York: Routledge, 2011), 79–97.

Chapter 10

Personality and Public Opinion

Jeffery J. Mondak and Matthew V. Hibbing[1]

Public opinion has many facets. Because of this, scholars who seek to understand public opinion approach the topic from multiple perspectives. The contributions in this volume demonstrate this point well. These chapters discuss public opinion in terms of meaning, measurement, subgroup differences, media effects, partisanship and ideology, political campaigns, and public policy. One persistent question faced by students of public opinion is why people differ in their views. In attempting to answer this question, one might consider the influences of immediate factors such as the statements of public officials and the corresponding content of media coverage. Analysts also might consider more long-term influences such as the impact of public opinion on a person's core values and basic political orientations. The position we advocate is that any full account of why people's opinions vary requires that we search broadly, and especially that we consider both immediate and long-term factors.

In this chapter, we address one of the longest of long-term influences, people's personalities. The discussion builds from the two-part premise that people differ with respect to fundamental psychological structures, and that these differences are consequential for what we think and how we act, including how we engage the political world. If our premise is correct, it would follow that we could better our understanding of public opinion by taking personality into account. Toward this end, the purpose of this chapter is to discuss how and why personality might matter for public opinion, and to provide examples of the sorts of effects personality might produce.

A link between personality and public opinion may not seem as obvious as possible differences in opinion among men and women, Democrats and Republicans, or Americans and Canadians. Recognizing this, our first task in this chapter is to develop, step by step, the case for why we advocate attention to personality. We do so by explaining what personality is, how and why people's personalities differ, and what researchers in psychology and in other fields have found regarding the consequences of personality for various facets of human behavior. Along the way, we make a slight detour in order to discuss the possibility that many differences among people, including differences in basic political orientations, might be partly based in biology. As will be seen, it is our contention that biological influences on aspects of our daily lives most likely operate at least partly *through* personality. If so, then attention to personality can be important in creation of a unified, multifaceted account of how various factors—long term, short term, biological, and environmental—come together to shape how we think and act.

After developing the rationale for how and why personality may matter for public opinion, we present evidence regarding examples of such effects. Drawing on data from a survey conducted in the United States in 2010, two types of influences are considered. First, we show that basic differences in people's personalities correspond with differences in a fundamental political orientation, ideology. Second, we test whether personality also matters for public opinion on a salient issue in contemporary American politics, same-sex marriage. Together, these examples demonstrate the basic point that personality traits influence people's opinions. We end our discussion by considering what this lesson implies regarding the nature of public opinion itself, along with what it means regarding other factors commonly thought to influence mass opinion.

Why Personality?

Personality may be of relevance for public opinion, but we first must understand what personality is before we seek to establish evidence of its influence. Psychologists have constructed many definitions of personality, and controversy continues among psychologists as to just what personality is. Fortunately, consensus does exist regarding the basic characteristics of personality. By reviewing the key characteristics of personality emphasized in trait research, we can develop a functional understanding of personality. This understanding, in turn, can inform the effort to link personality and public opinion.

The chief reason personality defies simple definition is that our personalities are not directly observable. Physical traits such as height, weight, and hair color can be defined and recorded in concrete terms, but greater ambiguity surrounds our psychological characteristics. With respect to personality, what psychologists have concluded is that people have persistent psychological tendencies. For example, some people are worriers, some are willing to try anything, and some are sticklers about keeping everything neat, tidy, and in its place. These consistent characteristics, or traits, are the outward signs pointing to the existence of a broader internal psychological structure—that is, of personality. Thus, we can define personality as being a multifaceted and enduring psychological structure that influences patterns in behavior.

A few aspects of this definition should be highlighted. First, personalities are thought to be multifaceted. In our own research, we focus mostly on personality traits. Personality traits capture many important psychological differences across individuals. As a result, a large-scale, multifaceted depiction of personality trait structure encompasses much of what we mean by personality. However, most psychologists contend that personality also includes components beyond traits, such as values, beliefs, and motives. Again, some disagreement continues among scholars as to the precise components that make up our personalities. In our view, such disagreement is inevitable because the central phenomenon in question, personality, cannot be observed or measured in any direct, objective manner. Fortunately, these lingering debates should not hamper the effort to study personality and public opinion provided that we focus on personality traits, which most contemporary scholars agree are central to personality.

A second noteworthy aspect of our definition is that personality is assumed to be an *enduring* psychological structure. What we mean by this is that personalities are relatively stable over time. They do not change from day to day, and they do not even change much from year to year. This feature helps establish why personality is important. There would not be much point in studying the possible effects of personality on behavior if personality itself lacked an enduring character. Psychologists measure the stability of personality by gathering data from the same people at multiple points in time, and then seeing whether a given individual's personality was similar each time it was measured. For the personality traits we study in our research, psychologists estimate stability levels averaging 0.94 (where 1.0 is perfect stability) with trait measures obtained in six-year intervals.[2] Part of the reason for this stability is that personality is substantially rooted in biology, a point that will be discussed further below.

The last feature of our definition that warrants emphasis is that personality is thought to influence patterns in behavior. For present purposes, this includes the opinions that people form and express. Personality can be thought of as establishing a person's central tendency. For example, if one individual scores high on the personality trait of extraversion and another person scores low on this trait, our general expectation would be that, across various situations, the first individual would behave in a more outgoing and sociable manner than the second. In other words, personality produces a similarity in behavior across circumstances. Importantly, this does not imply that a person's behavior will always be identical. Instead, people adapt their actions on a situational basis. In a given situation, it is safe to predict that the extravert will be more outgoing than the introvert. However, extraverts themselves can be expected to be more outgoing on a cruise ship than at a memorial service—and so can introverts. What this implies is that progress toward a full understanding of human behavior requires that we take into account features of the individual (such as personality), features of the situation (such as whether it is a cruise or a memorial service), and person–situation interactions.

The discussion thus far has outlined what we mean by personality, and it has begun to suggest why personality may be important for public opinion.

These are important steps, but further refinement is needed. Most critically, we require a means to represent some of the key facets of personality in concrete, measurable form. Rather than attempt to capture all aspects of personality, we will focus on several important personality traits. Since the late 1980s, psychologists have highlighted what have come to be known as the "Big Five" personality trait dimensions. The "Big Five" (sometimes also called the "Five Factor") research perspective has gained the most prominent position in contemporary research on personality. We follow this same course in our applied research on personality and political behavior.

The Big Five

The Big Five personality trait dimensions are openness to experience, conscientiousness, extraversion, agreeableness, and emotional stability. Although the earliest research on this framework traces to the 1950s and 1960s,[3] it was not until twenty years later that the use of five-factor approaches became common in research on trait psychology. Thanks largely to the pioneering efforts of psychologists Lewis Goldberg, Paul Costa, and Robert McCrae,[4] hundreds of studies on the Big Five now are being reported each year. Gosling and his colleagues have noted that the five-factor approach "has become the most widely used and extensively researched model of personality."[5]

Prior to the ascendance of the Big Five, scholars had examined dozens, and even hundreds, of different personality traits. What researchers eventually discovered was that the Big Five trait structure is seemingly universal in the sense that these same five trait dimensions are important aspects of people's personalities in nations and cultures all over the world.[6] This universality is important because it means that the many studies on the Big Five combine to provide a cumulative, well-integrated understanding of psychological differences. In addition to this cross-cultural breadth, five-factor models also enjoy breadth in terms of their representation of personality at the level of the individual. Although there is more to personality than the Big Five, these trait dimensions collectively capture the bulk of trait structure. This means that Big Five frameworks are especially useful for applied studies on the effects of personality, including for studies about personality and politics.

Applied research on the Big Five requires data on people's personality traits. Fortunately, we all tend to be relatively good judges of our own personalities.[7] Because of this, self-report data are common in research on personality. A study's participants are asked to rate themselves on various matters, with the resulting data then used by the researcher to construct measures of particular personality traits. Research exploring the properties of the personality traits themselves often will draw on very large data sets, with ten to fifty or more questions asked of participants for each trait dimension. In applied research, use of such exhaustive measures rarely is possible. For example, if a half-hour telephone or Internet survey about politics includes around 100 questions, only a small portion of those could be devoted to measuring personality. Recognizing this, several teams of researchers have worked to develop brief measures of the Big Five, measures that can provide functional representations of personality trait structure with a total of only five to ten survey questions.[8] Recent research on personality and politics has made use of such brief measures, and the tests we report below are based on data using a modified version of Gosling et al.'s ten-item personality measure.

Five-factor models provide well-established and straightforward means to explore the possible effects of personality on various aspects of human behavior. But if personality does matter for phenomena such as public opinion, what broader implications would be suggested? As noted above, we encourage students of public opinion to consider the many long-term and more immediate forces that combine to influence people's opinions. One particularly important point involves the possibility that both personality and aspects of political behavior may be shaped by biological factors. This possibility means that a full understanding of how and why personality and politics are related requires that we briefly consider the roles of biology and genetics.

Personality, Biology, and Politics

In contemplating why people think and behave as they do, we might imagine that the answer is to be found entirely in what individuals have learned and experienced in their lives. For instance, it may be that the reason one person approves of the job the president has been doing while another disapproves is simply that the two have based their judgments on different sets of information. From this perspective, were we to ask two individuals with similar life circumstances (e.g., income, education, place of residence) to evaluate a common set of information before evaluating the president, our expectation would be that they would reach similar judgments. In short, where the key features of the environment are the same, outcomes, including people's opinions, should be the same as well. If only the environment matters, then opinions should match whenever the environment is held constant.

Although our perspective on the bases of human behavior acknowledges a strong role for environmental forces, we think that there is more to the story. Public opinion is an excellent case in point. Most of us have had encounters with others in which we simply cannot comprehend why they think the way they do. In response, we say things such as "there's just no getting through to him," and "it's like she's living on another planet." Even when we walk through the facts one by one, the other person simply won't see things our way. And, of course, even when the other person explains his or her views to us, we, too, refuse to budge. The point suggested by such examples is that perhaps human behavior, including public opinion, is influenced not just by the information we encounter in the immediate environment, but also by deep-seated, long-standing orientations and perspectives.

Long-standing influences could, of course, be products of the environment. For instance, it might be that part of the reason people disagree on matters of public policy traces to their differing activities when they were children, such as experiences they had in the family, the neighborhood, and at school. These experiences may have left deep, lasting impressions, ones that continue to influence the person's views many years later. Although such early experiences no doubt are consequential, we contend that there also exist long-standing influences that are not purely environmental. More specifically, some variation in human behavior reflects the influence of biological factors. People differ in their genetic compositions, and these differences correspond with identifiable behavioral tendencies. Most importantly for present purposes, biological differences matter for both personality and for political behavior. Hence, by highlighting the connections among biology, personality, and public opinion, a richer and more comprehensive account of the personality–politics link can be developed.

The possible biological bases of human behavior are studied in numerous ways. One of the most common involves use of data provided by pairs of twins. Using data from identical and fraternal twins, we can estimate how much of the variation in some aspects of human behavior results from the influence of (1) biological forces, (2) the environmental experiences that two twins share, and (3) the environmental experiences that are unique to a given individual. Monozygotic (MZ) twins are genetically identical, whereas dizygotic (DZ), or fraternal, twins on average share 50 percent of their genes, the same as any other siblings. Suppose we are interested in whether biology matters for musical preferences, and we know that the correlation in musical preferences is 0.60 among MZ twins, versus 0.35 among DZ twins. This means that as genetic similarity rises from 0.50 to 1.0, the correlation in musical preferences increases twenty-five points. It follows that the full impact of genes on musical preferences, or what we would see as genetic similarity rises from 0 to 1.0, would be twice as much, or fifty points. If an analysis of this type permits us to conclude that there is some biological influence on the phenomenon under consideration, we would say that that phenomenon is *heritable*. In the present example, we would conclude that biology accounts for half of the variation in musical preferences, meaning that the heritability level in this case is 0.50. Environmental factors, divided into those encountered by both twins (the shared environment) and those unique to one twin (the unshared environment) would account for the other half.

A discussion of heritability and of tests conducted with data from MZ and DZ twins may seem rather far removed from personality and public opinion. However, an important connection exists. To appreciate this connection, the first point to note is that personality is heritable. All personality traits have been found to have a biological basis. For the Big Five trait dimensions, heritability levels have been estimated to be as high as between approximately 0.60 and 0.80.[9] In other words, a majority of the variation in personality across a population reflects the influence of biology. It follows that, to a substantial extent, our personalities already are shaped at birth. This strong grounding in biology likely helps to explain why people's personalities are so stable over time.

Some scholars have pushed this matter even farther, seeking to find out how it is that biological influences matter for personality. One approach is to conduct what is referred to as a genome-wide association study in order to determine if specific genetic markers correspond with particular personality traits. Research of this type generally has failed to associate specific genes with personality.[10] This is not especially surprising. There are tens of thousands of genes. Numerous genes likely act in highly complex combinations with one another to influence personality, meaning we should not expect scientists to identify something such as an extravert gene or a conscientiousness gene. Recognizing this, other scholars have searched for physiological correlates of personality. Here, studies have been more fruitful. For example, in one recent study focused on the Big Five, a team of researchers found that there are differences in the structures of people's brains, such as the sizes of particular brain regions, which correspond with variation in four of the Big Five trait dimensions.[11]

Collectively, this research establishes that there is a strong biological basis to personality, a point that psychologists and behavioral geneticists have emphasized for many years. More recently, political scientists have made considerable progress in demonstrating a parallel lesson, namely that many facets of political behavior also are influenced by biological forces. Although of more recent vintage, the research on biology and politics has proceeded on much the same track as work on biology and personality, with researchers making use of data from twin studies,[12] genetic association,[13] physiology,[14] and brain structure and function.[15] Collectively, work in this vibrant area has shown that there is a heritable, or biological, component to many aspects of political behavior. Those studies pertaining to ideology and policy issues are especially relevant for a discussion of public opinion. For instance, Alford et al., using data from twin studies, report a heritability level of roughly 0.50 for ideology.[16] Oxley et al. identify a correspondence between differences in physiological responses—physical sensitivities to threat—and variation in attitudes toward matters such as immigration policy, capital punishment, and the Iraq War.[17]

As with biology and personality, the research on biology and politics has given rise to questions about mechanism and process. At question is how and why biological influences act on political behavior. At first glance, the link between biology and politics may seem quite curious. Biological forces gain shape over thousands of years, whereas political matters such as where one stands on immigration policy seemingly are products of the moment. It would be rather far-fetched, for example, to propose that there is something like an Iraq War gene. Recognizing this, most scholars who study biology and politics assume that biology matters for broad, general orientations and predispositions, which, in turn, matter for political views. These general orientations relate to phenomena such as whether a person is sociable and welcoming or cautious and wary around others, and rigid and inflexible or open and adaptable with respect to new ideas and circumstances. Transferred to the political domain, such general orientations influence where people stand in terms of core political values and even specific policies.

Personality traits are likely to be among the general orientations connecting biological influences and political outcomes. Scholars studying biology and politics have hypothesized that this is the case.[18] Because personality traits are highly heritable, any influence of personality on political behavior seemingly would signal an antecedent role for biology: biological forces help shape our personalities, and our personalities, in turn, influence our patterns of political behavior. Although this causal chain makes good sense, two caveats are in order. First, definitive evidence of this causal process requires that biological factors, personality, and political behavior all be studied within a single research design. Studies of this sort currently are underway. Second, even if personality is *a* link between biology and politics, additional linkages are likely.[19]

We have discussed the apparent connections among biology, personality, and politics as a means to provide full background regarding the nature of personality effects on mass opinion. As its title emphasizes, this book is devoted to new directions in public opinion. In the past few years, research efforts on both biology and politics and on personality and politics have experienced a remarkable resurgence. These are important interrelated directions in current public opinion research. The connection between biology and personality helps to establish the significance of both as determinants of political behavior. In other words, one reason it is important to study personality and public opinion is that any effects of personality emanate largely from biological sources. By keeping these various relationships in mind, the study of personality and politics is seen, correctly, as one path in a larger, holistic map of the forces that give rise to public opinion.

Thus far, we have examined at length the rationales for why it may be that personality matters for public opinion, but we have not yet recounted what sorts of effects have been identified in past studies. Research we ourselves have conducted, along with research by several other teams of scholars, has shown that the Big Five personality traits do influence mass opinion. Our next step is to review what some of these studies have found. Later, we will introduce new data as a means to provide examples of a few key personality effects.

Personality, Ideology, and Opinion

Empirical studies regarding the effects of personality on political behavior cover considerable ground. Here, we will limit discussion in two manners.

First, although personality traits may influence numerous facets of political behavior, we will devote the greatest attention to public opinion, while making only passing reference to research exploring the effects of personality on matters such as political information and political participation. Second, most of our discussion is limited to applications involving the Big Five trait taxonomy. Political scientists studied personality and politics prior to the emergence of five-factor models and some scholars today employ alternate frameworks, but these studies will receive minimal attention here. The important point to keep in mind is that "personality and political behavior" is a much broader topic than "the Big Five and public opinion."

Our own research on political applications of the Big Five began in 1997, and we have been gathering personality data on surveys since 1998. More recently, a team of researchers at Yale University headed by Alan Gerber and Gregory Huber has followed suit, producing a series of studies that complement ours, using data from a series of surveys fielded starting in 2006. Our own contributions include an article that provides a general overview of applications of the Big Five to public opinion, political information, and other aspects of mass politics,[20] a much more extensive outline of our research agenda,[21] two examinations of effects of the Big Five on civic engagement and political participation,[22] and more specific treatments concerning the impact of the Big Five on patterns in social and political conversations,[23] jury service,[24] and the political attitudes and behaviors of state legislators.[25] Gerber and his colleagues have studied subgroup differences in Big Five effects on political behavior,[26] the specific impact of personality on participation,[27] and political information.[28]

Although the Big Five traits often are described in collective form, it is important to keep in mind that the taxonomy includes five distinct trait dimensions, each with its own behavioral correlates. All of the traits have been found to be related to multiple aspects of political behavior, but significant effects in the political domain are more common for openness, conscientiousness, and extraversion than for agreeableness and emotional stability. Further, extraversion most often predicts social forms of civic engagement such as participating in political discussion and attending meetings and rallies, whereas effects on political attitudes are less common. Hence, when applied to the study of public opinion, openness to experience and conscientiousness are the Big Five traits that generally should be expected to be of the greatest relevance.

People high in openness to experience exhibit imagination, curiosity, and analytical skill, and they seek information and engagement of all sorts. As the term "openness to experience" implies, these individuals are willing to try new things and to encounter new ideas. Conscientiousness includes a sense of dependability often represented in Big Five measures with reference to terms such as "reliable" and "organized." Conscientiousness also includes a volitional component captured by terms such as "hardworking" and "persevering." People scoring high in conscientiousness tend to be cautious and risk-averse.

Research on personality and public opinion has identified effects of the Big Five on ideology, values, and issue opinions. When scholars have examined the influence of the Big Five on political ideology they consistently have found effects for openness to experience and conscientiousness, along with occasional more modest effects for agreeableness and emotional stability. Openness is positively associated with political liberalism (and thus negatively associated with conservatism), meaning that people who score high in openness to experience have a greater likelihood of being liberal than of being conservative.[29] This relationship makes sense when we consider the nature of liberal ideology. A key part of political liberalism is the interest in new solutions to existing political problems and the willingness to embrace societal change.

The other consistent finding in studies regarding the Big Five and ideology has been a positive relationship between conscientiousness and political conservatism. Many of the same studies that identified links between openness and liberalism have found parallel effects of conscientiousness on self-identification as a conservative. This relationship, like the openness–liberal link, enjoys strong intuitive appeal. Political conservatives are cautious in policy making and reluctant to alter the status quo, and many conservatives value personal responsibility and tradition. These preferences are the hallmarks of individuals psychologically inclined toward conscientiousness.

Consistent effects of openness and conscientiousness have been identified in many studies involving the mass public, and these same relationships have been found with data from elected officials—members of the state legislatures in Arizona, Connecticut, and Maine.[30] A last point about the Big Five and ideology is that agreeableness and emotional stability have emerged in some studies, including the Dietrich et al. legislator project, as predictors of ideology. Although more modest than the effects for openness and conscientiousness, the evidence suggests that agreeableness corresponds with a tendency toward ideological liberalism and emotional stability predicts conservatism.

Elsewhere in this volume, the importance of people's values (Federico), including religions beliefs (Campbell and Layman) is noted. Personality also may be important in this area. Openness and conscientiousness both have been found to be related to people's core values. For example, in one of our works, conscientiousness produced very strong positive effects on moral traditionalism and moral judgment, and openness yielded equally strong negative effects.[31] Caprara et al. find similar results with respect to two other core values, universalism and security.[32] In that study, the authors posit that the pathway linking the Big Five and ideology runs through values. That is, openness and conscientiousness shape views regarding universalism and security, which, in turn, influence ideology.

Beyond ideology and values, effects of the Big Five also have been found on people's specific policy judgments. To a large degree, such effects reflect the impact of personality on ideology. However, in many cases personality has been found to be influential even when controlling for ideology.[33] We present an example of such a test below by exploring whether, controlling for ideology, the Big Five traits affect opinion on same-sex marriage. To our knowledge, possible relationships between the Big Five traits and attitudes toward same-sex marriage have not been studied directly, although several findings are informative. Riemann et al. administered a survey of political attitudes to a sample of German citizens.[34] Their measure of general conservatism included attitudes toward same-sex marriage, and significant relationships were found for openness and agreeableness, with both shown to be positively associated with liberal attitudes. Cullen et al. included a measure of openness in their study of the correlates of homophobia.[35] Using a sample of university students they found that openness was negatively related to homophobia, meaning that individuals with low scores on openness were more likely to be homophobic. Similarly, McCrae et al. found that low scores on openness were associated with attitudes which stigmatized people with HIV/AIDS in both the United States and Russia.[36] Finally, Costa et al. found that higher scores on openness were associated with liberal sex attitudes.[37]

Thus far, we have discussed at some length the rationale for why personality should be expected to influence public opinion, along with what sorts of effects have been seen in prior research. This material has provided important background, but the most tangible way to demonstrate the personality–opinion link is to introduce direct evidence. Toward this end, our final substantive task is to report data from a recent survey. With past research to guide us, our expectation is that personality traits—especially openness to experience and conscientiousness—should emerge as determinants of both political ideology and respondents' policy stances.

Exploring the Personality–Opinion Connection

The data we will examine are from a national Internet survey conducted in March, 2010.[38] The survey's 1,500 respondents answered numerous questions about politics, and also a ten-item Big Five personality battery. Our interest is in whether values on the Big Five measures correspond with respondents' political views. Specifically, we will assess the possible effects of the Big Five trait dimensions on ideology and attitudes toward same-sex marriage.

Ideological orientation is measured with data from an item on which respondents were asked to place themselves on a ten-point scale on which 1 was labeled "liberal" and 10 was labeled "conservative." All but six respondents provided answers. Responses were split nearly evenly between the liberal (49.6 percent) and conservative (50.4 percent) halves of the scale. The scale has a mean value of 5.80.

We measure attitudes toward same-sex marriage with data from a question that asked "How strongly do you approve or disapprove that same-sex couples can have the right to marry?" As with ideology, a ten-point scale is used, with endpoints labeled "strongly disapprove" (1) and "strongly approve" (10). All 1,500 respondents answered this question. Opinion was fairly evenly divided, with 53.5 percent of respondents expressing disapproval of same-sex marriage, and 46.5 percent indicating approval. The scale has a mean value of 5.27.

The Big Five personality traits are measured using data from ten survey items, two for each trait dimension. The questions asked of respondents are adapted from Gosling et al.'s (2003) "ten-item personality inventory," or TIPI.[39] In pilot tests conducted before our full surveys were administered throughout the Americas, we used the actual TIPI items. Especially outside of the United States, many of the respondents on the AmericasBarometer surveys—a series of polls administered in twenty-five nations in the Americas—have very low levels of education, and thus it is important that survey questions be tested carefully to make sure that respondents understand what they mean. In our pilot tests, many respondents struggled with some of the words on the TIPI, words such as "extraverted," "reserved," and "conventional." With the help of feedback from interviewers, we were able to develop a revised set of personality questions that was better understood by respondents.[40] As on the TIPI, respondents were asked to use a seven-point scale to indicate the extent to which they agreed or disagreed that a series of statements apply to them. A value of 1 means "strongly disagree" and a value of 7 means "strongly agree." For each trait, one item is worded positively and one is worded negatively. In Table 10.1, we list the Big Five trait dimensions, the survey items used to measure them, and also our central expectations regarding possible effects of personality on ideology and on attitudes regarding same-sex marriage.

Our final personality scales are constructed by reversing the five items that are worded negatively so that high scores indicate possession of the trait in question, adding the two items pertaining to each trait, and then recoding the final measures so that they range from 0 (the lowest observed value for the full Americas survey) to 1 (the highest observed value). All but one of the respondents in the United States answered all ten of the personality questions. The mean scores for the final scales are: openness, 0.67; conscientiousness, 0.67; extraversion, 0.47; agreeableness, 0.57; and emotional stability, 0.54. These 0–1 scales will be used as independent variables in statistical models—specifically, what are known as ordinary least squares regression models—to see if variation in people's personality traits predicts variation in ideology and opinion regarding same-sex marriage. The regression model enables us to assess the possible effects of the Big Five traits while also accounting for the possible influences of other factors.[41]

We begin our analyses by testing the possible effects of personality on ideology. The precise statistical estimates for this model are reported in Table 10.2. All four demographic variables produced statistically significant results.

Table 10.1 The Big Five and Public Opinion: Traits, Measures and Expectations

Trait dimension	*Survey measures*	*Expected relationship with ideology*	*Expected relationship with opinion regarding same-sex marriage*
Openness to experience	Open to new experiences and intellectual (5); uncreative and unimaginative (10, R)	High openness corresponds strongly with ideological liberalism	High openness corresponds with approval of same-sex couples having the right to marry
Conscientiousness	Dependable and self-disciplined (3); disorganized and careless (8, R)	High conscientiousness corresponds strongly with ideological conservatism	High conscientiousness corresponds with disapproval of same-sex couples having the right to marry
Extraversion	Sociable and active (1); quiet and shy (6, R)		
Agreeableness	Critical and quarrelsome (2, R); generous and warm (7)	High agreeableness may correspond weakly with ideological liberalism	High agreeableness may correspond weakly with approval of same-sex couples having the right to marry
Emotional stability	Anxious and easily upset (4, R); calm and emotionally stable (9)	High emotional stability may correspond weakly with ideological conservatism	High emotional stability may correspond weakly with disapproval of same-sex couples having the right to marry

Note

Survey measures were asked following this prompt:

> Here are a series of personality traits that may or may not apply to you. Using the 1–7 ladder, where 1 means 'strongly disagree' and 7 means 'strongly agree,' please tell me the number that indicates the extent to which you agree or disagree with that statement. You should rate the extent to which the pair of traits applies to you, even if one characteristic applies more strongly than the other. You see yourself as a _____ person.

Numbers in parentheses following the items indicate the order in which they were asked. An "R" within the parentheses means that values on this item were reversed in the final scale.

Table 10.2 The Influence of Personality on Ideology

Constant	4.77 (0.40)
Female	−0.55*** (0.14)
African American	−0.79*** (0.22)
Hispanic	−0.47** (0.21)
Age	0.02*** (0.00)
Openness to experience	−2.17*** (0.35)
Conscientiousness	1.88*** (0.35)
Extraversion	0.29 (0.31)
Agreeableness	0.46 (0.39)
Emotional stability	0.62* (0.34)
R^2	0.09
Number of cases	1,493

Source: U.S. component of the 2010 AmericasBarometer.

Note

Cell entries are OLS regression coefficients with standard errors in parentheses. The dependent variable is a ten-point measure of ideological self-placement, coded 1 (liberal) to 10 (conservative). *** $p < 0.001$, ** $p < 0.05$, * $p < 0.10$

Specifically, female respondents are, on average, somewhat more liberal than respondents who are male; African Americans and Hispanics are more liberal than respondents who are white; and older respondents are more conservative, as a whole, than are younger respondents.

Among the personality variables, the results are very much in line with the findings reported in past studies. Statistically significant effects found for the personality variables are summarized in Figure 10.1.[42]

First, openness to experience is strongly negatively related to being conservative. The estimate, or regression coefficient, for this trait is −2.17. This means that as openness shifts in value from 0 to 1, the ideology of the respondent is predicted to move over two points toward the liberal end of the ten-point ideology measure.

As expected, conscientiousness emerges as a significant predictor of ideological conservatism. The coefficient for this trait is 1.88, meaning that it is almost as large, although in the opposite direction, as the effect for openness to experience. The second section of Figure 10.1 displays this effect. The results for openness and conscientiousness both are substantively quite sizeable. For example, both are over twice the magnitude of the largest demographic effect, the −0.79 result for being African American. The influences of openness and conscientiousness on ideology are especially pronounced when the two traits are viewed in tandem. A person who is high in conscientiousness and low in openness is predicted to have an ideology value a full four points to the right of an individual with the opposite personality profile.

Among the other three Big Five traits, extraversion is rarely found to be linked to ideology, whereas agreeableness and emotional stability sometimes produce modest effects. Present results match well to this pattern. The

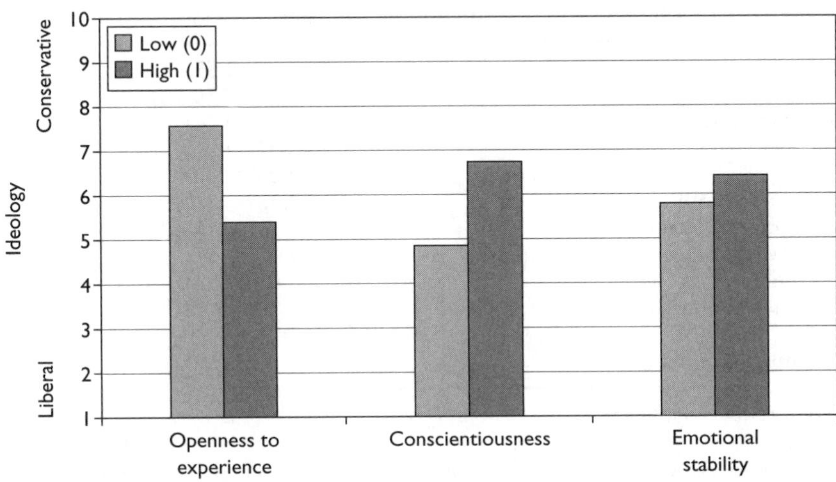

Figure 10.1 Estimated Effects of Personality Traits on Ideology.

regression coefficients for extraversion and agreeableness are small and statistically insignificant. Emotional stability proves to be related to ideology, but, as seen in Figure 10.1, the effect is less than one-third as large as those for openness and conscientiousness. Overall, the Big Five traits clearly do matter for ideology, but, as expected, the five trait dimensions do not perform comparably. In this data set, openness to experience is strongly associated with ideological liberalism, conscientiousness is strongly associated with conservatism, emotional stability modestly predicts conservatism, and agreeableness and emotional stability are unrelated to ideology.

These results show that personality influences one of people's most fundamental political orientations, but are there also effects on opinions about contemporary issues? Statistical estimates for our test concerning opinion on same-sex marriage are reported in Table 10.3.

The general pattern of results is highly similar to what we saw above for ideology. First, women and younger people are more approving of same-sex couples having the right to marry than are men and older people. However, unlike with ideology, there are no differences in opinion associated with variation in race and ethnicity. Second, openness to experience and conscientiousness once again produce extremely strong effects, and emotional stability again exerts a modest but statistically discernable influence.

The magnitudes of the openness and conscientiousness effects warrant emphasis. As Figure 10.2 reveals, both traits are estimated to produce greater than three-point swings on the 1–10 opinion scale.

The strongest impact emerges when we consider the joint influence of openness and conscientiousness. An average respondent is estimated to have a score of 8.43 on the same-sex marriage item if the person is high in

Table 10.3 The Influence of Personality on Approval of Same-Sex Marriage

Constant	7.88 (0.55)
Female	0.73*** (0.20)
African American	–0.26 (0.31)
Hispanic	–0.41 (0.29)
Age	–0.05*** (0.01)
Openness to experience	3.28*** (0.48)
Conscientiousness	–3.10*** (0.48)
Extraversion	0.05 (0.43)
Agreeableness	–0.63 (0.53)
Emotional stability	–0.79* (0.48)
R^2	0.13
Number of cases	1,499

Source: U.S. component of the 2010 AmericasBarometer.

Note
Cell entries are OLS regression coefficients with standard errors in parentheses. The dependent variable is a ten-point measure of approval of the right of same-sex couples to marry, coded 1 (strongly disapprove) to 10 (strongly approve). *** $p < 0.001$, * $p < 0.10$.

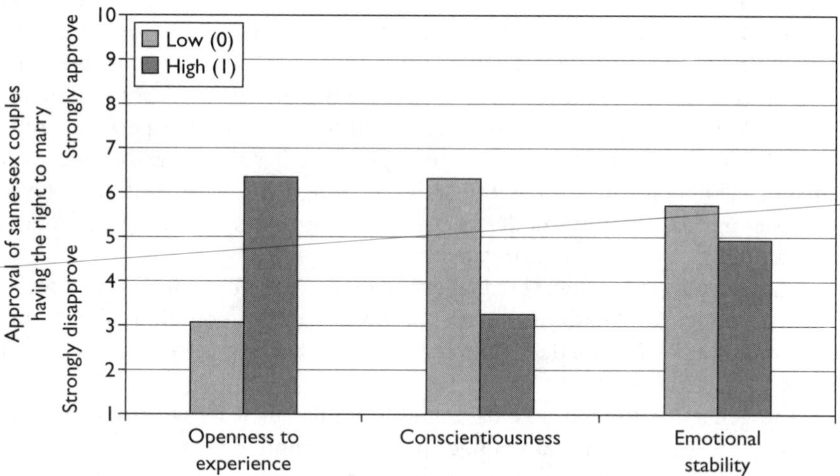

Figure 10.2 Estimated Effects of Personality Traits on Approval to Same-Sex Couples Having the Right to Marry.

openness to experience and low in conscientiousness, versus a score of 2.05 if he has the opposite profile in terms of these two traits. This suggests that, to a substantial extent, opinion on same-sex marriage is shaped by people's core biologically influenced psychological differences.

Our initial account of opinion on same-sex marriage suffers from an important limitation in that it examines the possible effects of personality traits and of demographic attributes, but it omits basic political orientations such as ideology. Public debate over same-sex marriage has transpired largely along ideological lines, with many liberals expressing support of same-sex couples having the right to marry, and many conservatives expressing opposition. Earlier, we saw that the same three personality traits that matter for opinion on same-sex marriage also matter for ideology. This raises the possibility that there is no direct relationship between personality and opinion in this case. Instead, it may be that personality shapes ideology, which, in turn, influences opinion on the issue of same-sex marriage. In other words, the effects of personality on opinion may be indirect rather than direct, with those effects operating through ideology.

We believe that it is important to understand not only whether personality matters for public opinion, but also how, and through what channels, any influences of personality operate. Thus, we must sort out the relationships among personality, ideology, and opinion. The most straightforward means to do so is to add ideology as a predictor of same-sex marriage.[43] If, as should be expected, ideology is related to opinion in this case, that would signal an indirect effect of personality. If inclusion of ideology causes the statistical estimates for the personality variables to weaken and slip to statistical insignificance, this would mean that personality exerts *only* an indirect influence on opinion about same-sex marriage. Conversely, if ideology generates a significant effect and the personality variables also continue to produce strong influences, this would mean that personality affects opinion regarding same-sex marriage both directly and indirectly.

The revised statistical estimates are reported in Table 10.4.

Table 10.4 Direct and Indirect Effects of Personality on Approval of Same-Sex Marriage

Constant	11.77 (0.47)
Female	0.27 (0.16)
African American	−0.90*** (0.25)
Hispanic	−0.79** (0.24)
Age	−0.03*** (0.00)
Openness to experience	1.52*** (0.40)
Conscientiousness	−1.60*** (0.40)
Extraversion	0.29 (0.35)
Agreeableness	−0.26 (0.44)
Emotional stability	−0.31 (0.39)
Ideology	−0.81*** (0.03)
R^2	0.42
Number of cases	1,499

Source: U.S. component of the 2010 AmericasBarometer.

Note

Cell entries are OLS regression coefficients with standard errors in parentheses. The dependent variable is a ten-point measure of approval of the right of same-sex couples to marry, coded 1 (strongly disapprove) to 10 (strongly approve). *** $p < 0.001$, ** $p < 0.01$, * $p < 0.10$.

Ideology produces what substantively is a quite large effect. Because values on ideology range from 1 to 10, the –0.81 coefficient means that the predicted score on the same-sex marriage item shifts by 7.29 points across the ideology scale. The important lesson with respect to personality is that part of the influence of the Big Five on opinion is indirect, with this influence operating through ideology. As to the trait variables, the estimate for emotional stability is small and statistically insignificant. Therefore, it appears that the impact of this trait dimension on opinion is only indirect. In contrast, the estimates for openness to experience and conscientiousness remain statistically significant. The new estimates for these variables are about half as large as the ones observed before we added ideology to our account. This suggests that these two traits produce both direct and indirect effects on opinion about same-sex marriage, with approximately half of the influence associated with each trait being direct and half being indirect.

We summarize the collective lessons from our empirical tests in Figure 10.3. First, arrows lead from each of the three personality traits to ideology. Specifically, openness is negatively associated with ideological conservatism, whereas conscientiousness and emotional stability are linked positively to conservatism. Second, conservatism is negatively associated with approval of same-sex couples having the right to marry. Third, openness and conscientiousness produce direct effects, over and above the impact operating via ideology, on opinion about same-sex marriage. This exercise serves to demonstrate that personality traits are important determinants of at least one facet of public opinion, and also that the effects of personality on opinion operate partly in conjunction with people's fundamental political orientations.

Conclusions

The purpose of this chapter has been to discuss the effects of people's personality traits on public opinion. Toward that end, we sought in the first portion of the chapter to explain the rationale for how and why personality and public opinion may be linked, and to review recent scholarship that speaks to such a

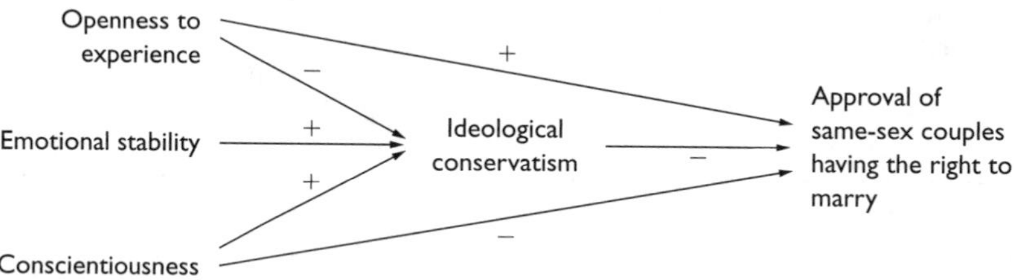

Figure 10.3 Direct and Indirect Effects of Personality Traits on Approval of Same-Sex Couples Having the Right to Marry.

connection. In the second section of the chapter, we presented a few illustrative tests. Those exercises yielded evidence that people's personality traits influence political ideology, and also that personality produces both direct and indirect effects on public opinion regarding a salient topic in contemporary politics, the right of same-sex couples to be married.

Although our immediate objective has been to discuss the possible relationship between personality and public opinion, two broader concerns have motivated this effort. First, taking personality seriously requires one to take long-term influences seriously. A central theme in this chapter, and in our own research agenda, is that much of the political behavior we observe on a day-to-day basis arises partly as the consequence of long-term forces. In contrast with more immediate influences, such as exposure to information during the course of a political campaign, long-term forces trace back many years. Indeed, some long-term influences are rooted in biology. Second, in studying the impact of personality and other long-term influences, we believe it is important to keep the big picture in sight. Many factors of various forms affect patterns in political behavior. Public opinion is not the exclusive product of personality traits any more than it is the exclusive product of what people see on the news. We will make the most progress toward understanding the bases of public opinion if we recognize that multiple influences are at work, and if we seek to discover how these influences combine.

In just the past few years, there has been a tremendous revitalization in research on personality and politics, coupled with a closely related wave of scholarly attention to the effects of biology on political behavior. As research in these areas continues, students of public opinion will have to think carefully about what these developments imply regarding matters such as why people hold different views and what prospects exist for people with divergent opinions to engage in civil, constructive discourse about political affairs. The tests presented in this chapter are good cases in point. Personality and other long-term influences do not determine public opinion, and the effects of these influences are not such that opinion is set in stone. Nonetheless, personality effects are deep-seated. The strong impact of personality on people's political views therefore helps to explain some of the fundamental divisions seen today, divisions such as those between liberals and conservatives, and between proponents and opponents of same-sex marriage. These examples are of sufficient importance to demonstrate that research on personality constitutes a significant new direction in the study of public opinion.

Notes

1. This chapter was supported by a grant from the National Science Foundation (Award 0962153). Data reported in this chapter were gathered as part of the U.S. component of the 2010 AmericasBarometer survey. The authors thank Damarys Canache and Mitchell Seligson for their contributions to this project.

2. P.T. Costa and R.R. McCrae, "Personality in Adulthood: A Six-Year Longitudinal Study of Self-Reports and Spouse Ratings on the NEO Personality Inventory," *Journal of Personality and Social Psychology* 54 (1988): 853–63.
3. See, for example, E.C. Tupes and R.E. Christal, *Recurrent Personality Factors Based on Trait Ratings* (Lackland Air Force Base, TX: U.S. Air Force, 1961), and E.C. Tupes and R.E. Christal, *Stability of Personality Trait Rating Factors Obtained under Diverse Conditions* (Lackland Air Force Base, TX: U.S. Air Force, 1958).
4. See, for example, L.R. Goldberg, "An Alternative 'Description of Personality': The Big-Five Factor Structure," *Journal of Personality and Social Psychology* 59 (1990): 1,216–29; L.R. Goldberg, "The Development of Markers for the Big-Five Factor Structure," *Psychological Assessment* 4 (1992): 26–42; Costa and McCrae, "Personality in Adulthood"; R.R. McCrae and P.T. Costa, "The Five-Factor Theory of Personality," in *Handbook of Personality: Theory and Research*, eds. O.P. John, R.W. Robins, and L.A. Pervin (New York: Guilford, 2008); and R.R. McCrae and P.T. Costa, *Personality in Adulthood: A Five-Factor Theory* (New York: Guilford, 2003).
5. S.D. Gosling, P.J. Rentfrow, and W.B. Swann, "A Very Brief Measure of the Big-Five Personality Domains," *Journal of Research in Personality* 37 (2003): 506.
6. McCrae and Costa, *Personality in Adulthood.*
7. A key way psychologists test the utility of self-report personality data is to gather personality descriptions about these individuals from other people who know them well so that self-reports and other-person reports can be compared. High correlations between self-reports and other-person reports consistently are recorded when such tests are conducted, which suggests that we see ourselves much as others see us.
8. See, for example, Gosling et al., "A Very Brief Measure"; and S.A. Woods and S.E. Hampson, "Measuring the Big Five with Single Items Using a Bipolar Response Scale," *European Journal of Personality* 19 (2005): 373–90.
9. R. Riemann, A. Angleitner, and J. Strelau, "Genetic and Environmental Influences on Personality: A Study of Twins Reared Together Using the Self- and Peer Report NEO-FFI Scales," *Journal of Personality* 65 (1997): 449–75.
10. K.J. Verweij, B.P. Zietsch, S.E. Medland, S.D. Gordon, B. Benyamin, D.R. Nyholt, B.P. McEvoy, P.F. Sullivan, A.C. Heath, P.A. Madden, A.K. Henders, G.W. Montgomery, N.G. Martin, and N.R. Wray, "A Genome-Wide Association Study of Cloninger's Temperament Scales: Implications for the Evolutionary Genetics of Personality," *Biological Psychology* 85 (2010): 306–17.
11. C.G. DeYoung, J.B. Hirsh, M.S. Shane, X. Papademetris, N. Rajeevan, and J.R. Gray, "Testing Predictions from Personality Neuroscience: Brain Structure and the Big Five," *Psychological Science* 21 (2010): 820–8.
12. See, for example, J.R. Alford, C.L. Funk, and J.R. Hibbing, "Are Political Orientations Genetically Transmitted?" *American Political Science Review* 99 (2005): 153–67; and J.H. Fowler, L.A. Baker, and C.T. Dawes, "Genetic Variation in Political Participation," *American Political Science Review* 102 (2008): 233–48.
13. J.H. Fowler and C.T. Dawes, "Two Genes Predict Voter Turnout," *Journal of Politics* 70 (2008): 479–94.
14. D.R. Oxley, K.B. Smith, J.R. Alford, M.V. Hibbing, J.L. Miller, M.J. Scalora, P.K. Hatemi, and J.R. Hibbing, "Political Attitudes Vary with Physiological Traits," *Science* 321 (2008): 1167–70.
15. D.P. Westen, P.S. Blagov, K. Harenski, C. Kilts, and S. Hamann, "Neural Bases of Motivated Reasoning: An fMRI Study of Emotional Constraints on Partisan Political Judgment in the 2004 U.S. Presidential Election," *Journal of Cognitive Neuroscience* 18 (2006): 1947–58.
16. Alford et al., "Are Political Attitudes Genetically Transmitted?"

17. Oxley et al., "Political Attitudes Vary with Physiological Traits."
18. Alford et al., "Are Political Attitudes Genetically Transmitted?" 157; and Fowler et al., "Genetic Variation in Political Participation," 244.
19. We address the possible causal pathways connecting biology, personality, aspects of the environment, and political behavior more fully in J.J. Mondak, M.V. Hibbing, D. Canache, M.A. Seligson, and M.R. Anderson, "Personality and Civic Engagement: An Integrative Framework for the Study of Trait Effects on Political Behavior," *American Political Science Review* 104 (2010): 85–110.
20. J.J. Mondak and K.D. Halperin, "A Framework for the Study of Personality and Political Behavior," *British Journal of Political Science* 38 (2008): 335–62.
21. J.J. Mondak, *Personality and the Foundations of Political Behavior* (New York: Cambridge, 2010).
22. J.J. Mondak, D. Canache, M.A. Seligson, and M.V. Hibbing, "The Participatory Personality: Evidence from Latin America," *British Journal of Political Science* 41 (2011): 211–21; and J.J. Mondak et al., "Personality and Civic Engagement."
23. M.V. Hibbing, M. Ritchie, and M.R. Anderson, "Personality and Political Discussion," *Political Behavior* (forthcoming).
24. A.J. Bloeser, C. McCurley, and J.J. Mondak, "Jury service as Civic Engagement: Determinants of Jury Summons Compliance," unpublished manuscript.
25. B.J. Dietrich, S. Lasley, J.J. Mondak, M.R. Remmel, and J. Turner, "Personality and Political Elites: The Big Five Trait Dimensions among U.S. State Legislators," *Political Psychology* (forthcoming).
26. A.S. Gerber, G.A. Huber, D. Doherty, C.M. Dowling, and S.E. Ha, "Personality and Political Attitudes: Relationships across Issue Domains and Political Contexts," *American Political Science Review* 104 (2010): 111–33.
27. A.S. Gerber, G.A. Huber, D. Doherty, C.M. Dowling, C. Raso, and S.E. Ha, "Personality Traits and Participation in Political Processes," *Journal of Politics* (forthcoming).
28. A.S. Gerber, G.A. Huber, D. Doherty, and C.M. Dowling, "Personality Traits and the Consumption of Political Information," *American Politics Research* 39 (2011): 32–84.
29. See, for example, D.R. Carney, J.T. Jost, S.D. Gosling, and J. Potter, "The Secret Lives of Liberals and Conservatives: Personality Profiles, Interaction Styles, and the Things They Leave Behind," *Political Psychology* 29 (2008): 807–40; R. Riemann, C. Grubich, S. Hempel, S. Mergl, and M. Richter, "Personality and Attitudes towards Current Political Topics," *Personality and Individual Differences* 15 (1993): 313–21; Gerber et al. "Personality and Political Attitudes"; Mondak "Personality and the Foundations of Political Behavior"; Mondak and Halperin "A Framework for the Study of Personality and Political Behavior."
30. Dietrich et al. "Personality and Political Elites."
31. Mondak "Personality and the Foundations of Political Behavior."
32. G. Caprara, M. Vecchione, and S.H. Schwartz, "Meditational Role of Values in Linking Personality Traits to Political Orientation," *Asian Journal of Social Psychology* 12 (2009): 82–94.
33. See, for example, Mondak "Personality and the Foundations of Political Behavior," 135–9.
34. Riemann et al., "Personality and Attitudes towards Current Political Topics."
35. J.M. Cullen, L.W. Wright, and M. Alessandri, "The Personality Variable Openness to Experience as it Relates to Homophobia," *Journal of Homosexuality* 42 (2002): 119–34.
36. R.R. McCrae, P.T. Costa, Jr., T.A. Martin, V.E Oryol, I.G. Senin, and C. O'Cleirigh, "Personality Correlates of HIV Stigmatization in Russia and the United States," *Journal of Research in Personality* 41 (2007): 190–6.

37. P.T. Costa, Jr., P.J. Fagan, R.L. Piedmont, Y. Ponticas, and T.N. Wise, "The Five-Factor Model of Personality and Sexual Functioning in Outpatient Men and Women," *Psychiatric Medicine* 10 (1992): 199–215.
38. The survey was administered between March 17 and March 29, 2010. It is the U.S. portion of the 2010 AmericasBarometer project. Other surveys were administered as part of this project in an additional two dozen nations in the Americas. In most nations, face-to-face interviews were conducted.
39. Gosling et al., "A Very Brief Measure of the Big-Five Personality Domains."
40. The original TIPI has a readability score of 41.7, and a readability level (the expected number of years of education needed to understand a passage) of 9.2. Our revised measure has a readability score of 50.4 and a readability level of 8.4. The survey was, of course, translated into several languages in order to be administered in nations throughout the Americas.
41. In addition to the Big Five variables, the statistical models we estimate include four control variables: the respondent's sex (1 if female, 0 if male), whether the respondent is an African American (1 if yes, 0 if no), whether the respondent is Hispanic (1 if yes, 0 if no), and the respondent's age.
42. All estimates are calculated for a hypothetical respondent who is a white male, age forty, and who has average values on the other personality traits.
43. Similar tests using data from a 2006 survey are reported in Mondak (2010, 137–9), with focus on opinion regarding the PATRIOT Act, the Iraq War, abortion, tax cuts, and illegal immigration.

Part III

The Public and Society

Chapter 11

Campaigns and Elections

John Sides and Jake Haselswerdt

On the day after Barack Obama's victory in the 2008 presidential election, the lead story in the *New York Times* said this: "The story of Mr. Obama's journey to the pinnacle of American politics is the story of a campaign that was, even in the view of many rivals, almost flawless." This sentiment—which implicitly attributes Obama's victory to his campaign activities—is commonplace in the news media. While the campaign is underway, media accounts similarly focus on every twist and turn, suggesting that all kinds of events matter—in 2008, anything from Obama's comment about "bitter voters who cling to guns" to Jeremiah Wright and William Ayers. The portrait that emerges is one of instability and unpredictability: with a blizzard of ads, money, spin, and counterspin, we don't know what voters will do and so we don't know who will win.

And yet, at a meeting of political scientists held over Labor Day weekend in 2008—even before the start of the Republican National Convention—a panel of political scientists each presented a forecast of the outcome. Almost all of them predicted the exact outcome within a couple of percentage points. The average of their predictions was 53 percent, and that's what Obama got. That is a little bit lucky, but still it raises some important questions. How is it possible that elections are so predictable even amidst the apparently volatility of the campaign? And if elections are so predictable, how much does the campaign matter?

To tackle these questions, we first discuss what is so lacking in news coverage: why the influence of campaigns might in fact be limited. We discuss how voters' choices depend in part on "the fundamentals," including long-standing political identities and larger political events and trends—all of which are largely outside of the control of campaigns and make both voters and elections predictable. This presents a further puzzle: if the fundamentals matter so much, then why do the polls vary during the campaign? In fact, the ups and downs in the polls do suggest a role for the campaign. We then consider the circumstances in which campaigns can matter and three different ways that campaigns matter: changing voters' minds, changing the criteria they use in making decisions, and "getting out the vote" or encouraging them to participate on Election Day. Ultimately, political campaigns do play some role,

although their contribution to the election's outcome may still be outweighed by events beyond the candidates' control.

The Predictability of Voters

Voters rarely approach a campaign as blank slates, devoid of ideas about politics or the candidates. In fact, in many elections, voters can draw on long-standing political identities to guide their choices, even without any detailed information about the candidates. Some relevant identities involve race, ethnicity, socioeconomic status, and religion. The power of race derives in part from the historical linkages between racial communities and political parties, linkages that are nurtured by the attention parties pay to the concerns of racial groups. For example, African Americans have a long-standing tie to the Democratic Party because it, more than the Republican Party, took up the cause of civil rights. Even 40 years after the Civil Rights Movement, the tie remains strong. It is nurtured by Democratic politicians, who pursue policies favored by most African Americans and who routinely engage in symbolic gestures, such as speaking before the NAACP or in predominantly black churches. It is also nurtured by African American leaders who provide important cues for their followers, suggesting explicitly or implicitly that Democratic candidates deserve support. Finally, it is nurtured by the simple fact that residential and other patterns of segregation ensure that African Americans associate mostly with each other, thereby making it less likely they will encounter opposite or alternative political views. For these and other reasons, the vast majority of African Americans—upwards of 90 percent in presidential elections—vote for Democratic candidates. One can easily tell a similar story about other groups—for example, white evangelical Christians, whose close ties to the Republican Party have arisen via a similar process. In all such cases, voters behave predictably based on social identities and their associated group interests, which limits the ability of the campaign to persuade them otherwise.

Voters are also predictable because of *party identification*, which was discussed in Chapter 7. Party identification is a psychological tie to a political party, which means that voters tend to think of themselves as members of a party and that they feel some affinity for it. It does not change for most people, despite dramatic political or personal events. In fact, some researchers have found party identification as stable as religious identification.[1] This is not to say that party identification never changes, but typically it changes only gradually.

The relevance of party identification to campaigns and elections is twofold. First, party identification influences how we see the world and process new information. The biases it creates (see Chapter 7) are very relevant to elections. For example, different groups of partisans watch the exact same candidate debate and somehow conclude that their candidate won. After the second presidential debate in 2008, a CNN poll found that 85 percent of Democrats believed that Obama won, and 64 percent of Republicans thought that McCain won.

Second, party identification also influences how we make political choices, notably voting. Voters who identify with a party are very loyal to that party's candidates. Although voters sometimes "defect" and vote for a candidate of the opposite party—due to that candidate's appealing personality, or some compelling policy issue, or to the lack of a credible candidate in their own party—this is the exception rather than the rule. In fact, defections have become increasingly rare. Partisans have become more loyal to their parties, and fewer and fewer voters "split their tickets" by voting for candidates of different parties for different offices.

The true nature of contemporary party identification flies in the face of much conventional wisdom, which suggests that party identification has weakened as more and more voters have come to identify as "independent." Pundits routinely claim that independents are numerous—the "largest group in the electorate," "the vast middle ground where elections are won and lost in America," and "the fast-growing swath of voters."[2] It is true that the number of people who call themselves independent has grown to outnumber the fractions calling themselves Democrats or Republicans. But most of these independents profess that they "lean" toward one of the two major parties and, in elections, are just as likely to vote for that party as many who identify with that party in the first place.[3] Both facts were illustrated in 2008. In that year's American National Election Study, a large election survey carried out by political scientists, only 12 percent of the sample, and 7 percent of self-reported voters, identified as independent and did not indicate any leaning toward a political party. These "pure" independents were fairly evenly split between Obama and John McCain (58–42 percent). However, independents who leaned Democratic were almost unanimously behind Obama: 91 percent reported voting for him. Independents who leaned Republican were almost as loyal to McCain: 82 percent voted for him.

The relevance of party identification for campaigns is obvious: no amount of clever advertising by one candidate will persuade many of those who identify with the opponent's party to change their minds. Campaigns often only reinforce party loyalty rather than encourage defections. This is the conclusion of many studies of American presidential elections stretching back to the 1940s.[4] And when campaigns do have an impact, it is often small. During the 2008 campaign, Obama's and McCain's poll numbers only ever changed by a few percentage points at most. Of course, in close elections, the decisions of less predictable and truly independent voters can be consequential. But media coverage—with its laser focus on these voters—understates how much of voting is an entirely predictable expression of social and partisan identities.

The Predictability of Elections

When political scientists were able to predict the 2008 election, they did so two months ahead of time, before the candidate debates and the vast majority of television advertising.[5] The predictability of elections stems from how fundamental factors affect how we vote and thus, who wins the election.

Two factors are most important, especially in presidential elections: the health of the economy, and whether the country is at war (particularly an unsuccessful war) or at peace.[6] Their importance seems sensible: prosperity and peace are foundational goals, without which it is difficult for government to accomplish other things. The reason both factors affect elections is because they underlie the public's evaluation of political figures. The public holds elected officials responsible for how well the economy is doing and whether the United States is at war (and, if so, whether it is winning). Presidents are held most responsible and, if the president is not running for reelection, then his party is held responsible. When the economy is doing well and the country is at peace, the incumbent president or his party will do better than when the economy is weak and war casualties are mounting. Voters behave "retrospectively"—looking backwards at the state of the country and evaluating incumbents accordingly.

Retrospective voting sounds sensible and fair, but in some ways it is not. For one, presidents and their co-partisans have limited control over the economy and many events that take place during war, so they probably do not deserve much of the credit or blame that they receive. In fact, retrospective voting sometimes appears to depend on events that have nothing to do with politics at all, much less the actions of incumbent leaders. For example, incumbent leaders do better in elections held soon after the local college football team has won: a victory is worth about an extra 1 percent for the incumbent, and 2 percent if the team is a well-known powerhouse.[7] Second, the public's judgment about the economy is not necessarily sound. Voters can be more influenced by media reporting about the economy than the economy itself. This helps explain why, in 1992, Bill Clinton benefited from perceptions of a weak economy, even though the recession was over.[8] Moreover, voters' memories are short: they are much more influenced by change in the economy in the year before the presidential election, and tend to ignore the prior years.[9] A president who presides over three years of a bad economy and then one final year of growth may do better than a president who presides over three years of growth and one final year of recession.

These points are illustrated in Figure 11.1. Both graphs in this figure depict the relationship between economic growth, measured as change in real per capita disposable income, and presidential election outcomes, measured as the incumbent party's percentage of the major-party vote. The top graph relies on a measure of economic growth over the last three years of the president's term, assuming that his policies would not take effect until the second year of

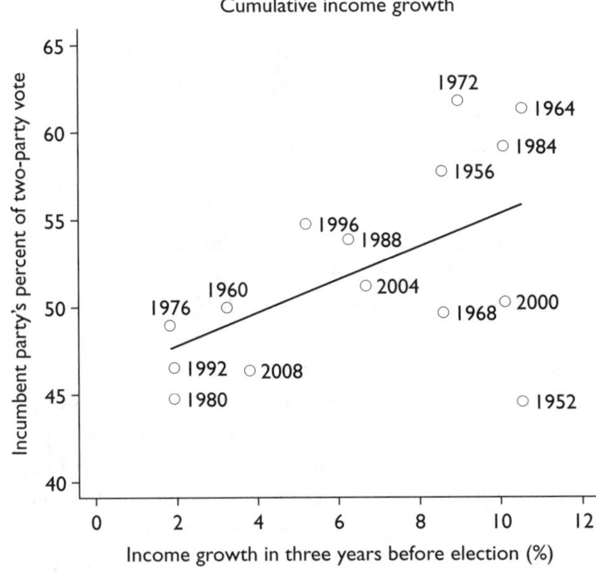

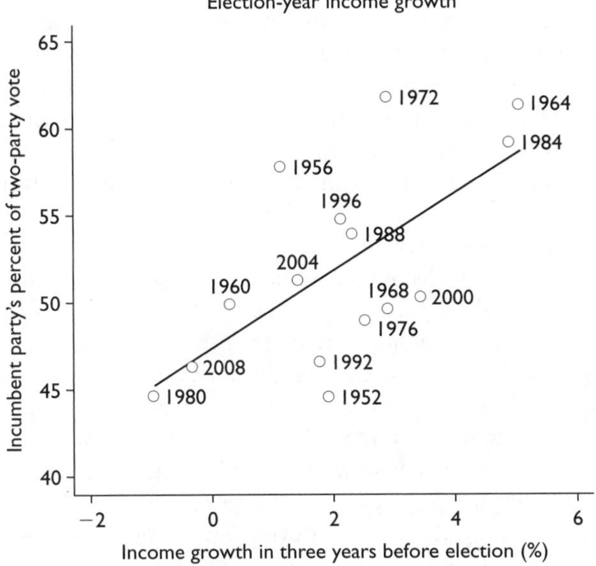

Figure 11.1 Income Growth and Presidential Election Outcomes, 1952–2008 (sources: Dave Leip's Atlas of U.S. Presidential Elections; Bureau of Economic Analysis).

his term. As economic growth increases, so does the incumbent party's share of the vote. But in the bottom graph, which relies on a measure of economic growth only in the election year, the relationship between the economy and election outcomes is stronger: the line capturing the relationship tilts upward more steeply, and the data points representing election years are more closely clustered around the line. Presidential election outcomes thus depend more on recent economic trends than on the trend across a president's term.

Presidential elections are not the only contests where the fundamentals, particularly economic performance, loom large. Similar factors affect congressional, state and local elections as well. On their face, congressional elections might seem difficult to predict because states and House districts, not to mention congressional candidates, are so diverse. And it is certainly true that the unique circumstances within districts matter. However, congressional elections also depend on national trends. Just as voters punish the president for a weak economy, they also punish representatives from the president's party. In election years when the economy is weak and the president unpopular, the president's party can expect to lose seats in Congress.[10] The 2010 election was no exception: the Democratic Party lost six Senate seats and more than 60 House seats. The economy is also an important factor in state elections, particularly gubernatorial elections, though a state's particular economic circumstances may be more important than national trends in such elections.[11]

The predictability of elections limits how much campaign strategy can accomplish. Certainly no amount of campaigning will change the state of the economy or improve prospects in war. These fundamental factors may be out of the control of any leader. Certainly they are out of the control of any challenger. Nonetheless, they strongly affect their chances of winning, and may render campaign strategy irrelevant in some cases. If an incumbent president is running amidst a weak economy, even a brilliant campaign may not be enough. Similarly, strategic wizardry may be superfluous when conditions are favorable. Consider the 2008 election, conducted amidst a recession and financial crisis. Was Obama's victory, as the *New York Times* suggested, the story of a flawless campaign? Or would a mediocre campaign have had much the same result, so difficult was it for the Republican Party to hold onto the presidency as home foreclosures were increasing and banks were failing?

In addition to the fundamental forces of the economy and war, there is another factor that can often overshadow even the best campaign: the presence of an incumbent running for reelection. There may be occasions when an incumbent is disadvantaged, such as during an economic crisis or a scandal, but in most cases incumbency is an asset. Even if things look bad for the incumbent's party, the incumbent will usually stand a better chance than a new candidate of the same party running in an open-seat race. This is because the incumbent is almost always better known than the challenger, and voters tend to favor more familiar candidates unless they are strongly supportive of the opposite party.

The size of the incumbency advantage varies with the visibility and nature of the office. In general, since higher offices attract more famous challengers, the incumbency advantage is reduced. Incumbent presidents definitely have an advantage; since World War II, seven of the ten presidents who ran for reelection won. But their advantage is not as great as that enjoyed by senators, who have enjoyed a reelection rate of 75 percent or higher since 1982. Even incumbent senators' advantage pales in comparison to that of their House counterparts, at least 86 percent of whom have been reelected in every election since 1982. In fact, in five of these elections, 98 percent of House incumbents running for reelection have been reelected. Even in the 1994, 2006, and 2010 elections, in which new House majorities were swept into office in spectacular fashion, 90 percent, 94 percent, and 86 percent of incumbents still managed to win reelection, respectively.[12] The incumbency advantage is so strong in these elections that many potential challengers choose not to run rather than risk a defeat that could set back their political careers. This is why, in the 2010 general election, 27 House incumbents ran totally unopposed. In most elections, incumbents do face a challenger, but it is rarely the most qualified or well-known challenger possible; high-quality challengers are especially likely to bide their time and wait for open-seat races that they have a good chance of winning.[13]

The nature of the office also determines the size of the incumbency effect. Research has shown that incumbent Members of Congress owe some of their advantage to constituent casework—essentially, favors that congressional staff do for constituents (e.g., helping to track down a Social Security check that was lost in the mail).[14] Members of Congress also enjoy the franking privilege, which allows them to send certain kinds of mail to their constituents without paying for postage, thereby increasing their name recognition. Furthermore, being a Member of Congress is a full-time job with a generous salary (currently $174,000), allowing members to devote themselves completely to politics. Many legislators in the American states and around the world do not enjoy a large staff, free postage, or a full-time salary, and their incumbency advantage is therefore reduced. Scholars have demonstrated that the more professionalized and "Congress-like" a state legislature becomes, the more reliably its incumbents are reelected.[15]

As we shall see, in the rare instances when incumbents are defeated, the challenger's campaign plays a crucial role. It is important to keep in mind, however, that these are in fact rare events. In many cases, the natural advantages of incumbency are too much for any campaign to overcome. This reality discourages many potential challengers or the opposing party from even trying.

When Campaigns Matter

Even though elections are often predictable, this does not mean the campaign is utterly irrelevant. For example, even if a weak economy helped Obama in 2008, he was not always ahead in the polls during the campaign. After the Republican National Convention, McCain surged to the lead for a couple weeks, making Democrats very nervous. Such changes in fortune are not uncommon in elections. There were weeks and even months where John Kerry and Michael Dukakis seemed destined to become the next president. Clearly, events that happen during the campaign can matter over and above the fundamentals, which, while powerful, do not entirely explain election outcomes. In fact, as we discuss later, campaigns may help ensure that the fundamentals end up influencing the election's outcome by making voters think more about the economy. But this does not mean that every campaign event will matter. To unpack the effects of campaigns, it is helpful to think about when exactly campaigns matter. Two factors are paramount: the number of undecided voters and the balance of resources among the competing candidates.

Campaigns will have larger effects when there are more voters who have not made up their minds. Although most voters can draw on social and partisan identities to make decisions about candidates, there will still be some who are uncertain about or unfamiliar with the candidates. Whenever these voters are more numerous, the campaign has a greater potential to affect voters' decisions.

For example, undecided voters are typically more numerous earlier rather than later in the campaign. As the campaign goes on, the information that voters acquire via news and advertisements will typically lead them to a decision. This helps explain why presidential nomination conventions, which are usually held in July or August of the election year, tend to have larger effects than the candidate debates that are usually held in late September or October.[16] At the time of the conventions, some partisans may not fully support their party's nominee and the convention's hoopla helps solidify their support and perhaps also persuades some independent voters to support that candidate.[17] In fact, the first of the two conventions tends to have a larger impact than the second, which suggests that the first convention solidifies enough opinions to reduce the pool of undecided voters.[18] By the time the debates roll around, the pool of undecided voters has shrunk even further and, as noted earlier, voters who have made a decision will rarely change their minds after the debate because they tend to believe that their preferred candidate won. The election in 2008 was no exception. Figure 11.2 presents the individual poll numbers and an average trend line for each candidate, with demarcations for various events: the announcement of the vice-presidential nominees, the conventions, the collapse of various financial institutions (Fannie Mae, Freddie Mac, Merrill Lynch,

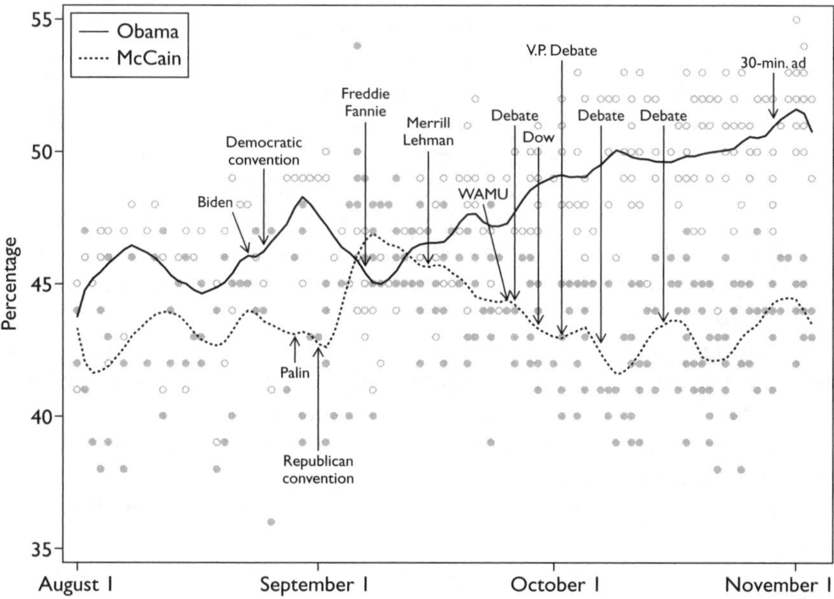

Figure 11.2 Campaign Events and Tracking Polls in the 2008 Presidential Campaign.

Lehman Brothers, and Washington Mutual), a large drop in the stock market (Dow), the candidate debates (presidential and vice-presidential), and Obama's 30-minute television advertisement late in the campaign. The effects of the two conventions, and particularly the Republican convention, are evident in late August. By contrast, there is little movement in the polls after any of the debates.

Undecided voters are also more numerous in elections other than presidential general elections. Compared to presidential primaries, congressional elections (especially open-seat races), and so on, presidential general elections tend to feature candidates who are relatively familiar and about whom voters have stronger opinions. Presidential primaries often feature a large and largely unknown pool of candidates, typically senators and governors who are familiar mostly in their home states and sometimes not even there. Moreover, voters cannot rely on party identification because all of the candidates are of the same party. This makes events during the primaries much more consequential, especially the outcomes of the earliest caucuses and primaries. In 2008, Obama's standing in the polls increased by about 20 points between the first caucus in Iowa on January 3 and the Super Tuesday primaries on February 5. This is a much larger increase than the conventions or debates have created in general elections, at least in the era of public opinion polling.

Campaign activity in congressional elections also matters. Many of these races feature a relatively well-known incumbent and a lesser-known challenger. Both incumbent and challenger campaigns can matter. Typically, the more the candidate spends, the more votes they receive. But campaign spending matters more for challengers because so few voters know them. Over time, challengers with more money to spend become better known than poorer challengers; voters are more able both to recall and to recognize their names, for example.[19] And this translates into a greater chance of winning. In congressional elections from 1972–2006, no challenger who raised less than $100,000 won. By contrast almost one-third of those who raised at least $1 million won.[20]

Campaign spending is arguably even more vital for challengers in elections for state legislature, state supreme court, and city council.[21] In these elections, which attract relatively little media coverage, voters are not likely to see, hear, or read anything about challengers unless it comes from their campaigns. Thus, campaigns can be crucial to the outcomes of such elections, even if the dollar amounts spent on them are miniscule compared to what is spent in higher-profile races.

A second factor affecting the impact of a campaign is the balance of information coming from the opposing sides. The logic here is straightforward: when the opponents have roughly the same amount of money to spend, produce similar numbers of advertisements in important media markets, and receive equivalent amounts of positive and negative news coverage, it is difficult for either one of them to gain any advantage. The net outcome of all of this campaign activity will not favor either candidate, and the polls will not move much at all. This is one reason why the polls during presidential campaigns are so static. At least until 2008, when Barack Obama chose to forego public financing and spent $730 million to McCain's $333 million, the presidential candidates were relatively evenly matched in resources.

It is when disparities between the candidates emerge that campaign activity can benefit the advantaged candidate. Several examples will illustrate. First, incumbent members of Congress are reelected at high rates in part because of resource disparities: the vast majority of incumbents out-spend their challengers. Second, disparities can emerge in news coverage during presidential campaigns. During a nominating convention, the party holding the convention receives a sudden increase in positive news coverage that is not counterbalanced by positive coverage of the other side.[22] This disparity helps explain why conventions give parties a bump in the polls. Third, even in presidential elections, disparities in television advertising can also emerge. In 2000, Bush outspent Gore in the battleground states late in the campaign, and the resulting advantage in advertising may have cost Gore four points of the vote—a large number in states where the outcome was so close (e.g., Florida).[23] In 2008, Obama did better in most areas of the country than did John Kerry in 2004. But Obama did particularly well the more he outspent McCain: in counties where Obama aired 1,000 more ads than McCain, he received about 0.5 percent more of the vote than John Kerry did in those same counties.[24] This is not a massive effect, suggesting how difficult it is to persuade voters in presidential elections, but it shows how disparities in campaign resources can matter.

How Campaigns Matter

If we want to know when and where political campaigns matter, the number of undecided voters and the balance of resources among the candidates are very helpful. The next question is *how* campaigns matter. Their effects on voters can take one of four basic forms: reinforcement, persuasion, priming, and mobilization. Each of these can contribute to the number of votes a candidate wins and thus to the election's outcome.

Reinforcement

Reinforcement occurs when campaigns solidify the preferences of voters. Some voters may have a natural tendency to vote for one party but still be uncertain how they will vote in some elections. Campaigns tend to bring these voters back into the partisan fold, leading them to a decision that is in line with their party identification.[25] Political operatives and commentators often call this activity "rallying the base," referring to the candidate's natural base of support. Reinforcement may be visible in polls, as voters move from the undecided column into a candidate's camp. It may also be relatively invisible. For example, in 2008, an uncertain voter who identified as a Democrat could have told a pollster that he supported Obama but done so out of partisan habit rather than any real affinity for Obama. If the campaign reinforced this choice, however, then the voter's answer to the pollster would not change but the sentiments underlying this answer would change a great deal—from tentative support to genuine enthusiasm. Thus, a lot of reinforcement cannot be measured with standard polls but it is certainly consequential. Candidates who cannot rally their own partisans will face especially long odds.

Persuasion

Persuasion is the most familiar campaign effect, and the one on which much popular commentary centers. It involves changing the attitudes of people, especially leading them to switch their support from one party to the other. In highly visible elections, such as presidential races, outright persuasion is not very common, thanks to the prevalence and power of the social and political identities discussed earlier. In the 2008 American National Election Study, respondents were interviewed in the month before and soon after the election. Of those who supported Obama in the pre-election poll and reported voting in the election itself, 97 percent voted for him. The same was true for McCain supporters, 94 percent of whom voted for him. But in less visible elections, for statewide or local offices, persuasion and thus defections are more common.[26]

How is it that campaigns come to persuade voters? One possibility has to do with policy issues. Voters whose views on policy are out of step with the party's platform (e.g., conservative Democrats or liberal Republicans) are more likely to defect in presidential elections, especially if they live in a battleground state that is closely contested by the candidates.[27] This suggests that persuasion depends at least in part on the information that campaigns convey about where the parties and candidates stand.

Another possibility is that persuasion depends on candidates' personalities or physical attractiveness. Some studies do show that these factors can affect voters' decisions. In one experiment, people shown the faces of competing candidates for only one second can pick the candidate who actually won the election about two-thirds of the time.[28] In another experiment, people were provided profiles of two opposing candidates. When an attractive picture of the first candidate was paired with an unattractive picture of the second, the attractive candidate did about 10 percent better than if their roles were reversed and the first candidate's picture was more unattractive.[29] Studies have also shown that candidates who are rated as physically attractive by third party observers tend to do better on Election Day.[30] Finally, campaigns can change perceptions of the candidates' attributes, for better or worse. In 2000, the news media's attention to exaggerated statements made by Al Gore led to a notable downturn in how honest voters perceived him to be.[31]

At the same time, other evidence suggests that personality and attractiveness may not matter all that much. For one, people's perceptions of personality—which candidate is more honest, a stronger leader, etc.—are strongly shaped by their party identification. It may be that voters' perceptions of the candidates essentially come *after* they have decided to support one of those candidates. Second, the apparent effect of attractiveness may be due to other factors entirely. Parties tend to run better-looking candidates in races they have a good chance of winning and uglier candidates in races they are unlikely to win—so the fact that better-looking candidates do better at the polls may have nothing to do with their looks.[32] And there is this irony: candidate appearance would be likely to matter most in less visible races with unfamiliar candidates, but these are precisely the races in which people are less likely to know what the candidates look like.

All in all, while persuasion of voters is certainly possible under the right circumstances, it is a difficult goal for campaigns to achieve. Furthermore, attempts at persuading voters of the opposite party to defect may be costly. If a Democratic candidate broadcasts some of her more conservative positions in an attempt to persuade Republican voters, she may undermine attempts to reinforce support among her natural Democratic base. For these reasons, in many elections, persuasion is the least prominent of the campaign effects.

Priming

Campaigns are not only about whom voters choose but *why* they choose them. Through the process of priming, campaigns can affect the criteria that voters use in making decisions. Candidates strive to make the election "about" the issues that favor them. They provide voters with information about those issues and ultimately help voters to link their own attitudes about those issues to their decisions at the ballot box.[33] The possibility of priming suggests how campaigns can matter even if elections are strongly affected by fundamental factors like the economy. The economy may not automatically be the most important criterion in voters' minds. The candidate who is advantaged by the state of the economy—the incumbent when the economy is strong, or the challenger when the economy is weak—will want to remind people about the economy and make it a more influential criterion. By contrast, the candidate disadvantaged by the economy will want to change the subject.

The importance of priming can be illustrated with the 2000 election. The essential puzzle in this election is why Gore did not win more of the popular vote, given how well the economy was doing at the time. In the bottom panel of Figure 11.1, the data point for the 2000 election is below the diagonal line, suggesting that Gore did not do as well as the state of the economy, which was growing robustly, would have predicted. One answer to the puzzle is that Gore simply failed to remind voters of the strong economy. He was, it seems, afraid to associate himself with the Clinton administration's record for fear that, as Clinton's vice president, he would be punished for Clinton's scandals. Thus, voters did not reward him for being part of an administration that presided over an economic expansion. Gore's strategy also contrasts sharply with Obama's in 2008, which entailed continual emphasis of the weak economy. A systematic study of presidential elections since 1952 shows the importance of priming: when candidates who benefit from the fundamentals emphasize them in their campaigns, they are more likely to win than candidates who, like Gore, focus on some other issue.[34]

Mobilization

A final way that campaigns matter involves mobilizing voters. This means helping them to register and get to the polls to vote. After all, it does not do a campaign much good if they persuade voters to support a candidate but those voters stay home on Election Day. Campaigns are increasingly interested in mobilization—sometimes referred to as get-out-the-vote (GOTV) or "the ground game," in contrast to the "air war" of campaign advertising. By using extensive databases of information about voters, candidates can better "micro-target" those voters who are likely to support them.

How do we know that campaigns actually mobilize? A first piece of evidence: higher levels of campaign spending in gubernatorial and U.S. Senate races are associated with higher turnout, particularly in years with no presidential election on the ballot.[35] Second, careful experimental studies have randomly assigned households to receive non-partisan GOTV reminders during elections. These studies show that GOTV does stimulate turnout, although personal forms of contact, particularly in-person conversations, are more effective than impersonal forms such as mail or phone calls.[36] Other studies have found that campaign activity mobilizes partisans in particular: when Democrats outspend Republicans, for example, the proportion of Democrats among voters goes up.[37] In 2008, Obama's extensive GOTV operation appears to have mattered: in several states, Obama did better, relative to Kerry in 2004, in counties in which he had opened field offices.[38]

These campaign effects—reinforcement, persuasion, mobilization, or priming—may all affect individual voters. Arguably even more important, however, is whether or not campaigns actually affect the outcomes. In other words, do the individual voters affected by the campaign "add up" to a number that actually makes one candidate win and the other lose? In some cases, campaign activity produces effects large enough to decide the election. A presidential campaign that successfully responds to the fundamentals does six points better overall.[39] The votes attributed to Obama field offices were sufficient to win him several states.[40] But ultimately it is harder for campaigns to change an outcome than simply to affect some individual voters. After comparing early poll numbers to the actual outcome, political scientist James Campbell finds that only five of 14 presidential campaigns from 1948–2000 appear to have changed the outcome.[41]

Conclusion

The news cycle demands a constant stream of fresh stories, interpretations, and analysis, and so naturally, during election season, journalists and commentators feature the twist and turns of the campaign itself. The results may make for more interesting news but they also tend to exaggerate what campaigns can really accomplish. Moreover, commentators often focus on aspects of the campaign that are particularly trivial and unlikely to affect anything, such as minor misstatements by the candidates. Instead, it is more accurate to say that campaigns can affect individual voters only when certain conditions are met—a large number of undecided voters, resource disparities among candidates—and even then may not sway enough voters in a particular direction to affect the overall outcome. None of this means that campaigns are inconsequential, particularly in close races. Moreover, even their occasional impact may have big policy consequences, given the differences between what a Democratic and Republican president, governor, or congressional majority will typically do while in office. But it does mean that the furious efforts of candidates often accomplish less than they would like, and certainly less than pundits perceive.

In reality, many crucial determinants of electoral outcomes lie outside of the control of candidates and campaigns. The best campaign advertising will not revive a flagging economy. The most dominant debate performance will probably fail to impress most viewers of the opposite party. The most charismatic challenger will probably have little hope of victory if the office he or she covets is currently occupied by a strong incumbent. While these realities may make following elections a less entertaining endeavor for journalists and other observers, they do point the way toward a richer understanding of what those elections are really about. Furthermore, they provide some reassurance for those concerned about the future of American democracy in the age of media overload. While money and tactics can play a role under the right circumstances, American voters are far more than passive recipients of campaign advertising or media strategies.

Notes

1. Donald Green, Bradley Palmquist, and Eric Schickler, *Partisan Hearts and Minds* (New Haven, CT: Yale University Press, 2002).
2. David Brooks, "What Independents Want," *New York Times*, November 5, 2009, retrieved from http://www.nytimes.com/2009/11/06/opinion/06brooks.html; Fareed Zakaria, "Obama Should Act More Like a President Than a Prime Minister," *Washington Post*, January 25, 2010, retrieved from http://www.washingtonpost.com/wp-dyn/content/article/2010/01/24/AR2010012402300.html?hpid=opinionsbox1; Matt Bai, "The Great Unalignment," *New York Times*, January 20, 2010, retrieved from http://www.nytimes.com/2010/01/24/magazine/24fob-wwln-t.html?ref=magazine.
3. Bruce E. Keith, David B. Magleby, Candice J. Nelson, Elizabeth Orr, Mark C. Westlye, and Raymond E. Wolfinger, *The Myth of the Independent Voter* (Berkeley, CA: University of California Press, 1992); John Sides, "Three Myths About Political Independents," *The Monkey Cage*, December 19, 2009, retrieved from http://www.themonkeycage.org/2009/12/three_myths_about_political_in.html.
4. Paul F. Lazarsfeld, Bernard Berelson, and Hazel Gaudet, *The People's Choice: How the Voter Makes Up His Mind in a Presidential Campaign* (New York: Columbia University Press, 1948); Steven E. Finkel, "Reexamining the 'Minimal Effects' Model in Recent Presidential Campaigns," *Journal of Politics* 55, no. 1 (1993): 1–31.
5. "Forecasting Recap," *PS: Political Science and Politics* 42, no. 1 (January 2009).
6. Douglas Hibbs, "Bread and Peace Voting in U.S. Presidential Elections," *Public Choice* 104, no. 1–2 (2000): 149–180; John Zaller, "Monica Lewinsky's Contribution to Political Science," *PS: Political Science and Politics* 31, no. 2 (1998): 182–189.
7. Andrew J. Healy, Neil Malhotra, and Cecilia Hyunjung Mo, "Irrelevant Events Affect Voters' Evaluations of Government Performance," *Proceedings of the National Academy of Sciences* 107, no. 29 (2010): 12,804–12,809.
8. Marc Hetherington, "The Media's Effect on Voters' National Retrospective Economic Evaluations in 1992," *American Journal of Political Science* 40, no. 2 (1996): 372–395.
9. Larry M. Bartels, *Unequal Democracy: The Political Economy of the New Gilded Age* (Princeton, NJ: Princeton University Press, 2008).
10. Gary Jacobson, *The Politics of Congressional Elections* (New York: Pearson Longman, 2009), 7th edition.

11. Lonna Rae Atkeson and Randall W. Partin, "Economic and Referendum Voting: A Comparison of Gubernatorial and Senatorial Elections," *American Political Science Review* 89, no. 1 (March 1995): 99–107; Deborah A. Orth, "Accountability in a Federal System: The Governor, the President and Economic Expectations," *State Politics and Policy Quarterly* 1, no. 4 (Winter 2001): 412–432.
12. "Reelection Rates Over the Years," Center for Responsive Politics, retrieved from http://www.opensecrets.org/bigpicture/reelect.php: 2010 figures from the authors' calculations.
13. Gary W. Cox and Jonathan N. Katz, "Why Did the Incumbency Advantage in U.S. House Elections Grow?" *American Journal of Political Science* 40, no. 2 (May 1996): 478–497.
14. Bruce E. Cain, John A. Ferejohn, and Morris P. Fiorina, "The Constituency Service Basis of the Personal Vote for U.S. Representatives and British Members of Parliament," *American Political Science Review* 78, no. 1 (March 1984): 110–125.
15. William D. Berry, Michael B. Berkman, and Stuart Schneiderman, "Legislative Professionalism and Incumbent Reelection: The Development of Institutional Boundaries," *American Political Science Review* 94, no. 4 (December 2000): 859–874; John M. Carey, Richard G. Niemi, and Lynda W. Powell, "Incumbency and the Probability of Reelection in State Legislative Elections," *Journal of Politics* 62, no. 3 (August 2000): 671–700.
16. James Stimson, *Tides of Consent: How Public Opinion Shapes American Politics* (New York: Cambridge University Press, 2004); Daron Shaw, "A Study of Presidential Campaign Event Effects from 1952 to 1992," *Journal of Politics* 61, no. 2 (1999): 387–422.
17. D. Sunshine Hillygus and Simon Jackman, "Voter Decision Making in Election 2000: Campaign Effects, Partisan Activation, and the Clinton Legacy," *American Journal of Political Science* 47, no. 4 (2003): 583–596.
18. Thomas M. Holbrook, *Do Campaigns Matter?* (Thousand Oaks, CA: Sage Publications, 1996).
19. Gary C. Jacobson, "Measuring Campaign Spending Effects in U.S. House Elections," in *Capturing Campaign Effects*, eds. Henry E. Brady and Richard Johnston (Ann Arbor: University of Michigan Press, 2006), 199–220; Laurel Elms and Paul M. Sniderman, "Informational Rhythms of Incumbent Dominated Congressional Elections," in *Capturing Campaign Effects*, eds. Henry E. Brady and Richard Johnston (Ann Arbor: University of Michigan Press, 2006), 221–241.
20. Jacobson, *The Politics of Congressional Elections*, 46. Dollar amounts are in $2006 and thus adjusted for inflation.
21. Anthony Gierzynski and David Breaux, "Legislative Elections and the Importance of Money," *Legislative Studies Quarterly* 21, no. 3 (August 1996): 337–357; Chris W. Bonneau, "The Effects of Campaign Spending in State Supreme Court Elections," *Political Research Quarterly* 60, no. 3 (2007): 489–499; Timothy B. Krebs, "The Determinants of Candidates' Vote Share and the Advantages of Incumbency in City Council Elections," *American Journal of Political Science* 42, no. 3 (July 1998): 921–935.
22. Holbrook, *Do Campaigns Matter?*; Richard Johnston, Michael G. Hagen, and Kathleen Hall Jamieson, *The 2000 Presidential Election and the Foundations of Party Politics* (New York: Cambridge University Press, 2004), 90.
23. Johnston et al., *The 2000 Presidential Election*, 85.
24. Michael M. Franz and Travis N. Ridout, "Political Advertising and Persuasion in the 2004 and 2008 Presidential Elections," *American Politics Research* 38, no. 2 (2010): 303–329.
25. Lazarsfeld et al., *The People's Choice*.
26. John Zaller, *The Nature and Origins of Mass Opinion* (New York: Cambridge University Press, 1992), Chapter 10.

27. D. Sunshine Hillygus and Todd G. Shields, *The Persuadable Voter* (Princeton, NJ: Princeton University Press, 2008).
28. Alexander Todorov, Anesu M. Mandisodza, Amir Goren, and Crystal C. Hall, "Inference of Competence from Faces Predict Election Outcomes," *Science* 308, no. 5728 (2005): 1623–1626.
29. Shawn W. Rosenberg and Patrick Cafferty, "The Image and the Vote: Manipulating Voters' Preferences," *Public Opinion Quarterly* 51, no. 1 (1987): 31–47.
30. Chappell Lawson, Gabriel S. Lenz, Andy Baker, and Michael Myers, "Looking Like a Winner: Candidate Appearance and Electoral Success in New Democracies," *World Politics* 62, no. 4 (2010): 561–593.
31. Johnston et al., *The 2000 Presidential Election.*
32. Matthew D. Atkinson, Ryan D. Enos, and Seth J. Hill, "Candidate Faces and Election Outcomes: Is the Face-Vote Correlation Caused by Candidate Selection?" *Quarterly Journal of Political Science* 4, no. 3 (2009): 229–249.
33. Andrew Gelman and Gary King, "Why Are Presidential Election Campaign Polls so Variable When Votes Are so Predictable?" *British Journal of Political Science* 23, no. 4 (1993): 409–451.
34. Lynn Vavreck, *The Message Matters: The Economy and Presidential Campaigns* (Princeton, NJ: Princeton University Press, 2009).
35. Robert A. Jackson, "Gubernatorial and Senatorial Campaign Mobilization of Voters," *Political Research Quarterly* 55, no. 4 (December 2002): 825–844.
36. Alan S. Gerber and Donald P. Green, "The Effects of Canvassing, Telephone Calls, and Direct Mail on Voter Turnout: A Field Experiment," *American Political Science Review* 94, no. 3 (2000): 653–663.
37. Thomas M. Holbrook and Scott D. McClurg, "The Mobilization of Core Supporters: Campaigns, Turnout, and Electoral Composition in United States Presidential Elections," *American Journal of Political Science* 49, no. 4 (2005): 689–703; Eric McGhee and John Sides, "What Drives Partisan Turnout?" *Political Behavior*, forthcoming.
38. Seth E. Masket, "Did Obama's Ground Game Matter? The Influence of Local Field Offices during the 2008 Presidential Election," *Public Opinion Quarterly* 73, no. 5 (2009): 1,023–1,039.
39. Vavreck, *The Message Matters.*
40. Masket, "Did Obama's Ground Game Matter?"
41. James E. Campbell, "When Have Presidential Campaigns Decided Election Outcomes?" *American Politics Research* 29, no. 5 (2001): 437–460.

Chapter 12

Media, Public Opinion, and Presidential Leadership

Matthew Baum

On September 9, 2009, over 32 million Americans watched President Barack Obama deliver a primetime television address on health care reform to a joint session of Congress.[1] Twelve days later, Obama appeared on the *Late Show With David Letterman.* For Obama, the first sitting U.S. president to appear on a late-night entertainment-oriented talk show, this was the second such appearance. It capped an intensive personal media push by the president to promote healthcare reform, including interviews on five Sunday news shows the previous day (on ABC, NBC, CBS, CNN, and Univision). That same month, Obama's Internet team sent weekly—and sometimes twice weekly—emails on health care to the roughly 13 million individuals in its famed email database.

Obama's media blitz was notable for the sheer number of public appeals, the diversity of outlets to which he carried his message, and the quite distinct tenor of the messages delivered across the differing outlets. In his nationally televised address, the president was, to paraphrase his predecessor, "a unifier, not a divider," offering a solemn appeal for national unity:

> In 1965, when some argued that Medicare represented a government takeover of health care, members of Congress—Democrats and Republicans—did not back down. They joined together so that all of us could enter our golden years with some basic peace of mind ... I still believe we can replace acrimony with civility.

In contrast, Obama's email appeals invited recipients to make donations, join discussion groups, participate in rallies, watch a video clip, visit his "Organizing for America" website, submit home-made videos, or call Congress to support the healthcare reform effort. They also issued partisan alerts, like: "Those who profit from the status quo—and those who put partisan advantage above all else—will fight us every inch of the way. ... The stakes are too high to let scare tactics cloud the debate."[2]

On *Letterman* Obama lightened his tone, for instance quipping in response to a question about racism in the anti-healthcare reform movement, "I think it is important to realize that I was actually black before the election." No mention of political parties or partisanship crossed the president's lips, except when he asserted that "it doesn't matter" if you are a Democrat or a Republican.

The liberal blogosphere dutifully replayed video highlights from all of Obama's appearances, thereby magnifying his message and delivering it directly to his base. For instance, on September 21, Huffingtonpost.com—at the time the most widely read political blog site on the Internet—featured "Highlights from Obama's Sunday Show Blitz," inviting readers to "vote for the best clip." The next day the site featured video clips from Obama's *Letterman* appearance.

Taken together, this arguably represents an unprecedented presidential media blitz aimed at a single policy initiative. It raises the question of why President Obama pursued such a strategy, and why he spoke in such starkly differing manners across different media outlets. The answer is that a combination of fragmenting media and audiences, along with journalistic norms favoring critical coverage of the president, especially during unified government, forced Obama to adopt a multi-tiered communication strategy. Through this strategy, he sought to reach (and persuade) an overall audience comparable in numbers and partisan diversity to those his predecessors from the 1960s to the 1980s largely took for granted virtually any time they appeared on national TV. The changing media landscape means the president must work harder to communicate with the public, and be far more precise in tailoring his messages to particular sub-constituencies who might otherwise dismiss his message, or tune him out entirely.

In doing so, presidents have two primary leadership strategy alternatives, which Tim Groeling and I refer to as *Preaching to the Choir* and *Converting the Flock*.[3] The former consists of reaching out to their political base in order to excite core supporters so they will show up in large numbers on election day, as well as enthusiastically support their major policy initiatives. The latter entails reaching out beyond the base, in order to recruit additional supporters and thereby expand their support coalition. Neither strategy is new; presidents have long pursued both, varying their emphasis depending on which groups support or oppose a given policy. However, the ground underneath which presidents have stood while pursuing these strategies has shifted dramatically, thereby altering their relative costs, benefits, and efficacies.

The first decade of the twenty-first century has been characterized by a perhaps unique historical circumstance in which three distinct types of media—each appealing to quite different audience types—coexist, cover news and politics, and compete for the attention of the American public. These are the traditional news media (dominated by the major broadcast networks and national newspapers), the "new media," most notably cable TV news and the Internet, and the soft news media, consisting of daytime and late-night talk shows, as well as entertainment-oriented and tabloid news magazine outlets.[4]

The audiences for these three media differ in important ways, with profound implications for their place in modern presidential communication strategies. I discuss each in turn, including their effects on public opinion. I then offer concluding observations regarding the future of political communication and its implications for presidential leadership.

Traditional News Media

For nearly four decades, the traditional news media—particularly network television—were the primary vehicle through which presidents communicated with the American people, and in so doing sought primarily to convert the flock. Network television was the informational commons, where a broad cross-section of Americans gathered to learn about the events of the day. When the president appeared on television, 50–60 million households routinely tuned in to hear what he had to say. No longer. Today barely more than half as many American households typically watch prime time presidential television appearances. The combined Nielson ratings for the evening newscasts of the "big three" broadcast networks (ABC, CBS, and NBC) have fallen from about 58 in 1969 to a little over 16 in 2008.[5] According to a 2008 Pew Center survey, the percent of Americans indicating that they regularly watch cable news now exceeds the percentage regularly watching network news (by 39 to 29 percent).

What little remains of the informational commons has itself become contested partisan territory, as the president's supporters are more and his opponents less likely to stay tuned when the president appears on TV. Figure 12.1 presents the trend, from 2002 to 2008, in partisan viewing of network

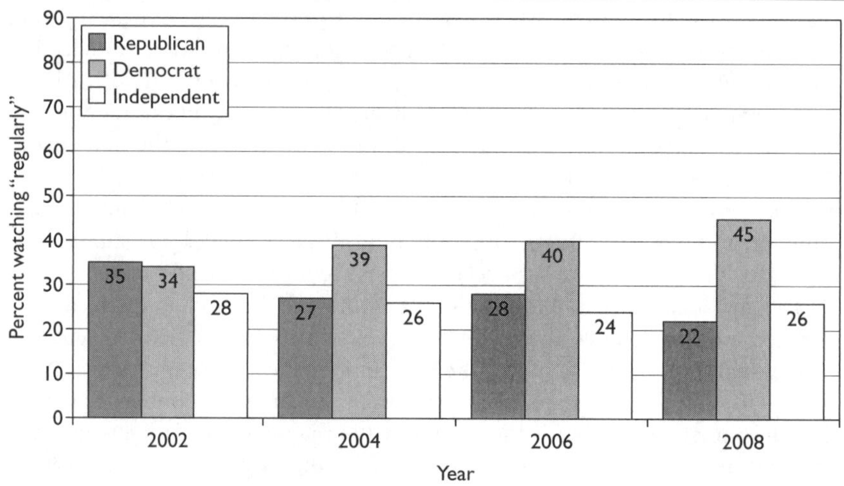

Figure 12.1 Partisan Trend in "Regular" Viewing of Network TV News.

news, based on self-reports in Pew Center surveys. According to these data, as recently as 2002 Republicans were seven percentage points more likely than Democrats to be regular viewers of network news (35 percent vs. 28 percent). By 2008 the regular network audience was composed of more Democrats than Republicans by over a two-to-one ratio (45 percent vs. 22 percent "regular" viewers). These figures suggest that nationally televised presidential addresses are increasingly unlikely to reach the same cross-section of Americans as they did in earlier decades.

According to data reported by Kernell and Rice,[6] the partisan skew in audiences for presidential television addresses has also increased substantially over time. Across the 18 prime time presidential addresses they investigated between 1971 and 1995, the gap in audience between members of the president's party and opposition partisans averaged 2.6 percent. Between 1996 and 2007, the average partisan gap across the 14 appearances for which data were available increased more than fourfold, to 11.8 percent. In short, over time what is left of the audience for presidential addresses has increasingly come to be dominated by the president's fellow partisans.

Moreover, the news values of the traditional news media have made it a particularly difficult environment for presidential communications. This problem has proven especially challenging for the Bush II and Obama administrations, the bulk of which have taken place during unified government. Elsewhere,[7] Tim Groeling and I document the tremendous network news bias toward negative, hostile coverage of presidents and their policies. We focused on a hard case for locating such a pattern: foreign policy. To the extent politics do "stop at the water's edge," then we should have been *least* likely to find a predominance of partisan attacks on the president in foreign policy. We examined news coverage of 42 U.S. foreign policy crises between 1979 and 2003 and found that nearly 80 percent of all rhetoric from Members of Congress (MCs) appearing on network evening newscasts within 61-day periods surrounding the events was critical of the president and his policies. While this skew was somewhat larger for domestic than foreign policy during these time periods, it clearly emerged for both domestic and foreign policy issues. It was particularly severe during unified government, when criticism of the president by his fellow partisan MCs was both *novel*—since the members of the president's party usually support him—and authoritative—given the party's leadership role in Congress. The ratio was far more favorable to the president on network Sunday morning talk shows, where MCs could speak in a largely unfiltered format. This suggests a strong network negativity bias on the heavily edited network news.

The predominant *style* of news coverage of the president has also shifted, with the president's own words increasingly supplanted by the interpretations of journalists. The average presidential soundbite on the evening news—that is, a president speaking in his own words—declined from about 40 seconds in 1968[8] to 7.8 seconds in 2004. This means that journalists' relatively negative coverage of the president increasingly dominates news broadcasts.

Where network television once afforded presidents an ideal opportunity to communicate with a broad cross-section of the public, today whenever a president takes to the airwaves he must compete with myriad alternative media for the public's attention. Indeed, broadcast networks have grown increasingly hesitant to surrender their airwaves for presidential communication. According to one report,[9] network executives lost roughly $30 million in advertising revenue in the first half of 2009 due to preemptions for Obama news conferences. This concern, in turn, prompted one of the "big four" networks (Fox) to decline the president's request for airtime on April 29, 2009.[10] Fox's decision prompted one network executive to comment:

> We will continue to make our decisions on White House requests on a case-by-case basis, but the Fox decision [to not broadcast Obama's April 29, 2009 press conference] gives us cover to reject a request if we feel that there is no urgent breaking news that is going to be discussed.[11]

This combination of audiences smaller in size and narrower in breadth, along with generally skeptical treatment by reporters of nearly any presidential statement or policy proposal, means that traditional news outlets have lost much of their utility to presidents as vehicles for converting the flock.

New Media

The so-called new media, by which I refer primarily to cable news channels and the Internet, differ in important ways from their traditional media cousins. Most notably, nearly all such outlets self-consciously seek to appeal to relatively narrow niches of the public. Rather than seeking to be all things to all people—as the major networks did during their heyday—new media outlets try to provide content that more closely fits the preferences of particular subgroups of the public. In news and politics, the primary dimension upon which new media outlets have differentiated themselves is ideology. For instance, in 2010 there are prominent cable news channels aimed primarily at liberals (MSNBC), conservatives (Fox), and moderates (CNN). On the Internet, the political blogosphere is dominated by ideologically narrow websites like Huffingtonpost.com and Dailykos.com on the left and Instapundit.com and Michellemalkin.com on the right.

Indeed, in news content analysis, Tim Groeling and I found substantial, and sometimes dramatic, differences in the ideological skew of news from left- and right-leaning Internet blogs, as well as on cable news outlets.[12] For instance, our data indicate that between 2004 and 2007 *Fox News* offered significantly less critical coverage of Iraq than CNN or the broadcast networks.

Consumers, in turn, are not passive recipients of whatever messages a given media outlet presents. Rather, they evaluate the credibility, and hence persuasiveness, of media messages in part by assessing the credibility of the messenger (the speaker) and the media outlet, as well as the costliness of the message. In a series of experiments,[13] Groeling and I found that typical individuals exposed to the identical praise or criticism of the president's handling of national security issues by MCs differed systematically in their assessments of the information's reliability, depending on the party of the speaker, the speaker's perceived incentives vis-à-vis the message (that is, whether praise or criticism of the president was, for that messenger, self-serving or costly), and the perceived ideological orientation of the media outlet. While media outlet reputations are perhaps most stark in the new media, increasing numbers of consumers—primarily, albeit not exclusively, Republicans—also view the *traditional* news media as ideologically biased (in a liberal direction), thereby allowing them to more easily discount information inconsistent with their prior beliefs.

As the range of options available to consumers seeking political information has expanded, making available media environments that closely match their personal political preferences, audiences have increasingly self-selected into ideologically friendly political news environments. For instance, Figure 12.2 summarizes data from Scarborough research showing that in 2000 the differential between Republican and Democratic viewers of CNN, Fox, and MSNBC were four, eight, and two percentage points, respectively.[14] By 2009, these gaps had expanded to 30, 20, and 27 points, respectively, with Democrats all but abandoning Fox in favor of CNN and MSNBC and Republicans moving in the opposite direction.

While, as with cable news, some Internet consumers seek out news from across the ideological spectrum—and some evidence[15] suggests they do so to a

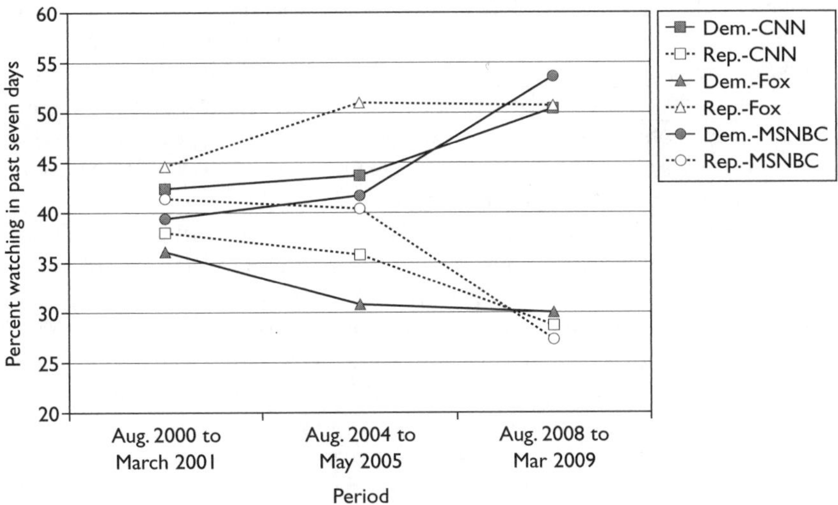

Figure 12.2 Trend in Partisan Viewing of CNN, Fox, and MSNBC.

greater extent on the Internet than on cable—the Internet is nonetheless a particularly amenable environment for ideological self-selection. For instance, according to an April 2007 Nielsen report,[16] 77 percent of readers of the left-leaning HuffingtonPost.com blogsite were registered Democrats, compared to only 3.8 percent registered Republicans.

Credibility assessments, in turn, allow consumers to discount any dissonant information to which they might continue to be exposed. This makes the new media particularly ill-suited for converting the flock, yet ideally suited for preaching to the choir. By providing "red meat to the base," presidents can rally supporters to organize in their communities to support policy proposals, as well as to turn out at elections. More effective local organizing of core supporters can indirectly enhance presidents' capacities to convert the flock, by transforming their core supporters into messengers charged with reaching out beyond the base. Indeed, much of the aforementioned Obama email campaign was aimed at inspiring core supporters to become active advocates of his healthcare reform policy in their communities.

Soft News Media

Regular consumers of political blogs and cable news outlets continue to constitute a fairly small minority of the American public. Many millions of other Americans who eschew most traditional news outlets, at least most of the time, and who rarely if ever read political blogs or watch cable news channels, are nonetheless exposed to at least *some* political news via the so-called soft news media, including daytime and late-night talk shows, as well as entertainment-oriented news outlets and tabloids.

Sam Popkin describes politicians as "crowd-seeking missiles." It is thus unsurprising that they seek to exploit the opportunity afforded them by the soft news media to reach out beyond their bases. They do so with good reason. Soft news outlets attract large crowds; nearly 7.2 million Americans watched the president exchange one-liners with Letterman. This represents more than double the 3.1 million who tuned in to Obama's interview the day before on ABC's *This Week with George Stephanopoulos*.[17]

Letterman's audience also differs substantially from those of most traditional news outlets. For instance, compared to the typical audience for traditional news shows such as *This Week with George Stephanopoulos*, *Letterman*'s audience is *less* politically engaged, *less* ideologically extreme and *less* partisan.[18] Consequently, a presidential appeal is *more* likely to persuade *Letterman*'s viewers than the relatively more partisan and ideologically extreme audiences of typical traditional news venues.[19] This persuasion gap is even larger for (mostly partisan) political Internet blog readers relative to traditional news venues.[20]

Soft news interviews tend to present candidates in a more favorable light than traditional political interview shows. For example, commenting on 2008 Democratic presidential candidate John Edwards' appearances on Leno, one reporter observes, "John and Elizabeth Edwards got substantially gentler treatment from Leno on 'The Tonight Show' than they did from Katie Couric on '60 Minutes.'"[21] In short, appearances on daytime and late-night entertainment talk shows, or other soft news programs, afford politicians one of their best opportunities to reach a large group of potentially persuadable voters in a relatively sympathetic venue. A mounting body of research, in turn, indicates that exposure to soft news influences voters' political attentiveness,[22] knowledge,[23] attitudes,[24] and even their voting behavior.[25] In reviewing the literature on soft news, Baum and Jamison[26] refer to these as the four Oprah effects. The soft news media thus arguably represent one of the *last*, and perhaps the *best* opportunity for political leaders to convert the flock. Recognizing this, it is unsurprising to find more and more political candidates and elected officials reaching out to soft news venues.

That said, not all soft news is alike. Existing alongside the lighter fare offered by Letterman, Leno, Regis, and *The View*, among other daytime and late-night talk shows, is a parallel niche of political satire-oriented talk shows, like *The Daily Show with Jon Stewart*, that cater to more politically sophisticated and ideological viewers, and whose audiences tripled in size from 2001–2005.[27] These shows assume a substantial amount of political knowledge on the part of audience members in order to "get the joke." Consequently, they are far more amenable to preaching to the choir than converting the flock.

Back to the Future?

Though in some ways unique, the current period is by no means the first time in American politics that partisan media have strongly influenced public debate. Rather, viewed in a broader context, overwhelmingly nonpartisan journalism, as we saw in roughly the first four decades following World War II, appears to have been an historical anomaly.

To better understand the implications of our increasingly polarized information environment, it is helpful to consider the partisan press of the nineteenth and early twentieth centuries. In that era, citizens who wanted an accurate picture of the political landscape could read multiple newspapers with differing partisan loyalties in order to triangulate on the "truth."[28] Such a strategy could offset to some extent the potentially harmful effects of partisan-oriented media. Yet this begs the question of whether typical citizens in the contemporary period, faced with far more varied alternatives, are likely to embrace a triangulation approach to news consumption. The present differs from the past in numerous important respects, not least of which is the explosion in the twenty-first century of entertainment mass media and other competitors for scarce public attention.

While it may be the case that politically attentive Americans in the twenty-first century are proportionately similar in number to their counterparts in prior news eras, a far larger portion of the contemporary population enjoys and exercises the franchise than was the case in the nineteenth century. Moreover, the ability of party organizations to reliably direct the voting of their members has declined with the death of party machines and the waning influence of state party bosses. Consequently, the *breadth* of consensus necessary to forge a bipartisan accord is far greater in the twenty-first century, and modern communication and polling technology allows nervous politicians to sense precisely when that consensus is eroding. Of course, gaining consent first requires capturing public attention, and even politically attentive citizens are unlikely to be able to attend to all of the competing messages in the modern media milieu.

Not only is it possible to consume nearly limitless political news from virtually any ideological perspective, it is also possible to consume equally limitless entertainment media, while rarely if ever encountering politics.[29] This raises the opportunity costs for typical consumers of seeking out alternative political perspectives. Survey evidence suggests that substantial portions of the public also appear to lack the motive to do so. Not surprisingly, as shown in Figure 12.3, these same data indicate that as the strength of an individual's political ideology increases, so too does that individual's preference for news that reinforces her pre-existing beliefs.[30]

If the era of three medias, and particularly its more polarizing elements, is characterized more by *reinforcement seeking* than by triangulation, forging and sustaining bipartisan consensus will likely prove a daunting and perhaps all but insurmountable task for future leaders. Evidence of this dilemma is

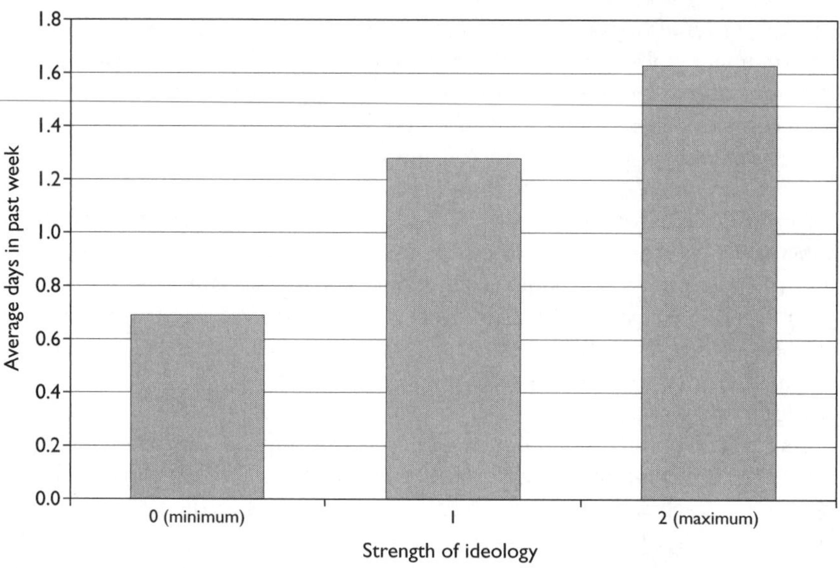

Figure 12.3 Average Days in Past Week Accessed Political Blogs on Internet, as Strength of Ideology Varies.

abundant in public reactions to the 2003 U.S. invasion and subsequent occupation of Iraq, a conflict that produced the greatest partisan divide ever recorded in scientific polling, both in terms of support for a U.S. military conflict and in terms of overall presidential approval.[31] Scholars continue to debate the media's role in sharpening, if not altogether producing, the partisan gulf in evaluations of the president and the Iraq War.[32] Jacobson, for instance, speculates that a combination of differences in content and partisan self-selection into friendly news environments—such as Fox for Republicans and conservatives, PBS, MSNBC, and CNN for Democrats and liberals, and network news for independents and moderates—may have contributed to partisan differences in perceptions of the war and the president leading it.[33]

As the prior discussion attests, self-selection, a concept dating back to Campbell and colleagues' theory of minimalism,[34] may well be sharpening partisan polarization, and this phenomenon seems likely to expand in the future. However, there exists a second, perhaps complementary, culprit: ideologically driven credibility assessments. In other words, contemporary citizens possess, arguably to a greater extent than their predecessors, the means to engage in a multi-pronged strategy for dissonance avoidance (that is, for avoiding information inconsistent with their pre-existing beliefs). Selective exposure, or avoiding dissonant information altogether, presumably represents the first such prong. However, even when this first defense mechanism fails and individuals are exposed to ideologically hostile news, they increasingly possess the means—by assigning ideological reputations to individual sources and media outlets—to systematically discount it. In other words, consumers appear also to selectively accept or reject information to which they are exposed based on its perceived credibility.[35] Credibility assessments in turn depend on the perceived ideological leaning of the outlet presenting the information, as well as on the content of the information itself (e.g., its perceived costliness for the outlet and the speaker). The combined influence of selective exposure and acceptance appears, at least in the cases of Iraq and overall assessments of President Bush's job performance, to have contributed substantially to the historically unprecedented levels of partisan polarization in America during President Bush's second term.

Conclusion

The picture I have painted of the contemporary media landscape is in some respects overly stark. For one thing, there is certainly overlap between the three medias, both in terms of content and audience. Viewers of traditional news media, especially network news, are more left-leaning than in the past, while as noted, the fastest growing segment of the soft news media—satiric political news shows like *The Daily Show*—caters primarily to politically sophisticated ideologues. Some Democrats consume conservative media, while some Republicans consume liberal media. All three medias, in turn, continue to afford presidents at least *some* capacity to both preach to the choir and convert the flock. Political messages frequently cross the boundaries of the three medias, as exemplified by the Obama media blitz described at the outset of this chapter. Hence, the media commons, and the common civic space for public affairs dialogue it created, has not entirely disappeared, nor has the capacity of presidents to use the media as a tool for building broader support constituencies via converting the flock.

That said, current trends toward ever more consumer self-selection and increasingly sophisticated information filtering and media targeting of consumer preferences all appear to portend a trend toward greater audience fragmentation and hence continued shrinking of the media commons. It seems inevitable that news providers will increasingly apply the same filtering technologies that allow media content distributors like Netflix and iTunes to determine the types of movies or music a customer is likely to prefer, and suggest to them precisely that, to news and public affairs content. The end result may be what Cass Sunstein terms "cyberbalkanization," where the media commons is largely supplanted by a "daily me" in which consumers encounter only the news and information they want, most of which tends to confirm rather than challenge their pre-existing attitudes.[36] Whether or not the media commons disappears entirely, there is little question that technological innovations and shifts in audience behavior are changing the way citizens consume news, with content growing increasingly personalized and subject to individual preferences regarding what, when, and where they entertain themselves or expose themselves to politically oriented information.

Of course, effective presidential leadership requires both exciting the base *and* building coalitions—and there is no reason to suppose that future presidents will succeed, at least over the longer term, by emphasizing one over the other. Along with, and perhaps in part *because of*, the three medias, politics in America are at a crossroads. Traditional communications channels are increasingly foreclosed, even as new ones emerge. Different channels, in turn, reach different audiences, and so privilege different communication strategies, different forms of leadership, and ultimately different policies. Given the enormity and speed of the changes in this marketplace, and their potential consequences for democratic participation and the strategic landscape confronting politicians, the evolution of the communication environment within which our politics are contested seems likely to play a central role in shaping the future course of American democracy.

Notes

1. Source: nielsenwire.com.
2. Source: barackobama.com email, September 9, 2009.
3. Matthew A. Baum and Tim Groeling, *War Stories: The Causes and Consequences of Citizen Views of War* (Princeton, NJ: Princeton University Press, 2010).

4. Though I do not focus on it here, most of the arguments I make concerning partisan political blogs apply to political talk radio as well.
5. Sources: Matthew A. Baum and Sam Kernell, "Has Cable Ended the Golden Age of Presidential Television?" *American Political Science Review* 93, March (1999): 1–16; retrieved from http://www.stateofthemedia.org/2009/chartland.php? id=1008&ct=line&dir=&sort=&col1_box=1&col2_box=1&col3_box=1.
6. Samuel Kernell and Laurie L. Rice, "Cable and Partisan Polarization of the President's Audience" (unpublished manuscript, University of California, San Diego, 2010).
7. Baum and Groeling, *War Stories*.
8. Daniel Hallin, *We Keep America on Top of the World: Television Journalism and the Public Sphere* (London: Routledge, 1994).
9. John Consoli, "Obama Drama: Nets Take a Stand Against Primetime Preemptions," *Hollywood Reporter*, May 7, 2009.
10. The *Fox News* Channel did, however, air the press conference.
11. Consoli.
12. Baum and Groeling, *War Stories*.
13. Baum and Groeling, *War Stories*.
14. Reported in Kernell and Rice; and Will Feltus, "Cable News Bias? Audiences Say 'Yes.'" National Media Research, Planning and Placement, 2009, retrieved from http://nmrpp.com/CableNewsBiasAudiences.pdf.
15. Matthew Gentzkow and Jesse M. Shapiro, "Ideological Segregation Online and Offline," *NBER Working Paper 15916* (April), 2010.
16. David All, "Is Yahoo!'s Online Debate Going to be Fair and Balanced?"April 26, 2007, retrieved from http://techpresident.com/blog-entry/yahoo's-online-debate-going-be-fair-and-balanced.
17. Appearances by presidential aspirants on *daytime* talk shows also attract large audiences. For instance, 8.7 million households watched presidential candidate Al Gore's September 11, 2000 appearance on the *Oprah Winfrey Show*.
18. Matthew A. Baum, *Soft News Goes to War: Public Opinion and American Foreign Policy in the New Media Age* (Princeton, NJ: Princeton University Press, 2003).
19. Matthew A. Baum, "Talking the Vote: Why Presidential Candidates Hit the Talk Show Circuit," *American Journal of Political Science* 44, April (2005): 213–234.
20. Baum and Groeling, *War Stories*.
21. Matea Gold, "Candidates Embrace the Chat: Daytime Gabfests and Latenight Comedy TV Become Essential Stops on the Presidential Trail to Reach 'Regular Folks,'" *Los Angeles Times*, September 29, 2007.
22. Matthew A. Baum, "Sex, Lies and War: How Soft News Brings Foreign Policy to the Inattentive Public," *American Political Science Review* 96, March (2002): 91–109; Baum, *Soft News Goes to War*; Liesbet Van Zoonen, Floris Muller, Donya Alinejad, Martijn Dekker, Linda Duits, Pauline van Romondt, and Wendy Wittenberg, "Dr. Phil Meets the Candidates: How Family Life and Personal Experience Produce Political Discussions," *Critical Studies in Mass Communication* 24, October (2007): 322–338.
23. Baum, *Soft News Goes to War*; Matthew A. Baum, "Soft News and Political Knowledge: Evidence of Absence or Absence of Evidence?" *Political Communication* 20, April (2003): 173–190; Paul Brewer and Xiaoxia Cao, "Candidate Appearances on Soft News Shows and Public Knowledge About Primary Campaigns," *Journal of Broadcasting and Electronic Media* 50, March (2006): 18–35; Dannagal G. Young and Russell M. Tisinger, "Dispelling Late-Night Myths: News Consumption among Late-Night Comedy Viewers and the Predictors of Exposure to Various Late-Night Shows," *Harvard International Journal of Press/Politics* 11, Summer (2006): 113–134.

24. Matthew A. Baum, "Circling the Wagons: Soft News and Isolationism in American Public Opinion," *International Studies Quarterly* 48, June (2004): 313–338; Baum, "Talking the Vote"; Paul Brewer and Emily Marquardt, "Mock News and Democracy: Analyzing The Daily Show," *Atlantic Journal of Communication* 15, November (2007): 249–226.
25. Markus Prior, *Post-Broadcast Democracy: How Media Choice Increases Inequality in Political Involvement and Polarizes Elections* (Cambridge/New York: Cambridge University Press, 2007); Matthew A. Baum and Angela Jamison, "The Oprah Effect: How Soft News Helps Inattentive Citizens Vote Consistently," *Journal of Politics* 68, November (2006): 946–959.
26. Matthew A. Baum and Angela Jamison, "Soft News and the Four Oprah Effects," in *Oxford Handbook of Public Opinion and the Media*, eds. Lawrence Jacobs and Robert Shapiro (Oxford: Oxford University Press, forthcoming 2011).
27. Michael Xenos and Amy Becker, "Moments of Zen: Effects of the Daily Show on Information Seeking," *Political Communication* 26, July (2009): 317–332.
28. For example, in their famous "Middletown" study of what they regarded as a typical American city in the 1920s, Robert and Helen Lynd (1929, 471) found that

    > The local morning paper distributes 8,851 copies to the 9,200 homes of the city, and the afternoon paper 6,715, plus at least half of an additional 785 sold on the street and news-stand. In addition, the circulation of out-of-town-papers ... now totals 1200 to 1500 a day.

    Robert Lynd and Helen Merrell Lynd, *Middletown: A Study in Modern American Culture* (Orlando, FL: Harcourt Brace, 1929).
29. Prior, *Post-Broadcast Democracy.*
30. Baum and Groeling, *War Stories.*
31. Gary C. Jacobson, *A Divider, Not a Uniter: George W. Bush and the American People* (New York: Pearson Longman, 2006).
32. E.g., Steven Kull, Clay Ramsay, and Evan Lewis, "Misperceptions, the Media, and the Iraq War," *Political Science Quarterly* 118 (2003/2004): 569–598; Stefano Della Vigna and Ethan Kaplan, "The Fox News Effect: Media Bias and Voting," (manuscript, Berkeley, California, March 30, 2003, retrieved from http://elsa. berkeley.edu/~sdellavi/wp/foxvote06-03-30.pdf); Gary C. Jacobson, "The War, the President, and the 2006 Midterm Congressional Elections," Paper presented to the annual meeting of the Midwest Political Science Association, the Palmer House Hilton, Chicago, April 12–15, 2007.
33. Jacobson, "The War."
34. Angus Campbell, Philip E. Converse, Warren E. Miller, and Donald E. Stokes, *The American Voter* (New York: Wiley, 1960).
35. Baum and Groeling, *War Stories.*
36. Cass Sunstein, *Republic.com 2.0* (Princeton, NJ: Princeton University Press, 2007).

Chapter 13

Public Opinion and Public Policy

Andrea Louise Campbell

The relationship between public opinion and public policy is a two-way street.[1] In one direction, we observe public preferences influencing government activity and policy outcomes, as we would expect in a democracy. That said, the correspondence between what the public says that it wants and what it gets out of government varies across time and across issues. Moreover, some groups in society—the economically privileged and the highly politically active, for instance—tend to achieve more of their policy goals, raising concerns about the policy consequences of economic and political inequality.

In the other direction, we see public policy influencing public opinion. As previous chapters revealed, there are many factors shaping the public's preferences. Here we add existing policy to the list. What Americans think the government should do now and in the future depends in part on how they regard what government has done in the past. Hence government policy is highly consequential because it influences what the public desires subsequently, shaping future policy outcomes.

This chapter explores existing scholarship on this two-way relationship between public opinion and public policy. It then utilizes a case study of Medicare reform—the 2003 addition of a prescription drug benefit to the federal health insurance program for older Americans—to demonstrate both the ways in which public opinion can shape policy outcomes and the ways in which the influence of the public is constrained when it comes head-to-head with the preferences of powerful interest groups and lawmakers themselves. The Medicare case also sheds light on how public policies influence subsequent public opinion and the political environment in which future policy making takes place. Although there is still much to learn about the relationship between public opinion and public policy, we can begin to assess how well our democracy in practice measures up to the ideal extolled by democratic theorists.

Public Opinion as an Influence on Public Policy

A hallmark of democratic governance is the notion of popular sovereignty, the idea that government policy should reflect the preferences of its citizens. As John Stuart Mill said, "There is no difficulty in showing the ideally best form of government is that in which the sovereignty, or the supreme controlling power in the last resort, is vested in the entire aggregate of the community."[2] The founders may have expressed skepticism about the capacities of ordinary citizens and the role of public opinion, designing a number of institutional barriers to its direct effects,[3] but modern theorists, such as V.O. Key Jr., firmly emphasize the central role of the public and its preferences: "Unless mass views have some place in the shaping of policy, all the talk about democracy is nonsense. As Lasswell has said, the 'open interplay of opinion and policy is the distinguishing mark of popular rule.'"[4] As another modern theorist, Robert Dahl, put it, democratic governance is prefaced on "the continuing responsiveness of the government to the preferences of its citizens, considered as political equals."[5] And empirical social scientist Chris Achen considers one of the central features of democratic theory to be "*control of outcomes*" (emphasis in the original).[6] Thus if the American democratic state is functioning as expected, there should be a robust correspondence between the public's professed preferences and public policy.

Political scientists have spent decades examining whether in fact public opinion does influence policy outcomes. The basic finding[7] is that representation occurs, and seems to occur fairly often, at the aggregate level, although there is important variation across issues and different kinds of individuals. The public is more likely to see its views reflected on highly salient issues, and the preferences of some citizens, particularly the well resourced and organized, are better represented than others.

There are several pathways by which public opinion shapes public policy: electoral accountability, politicians' view of their job, and group-based pressures and political parties.[8] Elections are a chief mechanism by which voters can make their views felt, elevating to office those who promise to reflect their views and removing politicians who have failed to do so.[9] A piece of evidence supporting this mechanism is that overall responsiveness tends to increase as elections draw nearer, presumably as a consequence of politicians attempting to curry favor with voters.[10] Another possibility is that voters choose representatives who are like them and who in turn pass policies congruent with their supporters' preferences. A second mechanism is the "social pressure" elected officials feel to respond to their constituents, acting either as delegates or trustees.[11] Delegates respond to specific instructions from constituents while trustees pursue policies they judge to be best for those they represent.[12] A third link between public opinion and public policy is the role of political parties and interest groups. Parties are crucial aggregators of interests in American politics, but there is concern that with the rise of candidate-centered elections and the importance of money in campaigning that parties represent the interests of the well-heeled and ideologically extreme more than those of broader publics.[13] Interest groups are the other important opinion aggregators, and the influence of interest groups on representation has been much debated as well. Early pluralist thinkers such as David Truman and Robert Dahl believed that organized groups, which would naturally emerge in response to political issues, enhanced representation, while later critics such as E.E. Schattschneider argued that the privileged were far more likely to organize and that many interests are in fact left without representation.[14] Contemporary research is divided, with some scholars believing that representation is enhanced in policy areas that are thickly populated by interest groups[15] with others arguing that "special interests" undermine the relationship between public opinion and public policy rather than reinforce it, exacerbating inequalities in representation.[16] Most of this latter research focuses on the skewed distribution of the "pressure system" in favor of business interests and the affluent and well educated, and predicts that these compositional biases will lead to unequal policy outcomes.[17]

Scholars have employed several different approaches in measuring the relationship between public opinion and public policy. Virtually all of these approaches measure public opinion with responses to surveys, either opinion on specific issues[18] or aggregate measures of policy liberalism or "mood" that combine many survey items and issues.[19] Measures of the outcome, public policy, include specific policy outcomes,[20] roll-call votes,[21] or "policy liberalism," the latter typically an aggregate measure across issues, such as the net liberal direction of *Congressional Quarterly* key votes.[22] "Responsiveness" is then usually assessed by examining the correspondence between public opinion and policy outcomes in some space or time. Analysis proceeds in one of several different ways.[23] The earliest empirical studies began by looking across different units such as congressional districts,[24] then later cities[25] and states,[26] and assessing the cross-sectional relationship between public opinion and public policy within each of those units. A second approach looked over time and across issues to see whether policy moved in a direction favored by the majority of Americans.[27] A third approach examined changes in public opinion and sought to discern whether changes in policy followed, either on specific issues[28] or in responses to changes in the aggregate "public mood."[29]

Overall, the magnitude of representation found in these studies is quite substantial. Comparing national surveys with policy outcomes, Monroe determined that policy was consistent with opinion 63 percent of the time between 1960 and 1979[30] and 55 percent of the time between 1980 and 1993.[31] Page and Shapiro similarly found that policy change is consistent with the direction of opinion change about two-thirds of the time.[32] Erikson, Wright and McIver found a very strong relationship between state policy and state opinion liberalism in their cross-sectional study,[33] and Stimson, MacKuen and Erikson discerned a nearly "one-to-one translation of preferences into policy" in their examination of congruence between policy change and policy mood, with the greatest congruence in elected institutions such as Congress and the least with non-electoral institutions such as the Supreme Court.[34]

The high degree of representation notwithstanding, a number of important methodological and substantive issues remain. One concern is that scholars typically utilize survey results to define "public opinion,"[35] whereas there are "at least" three other sources of public preferences that guide policy makers: activated public opinion, referring to the views of those "actively participating in political life" through political participation, organizational memberships, and social movements; latent public opinion, or the "underlying values and fundamental preferences of citizens" such as the desire for good economic performance; and perceived majority opinions, or the "assumed preferences of citizens … which may or may not accurately reflect actual preferences."[36] The reliance on surveys not only may mis-measure public opinion by failing to include these other sources but also may artificially inflate the congruence between opinion and policy because only the most salient issues get included on surveys. Moreover, Adam Berinsky argues that survey analysis may not be representative of actual public opinion because it excludes certain interests (those who say "don't know," who turn out to be systematically different from those who do respond).[37] A related concern arises around the sampling of issues, that is, the way in which researchers go about their work may inflate the relationship as well. Does one choose what questions individuals get surveyed on and match to policy, or choose some policies and match to survey responses? Paul Burstein asserts that the former practice—widely utilized in this literature—leads to bias because surveys ask about the most salient issues, and salience leads to better representation. Indeed, when he takes what he calls a random sample of congressional votes and then looks at corresponding polls, he finds less responsiveness than do other scholars.[38] It also appears that the greater the level of aggregation (e.g., looking at an aggregated public mood indicator rather than opinion on individual policies), the greater the correspondence with policy outcomes (e.g., Stimson, Erikson and McKuen's one-to-one relationship[39] versus Monroe's 55 percent).[40] It is difficult to know which measure of representation is "better," or whether the public feels better represented when its overall mood is reflected in policy or its opinion on specific issues.[41]

We might also wonder whether public opinion is an independent force or is itself shaped by political elites. The causality question—who leads whom?—arises.[42] The more problematic version is that elites can manipulate public opinion through misinformation campaigns.[43] Somewhat more benign is the "crafted talk" argument—that politicians pursue their own policy goals and use public opinion polls to identify the "language, symbols, and arguments that will 'win' public support for their policy objectives."[44] Certainly framing effects are common in public opinion, with different question wordings and contexts—whether within the survey itself or in the real world—having significant effects on reported opinions.[45] Most likely the relationship between public opinion and public policy is reciprocal, with political elites having an ear to the ground to discern what issues will play well with the public.[46] Or as Stimson, MacKuen, and Erikson put it in their model of "dynamic representation": "[l]ike antelope in an open field, [policy makers] cock their ears and focus their full attention on the slightest sign of danger" in the form of electoral consequences arising from failures of representation.[47]

Beyond these measurement issues are substantive concerns about the preference–policy relationship. One is whether responsiveness has changed over time. Lawrence Jacobs and Robert Shapiro point to the rise of presidential and congressional polling and utilize the case of President Clinton's failed health care reform as evidence of a "loss of democratic responsiveness"—politicians use polls not to discern public preferences but to guide their rhetoric in selling the policies they themselves desire.[48] Morris Fiorina similarly argues that responsiveness has declined—that there is now a "disconnect" between citizens and the "political class"—because political elites are far more polarized than are the moderate voters they purport to represent and because such elites set the political agenda and pursue their own issue priorities.[49] In contrast, Paul Quirk argues that responsiveness has improved over time, indeed problematically so, with too much deference to mass opinion, which is often uninformed or even biased by a misleading information environment. He argues that "politicians do pander," aided by the erosion of institutional protections against the "excess of democracy" the Founders warned against: the elimination of indirect election of the Senate; the congressional sunshine laws of the 1970s; the rise of the "plebiscitary presidency"; and the growth in the use of the initiative and referendum.[50] Empirical examinations of specific periods have found that responsiveness rose for several decades into the 1970s[51] and declined thereafter[52] in ways that square with Fiorina's account. Overall, however, the relatively small number of empirical studies and differences in their measures of responsiveness make drawing conclusions about trends difficult.[53]

Another concern is the important question of inequality and *whose* preferences are represented in policy outcomes. Early work on the opinion–policy relationship ignored questions of inequality and examined public opinion as a whole.[54] More recently, scholars have taken up the crucial question raised by the democratic theorists—"How does a 'democratic' system work amid inequality of resources?"[55]—and studied whether the affluent or the highly participatory are better represented than are the poor or the politically quiescent.[56] As with the question of change in responsiveness over time, the jury is still out and more research is needed. However, several extant studies point to pronounced inequalities. Martin Gilens examined hundreds of survey questions on proposed policy changes between 1981 and 2002 and found that most of the time policy does not change, reflecting the status-quo bias built into American governing institutions. However, when policy does change and policy preferences differ across income groups, policy outcomes strongly reflect the preferences of the most affluent—those at the 90th income percentile—but neither those of the poor nor middle income Americans.[57] Similarly, Larry Bartels finds in an examination of senatorial roll-call votes that the preferences of the affluent were weighted 50 percent more than those of middle income citizens, while the preferences of the poor were not reflected in their senators' voting behavior at all.[58] Lawrence Jacobs and Benjamin Page show that foreign policy (as measured by foreign policy opinion among policy makers) more closely matches the preferences of business leaders and experts than those of the public.[59] James Druckman and Lawrence Jacobs examine internal White House polls and find that Ronald Reagan's positions on core economic issues (taxes, spending, and Social Security reform) corresponded much more to the policy preferences of the affluent poll respondents than to those of the typical respondents.[60] And in a second look at the strong aggregate correlation between state-level opinion and policy, Elizabeth Rigby and Gerald Wright examine the responsiveness of state-level policy to different income groups and find evidence of inequality in economic policy in poor states. In wealthy states, there are few economic policy preference differences across income groups and no inequalities in responsiveness. However, in poorer states, the preferences of the affluent do differ from those of middle and low income residents, and there is a pronounced gradient in responsiveness, with policy corresponding closely with the preferences of the affluent and falling off for middle and lower income groups.[61]

The mechanisms by which the affluent prevail in getting their policy stands reflected in policy deserve more research, although there is support for the electoral accountability path, with scholars finding that those who are politically active appear to be better represented. The preferences of voters are better reflected in senatorial roll-call voting than are the preferences of nonvoters,[62] and social welfare spending is less generous in states where the poor constitute a smaller proportion of those who turn out to vote.[63] Another hypothesized pathway is through interest groups: since the well-heeled are more likely to be organized, perhaps interest groups acting on their behalf amplify their influence on policy outcomes. Recent research by Martin Gilens, however, suggests that interest groups and the affluent operate independently; interest groups sometimes share the preferences of the affluent and sometimes they do not. The affluent are far more likely to see their preference enacted when interest groups push in the same direction, but they prevail even without the assistance of organized groups.[64]

Some dissenters argue that policy preferences do not differ much across income groups and hence inequality in representation is of little concern.[65] When asked whether they believe the government is spending too much, too little, or about the right amount on cities, crime, defense, education, the environment, foreign aid, health, and welfare, respondents of different income levels differed substantially only on their welfare attitudes. But these researchers divide income into terciles only, which may mask the distinctive preferences of the very affluent, and they rely primarily on General Social Survey spending questions that are broad and unsurprisingly elicit similar reactions from different income groups.[66] A more extensive array of data reveals that there are large differences in preferences on redistributive issues across income groups, differences that are greater than those by education or gender.[67] Moreover, it is important to differentiate between economic and social policy. Because the affluent display cross-cutting preferences—they are economic conservatives but social liberals—using summary scores like ideology clouds analysis.[68] When policies are divided into economic or social issue areas, or when individual policies are examined, inequalities in responsiveness by income emerge.

Finally, Larry Bartels asks whether we are measuring the right thing by looking at responsiveness rather than congruence, that is, change versus level.[69] Many studies examine whether change in policy follows change in opinion, that is, how responsive policy is to marginal changes in public preferences. However, Bartels examines preferred levels of government spending across countries and finds large discrepancies between perceived and preferred levels of spending, with governments spending far less than their publics desire. In a related vein, Cook and Barrett found a significant mismatch between the spending preferences of the public and Members of Congress, with the public far more expansive.[70] It could be that policy makers recognize fiscal constraints on spending or tradeoffs across programs that publics do not, but this discrepancy between desired and actual spending does raise questions about how to measure the relationship between public opinion and public policy, and also about how much responsiveness is desirable. Policy makers could respond to demands for more spending, but pay the price later when voters become restless about the scope of government or ensuing tax increases or deficits.[71]

Policy Effects on Public Opinion

A smaller and more recent literature examines the effect of public policy on public opinion. Political scientists have long known that preferences are shaped by many influences, including childhood socialization, group memberships, identity, media, the political environment, and elite leadership. Yet there is the additional possibility that the public reacts to public policies themselves, recognized at least as early as Schattschneider's exhortation that "new policies create a new politics."[72] Only recently have scholars started to examine this effect empirically, which reverses the causal arrow to run from policy to opinion.

One version of this effect is the literature examining trends in attitudes over time and reactions to existing policies. Christopher Wlezien identified a "thermostatic" pattern in public opinion whereby the public's preferences for more or less spending on defense and several social policy areas is negatively related to recent policy. That is, when appropriations increase, the public becomes more likely to say spending in that area should be decreased, and vice versa.[73] James Stimson similarly argues that aggregate public opinion trends reveal a public that seems to drift away from the policy stances of the president it has most recently elected.[74]

The policy feedbacks literature takes this notion that existing policy can affect subsequent attitudes even further, asserting that these effects cycle back into the political system creating a policy–preference spiral in which policies affect preferences, which affect subsequent policies, and so on. Early theorists in this area, such as Helen Ingram and Anne Schneider, and Paul Pierson suggested that the ways in which policies are designed—what they do, for whom, and by what means—affects the attitudes of the public and the particular groups targeted by the policies.[75]

Subsequent empirical work has supported these hypotheses, showing for example that although Social Security and "welfare" are both anti-poverty programs, they have very different designs and therefore very different impacts on attitudes. Social Security is a universal program with contributory payroll tax financing. Virtually all seniors receive monthly pension benefits; they feel these benefits are earned; and the program's administration is based on well-defined rules and has a pro-client orientation in seeking to assist its clients to get the benefits to which they have contributed. The poor benefit because the Social Security formula redistributes from high to low income earners and pulls most seniors out of poverty, but in a hidden and non-stigmatizing way.[76] In contrast, welfare or AFDC/TANF is a means-tested program for poor families financed out of general tax revenues. Benefits are not high enough to pull families above the poverty line and are awarded not by automatic formula but by case workers who appear to clients to have great discretion and indeed arbitrary and capricious powers.[77] These differing policy designs have vastly different effects on client attitudes. Senior citizens have high levels of political efficacy and political interest and strong feelings about the nature of government provision, rejecting alternative models such as Social Security private accounts and Medicare vouchers which would change the design of their programs in ways they view as inimical to their interests. Welfare recipients have lower levels of political efficacy and interest than even their low levels of income and education would predict due to their policy experiences. They come to view the entire government as arbitrary and capricious as "the welfare," and largely fail to participate in politics.[78]

Another example of the effects of program designs on public opinion comes from the "tax expenditure" system. Many social policies in the United States are direct spending programs in which the government directly spends money to provide cash or in-kind benefits. Examples include Social Security, Medicare, welfare, food stamps, unemployment insurance, and public housing. But many other social policies are delivered indirectly through the tax code in the form of tax credits or tax exemptions. These tax expenditures provide a benefit or subsidize an activity by reducing or eliminating income taxes on the money an individual spends. Examples include the home mortgage interest deduction, whereby homeowners can deduct the interest on their home loan from their taxable income, and the tax exclusion for employer-provided health insurance, in which neither employers nor employees pay taxes on the amount they contribute for the employees' health insurance.

This "hidden welfare state" is nearly as large as the visible welfare state,[79] and yet scholars have long speculated that it would have very different effects on public attitudes, that individuals receiving a benefit that does not come as a visible cash payment or service but rather as a savings on their taxes would not perceive it as a government benefit. New data demonstrate that this is in fact the case. Beneficiaries of the home mortgage interest deduction (an indirect program) are far less likely to say that the program "helped them a lot" than are beneficiaries of government-provided housing (a direct program). Similarly, beneficiaries of a Hope or Lifetime Learning tax credit for higher education are far less likely to say that the program helped them a lot than are beneficiaries of direct student loans.[80] Thus the government foregoes billions of dollars in tax revenues to provide benefits which many do not perceive as government benefits. The impact of these policy designs on public attitudes is extremely consequential. Americans recognize that the government spends a great deal of money on the young through public education and on the old through Social Security and Medicare. The government also "spends" billions on those between ages 18 and 65, but much of this is in the form of tax expenditures. Because such programs are hidden, people don't recognize them as government benefits and think government does little for them, feeding skepticism about government and making it more difficult to implement further government programs. Hence public policies and their designs have enormous effects on public opinion.

Public Opinion and Medicare Reform

The interplay between public opinion and public policy is complex. We wonder how much influence the public's preferences have in shaping policy outputs, especially in issue areas where other powerful actors may have different preferences. In turn we wonder how policy outcomes affect subsequent opinion and the possibilities for further policy making.

The Medicare Prescription Drug Improvement and Modernization Act of 2003 (MMA) represents a useful case study in examining the relationship between public opinion and public policy, illustrating many of the dynamics mentioned above (although as a single case study not necessarily testing them definitively).[81] At the moment of passage, the MMA was the largest social policy expansion in a generation, adding a new prescription drug benefit to

Medicare, the federally run health insurance program in the United States for senior citizens and the permanently disabled, and making other important changes in the program. The story of the prescription drug benefit demonstrates both the potential for and the limits on citizen shaping of public policy as well as showing how existing policies can reshape the political landscape and subsequent possibilities for policy making.

The origins of the legislation show how limited knowledge can be among the public, even in issue areas of great apparent relevance, as well as the agenda setting power of political elites. President Bill Clinton first publicly raised the idea of adding a prescription drug benefit to Medicare in his January 1999 State of the Union address. The economy was booming and there was a rare surplus in the federal budget that made social policy expansion possible. In good economic times public opinion is more expansive toward social welfare policy and open to a greater public role.[82] Why not use the surplus to enhance the Medicare benefit?

The proposal was immediately popular among seniors, but interestingly Clinton's motivation in introducing the idea did not originate in public opinion per se but rather was a product of both policy convictions and political motivations. Prescription drug coverage was a non-issue among seniors beforehand: a June 1999 Kaiser Family Foundation poll asking Americans what they thought was the most important health care problem facing the United States found that only 4 percent of those aged 65 and over said "prescription drugs prices." Most seniors at the time had some kind of drug coverage, hence little surprise they weren't agitating for a new benefit, but experts knew that coverage was endangered even if seniors themselves did not yet. Employers were beginning to drop drug coverage for their retirees; drug prices were climbing rapidly; and monthly premiums for supplemental medigap insurance plans that covered prescription drugs were rising steeply. If senior drug coverage wasn't a problem at the moment, it soon would be, and lawmakers acted in an anticipatory manner.[83]

Political motivations also drove Clinton's proposal: Republicans had been trying since the mid-1990s to change the structure of Medicare, which they viewed as the embodiment of big government. They sought to transform it from a defined contribution social insurance entitlement program in which the government paid for seniors' medical expenses after the fact, with no limit on spending, into a defined benefit voucher program, a more limited and fiscally predictable program in which seniors would be given a voucher to purchase health insurance in the private market, which would take advantage of competition among insurers to hold down premiums and would cap the government's financial obligation for seniors' health insurance. Clinton's prescription drug proposal was intended to add a popular new benefit to traditional Medicare to stave off these free market reform proposals from the Republicans.

If Clinton sought to enhance Medicare benefits to protect the program politically, we might ask: why prescription drugs? The answer sheds additional light on the nature of public attitudes and understanding and the role of public opinion in policy making. As a health insurance program, Medicare had (and still has) several significant shortcomings: besides lacking prescription drug coverage, it charged deductibles and copayments with no annual cap, raising the possibility of catastrophic out-of-pocket costs for very ill seniors; nor did the program cover long-term care other than short nursing home stays after hospitalization. Studies showed that the expected out-of-pocket costs for an average senior over a lifetime are far greater for long-term care than for prescription drugs.[84] And yet when Medicare was expanded for the first time since 1965, it was coverage for drugs that was added. Why? Prescription drugs are highly salient. They are an everyday expense for the vast majority of seniors, with 90 percent taking at least one drug, and half of those taking five or more.[85] In contrast, catastrophic out-of-pocket expenses only hit a few, and most seniors are either ignorant about long-term care (thinking Medicare does cover it) or in denial, underestimating their risk of needing nursing home or home health care.[86] Seniors may not have known their drug coverage was endangered, but when the government offered to pay for their prescriptions, they reacted with enthusiasm.

We might also ask: Why enhance a program for seniors, who already benefit from the federal government's largest domestic programs, when the budget surplus could have been used for any number of other policy needs, such as education or the environment, or, in the health realm, expanding coverage to the uninsured? The answer lies in policy feedback effects deriving from previous policies, which made seniors an ideal target for social policy expansion. Over time older Americans had been transformed from one of the least participatory to the most participatory age group in American politics, helping to explain why politicians might be interested for electoral reasons in showering them with new benefits. The development of Social Security and Medicare over time had enhanced politically relevant resources for seniors, providing them with steady incomes and making retirement a reality; fostering their political interest by tying their well-being so visibly to government policy; and defining them as program recipients and therefore a politically relevant group ripe for mobilization by political parties and interest groups such as AARP.[87] Attitudinally, seniors were a favored group as well: Americans had grown accustomed to a significant government role in seniors' health care since the 1965 inception of Medicare, a kind of attitudinal feedback—why not enhance it? Because Medicare was a non-stigmatized program owing to its universal structure and contributory payroll tax financing, expanding it was unproblematic politically. And seniors were a sympathetic and blameless group, with drug needs arising from the inevitable problems of aging. In line with many other surveys at the time, 89 percent of respondents in a May 2000 *ABC News* poll supported "*having the Medicare insurance program cover prescription drug expenses for senior citizens.*"[88]

Thus, once on the agenda, a prescription drug benefit was inevitable. But the acute question was what form it would take. Clinton raised the idea, but meanwhile the Republican party achieved unified control of government in the 2000 election and was left with this popular proposal on its plate. The difficulty for the party was that the last thing many Republican lawmakers wanted to do was to expand a big government program. However, seniors are an important constituency for both parties, and so Republicans felt they had to craft a drug benefit of some sort.[89]

The initial strategy was to use the new drug benefit as a carrot to lure seniors out of traditional Medicare by limiting the drug benefit to those seniors who enrolled in private managed care plans such as health maintenance organizations (HMOs); if Republicans couldn't voucherize Medicare, at least they could enhance the presence of market-model health plans in the program. However, this idea was met with opposition not only among seniors—wary of managed care plans as an effort to lure them into HMOs during the 1990s had backfired severely—but also from within the Republican party itself. Republican senators and Members of Congress from rural states told their colleagues that there were no managed care plans in their states, or only one, so they could not countenance limiting the prescription drug benefit to those in private plans. Instead, the prescription drug benefit became a voluntary add-on to traditional Medicare, so-called Part D drug plans that seniors buy from insurance companies. Seniors would not have to leave traditional Medicare, which they regarded highly, in order to secure the new drug benefit.[90]

Thus, public opinion—working through electoral accountability—helped secure and shape the prescription drug benefit. Much of seniors' power and influence is owing to policy feedback effects of earlier programs for seniors which helped make them a formidable constituency.

However, the MMA case study also illustrates limits in the power of public opinion to shape policy details. The political preferences of policy elites as well as the influence of interest groups overrode the preferences of the public when it came to the specific design of the drug benefit. Polls showed that large majorities of seniors wanted a Medicare option for drug coverage (not just Part D plans from private insurance companies), government negotiating power over drug prices (as the Veterans Health Administration had), and reimportation of less expensive drugs from abroad (prior to the MMA, many seniors bought their drugs on trips to Canada or Mexico and wanted access to these cheaper drugs expanded). The final legislation included none of those provisions, because they were opposed by organized interests, in particular the pharmaceutical and insurance industries. Drug manufacturers were very happy to have their biggest customers enjoy new government subsidy of their prescription needs, but they did not want the government negotiating drug prices for the 44 million Medicare beneficiaries, a huge proportion of manufacturers' customer base. Nor did they want cheaper drugs imported from other countries whose national health systems did negotiate lower drug prices. And the insurance industry, charged with inventing an entirely new insurance product, stand-alone drug insurance plans, did not want competition from an option from within Medicare, which would surely have become the default for seniors, undermining private insurers' market share and potential profits.

We might imagine AARP, as a group organizing seniors themselves, to serve as the kind of interest group that leads to greater representation, in the way pluralist scholars such as Dahl and Truman predicted. The organization's role here is mixed: it did secure better subsidies for low income seniors and for businesses to retain drug coverage of former employees; but it also endorsed the legislation at the last minute, providing political cover for wary lawmakers on both sides of the aisle despite having failed to secure more provisions in line with senior desires. The MMA roll-call vote was the longest open tally in congressional history as Republican party leaders engaged in protracted arm-twisting and bargaining; without AARP's endorsement, it probably would not have become law.

In the end, seniors did not get the structure they wanted. They also complained bitterly about other aspects of the policy design, such as the donut hole coverage gap in which seniors had to pay 100 percent out-of-pocket for drug costs in a $3600 band above the standard coverage and before catastrophic coverage kicked in—an odd structure not found elsewhere in the insurance world but necessitated by the budget constraint imposed on the new drug program (which had been proposed during a budget surplus but formulated after the return of federal government deficits). Also unpopular was the late enrollment penalty—if seniors do not sign up for a drug plan within six months of initial eligibility, they forever pay an accumulating 1 percent on their monthly payments for each month they delay, a provision necessitated by making the prescription drug plan voluntary.[91] And while the Republican framers of the law extolled the virtues of choice of drug plans—"choice creates competition, and competition drives down price," as Newt Gingrich put it[92]—seniors got more choice than they wanted or could handle cognitively. When asked the optimal number of drug plans to choose from, the modal answer among seniors in one survey was three to five.[93] Laboratory experiments have shown that seniors are best able to select an optimal plan when presented with three plans rather than ten or 20.[94] But in the real world seniors have to choose from among 40 or more.[95]

Despite their initial complaints and dissatisfaction over these design elements, seniors are largely happy with the drug benefit outcome. Behavioral economists have long argued that people are "satisficers," happy with "good enough."[96] Sixty percent of all Medicare beneficiaries have Medicare prescription drug coverage, either through stand-alone Part D plans (38 percent) or Medicare Advantage drug plans (21 percent),[97] and survey data show that senior favorability toward the new drug benefit increased over time. The percentage of Medicare recipients having a favorable impression of the new drug program increased from 47 percent in December 2005, on the eve of Part D implementation, to 63 percent in May 2007.[98] There is little agitation among seniors for change and no movement by policy makers to provide the three things seniors wanted but organized interests opposed.[99] And having so much choice has caused most seniors to freeze up rather than search for a better plan during the annual open enrollment period; only 9 percent switch from year to year, when more than 40 percent would be better off doing so.[100] Despite flaws in legislation, public opinion moves on to other concerns, such as coverage and the overall health care reform.

Thus public opinion can broadly shape policy outcomes. Policy makers anticipated a future need of seniors and the popularity that a Medicare prescription drug benefit would garner. Once the idea was presented, public opinion backed the idea with enthusiasm. However, the public had less to say on the specifics of the law, and interest groups easily prevailed in vetoing popular provisions inimical to their interests.

What about the other direction of causality, policy change in turn affecting public opinion? The policy feedbacks literature would suggest that changing the structure of Medicare by increasing the role of private insurers could change seniors' attitudes about the role of markets versus the government in their health care, lead them to embrace privatization in other areas like Social Security, or even reduce seniors' political cohesiveness and group identity by splitting them across different health plans. After all, over half of seniors are receiving their drug benefits from private insurers, and one-quarter have left traditional Medicare altogether and joined privately managed care plans in accordance with another provision in the MMA. Might these seniors' attitudes change compared to other seniors who remained in traditional, government-run Medicare?

However, survey data show that such attitudes have not changed, at least not in the short term. Compared to seniors who stayed in traditional Medicare, those who signed up for private drug plans or who enrolled in a privately managed care plan do not experience diminished feelings of solidarity with other seniors, nor are they less supportive of Medicare spending or more likely to advocate the market over the government in seniors' health care or other issue areas like Social Security privatization.[101] It could be that these structural changes do not have that much of an impact because Medicare has always used private doctors and hospitals, so that the privatized aspect of drug plan administration is not that vivid to people. Or it could be that these kinds of state-market attitudes are shaped not only by program experiences but the many other influences on public opinion, which may be much more durable.

Another example of the failure of a major policy design change to alter attitudes suggests that this is the case. In 1996 welfare was transformed in fundamental ways. The AFDC program was replaced with TANF, stripping welfare of its entitlement status and placing new work requirements and lifetime limits on the program, provisions that were very popular with the public. Hypotheses arising from the feedbacks literature would suggest that the new design of welfare, especially because it implements changes the public desired, would change attitudes about welfare and welfare recipients. No longer could a recipient be on welfare for a lifetime, and now recipients would have to work to receive benefits. Despite these changes in policy design, no attitudinal change has occurred: Americans are no more favorably disposed toward welfare than they were before the reform.[102] The lack of change in attitudes suggests the considerable influence of other factors beyond public policy, such as childhood socialization, ideological commitments and media messages. It may also be the case that attitudinal change is a long-term process. Perhaps we will not observe new attitudes toward, say, Medicare until new cohorts age into Medicare eligibility, and, having never experienced the program under its old, government-centric design, embrace a greater role for the market as they experience the "new normal" of privatized provision.

Conclusion

Thanks to the work of many scholars over time, we know more and more about the relationship between public opinion and public policy. Although there are many areas where more research is needed, we can draw a number of conclusions with confidence.

Among the myriad influences on public policy—the ideological and policy preferences of lawmakers, the desires of organized interests, norms and models arising from existing policy, budget constraints imposed by ongoing governmental operations, and so on—public opinion does play a role. But this role is constrained in important ways. The public has its greatest influence on salient issues; in more esoteric realms in which the public cannot discern its interest or believes it has none, other elite-level influences tend to prevail. Where the public does have influence, it usually shapes the general direction of policy rather than fine-grained specifics, where, again, other interests tend to stipulate the details. And the consensus among many scholars is that inequality in representation is a significant problem, one that threatens to undermine the very legitimacy of democratic governance. Democratic theory is predicated on the equal distance of all citizens from government, but clearly some citizens are viewed as more central, and their preferences tend to prevail over those of the less privileged and less participatory.

Important too is the influence of existing policy on the public's attitudes (precisely because those attitudes tend to feed back into the political system, determining the possibilities for future policy making). The observation that public opinion reacts in thermostatic fashion, moving away from the status quo to prefer, say, more or less spending or a stronger or weaker role for government than exists at the moment, begs the question: Is government doomed to perpetually disappoint its citizens? Or is the very fact of opinion and policy tacking from side to side ideologically a measure of responsiveness? What we do know is that public policy is only one of many influences on public preferences, and changing policy does not always succeed in winning over the public, whether because other influences remain dominant, or simply because the public does not realize the policy change took place.

Thus the relationship between public opinion and public policy looks to be a variable one, stronger on some issue areas and for some subgroups in society, weaker in other areas and for less privileged groups. As with other aspects of public opinion, the public's widespread lack of knowledge and inattentiveness to politics undercuts its ability to shape policy outcomes, something that ultimately only the public can choose to change.

Notes

1. Many thanks to Mike Sances for his superb research assistance.
2. John Stuart Mill, *Considerations on Representative Government* (Chicago, IL: Henry Regnery, 1962), p. 57.
3. See Alexander Hamilton, James Madison, and John Jay, *The Federalist* (New York: Anchor, 1961).
4. V.O. Key Jr., *Public Opinion and American Democracy* (New York: Alfred A. Knopf, 1964), p. 7.
5. Robert A. Dahl, *Polyarchy: Participation and Opposition* (New Haven, CT: Yale University Press, 1971), p. 1.
6. Christopher Achen, "Measuring Representation," *American Journal of Political Science* 22 (1978): 475–510.
7. For valuable overviews of this literature, see Paul Burstein, "The Impact of Public Opinion on Public Policy: A Review and an Agenda," *Political Research Quarterly* 56 (2003): 29–40; Carroll J. Glynn, Susan Herbst, Garrett J. O'Keefe, and Robert Y. Shapiro, with Lawrence R. Jacobs, "Public Opinion and Public Policymaking," in *Public Opinion*, eds. Carroll J. Glynn, Susan Herbst, Garrett J. O'Keefe, and Robert Y. Shapiro (Boulder, CO: Westview Press, 1999), pp. 299–340; and Jeff Manza and Fay Lomax Cook, "A Democratic Polity? Three Views of Policy Responsiveness to Public Opinion in the United States," *American Politics Research* 30 (2002): 630–67.
8. Glynn et al., "Public Opinion and Policy Making."
9. Anthony Downs, *An Economic Theory of Democracy* (New York: Harper, 1957).
10. Edward R. Tufte, *Political Control of the Economy* (Princeton, NJ: Princeton University Press, 1978).
11. Glynn et al., "Public Opinion and Policy Making."
12. R. Douglas Arnold, *The Logic of Congressional Action* (New Haven, CT: Yale University Press, 1990).
13. Morris P. Fiorina, *Disconnect: The Breakdown of Representation in American Politics* (Julian J. Rothbaum Distinguished Lecture Series) (Norman, OK: University of Oklahoma Press, 2009).
14. David B. Truman, *The Governmental Process: Political Interests and Public Opinion* (New York: Knopf, 1951); Robert A. Dahl, *Who Governs? Democracy and Power in an American City* (New Haven, CT: Yale University Press, 1961); E.E. Schattschneider, *The Semi-Sovereign People: A Realist's View of Democracy in America* (Austin, TX: Holt, Rinehart and Winston, 1960).
15. Burstein, "The Impact of Public Opinion on Public Policy."

16. Jacob Hacker and Paul Pierson, "Winner-Take-All Politics: Public Policy, Political Organization, and the Precipitous Rise of Top Incomes in the United States," *Politics and Society* 38 (June 2010): 152–204.
17. Schattschneider, *The Semi-Sovereign People*; Frank R. Baumgartner and Beth L. Leech, *Basic Interests: The Importance of Groups in Politics and in Political Science* (Princeton, NJ: Princeton University Press, 1998).
18. Benjamin I. Page and Robert Y. Shapiro, *The Rational Public: Fifty Years of Trends in Americans' Policy Preferences* (Chicago, IL: University of Chicago Press, 1992); Alan D. Monroe, "Consistency between Policy Preferences and National Policy Decisions," *American Politics Quarterly* 7 (1979): 3–18; Alan D. Monroe, "Public Opinion and Public Policy, 1980–1993," *Public Opinion Quarterly* 62 (1998):6–28; Martin Gilens, "Inequality and Democratic Responsiveness," *Public Opinion Quarterly* 65 (2005): 778–96.
19. James A. Stimson, Michael B. MacKuen, and Robert Erikson, "Dynamic Representation," *American Political Science Review* 89 (1995): 543–65; James Stimson, *Tides of Consent: How Public Opinion Shapes American Politics* (New York: Cambridge University Press, 2004).
20. Page and Shapiro, *The Rational Public*; Monroe, "Consistency between Policy Preferences and National Policy Decisions": Monroe, "Public Opinion and Public Policy, 1980–1993"; Gilens, "Inequality and Democratic Responsiveness."
21. Warren E. Miller and Donald E. Stokes, "Constituency Influence in Congress," *American Political Science Review* 57 (1963): 45–56; Larry Bartels, *Unequal Democracy: The Political Economy of the New Gilded Age* (Princeton, NJ: Princeton University Press, 2008).
22. Stimson et al.'s policy liberalism measures include: for Congress the net liberal direction on *Congressional Quarterly* key votes, the size of the liberal coalition on those votes, and interest group ratings of members; for the president the liberalism of his support coalition in Congress, the liberalism of the president's stand on key votes, and solicitor general briefs; for the Court a content-analysis based measure of net liberalism of majority opinions. See Stimson et al., "Dynamic Representation."
23. Larry Bartels distinguishes between responsiveness—a change in policy following a change in opinion—and policy congruence—a static measure of correspondence between preferences and policy as will be discussed below. See also Christopher Achen's discussion of three theoretically and empirically distinct measures of representation in his "Measuring Representation"; Larry Bartels, "The Opinion–Policy Disconnect: Cross-National Spending Preferences and Democratic Representation," Paper prepared for presentation at the Annual Meeting of the American Political Science Association, Boston, MA, August 2008.
24. Miller and Stokes, "Constituency Influence in Congress."
25. Jeffrey M. Berry, Kent E. Portney, and Ken Thomson, *The Rebirth of Urban Democracy* (Washington, DC: Brookings, 1993).
26. Robert S. Erikson, John P. McIver, and Gerald C. Wright, *Statehouse Democracy: Public Opinion and the American States* (New York: Cambridge University Press, 1994).
27. Monroe, "Consistency between Policy Preferences and National Policy Decisions"; Monroe, "Public Opinion and Public Policy, 1980–1993."
28. Page and Shapiro, *The Rational Public.*
29. Stimson et al., "Dynamic Representation."
30. Monroe, "Consistency between Policy Preferences and National Policy Decisions."
31. Monroe, "Public Opinion and Public Policy, 1980–1993."
32. Page and Shapiro, *The Rational Public.*

33. Erikson et al., *Statehouse Democracy.*
34. Stimson et al., "Dynamic Representation."
35. We might wonder whether there is indeed a "public opinion" to translate into public policy in the first place, with skeptics examining individual-level opinion arguing that citizens have reasons to be rationally ignorant about politics (Downs, *An Economic Theory of Democracy*) and lack true attitudes on many issue areas (Philip E. Converse, "The Nature of Belief Systems in Mass Publics," in *Ideology and Discontent*, ed. David Apter (New York: Free Press, 1964), 206–61). Aggregating opinions across many individuals, as most scholars in this arena do, in theory leads to the canceling out of individual-level error in opinion (see Page and Shapiro, *The Rational Public*).
36. Manza and Cook, "A Democratic Polity?" p. 632. On latent public opinion, see also John R. Zaller, "Coming to Grips with V. O. Key's Concept of Latent Opinion," in *Electoral Democracy*, eds. Michael MacKuen and George Rabinowitz (Ann Arbor, MI: University of Michigan Press, 2003), 311–36.
37. Adam J. Berinsky, *Silent Voices: Public Opinion and Political Participation in America* (Princeton, NJ: Princeton University Press, 2005).
38. Paul Burstein, "Why Estimates of the Impact of Public Opinion on Public Policy Are Too High," *Social Forces* 84 (2006): 2273–90.
39. Stimson et al., "Dynamic Representation."
40. Monroe, "Public Opinion and Public Policy, 1980–1993."
41. We do know that many Americans do not think their opinions generally matter for policy outcomes. Large majorities say that Congress is "generally out of touch with average Americans" and that "people in government" do not "understand what most Americans think." See Steven Kull and Clay Ramsay, "How Policymakers Misperceive U.S. Public Opinion on Foreign Policy," in *Navigating Public Opinion*, eds. Jeff Manza, Fay Lomax Cook, and Benjamin I. Page (Oxford: Oxford University Press, 2002), pp. 201–18.
42. For discussions of the causality question, see Gilens, "Inequality and Democratic Responsiveness," 789–93; Brandice Canes-Wrone, *Who Leads Whom? Presidents, Policy, and the Public* (Chicago, IL: University of Chicago Press, 2005); Kim Quaile Hill and Angela Hinton-Andersson, "Pathways of Representation: A Causal Analysis of Public Opinion-Policy Linkages," *American Journal of Political Science* 39 (1995): 924–35; Stimson et al., "Dynamic Representation," p. 546.
43. Page and Shapiro, *The Rational Public*, Chapter 9.
44. Lawrence Jacobs and Robert Y. Shapiro, "Politics and Policymaking in the Real World: Crafted Talk and the Loss of Democratic Responsiveness," in *Navigating Public Opinion*, eds. Jeff Manza, Fay Lomax Cook, and Benjamin I. Page (Oxford: Oxford University Press, 2002), 54–75.
45. James Druckman, "The Implications of Framing Effects for Citizen Competence," *Political Behavior* 23 (2001): 225–56.
46. Hill and Hinton-Andersson, "Pathways of Representation."
47. Stimson et al., "Dynamic Representation," p. 559.
48. Jacobs and Shapiro, "Politics and Policymaking in the Real World."
49. Fiorina, *Disconnect.*
50. Paul J. Quirk, "Politicians Do Pander: Mass Opinion, Polarization, and Law Making," *The Forum* 7 (2009), retrieved from http://www.bepress.com/forum/vol. 7/iss4/art10/.
51. Stephen Ansolabehere, James M. Snyder Jr., and Charles Stewart III, "Candidate Positioning in U.S. House Elections," *American Journal of Political Science* 45 (2001): 136–59; Page and Shapiro, "Effects of Public Opinion on Policy."
52. Ansolabehere et al., "Candidate Positioning in U.S. House Elections"; Monroe, "Public Opinion and Public Policy, 1980–1993."

53. For a tabulation of the major results, and an argument that the literature is not definitive on the question of changes in responsiveness over time, see Burstein, "The Impact of Public Opinion on Public Policy."
54. Miller and Stokes, "Constituency Influence in Congress"; Page and Shapiro, "Effects of Public Opinion on Policy."
55. Dahl, *Who Governs?*, p. 3.
56. See also the report of the APSA Task Force on Inequality and American Democracy, *American Democracy in an Age of Rising Inequality: Report of the American Political Science Association Task Force on Inequality and American Democracy* (Washington, DC: American Political Science Association, 2004), retrieved from http://www.apsanet.org/imgtest/taskforcereport.pdf.
57. Gilens, "Inequality and Democratic Responsiveness."
58. Bartels, *Unequal Democracy*, Chapter 9.
59. Lawrence R. Jacobs and Benjamin I. Page, "Who Influences U.S. Foreign Policy?" *American Political Science Review* 99 (2005): 107–23.
60. James Druckman and Lawrence R. Jacobs, "Segmented Representation: The Reagan White House and Disproportionate Responsiveness," in *Who Gets Represented?* eds. Peter Enns and Christopher Wlezien (New York: Russell Sage Foundation, 2011), 166–88.
61. Elizabeth Rigby and Gerald C. Wright, "Whose Statehouse Democracy? Policy Responsiveness to Poor versus Rich Constituents in Poor versus Rich States," in *Who Gets Represented?* eds. Peter Enns and Christopher Wlezien (New York: Russell Sage Foundation, 2011), 189–222.
62. John D. Griffin and Brian Newman, "Are Voters Better Represented?" *Journal of Politics* 67 (2005): 1206–27.
63. Kim Quaile Hill and Jan E. Leighley, "The Policy Consequences of Class Bias in State Electorates," *American Journal of Political Science* 36 (1992): 351–65.
64. Martin Gilens, "Interest Groups and Inequality in Democratic Responsiveness in the U.S.," Prepared for the Annual Meetings of the American Political Science Association, Toronto, Ontario, September 3–6, 2009.
65. Stuart N. Soroka and Christopher Wlezien, "On the Limits to Inequality in Representation," *PS: Political Science and Politics* 41 (2008): 319–27.
66. Martin Gilens, "Preference Gaps and Inequality in Representation," *PS: Political Science and Politics* 42 (2009): 335–41.
67. Patrick Flavin, "Differences in Income, Policy Preferences, and Priorities in American Public Opinion," Presented at the annual meeting of the Midwest Political Science Association in Chicago, April 2–5, 2009.
68. Rigby and Wright, *Whose Statehouse Democracy?*
69. Bartels, "The Opinion–Policy Disconnect."
70. Fay Lomax Cook and Edith J. Barrett, *Support for the American Welfare State: The Views of Congress and the Public* (New York: Columbia University Press, 1992).
71. Zaller, "Coming to Grips."
72. E.E. Schattschneider, *Politics, Pressures, and the Tariff* (New York: Prentice-Hall, 1935), 288.
73. Christopher Wlezien, "The Public as Thermostat: Dynamics of Preferences for Spending," *American Journal of Political Science* 39 (1995): 981–1000.
74. Stimson, *Tides of Consent*.
75. Helen Ingram and Anne Schneider, "Constructing Citizenship: The Subtle Messages of Policy Design," in *Public Policy for Democracy*, eds. Helen Ingram and Steven Rathgeb Smith (Washington, DC: Brookings, 1993), 68–97; Paul Pierson, "When Effect Becomes Cause: Policy Feedback and Political Change," *World Politics* 45 (1993): 595–628.

76. Andrea L. Campbell, *How Policies Make Citizens: Senior Political Activism and the American Welfare State* (Princeton, NJ: Princeton University Press, 2003).
77. Joseph Soss, "Lessons of Welfare: Policy Design, Political Learning, and Political Action," *American Political Science Review* 93 (1999): 363–80.
78. Campbell, *How Policies Make Citizens*; Soss, "Lessons of Welfare."
79. Christopher Howard, *The Hidden Welfare State: Tax Expenditures and Social Policy in the United States* (Princeton, NJ: Princeton University Press, 1997).
80. Suzanne Mettler, "Visible Lessons: How Experiences of Higher Education Policies Influence Participation in Politics," unpublished manuscript, Cornell University, November 2, 2009.
81. Material in this section is adapted from Kimberly J. Morgan and Andrea Louise Campbell, *The Delegated Welfare State* (New York: Oxford University Press, forthcoming).
82. Wlezien, "The Public as Thermostat," although for a contrasting view (the public as contractionist during bad economic times), see Cindy D. Kam and Yunju Nam, "Reaching Out or Pulling Back: Macroeconomic Conditions and Public Support for Social Welfare Spending," *Political Behavior* 30 (2008): 223–58.
83. C.f. Arnold, *The Logic of Congressional Action.*
84. James R. Knickman and Emily K. Snell, "The 2030 Problem: Caring for Aging Baby-Boomers," *Health Services Research* 37 (2002): 849–84.
85. Dana Gelb Safran, Patricia Neuman, Cathy Schoen, and Michelle S. Kitchman, "Prescription Drug Coverage and Seniors: Findings from a 2003 National Survey," *Health Affairs Web Exclusive* 24 (January to June 2005): W5–W19.
86. Robert B. Friedland, "The Coverage Puzzle: How The Pieces Fit Together," Paper presented at the National Academy of Social Insurance annual conference, Washington, DC, 2002.
87. Campbell, *How Policies Make Citizens.*
88. *ABC News* Poll, May 7–9, 2000 and based on 1013 telephone interviews. Sample: national adult. [USABC.051000.R6]. Accessed from the Roper Center Public Opinion Archives July 2, 2010.
89. Andrea L. Campbell and Robert H. Binstock, "Politics and Aging in the United States," in *Handbook of Aging and the Social Sciences*, 7th edition, eds. Robert H. Binstock and Linda K. George (Boston, MA: Academic Press, 2010), 265–79.
90. Republicans did create a managed care program—Medicare Advantage—by increasing subsidies to insurers to 114 percent of traditional Medicare in order to lure them back into the Medicare market. Most Medicare Advantage health plans do cover prescription drugs—although as stated that is not the only way to get drug coverage—and, as of 2010, about one-quarter of seniors had enrolled (Kaiser Family Foundation, "Medicare Advantage 2010 Data Spotlight: Plan Enrollment Patterns and Trends," June 2010, retrieved from http://www.kff.org/medicare/upload/8080.pdf).
91. The assumption from the beginning, even under Clinton, was that the drug benefit would be voluntary. An earlier attempt to expand Medicare benefits to cap annual catastrophic costs, a mandatory benefit expansion financed by increases in Medicare premiums and a tax surcharge on the most affluent 40 percent of seniors, was met with a firestorm of protest and repealed by Congress 17 months after its 1988 enactment (Richard Himelfarb, *Catastrophic Politics: The Rise and Fall of the Medicare Catastrophic Coverage Act of 1988* (University Park, PA: Pennsylvania State University Press, 1995)). But making the drug benefit voluntary would induce adverse selection—only those with high drug needs would enroll—undermining the insurance concept. Hence the late enrollment penalty was introduced to encourage healthier seniors to enroll, expanding the risk pool.

92. Quoted in Robert Pear, "Some Senators Fear Employers Will Drop Retirees' Drug Plans," *New York Times*, June 14, 2003, Section A, 12.
93. Morgan and Campbell, *The Delegated Welfare State.*
94. Y. Hanoc, T. Rice, J. Cummings, and S. Wood, "How Much Choice is too Much? The Case of the Medicare Prescription Drug Benefit," *Health Services Research* 44 (2009): 1157–68.
95. Jack Hoadley, Juliette Cubanski, Elizabeth Hargrove, Laura Summer, and Tricia Neuman, "Part D Plan Availability in 2010 and Key Changes since 2006," Kaiser Family Foundation, November 2009, retrieved from http://www.kff.org/medicare/upload/7986.pdf.
96. Herbert A. Simon, *Reason in Human Affairs* (Stanford, CA: Stanford University Press, 1983).
97. Kaiser Family Foundation, "Prescription Drug Trends," May 2010, p. 5, retrieved from http://www.kff.org/rxdrugs/upload/3057–08.pdf.
98. Morgan and Campbell, *The Delegated Welfare State.*
99. Although the health care reform passed in 2010 does gradually fix the donut hole coverage gap—perhaps the most egregious problem with the benefit from a health perspective, as some seniors cut their doses or stop taking their medicines altogether when they hit the donut.
100. P. Neuman, M.K. Strollos, S. Guterman, W.H. Roger, A. Li, A.M.C. Rodday, and D.G. Safran, "Medicare Prescription Drug Benefit Progress Report: Findings From a 2006 National Survey of Seniors," *Health Affairs* 26 (2007):W630–43; J.T. Abaluck and J. Gruber. "Choice Inconsistencies Among the Elderly: Evidence from Plan Choice in the Medicare Part D Program," *NBER Working Paper 14759*, February 2009, retrieved from http://www.nber.org/papers/w14759.
101. Morgan and Campbell, *The Delegated Welfare State.*
102. Joseph Soss and Sanford F. Schram, "A Public Transformed? Welfare Reform as Policy Feedback," in *Remaking America: Democracy and Public Policy in an Age of Inequality*, eds. Joseph Soss, Jacob S. Hacker, and Suzanne Mettler (New York: Russell Sage, 2007), 99–118.

Conclusion

Assessing Continuity and Change

David O. Sears

Formal academic survey research on public opinion about politics began in the 1940s. In the early years, several milestone projects were published that not only set the agenda for later researchers, but pointed the way. Here we are, seven decades later, and research has burgeoned in the interim. The authors of this collection have done a wonderful job, in my judgment, of summarizing the current state of the art (and science).

The question I have set for myself in this concluding chapter is to assess the "new directions" part of this work's title. Pioneers sometimes stake out the territory so thoroughly that little remains for those who follow but to fill in the gaps with predictable results. If that has been the case, surely great disappointment would reign in the halls of the National Science Foundation.

But sometimes the founding paradigm(s) are challenged by new perspectives. And sometimes the external environment changes in ways that force us to rethink the conventional wisdom. In some cases, even, the pioneers had it wrong. After all, Europeans named native Americans "Indians" believing they had reached "India," not North America. And sometimes vast territories are ignored by pioneers and only later become recognized for what they are. Sixteenth and seventeenth century maps of North America remain exquisitely detailed and accurate for the Atlantic coastline, and even a few miles inland, but beyond that, it was all *terra incognito.*

So I will attempt to assess the relative balance of continuity and change in the chapters of this volume. As might be expected, all of these possibilities are true in some respects. I hope I can do justice to the nuanced and extensive treatments of the topics covered by the authors. For convenience I have grouped the research covered in this volume into six categories: voting behavior; campaigns and media effects; personality, motivation, and emotion; social groups in mass politics; the effects of changes in society exogenous to academic research on politics; and the implications of this research for the quality of democratic governance.

The Pioneers

The earliest major academic studies of public opinion and voting behavior were, of course, those of Paul Lazarsfeld and his sociological colleagues at Columbia University. They conducted studies of two limited communities, and emphasized the stability through presidential campaigns of voting preferences rooted in demographic differences and primary group relationships. They found disappointingly slim returns from an ambitious examination of propaganda and media influence. Those latter findings were later generalized by Klapper's influential 1960 literature review on the effects of mass communications.[1] He concluded that under normal circumstances they effectively reinforced prior attitudes rather than changing them very much, a viewpoint that later became known as the "minimal effects model." In my classes I usually contrast this view with a slim 1939 volume called *The Fine Art of Propaganda* which in a more qualitative style detailed the "tricks of the trade" that purportedly gave artful propagandists like Father Charles Coughlin and Joseph Goebbels such powerful sway over gullible mass publics.[2]

A radically different style of research using nationally representative sample surveys came to some overlapping, and some different, conclusions with the publication in 1960 of *The American Voter*.[3] It developed a systematic theory of voting behavior later known as "the Michigan School," since all four authors were professors at the University of Michigan. This early work of political science largely replaced sociology with both politics and individual psychology as the starring players in the story, but with a similar underlying theme: that individual voting preferences were not easily changed. The primary reason they gave, however, was that voting choices and many other features of political public opinion were organized by powerful attachments to the political parties, "party identification," that were acquired early in life and rarely changed very much in later years.

In both early versions of the voting literature, social groups were treated centrally, especially as being the fundamental grounding for attachments to the parties. The Lazarsfeld volumes tended to emphasize demographic groups such as social class or religious denominations, measured with objective group membership, as the vehicle for their influence. *The American Voter* adopted the more social psychological concept of reference group influence, measured with subjective orientations such as group identification and perceived group norms, as a way to analyze the political impact of social class, labor unions, and other such groups.

In that era, the study of personality had become a flourishing field within the discipline of psychology. Personality assessment had been the dominant activity of clinical psychologists, psychoanalytic theory was much in vogue among intellectuals, and personality was such a strong focus of attention that the premiere journal for social psychologists was renamed the "Journal of

Personality and Social Psychology." Perhaps the most visible research project for psychologists with an interest in politics was Adorno et al.'s *The Authoritarian Personality*, developing the thesis that anti-semitism (and a variety of other disapproved political attitudes) had its immediate roots in personality dispositions.[4] However neither the Columbia nor the Michigan schools, different as they were, paid much attention to personality differences. Nonetheless the personality and politics paradigm did become perhaps the most visible contribution of psychology as a discipline to the general domain of political behavior.

Finally, because of the apparent indifference of the voters to much of the substance of political campaigns, except perhaps as rationalizations for decisions made much earlier, both the Columbia and Michigan studies created great complications for those who wished to defend democratic citizenries' capabilities for governing their own affairs. These studies were widely interpreted as sharply questioning the competence of democratic citizens to govern themselves. Many were forced to fall back, with a depressed sigh, on Churchill's famous dictum that "democracy is the worst form of government except for all the others that have been tried."

Voting Behavior

One consequence of the pioneers' efforts in the area of voting behavior was a growing gap between political behavioralists, who saw relatively little impact of campaigns, and media commentators and campaign consultants, whose livelihood depended on asserting their effectiveness. Did the pioneers get it right? Put another way, to what extent and where do we see continuity or change? Where do we see "new directions" in this domain? Here I am relying principally on the chapters by Baum, Hetherington, and Sides and Haselswerdt.

For one thing, individual voters' preferences in presidential elections remain highly predictable from measures that can be assessed long before the formal general election campaigns begin in September, on the basis of demographic differences and party identification. In a way the case for that predictability is even stronger today than it was decades ago, given the subsequent discovery that independent "leaners" resemble partisans more than they do "true independents"—as discussed in the Sides and Haselswerdt chapter. Moreover, party identification is the most stable of political attitudes, and the most powerful influence on other attitudes, as Hetherington demonstrates. It remains the single most important individual attitude in American mass politics.

However party identification is not so tidily ascribed to parental influence as once thought, for three reasons. Some parents are disengaged from politics, and have little lasting influence on their children. The embeddedness of party identification in social groups, such as racial or religious groups, means that some will realign their party identifications more appropriately with their other group attachments later in life. And there is evidence that the individual's early political experiences may foster some departures from parental norms, as discussed in Hetherington's chapter.

Campaigns and Media Effects

The Sides and Haselswerdt chapter is a useful analysis of current perspectives on campaign influences. Reinforcement remains more common than persuasion in presidential elections. But researchers pay more attention today than did the pioneers to lower profile elections, such as primaries, sub-presidential elections, or ballot propositions. Persuasion via the media seems to be more common in those cases than in presidential general elections. Perhaps Klapper would have anticipated that from his lesser-known principle,[5] that change is more common when "mediating factors," such as group norms, party identification, and selective reception, are absent. In such cases the voter's policy preferences and personality may have more influence, even though party identification still dominates when relevant. A surrogate for media attention, the money spent by a campaign, similarly seems to have more influence on races for other offices down the ballot, and for congressional challengers. And there is evidence that priming attention to the economy by a campaign can influence the outcome. Get-out-the-vote campaigns can also influence the outcome sometimes.

In the end, party identification, a highly stable attitude, still is by far the single most powerful influence on individual voting decisions, especially in presidential elections. But the conditions under which campaigns, as principally conveyed through the media, have important effects are clearer now than they were in the 1950s and 1960s. In that sense the gap between political behaviorists' tendency to downplay the effectiveness of campaigns, and campaign consultants' trumpeting of their own successes, seems to have diminished. Money and tactics play a role in campaigns, but voters are far more than passive recipients of ads and strategies, contrary to the view developed in *The Fine Art*.

The Baum chapter more directly presents a contemporary view of media influence in politics. Nevertheless, there is much that is familiar from the earlier reign of the minimal effects model. The old idea of selective exposure is back with a vengeance, with slumping audiences for nominally neutral mainstream media such as newspapers and network news, and increased attention to highly partisan new media such as cable television and the blogosphere. Selective interpretation, reflected in partisan credibility assessments, catches whatever slips through the selective exposure net, leading to further reinforcement of the voter's prior preferences. That would be a familiar world for the old advocates of the minimal effects model. Nevertheless, we are cautioned, the audience for the new media tends disproportionately to be highly ideological and small. As Baum says, that makes them better for preaching to the choir than for converting the flock.

What has changed in public response to the media, then? There is perhaps greater recognition of individual differences in such obstacles to persuasion, with stronger partisans considerably more selective in exposure and interpretation than weaker partisans (though with the complication that the latter are less likely to pay attention to politics). On the other hand, the large audiences for normally apolitical entertainment television are quite vulnerable to political persuasion on the rare occasions when politics arises, given the absence of those pesky "mediating factors." Zaller's "RAS" model nicely balances reception and acceptance as sometimes conflicting influences on persuasion.[6] There also is greater appreciation for elites' and campaigns' ability to prime the issues they "own" and thereby swing things their way. Vavreck supplies a useful analysis of how differently the 2000 Gore and 2008 Obama campaigns dealt with the economy, with the latter pounding on the dismal Republican record, and the former perhaps passing up the opportunity to boast about the strong Democratic record.[7]

Another change is greater attention to elites' behavior as a central factor in the mass public's response. In the pioneers' day, there was considerable ideological overlap between the two parties, at both the elite and mass level. Hetherington's chapter reviews the profound changes in party elites over the past half century, describing the general consensus that they are far more politically polarized than was the case in the pioneers' day. There is some dispute about whether the mass public has become more polarized as well, but little argument about the fact that the public has in response sorted itself into ideologically more consistent camps, with Democrats being more liberal and Republicans more consistently conservative. This sorting process seems to have penetrated far beyond partisan politics even into preferences for different sports (Republican NASCAR fans, and Democratic soccer fans) or entertainment shows.

Why have voters more consistently sorted themselves out by party? Partly it is because elites are more polarized, and so offer voters more polarized choices, as Fiorina says.[8] But hot button issues, especially those with a link to race (such as black candidates or affirmative action or welfare) or religiously based moral traditionalism (such as abortion or gay rights) have become more prominent, which excite the base and attract the cross-pressured. Cable and the Internet, which have relatively small audiences (though overrepresenting the politically attentive), facilitate sorting. The civil rights movement, once it had finally been endorsed by the Democratic White House in 1963, broke the old anomalous race-centered party system in the south, sorting most white southerners into the Republican party and almost all black southerners into the Democratic party.

The political implications of these changes are profound. As Hetherington points out, an elite committee of the APSA in 1950 advocated the strengthening of the two major political parties, which at the time were often charged to be so similar that they were described as "Tweedledee and Tweedledum." APSA! Be careful what you wish for! The increased strength of party identification at all levels has had a paralyzingly powerful impact in Congress and legislative halls in state capitals all over the country. Yet Baum reminds us that the parties and media were highly polarized a century ago, so perhaps the anomaly is the period immediately after World War II. That is when empirical political behavior research first began to flourish and so perhaps looms larger than it should.

Groups in Politics

Another theme in this volume concerns groups in politics, as reflected in the chapters by Jane Junn, Tali Mendelberg, and Erica Czaja; Nancy Burns and Donald Kinder; and David Campbell, Geoffrey Layman, and John Green. Again we see both clear continuities and some marked changes.

The pioneers did not take a uniform view of how groups operated in politics. *The People's Choice*[9] took objective demographic categories—membership groups—as key influences on the vote. *Voting*[10] broadened that perspective to examine the direct social influence of primary groups, especially in the families and the workplaces of the moderate-sized community it studied. *The American Voter*,[11] using reference group theory, examined subjective orientations toward secondary groups such as social class, labor unions, and religious denominations. Other Michigan studies in the same vein examined closeness to secondary groups as a factor in the vote, and placed groups, rather than conventional ideologies, as the central feature of most voters' thinking.[12]

Much has changed in how groups are treated in the political science literature. Most notably, the reality has changed. Race, gender, and religiosity have become more central to American politics, and justifiably have a large footprint in this volume. In the 1950s blacks were almost politically invisible, largely prevented from voting in the south and concentrated in a few large metropolitan areas in the north, often with low participation rates.[13] The Columbia studies focused on moderate-sized communities with few blacks. Blacks made only a cameo appearance in *The American Voter*, and almost none at all as a group affecting whites' votes. Women were generally assumed simply to double their husbands' votes. Religion was thought to influence politics primarily through the partisan allegiance of Catholics and Jews to the New Deal Coalition, and northern Protestants to the Republicans. Individual differences in religiosity did receive modest attention in *The American Voter*, but the real spotlight on that variable came only in the Michigan team's later account of the 1960 election, which presciently put the spotlight on variations in religiosity within Protestant and Catholic denominations.[14] With the possible exception of *The American Voter*'s interest in labor unions, none treated interest groups as proactive motivators, organizers, and mobilizers. Even European ethnic groups did not receive much attention in those early works, despite their prominence in the political machines of the day.

That soon changed, as the politics of the 1960s were full of mobilization of groups in the mass public. The civil rights struggle received the earliest attention, especially with the passage of the Civil Rights Act in 1964 and the Voting Rights Act in 1965. Accordingly the Michigan account of the 1964 election put race front and center.[15] It was soon followed by a resurgent feminist movement, Chicano and Asian American movements, and later the Christian right, and lower-keyed advocacy on behalf of the elderly, disabled, gun owners, immigrants, children, and animals. Those political movements have especially brought race, gender, and religion forcefully to our attention. That revised story is what we see in this volume.

I would offer a somewhat more general interpretation of the change than do the current authors. The massive grassroots civil rights movement of the 1950s and early 1960s was the model for the entry of these other groups into mass politics, both as agents and as targets. Blacks themselves became the models for the understanding of group consciousness and activism within other groups, and whites' responses to blacks became the models for understanding opposition to other group-based movements. So, for example, the key concepts that Junn, Czaja, and Mendelberg use for understanding non-European ethnic groups such as Hispanics and Asians are drawn from research focusing on blacks: prejudice and discrimination, identity and group consciousness, linked fate, and the black utility heuristic. But they add a focus on understanding the political incorporation of such heavily immigrant groups, not a factor particularly central to blacks today or to other groups in the 1950s. The Nancy Burns and Donald Kinder chapter is explicitly framed around a comparison of gender with race.

Comparing blacks with Hispanics, Asians, and women highlights the distinctiveness of blacks as a political group in America, in my view—what we have called "black exceptionalism."[16] Despite the obvious similarities between women and blacks, in terms of discrimination and exclusion, Burns and Kinder find major differences between the two groups. The "gender gap," however persistent, is far smaller than the racial divide on racial issues. Blacks show much stronger group identification, common fate, and anger than do women, and root their attitudes about issues that affect them collectively more strongly in group consciousness. That is, black group consciousness is more prevalent, stronger, and more politically potent than is the case for women's gender consciousness. Burns and Kinder quite reasonably ascribe that to the contrasting forms of social organization for the two groups, especially the unusually strong segregation of blacks from whites and, in contrast, the intimate relations that most women have with men. Intimate relations with an out-group impair both in-group solidarity and hostility toward the out-group, whereas separation stimulates them. One recent political consequence is that racial resentment was a much stronger influence on anti-Obama attitudes in 2008 than gender resentment was on anti-Hillary Clinton attitudes.[17]

Indeed blacks prove not to be as helpful a model for understanding even other racial or ethnic groups as one might think. I would interpret Junn, Mendelberg, and Cjaza's examination of Asians and Latinos as yielding further evidence of black exceptionalism. As already mentioned, they borrow the language of black group consciousness, using terms like common fate, etc.[18] But Asians are much less likely to use the term "Asian American" to describe their own identities than blacks are to use "African American."[19] The acquisition of partisan identification among Latinos and Asians depends more on the length of time they have been in the country than the standard processes of socialization described by *The American Voter*, which continue to dominate among both blacks and whites. Moreover, blacks are the most homogeneously Democratic group in the nation, whereas both Asians and Latinos are considerably more divided. For example, Japanese Americans and Mexican Americans are quite Democratic, and Vietnamese and Cuban Americans strongly tilt Republican. SES does not create divisions in African Americans' strong support for policies benefiting blacks, but higher social class does reduce Asians' and Latinos' support for policies particularly benefiting their groups.

In other words, the origins of public opinion for African Americans differ in numerous ways from its origins among Latinos and Asians, due to the different historical circumstances these groups have faced over time. The life circumstances of blacks in the United States have always been quite unique, and today those exceptional circumstances continue to make black public opinion distinctive.

Finally, links between party and a social group may be quite durable, even if not permanent, as Burns and Kinder say. For example, the racial divide in partisanship has expanded sharply since the 1950s, reaching an all-time high in 2008, presumably due to the unique circumstance of an election pitting a black major party candidate against a white one.[20] The Campbell, Layman, and Green chapter on the link between religious beliefs and party identification, however, is a useful caution that the conventional wisdom about the link of group membership to issue positions may easily be oversimplified. Religiosity is not always associated with conservative issue attitudes, any more than blacks are more liberal than whites on all issues.

Another example of the sometimes dynamic nature of the link between groups and parties is one that, somewhat surprisingly, does not show up in this volume. Geographic divides have received much popular attention over the past several presidential elections, given the ubiquity of the blue-state vs. red-state maps. In the immediate postwar period, the south (the former Confederacy) was almost solidly Democratic in presidential elections, whereas today it is heavily Republican. Why? The reason is instructive. The best evidence is that the switch has much to do with the peculiar historical circumstance surrounding race, that first slavery, and then formalized discrimination, lasted far longer, and was embedded in local institutions more thoroughly, in the south than elsewhere. During the 1960s the national Democratic party abandoned its long-time protection of white supremacy, with the consequence that the more racially conservative white south gradually shifted heavily to the Republican party.[21]

Personality, Motivation, and Emotion

Personality, motivation, and emotion were central topics for personality and social psychologists in the 1950s and early 1960s. *The Authoritarian Personality* by Adorno and colleagues used both depth interviews and questionnaires to link underlying personality traits to political and social attitudes.[22] In political science, Herbert McClosky developed a pioneering analysis linking political conservatism to a variety of unappealing personality traits.[23] The term "political psychology" was probably linked most closely in political scientists' minds to exactly that kind of "personality and politics" work, linking personality traits to political attitudes.[24]

However such analyses soon fell out of favor. *The Authoritarian Personality* was excoriated by sociological critics steeped in the ways of survey research, a bashing from which it never fully recovered.[25] *The American Voter* scarcely mentions personality at all as a factor in presidential voting. Philip Converse challenged the presumption that wide-ranging ideological belief systems were widespread in the mass public, shedding some doubts about bold claims that such quasi-political attitudes as ethnocentrism, xenophobia, or authoritarianism were strongly grounded in personality.[26] Within the discipline of psychology, Walter Mischel published a widely heralded challenge to the notion that personality traits had powerful trans-situational effects on behavior, dampening the interest of many personality and social psychologists in pursuing them.[27] It was soon followed by the "cognitive revolution" in social psychology, which sought purely cognitive, non-affective explanations for errors and biases in judgment. The very idea of stable, consistent personality traits itself became disparaged as an artefact of cognitively based errors of perceivers' judgments, described as the "fundamental attribution error."[28]

As often happens, personality analyses cycled back into vogue in the 1990s with the growing attention to the "Big Five" personality inventory.[29] As Federico indicates in his treatment of contemporary research on ideology, reappearing in public opinion research was a revisionist "right-wing authoritarianism," centered more in social learning theory than in psychoanalytic theory, developed by Robert Altemeyer.[30] A re-do of the old McClosky personality and conservatism argument was a controversial article by John Jost, Arie Kruglanski, and Jack Glaser that treated political conservatism as a product of motivated reasoning, in which ideological conservatism eased anxieties aroused by ambiguity and uncertainty.[31]

Most recently, studies of both personality and public opinion have seen a resurgence of interest in their possible genetic determinants, based on twin studies. Jeffery Mondak and Matthew Hibbing take an unusually strong position on the biological basis of personality, its durability through the life span, and its broad effects on behavior. This position is quite contrary to earlier dominant views of personality, whether the 1950s-era view of its origins in early experience, or the situationism of the 1980s that tended to downplay the role of personality in determining behavior. However, Mondak and Hibbing's findings are not very clear on the absolute strength of the association of personality with political attitudes. Other research on the political linkages of the Big Five often has found rather weak associations.

These forays into the personality determinants of ideology have come more from the discipline of psychology than from political science. In general they assume the widespread existence of an underlying left–right ideological dimension in the mass public, perhaps based in two sub-dimensions, of equality vs. inequality and openness vs. order, and that ideology is coherently associated with personality. Psychologists have generally not integrated such assumptions with political scientists' long history of research, going back to Converse's classic paper, indicating that the coherence of public opinion and the understanding of conventional political ideologies are much greater among political elites than in the public as a whole.[32] For example, the "top of the head" view of survey responses promoted by John Zaller and Stanley Feldman would not lead us to expect strongly coherent policy preferences emerging from either ideology or personality.[33]

Christopher Federico does cite this line of research, acknowledging that citizens' preferences are usually not firmly based in ideological commitments, and that any sub-dimensions of ideology are likely to be more coherently reflected in the thinking of elites and the attentive public than in that of the average voter. Similarly, Mondak and Hibbing qualify their strong assertions about the biological basis of personality somewhat by speculating that biology may matter more for broad, general orientations and predispositions than for specific issue positions. But squaring that view with research questioning the ubiquity of broad ideological liberalism or conservatism is a project for the future. Perhaps that lack of integration is in part due to the unrepresentative participant pools often used by psychologists, such as college students or individuals closely attuned to political blogs.[34] Mondak and Hibbing supply little detail about the survey they rely on, but such Internet surveys sometimes overstate the constraint of political attitudes with other orientations because of oversampling the politically interested. In any case, the role of personality in public opinion is difficult to assess absent more precise integration of those two literatures. One possible avenue of reconciliation may lie in Converse's later observation that information has a low mean but high variance in the general public.[35] Psychologists' assertions about personality and ideology rarely acknowledge either reality, however.

Finally, the attention to discrete emotions in Ted Brader's chapter is another clear "new direction." In the pioneers' day, affect was generally treated by attitude researchers as a single bipolar dimension ranging from positive to negative. Discrete emotional reactions were generally treated as slight variations on the general evaluative theme, even in semantic meaning or impression formation.[36] More complex theories of emotion with roots in contemporary biological and evolutionary theorizing, such as theories of "fight or flight," have led to a richer sense of emotional expression. The case Brader makes for the differential political effects of diverse discrete emotions is impressive. Diverse emotions, he finds, can differentially affect exposure to and learning of information, party loyalty, style of information processing, and even political participation.

Exogenous Changes

Not all changes in the account of public opinion given by academic researchers come from changes endogenous to their scholarly fields, such as fresh theories or new empirical findings. To some extent change is also produced by factors quite exogenous to academic research. Three such changes are examined in this volume: increased rate of immigration (Junn, Mendelberg, and Czaja), the structure of the media (Matthew Baum), and technological changes that have influenced methods of collecting data on public opinion (D. Sunshine Hillygus).

Change in the ethnic composition of the nation has been perhaps the most dramatic external change that has directly affected public opinion. Extensive immigration from Latin America and Asia has resulted in a rapid diversification of the nation. That immigration was not dreamed of by the pioneers of our field, and was even unanticipated by those who wrote the enabling legislation in the mid-1960s. I have already discussed how that has changed our treatment of race. Any simple effort to model an analysis of public opinion among Latinos and Asians on public opinion among African Americans, the major racial minority group extant in the 1950s, would go awry. Arguably a closer analogue would be the European immigrants of a century ago, and their descendants. Generation in the United States would be a stronger predictor of many political outcome variables than the subjective orientations so important in analyses of black opinion, consistent with what Junn, Mendelberg, and Cjaza have written. It is more of an open question as to whether Latinos and Asians as targets of others' opinions can be understood in the same terms as African Americans.[37]

Changes in the media over time represent another important exogenous change that influences the story we tell about public opinion. One central set of changes has been in the way the public gets political news. Most obvious has been diminishing newspaper readership and audiences for network news programs. Both newspapers and network news have generally reflected somewhat balanced and moderate political viewpoints, and attracted broad audiences across the political spectrum, at least in the period since World War II. Instead now there are surging numbers of cable outlets, political blogs on the Internet, and high profile radio talk shows. These outlets prominently feature stridently partisan political views, and seem to invite highly selective exposure. Baum would also include the growing importance of the more sporadically presented "soft news" in entertainment programs such as *Saturday Night Live*, *Oprah*, *David Letterman*, or *Jon Stewart*.

These changes probably have not greatly enlarged the store of political information in the general public, nor led to more informed political choices. Rather, they seem to have led to increased polarization, certainly of elites and very likely of the more politically attentive members of the public. They are part of what Herbst notes is the yin and yang of the atomized, as opposed to communal, public, perhaps reflecting a swing back to the latter. Audiences for political cable or radio talk shows or for particular blogospheres are members of new communities, if often imagined ones rather than face to face, quite unlike newspaper readers or the viewers of network news, who remain very much on their own in trying to make sense of the complexities of the political world.

Exogenous changes have also affected the very gathering of data on public opinion that we all rely on. As Hillygus says, there is a proliferation of polls, but people have become harder to reach. Here too we see a blend of continuity and change. Immediately after World War II, quota sampling, community based samples, and face to face interviewing were the norm, at least for academic surveys. That soon evolved to probability sampling and national samples. Later on, telephone surveys began to replace face to face home interviews, as costs began to escalate. Response rates began to fall. Now we are entering an era of landline only, or landline plus cell phone, telephone samples, with very low response rates, or, as she puts it, opt-out or opt-in online samples, where sometimes even the concept of a response rate may not apply.

Encouraging research progress has been made in identifying the sources of error in public opinion surveys beyond sampling error. Hillygus touches on some and on the notion of "total survey error," and is justly critical of the media for publishing polls without mentioning the numerous other possible sources of error. Among them are our editor's ingenious ways of determining that on some racial items, "don't know" responses may serve to conceal socially undesirable underlying racial attitudes.[38] I must note, however, that the measures of racial resentment or symbolic racism often used by political psychologists draw almost no "don't know" responses, presumably because they do not measure prejudice very blatantly.[39] That is yet another reason to believe that they are particularly valid measures of underlying racism.[40] Full disclosure compels me to reveal ongoing research in which we find that some other commonly used measures (the ANES thermometer and stereotype measures) are particularly vulnerable to error, presumably because they *do* measure prejudice against stigmatized racial groups so blatantly.[41]

Hillygus goes on to the wise conclusion that every survey is flawed in some way or another, though some more than others, which she neatly summarizes by contrasting the "gold" vs. the "tin" standards of survey excellence. However, I think she does not go far enough. It is usually not possible to assess the actual bias introduced by any given factor in any given survey, because we can't compare the results with those produced with the potentially biasing factor absent. We can, however, cite other (sometimes experimental) research that has assessed the biasing effects of that factor elsewhere. Then we can speculate that the procedures used in our survey may have introduced the biasing effects of that factor. However the best we can usually do is to speculate. The only real way to assess the degree of bias is to see if the same results are replicated with surveys using different methods. Let me repeat the point for emphasis. Since no survey is perfect, and since we cannot normally assess biases within any given survey, the only way to be sure of our findings is to see if they replicate in other surveys that are done differently.

Hillygus does use this true gold standard criterion of replication with telling effect when appraising the effects of falling response rates. She properly suggests that dwindling survey response rates may not be as severe a problem as we feared a couple of decades ago. Some careful studies have shown that survey findings are quite similar if otherwise identical surveys are allowed to have either higher or lower response rates. At least that is the current wisdom.

However, excuse me for a mild tut-tut. Falling response rates have driven many to an interest in the new technology of online surveys, obviously not available in the 1950s. One might welcome application of the same replication criterion in the comparison of "opt-out" online surveys, of the sort Knowledge Networks uses, with "opt-in" online surveys, of the sort YouGov/Polimetrix uses. Hillygus praises the former for using probability sampling, and rejects the latter for using a distant cousin of the quota sampling discredited as a result of the 1948 debacle (remember the *Chicago Tribune* headline, "Dewey defeats Truman").

With the editor's indulgence, I will immodestly (but blushingly) cite our own research as an example of using replication as the primary criterion for assessing methodological biases. Our recent analysis of the 2008 presidential election compares the YouGov/Polimetrix online "opt-in" CCAP survey, with over 18,000 cases, with the putative "gold standard" ANES, based on a far smaller sample.[42] In all but one case, the major findings are almost identical. The exception concerns the findings for Latinos, where the small ANES subsample would probably lead most of us not to be surprised by less than perfectly reliable findings. From this study, using the standard of replication, opt-in seems to have been just fine, at least for the analysis of voting behavior.

Having said that, my instincts would lead me to be cautious about studying problems centrally involving interest in and information about politics with any sampling procedure that allows respondents to self-select into the survey based on its topic (which, alas, also include telephone surveys and the ANES to a significant degree these days).[43]

Junn, Mendelberg, and Cjaza's chapter highlights another impact that exogenous changes have had on survey methodology. The proportion of Americans with Asian or Latino ancestry has skyrocketed. Obviously, none of the reasons for that demographic change have to do with public opinion surveys, so it is truly exogenous. Yet, as they point out, this change has had major ripple effects on survey research. How does one study such groups, which still do not show up in sufficient numbers to yield reliable results in most national surveys? The standard approach to surveying small subpopulations is to oversample them. That has traditionally worked fairly well for sampling African Americans, who are highly residentially segregated.[44] Moreover, at least on partisan and racial issues, they constitute a rather attitudinally homogeneous subpopulation. For either face to face or telephone surveys, oversampling such a concentrated subpopulation, using exactly the same survey instrument, is not only easy but likely not to give severely biased results.

But what about Latinos and Asians? As with blacks, they are too few in numbers to make their subsamples of standard academic surveys analyzable. So, as in other realms, the social scientist's first impulse is to use the African American model to solve the problems posed by these newer ethnic minorities. But, as Junn says, the differences are large. Neither group is remotely as residentially segregated as are blacks. To be sure, there are concentrations, such as, out our way, in East Los Angeles (Latinos), or in Koreatown or the San Gabriel Valley (Chinese), or Westminister (Vietnamese). But each of these subpopulations is also far more dispersed than are blacks. And those dispersed elsewhere are different, in terms of generation in the United States, in language preferences, and probably in other ways. Both the Latino and Asian subpopulations are also ethnically and politically diverse. One would not expect an oversampling of Latinos in Miami to look politically like ones from Los Angeles or San Antonio. So oversampling Latinos and Asians is a trickier business than oversampling blacks.

Democratic Governance

The basic precept of democratic governance is the continuing responsiveness of government to the people. That means there should be some association between public opinion and public policy, though of course political theorists as well as politicians differ about how tight they believe the link should be. Early research on political behavior questioned the competence of the public to guide public policy. Both the Columbia and Michigan pioneers believed that the public has, on average, modest information about politics, fairly inconsistent issue preferences, not especially stable political attitudes, and impoverished understanding of conventional political ideologies.[45] Mitigating those shortcomings was the idea that voters could take cues from elites, in essence developing "ideology by proxy." Alternatively, voters might develop specialized expertise, such that for every issue there might be an interested and informed "issue public." The issue publics for different issues might not overlap very much, so that the public as a whole might show generally poor information levels, but still exercise some wise judgment in specific issue areas.[46]

At the same time Downs and Key took contrarian positions, Key famously maintaining that "voters are no fools," and Downs asserting in a variety of ways that voters actually resemble rational thinkers more than the behavioral pioneers believed.[47] They, of course, foreshadowed the later development of portraits of democratic voters as more sensible and rational portraits developed by those influenced by and sympathetic to rational choice theory.[48]

Today, perhaps, the conventional wisdom is that "the miracle of aggregation" leads public opinion in the aggregate to look a good bit more rational than a cold-eyed examination of individual attitudes would suggest, and indeed, perhaps "enlightened enough" in Martin Gilens' words. He suggests a number of other findings that suggest public opinion may not be so chaotic and irrational after all. First, deliberative polls often find rather little change in public opinion after ordinary people have been exposed to intensive bursts of information and have had a chance to discuss it. Second, he describes simulations of a public composed of the well informed, produced by imputing the preferences that the poorly informed *would* have if they were better informed. Such simulated well-informed publics yield estimates of public opinion close to the aggregate opinion of the actual public. Third, framing and question wording effects obtained in artificial survey experiments sometimes give the impression that the public emotionally overreacts to the particularly loaded symbols they are presented with, such as "welfare" or "death tax," ignoring the realities of the policies they purportedly refer to. But, as Gilens says, such dramatic examples may not be typical, they may lead the public to think about quite different policies rather than being swayed in their attitudes about a given policy, and such swings may not be especially robust in the face of elite competition. It is tempting, therefore, to conclude with Key and Gilens that, at least in the aggregate, public opinion may resemble what a much more informed citizenry would prefer. The "signal" of the informed comes through despite the "noise" of the rabble.

That may be too generous, however, for three reasons I can think of. The inescapable fact remains that once having looked inside the sausage factory of public opinion, we cannot easily forget the grim reality we have seen. Relatively few members of the general public are well informed about politics, or have consistent and stable preferences on most issues. Moreover, the best informed are the *most* likely to disregard facts inconveniently inconsistent with their priors.[49] Second, partisan elites are constantly trying to manipulate the public, often successfully. Just as often, however, they are pandering to an ill-informed and emotional public, which is no better for rational public policies. When they are not engaged in manipulation or pandering, they are engaged in deception, as Andrea Campbell illustrates so vividly in her case study of Medicare reform. Perhaps public opinion influences the general direction of public policy, but in terms of the actual impact of the policy on citizens' lives, the devil truly is in the details. And third, there is the problem of social inequality, as Gilens' and Campbell et al.'s chapters so tellingly indicate. The well-off are not only more powerful but are more politically competent than the little guy. And they have disproportionate influence over who decides on the details.

The pioneers would have found familiar landscape in those observations. But we do have some "new directions" in democratic governance as well, emphasized by Baum. He suggests that political consensus is much more difficult to achieve today than it was, given some important political changes. One is the strikingly increased elite polarization. Political machines are far weaker, so deal making is more complicated. The media environment has changed as well. The traditional news media are less important, replaced to some extent by the more polarizing new media. Media audiences have fragmented, becoming smaller, politically narrower, and more partisan. A shrinking "media commons" is replaced with increased selective exposure and selective interpretation. The proportion of the population voting is also far higher than it was a century ago, making the task of persuasion more difficult.

And the goal of achieving national consensus and unity may be especially difficult for the individual whose job that is, the president. "[T]he ground underneath which presidents have stood" while trying both to mobilize their base and recruit new supporters has shifted dramatically, in Baum's felicitous terms, making the task of sustaining bipartisan consensus more daunting, even in time of war. It has become harder for the president to mobilize the public, for better or worse. The content of the media has changed as well, becoming more negative and skeptical. Presidents have less direct access to the public, as the media increasingly feature journalists' own interpretations, rather than presenting presidential speeches and news conferences in the leaders' own words.

But then let us remember that the Founders expected that democracy would be disputatious. They were not rebelling against a Europe filled with benign leaders who thoughtfully and responsively considered the preferences of the people. They were rebelling against selfish autocrats who rode roughshod over ordinary people. They did not expect democracy to be pretty or that all interested parties would pull together cooperatively all the time. The ills of our democracy are what they are, and the public bears some responsibility for them, engaging in sins of commission and omission alike. And it seems inevitable, if regrettable, that democratic systems are no cure-all for the natural differences in wealth and power that develop in any human society.

In all these areas, I am impressed by the authors' abilities to layer the "new directions" that the study of public opinion has taken on top of the foundations laid down by the pioneers half a century ago. It has been my privilege to add these few comments to what they have achieved.

Notes

1. Klapper, Joseph T. (1960). *The Effects of Mass Communications*. Glencoe, IL: Free Press.
2. Lee, Alfred Mclung and Elizabeth Briant Lee, eds. (1939). *The Fine Art of Propaganda: A Study of Father Coughlin's Speeches*. New York: Harcourt, Brace and Company.
3. Campbell, Angus, Philip Converse, Warren E. Miller, and Donald Stokes. (1960). *The American Voter*. New York: John Wiley.
4. Adorno, Theodor W., Else Frenkel-Brunswik, Daniel J. Levinson, and Nevitt R. Sanford (1950). *The Authoritarian Personality*. New York: Harper and Row.
5. Klapper (1960).
6. Zaller, John. (1992). *The Nature and Origins of Mass Opinion*. New York: Cambridge University Press.
7. Vavreck, Lynn (2009). *The Message Matters: The Economy and Presidential Campaigns*. Princeton, NJ: Princeton University Press.
8. Fiorina, Morris P., Samuel J. Abrams, and Jeremy C. Pope (2006). *Culture War? The Myth of a Polarized America*, 2nd edition. New York: Pearson Longman.
9. Lazarsfeld, Paul F., Bernard Berelson, and Hazel Gaudet (1948). *The People's Choice* (2nd ed). New York: Columbia University Press.
10. Campbell et al. (1960).
11. Campbell et al. (1960).
12. Campbell, Angus, Gerald Gurin, and Warren E. Miller (1954). *The Voter Decides*. Evanston, IL: Row, Peterson and Company; and Converse, Philip. E. (1964). "The nature of belief systems in mass publics." In David E. Apter (Ed.), *Ideology and discontent* (pp. 206–261). New York: Free Press of Glencoe.
13. Today, of course, blacks' pivotal roles in the desegregation of the armed forces and in Harry Truman's victory in 1948 are more widely recognized.
14. Converse, Philip E., Angus Campbell, Warren E. Miller, and Donald E. Stokes (1961). "Stability and change in 1960: A reinstating election." *American Political Science Review*, 55, 269–280.
15. Converse, Philip E., Aage R. Clausen, and Warren E. Miller (1965). "Electoral myth and reality: The 1964 election." *American Political Science Review*, 59, 321–336.
16. Sears, David O. and Victoria Savalei (2006). "The political color line in America: Many peoples of color or black exceptionalism?" *Political Psychology*, 27, 895–924.
17. Tesler, Michael and David O. Sears (2010). *Obama's Race: The 2008 Election and the Dream of a Post-Racial America*. Chicago, IL: University of Chicago Press.
18. Dawson, Michael C. (1994). *Behind the Mule: Race and Class in African American Politics*. Princeton, NJ: Princeton University Press.
19. Sears, David O., Mingying Fu, P.J. Henry, and Kerra Bui (2003). "The origins and persistence of ethnic identity among the 'new immigrant' groups." *Social Psychology Quarterly*, 66, 419–437.
20. Tesler and Sears (2010).
21. Valentino, Nicholas A. and David O. Sears (2005). "Old times there are not forgotten: Race and partisan realignment in the contemporary South." *American Journal of Political Science*, 49, 672–688.
22. Adorno, Theodor W., Else Frenkel-Brunswik, Daniel J. Levinson, and R. Nevitt Sanford (1950). *The Authoritarian Personality*. Oxford, England: Harpers.
23. McClosky, Herbert (1958). "Conservatism and personality." *American Political Science Review*, 52, 27–45.
24. Greenstein, Fred I. (1969). *Personality and Politics*. Chicago, IL: Markham; and Greenstein, Fred I. and Michael Lerner, eds. (1971). *A Source Book for the Study of Personality and Politics*. Chicago, IL: Markham Publishing.

25. Hyman, Herbert H., and Paul B. Sheatsley (1954). "The authoritarian personality: A methodological critique." In R. Christie and M. Jahoda (Eds.), *Studies in the Scope and Method of the Authoritarian Personality* (pp. 51–123). Glencoe, IL: The Free Press.
26. Converse (1964).
27. Mischel, Walter (1968). *Personality and Assessment.* New York: Wiley.
28. Jones, Edward E. and Victor A. Harris (1967). "The attribution of attitudes." *Journal of Experimental Social Psychology*, 3, 1–24.
29. Goldberg, Lewis (1993). "The structure of phenotypic personality traits." *American Psychologist*, 48, 26–34.
30. Altemeyer, Bob (1988). *Enemies of Freedom: Understanding Right-wing Authoritarianism.* San Francisco: Jossey-Bass.
31. Jost, John T., Jack Glaser, Arie Kruglanski, and Frank Sulloway (2003). "Political conservatism as motivated social cognition." *Psychological Bulletin*, 129, 339–375.
32. Converse (1964).
33. Zaller, John and Stanley Feldman (1992). "A simple theory of the survey response: Answering questions versus revealing preferences." *American Journal of Political Science*, 36, 579–616.
34. Adorno et al. (1950); and Sears, David O. (1986). "College sophomores in the laboratory: Influences of a narrow database on social psychology's view of human nature." *Journal of Personality and Social Psychology*, 51, 515–530.
35. Converse, Phillip E. (2000). "Assessing the capacity of mass electorates." *Annual Review of Political Science*, 3, 331–353.
36. Osgood, Charles E., George J. Suci, and Percy H. Tannenbaum (1957). *The Measurement of Meaning.* Urbana, IL: University of Illinois Press; and Rosenberg, Seymour and Andrea Sedlak (1972). "Structural representations of implicit personality theory." In Leonard Berkowitz (Ed.), *Advances in Experimental Social Psychology Vol. 6* (pp. 235–293). New York: Academic Press.
37. Jack Citrin and David O. Sears, "The politics of multiculturalism and the crisis of American identity," manuscript in preparation; Sears et al. (2003); and Sears and Savalei (2006).
38. Berinsky, Adam J. (2004). *Silent Voices: Public Opinion and Political Participation in America.* Princeton, NJ: Princeton University Press.
39. Tesler and Sears (2010); and Kinder, Donald R. and Lynn M. Sanders (1996). *Divided By Color: Racial Politics and Democratic Ideals.* Chicago, IL: University of Chicago Press.
40. For other reasons, see Sears, David O. and P.J. Henry (2005). "Over thirty years later: A contemporary look at symbolic racism." In Mark Zanna (Ed.), *Advances in Experimental Social Psychology, Vol. 37* (pp. 95–150). San Diego, CA: Elsevier, Academic Press.
41. Sears, David O., and Victoria Savalei, "Blunt or sharp instruments: Measuring affect toward ethnic and racial groups in contemporary America." Presented at the annual meeting of ISPP, Dublin, Ireland, July 17, 2009; and Sears, David O. and Victoria Savelei, "The determinants of even-handedness in evaluations of racial and ethnic groups." Presented at ISPP, San Francisco, July 7, 2010.
42. Tesler and Sears (2010).
43. On the robustness of survey findings despite major changes in American society and survey procedures, I might also mention the replication of the great majority of findings from *The American Voter* (1960), using data collected in the 1950s, in *The American Voter Revisited* (2008), using data collected over the half century since.
44. Massey, Douglas S. and Nancy A. Denton (1993). *American Apartheid Segregation and the Making of the Underclass*, Cambridge, MA: Harvard University Press.

45. Berelson, Bernard R., Paul F. Lazarsfeld, and William N. McPhee (1954). *Voting: A Study of Opinion Formation in a Presidential Campaign*. Chicago, IL: University of Chicago Press; and Converse (1964).
46. Campbell et al. (1960); and Converse (1964).
47. Downs, Anthony (1957). *An Economic Theory of Democracy*. New York: Harper-Row; and Key, V.O. Jr. (1966). *The Responsible Electorate*. Cambridge, MA: Harvard University Press.
48. Fiorina, Morris P. (1981). *Retrospective Voting in American National Elections*. New Haven, CT: Yale University Press; Page, Benjamin I. and Robert Y. Shapiro (1992). *The Rational Public: Fifty Years of Trends in Americans' Policy Preferences*. Chicago, IL: University of Chicago Press; and Popkin, Samuel (1994). *The Reasoning Voter: Communication and Persuasion in Presidential Campaigns*, 2nd edition. Chicago, IL: University of Chicago Press.
49. Zaller (1992).

Index